Urbanization in Nigeria

Akin L. Mabogunje, M.A., Ph.D.

Professor of Geography, University of Ibadan, Nigeria

01.364
1112u

Africana Publishing Corporation . New York

Published in the United States of America
by Africana Publishing Corporation,
101, Fifth Avenue,
New York, N.Y. 10003.

First printing 1969
Second printing 1971

Library of Congress catalog card No. 76-80853

ISBN 8419-0002-7

Printed in Great Britain

Preface

The primary aim of this book is to provide for the first time a conspectus of traditional and modern urbanization in Nigeria. Although there is now no dispute as to the existence of a pre-European urbanism in this part of the world, neither its character nor its extensiveness has ever been fully explored. Moreover, accepting the existence of traditional urbanism in Africa has never meant seeing this development as due to processes which have operated in similar manner elsewhere in the world.

The focus of the study is thus in a sense comparative. It seeks comparison through examining empirically derived generalizations about urbanization and individual urban centres based on studies in other parts of the world. In this way, the book concentrates as much on the similarities as on the differences between Nigerian and non-Nigerian cities.

If the existence of a traditional system of towns and cities is the first major fact about urbanization in Nigeria, the dynamic impact of modernization begun by the colonial régime and continued by the independent governments of the country is the second. A substantial section of the book is devoted to examining the nature of this impact on the system of cities and on individual cities. It has been suggested that much of the examination is based on an economic interpretation of urbanization. For this, no apology is offered. Towns and cities are seen as crucial nodes in the spatial economy. Their size, number, distribution and characteristics are assumed to be useful indications of the state and conditions of the economy.

The analysis of various aspects of the impact of modern development on Nigerian cities and towns is the special concern of Chapter 6. It involves the use of sophisticated statistical techniques as well as somewhat technical terms and concepts. Therefore, a reader without a basic training in the social sciences may find the chapter a little difficult to follow. He is, however, advised to persevere since this chapter is perhaps the most important in the book. It is here that the major ideas as to what is happening today in the overall urban development in Nigeria are discussed and evaluated. Nonetheless, a reader more interested in

getting some indication of the characteristics of Nigerian cities ar
towns rather than in the reasons behind those characteristics can qu
conveniently omit reading the chapter.

One apology is offered: it has not been possible for the analysis to u
statistical data of a date more recent than 1952-53. This unfortuna
situation has arisen because of the cloud that surrounds the recent 196
census of the country and the fact that up to now no breakdown of th
census figures has been provided beyond the total population of indiv
dual settlements. However, while the 1952-53 figures may be dated,
is believed that much of the inference that can be made from them re
mains valid even today. Moreover, since there has been no comparabl
analysis of the results of that census up-to-date, most of the facts re
vealed in this study are virtually new.

One other point which needs to be made about this study relates t
the effect of the recent upheavals and strife in Nigeria. Since May 196
there has been a considerable movement of people back to their regio
of origin. This is particularly true of Northern Nigeria where peoples o
Eastern Nigeria origin have moved out in large numbers. It is less tru
of Lagos, Western and Mid-Western Nigeria, although these areas als
lost some population while gaining others. Since most migration i
Nigeria has been to the cities, the effect of the recent events will be mos
marked in these places. The *sabon-gari* of Kano, for instance, is said t
be now no more than a ghost-town. The same is true of Zaria an
especially of Jos. By contrast, towns of Eastern Nigeria are, as it were
bursting at the seams with the sudden influx of 'repatriates'. The exten
to which these changes distort the picture described in this book is stil
too early to assess. But even if this were to be great, the book will still be
of value as a study of the process of urbanization in a pre-industria
society.

This book derives in part from my doctoral dissertation. However
much of the thinking that has influenced its present form began only
during my nine-month stay as Visiting Scholar in the United States of
America in 1963. Before then, my insight into the urban situation in
Nigeria was handicapped by my lack of acquaintance with sophisticated
analytical methods. This deficiency was corrected during those pleasant
months I spent with the staff of the Department of Geography and
Economics at the Northwestern University, Evanston, Illinois. To all
those colleagues who were disposed to engage in the arguments that
helped to straighten my thinking, I wish to acknowledge my gratitude.

In particular, I wish to express thanks to Professors W. L. Garrison and Duane F. Marble who were very generous with their computer-time for the factor-analysis of the 1952 Census of Nigeria as they relate to the urban areas; to Professor H. C. Darby, now of Cambridge University, England, for his earlier supervision of my doctoral dissertation while we both belonged to University College, London; to Mrs S. O. Bankole who has worked untiringly at typing the manuscript; to my Research Assistant, Mr S. O. Onakomaiya, who did much of the other computation and analysis; and to Mr T. K. P. Amachree, who has produced most of the maps and diagrams.

I also wish to acknowledge with thanks my indebtedness to the Computing Centre of Northwestern University, Evanston, Illinois, USA for the use of their IBM 7090 Computer in 1963.

Last but not least, I wish to express my sincere appreciation to my wife for her constant spurring to keep me working at this book to the finish.

University of Ibadan   A. L. Mabogunje

Contents

List of Plates

List of Figures

List of Tables

Acknowledgments

The author and publisher are grateful to the following for permission to reproduce the photographs:

The Editor of *Nigeria Magazine* for Plates 2, 4, 5, 6, 7, 8, 12, 15, 22, 23, 24, 25, 28 and 29.

Western Nigeria Information Service for Plates 3, 10, 11, 14, 16, 17, 18 and 19.

Federal Information Service, Lagos, for Plates 21, 26 and 27.

Aerofilms Ltd., London, for Plate 9.

1 Introduction

One of the most impressive phenomena of the twentieth century has been the growth of cities. At no time in human history have men shown such strong inclination to agglomerate in large numbers in a few centres. Davis has shown that while in 1800 only 2·4 per cent of the world's population lived in cities of more than 20,000 people, by 1950 the proportion had risen to 20·9 per cent.[1] The position is equally impressive for the proportion of the population living in cities with a population of more than 100,000. Davis found that while in 1800 the percentage was 1·7 by 1950, this has now risen to 13·1. The number of cities also rose. Of those with a population over 100,000, the number increased from less than 50 in 1800 to over 900 by 1950.

Although it is true that this phenomenal growth in the number of cities and of city-dwellers was taking place over a period in which world population was also rapidly increasing, the remarkable fact is that the rate of urban growth was so many times greater than the rate of growth of the total world population. Thus, while the world's population increased from 836 million in 1800 to about 2·4 thousand million by 1950—a threefold increase—the world urban population, if we confine ourselves to cities with a population over 100,000, increased from 15·6 million to 313·7 million, a more than twentyfold increase.

TABLE I   PERCENTAGE OF THE WORLD'S POPULATION LIVING IN CITIES, BY REGIONS, 1950

	In cities of 20,000 plus	In cities of 100,000 plus
WORLD	21	13
OCEANIA	47	41
NORTH AMERICA (CANADA AND USA)	42	29
EUROPE (EXCEPT USSR)	35	21
USSR	31	18
SOUTH AMERICA	26	18
MIDDLE AMERICA AND CARRIBBEAN	21	12
ASIA (EXCEPT USSR)	13	8
AFRICA	9	5

Source: K. Davis, op. cit.

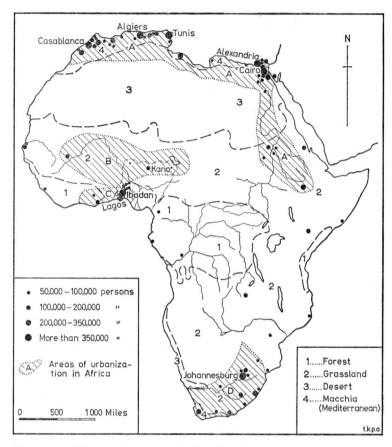

Figure 1   Africa: major areas of urban development

This rapid rate of urbanization has not been uniform everywhere in the world. Britain, for instance, was in the van of urban development and had reached by 1801 a position not achieved by any other country until after 1850. Davis gave the following table to emphasize the unevenness of urban development in the world even by 1950. From this table, Africa stands out as the continent least urbanized in the world with only 9 per cent of its total population of 250 million living in cities of over 20,000.

Even within Africa, there is considerable unevenness. Four areas of major urban development can be identified (Fig. 1). Three of these are found north of the equator. They comprise the Mediterranean regions of North Africa including the Nile valley, the new grassland region of the Western Sudan and the eastern forested area of the Guinea coast. These three areas are also significant because their urban development pre-dated the European penetration of the continent. The fourth area in South Africa represents the major area of purely European effort in urban development.

Nigeria includes within its area parts of the urban development in both the Western Sudan and the forest country. Reviewing the pattern of population concentration in Africa in 1950, Trewartha and Zelinsky noted that, if the population figures of 5,000 were to be used to define an urban settlement, Nigeria, although accounting for only about 20 per cent of the total population of tropical Africa has nearly 35 per cent of its urban population.[2] This unusual concentration of urban population poses an exciting challenge to our understanding of urbanization in pre-industrial circumstances.

In recent writings, urbanization has tended to be closely linked with economic development. The exact nature of the relationship has, of course, never been explicitly stated. Hoselitz, for instance, noted that while, on the one hand, there is general agreement that the growth and development of cities is a necessary condition of economic development, on the other hand, there are the findings which tend to show that the richer a country, the more urbanized it is and the larger a city in any country, the wealthier it is.[3] In short, there is as yet no definitive statement as to whether the existence of cities provided the reason for economic development or whether economic development represents the main cause of cities. This ambivalence, of course, may be simply calling attention to the fact that the relation is complex and that our knowledge of the subject is still very circumscribed.

However, Hoselitz's recognition of the fact that not all cities could be shown at all times to be generative of economic development is important and merits further exploration for our present purpose. Hoselitz, following on this recognition, distinguished two types of city which he called *generative* and *parasitic*. A city is generative if its impact on economic growth is favourable, i.e. if its formation and continued existence and growth is one of the factors accountable for the economic development of the region or country in which it is located. A city is parasitic if it exerts an opposite impact.

The major point to be made here is the need to emphasize the time dimension in considering whether a particular city or group of cities is generative or parasitic within an economic system. In this respect, an economic system is conceived as a system of organizing space so as to minimize distance-cost involved in the production and distribution of goods and services. The major elements of this spatial organization are in particular the cities and the routeways. Cities are essentially the points of articulation of an economic system and their efficient functioning is circumscribed by the detail characteristics of the economic system, that is, its productive capacity, its transport system and technology, and the general level of income of the populace. These characteristics, moreover, determine the number, size and distribution of the cities. In short, for any given economic system, it is theoretically conceivable that there is a given pattern of urban centres which makes for efficient economic interaction. If such an economic system were to change drastically or be supplanted, we can expect that the pattern of cities will change. Thus, if we can think of the medieval economic system with its major dependence on agriculture, extensive trading activities, limited manufacturing enterprise, animate source of power and transport, wide diffusion of political power and relative insecurity of life, we can conceive of a system of cities which will be efficient in the context of those days. Such a system, however, is bound to be inadequate and highly inefficient in the modern situation of inanimate power sources, machine-based industries, more voluminous trade, a highly productive agricultural system and greater centralization of political power.

Ideally, therefore, every economic system should generate its own appropriate system of cities. However, as Isard observed, cities represent accumulated fixed investments which, in conjunction with their vested social institutions, tend to entail major geographic immobilities and rigidities and, for the most part, preclude relocation.[4] Thus, even when an economic system has been supplanted by another, its cities remain for long afterwards. Whether they continue to be generative of economic growth within the new system or are parasitic is then a function of their position in the new spatial integration that must follow from a change in the economic system.

Previous studies

The idea that the emergence or the imposition of a new economic system involves a different pattern of spatial integration and a different system of cities is important to bear in mind in any consideration of urbanization in those countries of Asia and Africa which have recently been exposed to European influences especially by way of colonialism. This is particularly evident in those countries which, before the advent of the Europeans, already had a system of cities related to pre-industrial economic conditions.

Unfortunately, while there exist numerous studies on individual urban centres or on social implications of urbanization in general, there are very few studies dealing specifically with this aspect of the problem. In Asia, these few studies have tended to concentrate on the historical antecedents of the cities. In Japan, for instance, Lee indicated that there had taken place five major periods of urban growth beginning from 660 B.C.[5] The earlier periods cover spans of over 500 years, although the more recent have been between 100 and 200 years. With each new period, some of the old centres became redundant and were abandoned, but many others either survived in a state of suspended animation or become actively integrated into the new system. In a similar vein, Trewartha noted that 'in spite of the fact that the last half century has seen a remarkable growth in urban population (in Japan), it appears that relatively few large cities actually have been called into existence by the exigencies of the modern era. Chief among these cities are the great deep-water ports of Kobe and Yokohama, the new urban centres of semi-frontier Hokkaido and the industrial port cities of Northern Kyushu. Others, like Osaka, Nagoya and Sakai, ancient in origin and fame have been greatly expanded and altered during the era of industrial and commercial revolution.'[6]

The same story is told for China where Pak Si Wu identifies six major periods of urban development starting from 2205 B.C.[7] Lee believes that a seventh period may be added, dating from 1950 and related to the economic programme of the Communist régime.[8] This programme involves the systematic dismantling of factories and the large-scale evacuation of population from seaboard cities. The abandonment of these cities is based on the premise that if the natural resources found in the various areas within the nation are to be utilized effectively, cities and industries must be located there and not on the Pacific seaboard; moreover, that the coastal cities have grown in importance and wealth only because of Western influence and not because of local conditions. In consequence, inland cities are now being encouraged to manufacture consumer goods and to trade with each other. In this way, it is hoped that cities which were thriving municipalities in former eras may regain their lost status.

Even before this new emphasis, much of the recent urbanization in China had been around traditional urban centres, in particular the *hsien* capitals, most of which date from the second period of urban development beginning from about 200 B.C. These centres were the headquarters of the lowest administrative units. Through them the imperial government exercised its authority over the rural communities. They also served as the economic focus, the cultural centre, the transportation node, the central market and, in most cases, were the most populous settlement of their *hsien* or rural district. Sen-don Chiang noted that the *hsien* capitals still serve as a base for the growth of urban population in present-day China. Among 189 communities announced as 'cities' by Peking up to 1958, 160 were originally *hsien* capitals.[9] Unfortunately Chiang did not indicate how many *hsien* capitals were now merely surviving in the system and how many had disappeared.

With regard to India, it is remarkable that although this country has one of the oldest traditions of urbanization in the world, dating from the Neolithic and claiming such famous excavated sites as that of Mohenjo-daro, the study of its urbanization has been very limited. The major distinction has been between the pre-British period and the modern period dating from the seventeenth century. Crane observed in his brief study that 'India was, comparatively speaking, a highly urbanized area, but after its own fashion, when the first European travellers appeared on the scene. Travellers in the fifteenth and sixteenth centuries made it clear that India had a degree of urbanization unsurpassed by the Western world at that time.'[10] Crane, nonetheless, went on to point out that to a large extent the major cities (of India) have been the creation of European effort and enterprise. Each consists typically of a European and an indigenous city. Hence, one may speak of two urbanisms in India.'

More recent studies on urbanization in Asia have tended to be sociological and to be concerned in particular with the problems of the rapidly growing centres. The most important of these has been the volume on *Urbanization in Asia and the Far East*, edited by Hauser and resulting from an International Conference organized by the United Nations in 1956. Although the papers included in this volume covered a wide range of problems connected with the phenomenal growth of urban centres, no single one looked at urbanization as a continuing process of spatial adjustments to new economic conditions.

When we turn to Africa, we are faced with still scantier information. Part of the explanation for this is, of course, that over a large part of the continent, urban development has been a recent phenomenon related to the European colonialization of Africa. Over most areas, especially in East, Central and South Africa, the African found himself a stranger in the city and his precsee created many problems especially with a European settler group anxious to monopolize the major benefits of urban concentrations. Most studies of urbanization in Africa have thus until recently, come from these areas of the continent and have been concerned largely with sociological questions related to the African adjustment to city life and to the routine of an industrial economic system.[11] The major study on urbanization in Africa organized in 1956 by the International African Institute under the auspices of UNESCO covered much the same ground.[12] In West Africa, however, a few studies have begun to evaluate the significance of this dynamic perspective on urbanization. The two most important of these are the brief studies by Bascom on urbanization among the Yorubas and the series of papers on various aspects of urbanism in West Africa published in the special number of the *Sociological Review* in 1959.[13]

Apart from the paucity of comprehensive studies of urbanization in Asia and Africa, most of the studies so far conducted are open to two major criticisms. The first is that they have been largely descriptive and the insights they have provided are in terms of some intuitive notion of differing types of urbanization related to different historical origins. One reason for this weakness is the unfamiliarity, until recently, of many social scientists with many of the fairly sophisticated analytical techniques which would have made it possible to encompass the complexity involved in the study of urbanization on this scale. One of these analytical techniques is that of multivariate analysis which seeks to reduce a large number of variables related to a particular population of observations into a much smaller number of independent dimensions. Recently, an impressive study of British towns using component analysis (a type of multivariate analysis) was carried out by Moser and Scott.[14] Although the major concern of their study was to 'classify (British) towns on the basis of their social, economic and demographic characteristics', their technique offered great possibilities for work of a much wider scope concerned with testing a number of hypotheses about the process of urbanization in any country.

A second weakness of most of the studies that have been made so far is the over-concentration on the sociological problems of the few rapidly growing urban centres in countries which have just begun to adjust themselves to a new economic order. Great concern is shown for such problems as overcrowding, unemployment, delinquency, the plight of the new immigrant, and the decline of traditional values. Yet, in countries with an earlier pattern of urban concentration, an equally pressing though different type of problem is posed by the situation of those traditional urban centres which are no longer functional in the current economic circumstance. In other words, to revert to Hoselitz's terminology, not only the 'generative' but also the 'parasitic' urban centre deserve attention, the latter no less than the former, if only to gain some understanding of the implications of urban parasitism within an economic system.

Scope of the present work

The present work is therefore concerned not so much with the social problems of urbanization but rather with urbanization itself, as a process operating through time. The study is based upon a few assumptions which are here explicitly stated. First, it assumes that every nation state is a single economic entity within which the economic activities of the inhabitants are governed by much the same form of legislations and regulations. From this it follows that national boundaries are seen as constituting some of the most effective economic barriers in the world. Second, the study assumes that, given certain common goals or aspirations, the economic behaviour of human beings is the same irrespective of their race or culture. This is not to deny the importance of racial or cultural characteristics in many areas of human endeavour. Rather it is to help emphasize the great need always to look for underlying similarities among phenomena whose manifestation may appear diverse and unrelated because of differences such as those of race, culture or geographical situation. As Bronowski puts it, 'it is the constant urge of science as well as of the arts, to broaden the likeness, for which we grope under the facts. When we discover the wider likeness, whether between space and time, or between the bacillus, the virus, and the crystal, we enlarge the order in the universe; but more than this, we enlarge its unity.'[15]

The present study therefore has a strong theoretical orientation. It does not see the urbanization process in Nigeria as unique in any way but tries to show that it reflects the operation of much the same forces as have led to urban growth and development in other parts of the world. The study also makes a distinction between the process of urbanization and the resulting structure of individual urban centres. To emphasize this latter point, the book has been divided into two parts. The first deals with urban growth in Nigeria; the second with a typology of Nigerian cities. Both sections begin with a theoretical consideration of what is to be expected. This serves as a useful model against which can be measured how much the Nigerian situation deviates from the norm.

In Part One, which deals with patterns of urbanization, an attempt is made to review ideas about a theory of urbanization derived from current views in the social sciences. Two chapters then describe traditional urbanization in Nigeria before the beginning of the colonial period. The two areas of such urbanization were the Hausa area of Northern Nigeria and the Yoruba area of Western Nigeria. Each area is treated in a chapter. This is followed by a review of factors stimulating a modern revival of urbanization under the colonial régime. The emphasis here is on emergence of a new economic order and its imposition of a new pattern of spatial integration on the country. With the end of the colonial era, it is suggested that we may be at the beginning of novel changes both in the economic system and in the system of cities. The final chapter in this section is concerned with the analysis of the situation based largely on an extension of Christaller's theory of central places and the multivariate technique of factor analysis.

Part Two also opens with a review of theories concerning the structure of cities. It reviews the assumptions of these theories and indicates the type of perspective which they provide for an understanding of the structure of Nigerian cities. The next four chapters concentrate on two cities—Ibadan and Lagos—to exemplify the basic differences among cities in Nigeria. Ibadan is chosen because, in a sense, it represents the apogee of pre-European urbanization. Although it is a Yoruba city, its situation and problems are shown to be very similar to those of older cities like Kano and Zaria in Northern Nigeria. Lagos, on the other hand, is the metropolitan creation of the colonial era and its character and conditions are reflected in similar centres such as Port Harcourt, Aba and Kaduna.

A concluding chapter considers the trend of urbanization in the country. In particular, it tries to emphasize the diverse and ever-changing aspects of this trend and the type of impact on the city structure that may be expected. It then tries briefly to highlight areas of continuing problems especially those relating to the differing economic viability of the urban centres, to their traffic congestion and to the efficiency of their administrative machinery.

References

1. Kingsley Davis, 'The Origin and Growth of Urbanization in the World', *American Journal of Sociology*, Vol. 60, March 1955, p. 434, see Table 1.
2. G. T. Trewartha and W. Zelinsky, 'Population Patterns in Tropical Africa', *Annals of the Association of American Geographers*, Vol. 34, No. 2, June 1954, pp. 135-162.
3. Bert F. Hoselitz, 'Generative and Parasitic Cities', *Economic Development and Culture Change*, Vol. 3, No. 3, April 1955, pp. 278-279.
4. Walter Isard, *Location and Space-Economy*, New York, 1956, p. 183.
5. R. H. Lee, *The City*, New York, 1955, pp. 72-84.
6. G. T. Trewartha, 'Japanese Cities. Distribution and Morphology', *Geographical Review*, Vol. 24, No. 3, July 1934, p. 406. See also R. B. Hall, 'The Cities of Japan, Notes on their distribution and inherited forms', *Annals of the Association of American Geographers*, Vol. 24, No. 4, December 1934, pp. 175-200.
7. Pak Si Wu, '*Urbanization in China: A study of Shanghai and Peiping* (unpublished Master's thesis, University of Chicago Libraries, December 1940).
8. R. H. Lee, op. cit., pp. 54-55.
9. Sen-don Chiang, 'Some Aspects of the Urban Geography of the Chinese Hsien Capital', *Annals of the Association of American Geographers*, Vol. 51, No. 1, March 1961, pp. 43-44.
10. R. I. Crane, 'Urbanization in India', *American Journal of Sociology*, Vol. 60, No. 1, March 1961, pp. 43-44.
11. See, for instance, P. Ibbotson, 'Urbanization in Southern Rhodesia', *Africa*, Vol. 16, No. 2, April 1946, pp. 73-82; G. E. Stent, 'Migrancy and Urbanization in the Union of South Africa', *Africa*, Vol. 18, No. 3, July 1948, pp. 161-183; J. D. R. Jones, 'The effects of Urbanization in South and Central Africa', *African Affairs*, Vol. 52, No. 206, January 1953, pp. 37-44.
12. International African Institute, *Social Implications of Industrializ-tion and Urbanization in Africa south of the Sahara*. Prepared under the auspices of UNESCO by the International African Institute, London, Tensions and Technology Series, UNESCO, Paris, 1956, 743 pp.

13. W. Bascom, 'Urbanization among the Yoruba', *American Journal of Sociology*, Vol. 60, No. 5, March 1955, pp. 446-454; 'Urbanism in West Africa', *The Sociological Review* (special number), Keele, University College of North Staffordshire, England, 1959, 131 pp.
14. C. A. Moser and Wolf Scott, *British Towns*, Centre for Urban Studies, Report No. 2, London, 1961, 169 pp.
15. J. Bronowski, *The Common Sense of Science*, London, 1960, p. 138.

Part One   Patterns of Urbanization

2 The Theory of Urbanization

The need for theory

No formal theory of urbanization exists. The literature of the social sciences, however, abounds in general statements of a theoretical nature which seek to explain the phenomena of human agglomeration in space. Much of this literature concerns specifically the experience of Europe and those other areas of the world where European influence has penetrated. Moreover, to some extent, this literature implicitly tends to regard urbanization as a peculiarly European and American phenomena with some of the studies assuming that modern industrial development is the only basis for urban agglomeration.

The role of theory in science is to explain the underlying connections between groups of related phenomena. Any theory, however, represents a simplification or a generalization of reality and does not therefore completely describe particular situations. What it loses by way of details, it makes up by providing new insights into the relationship between various phenomena which at first sight may appear diverse and without connections.

Urbanization, or the process whereby human beings congregate in relatively large number at one particular spot of the earth's surface, is a universal phenomena of considerable antiquity. This definition of urbanization is no doubt vague, especially with regard to the phrase 'relatively large number'; but this is deliberate. For the definition of an urban centre or a locality which has undergone or is undergoing the process of urbanization varies considerably depending on what period of time we are considering and, for any one period, what part of the world.

The identification of the process as involving mainly a numerical increase of population on a limited area is also deliberate. Various definitions of urbanization or of an urban centre exist. Perhaps the best known is that of Louis Wirth which defines an urban centre as 'a relatively large, dense and permanent settlement of socially heterogeneous individuals'.[1] While accepting size as a criterion, Wirth added other factors which appear more to be dependent on size than to be preconditions for urban development.

At any rate, the problem is to explain the development of towns and cities in different parts of the world and at different periods. For such an explanation to be of theoretical significance, it must be logically consistent and valid, irrespective of the time and place under consideration. It is easy to assume that industrialization is the major explanation for urban development. In particular, the present-day situation in which the highest level of urbanization is found in those parts of the world where industrialization has reached an advanced stage may appear to confirm this view. There is, of course, no doubt that industrialization has some relation with urbanization; that as the level of industrial development in a country rises, so does the level of urbanization; that as these two related processes increase, so does the characteristic heterogeneity of the population. But these relationships need not have held in this manner at the very beginning of the process, unless of course we define industrialization in much wider terms than the more commonly accepted one of 'the process of technological development by the use of applied science, characterized by the expansion of large-scale production with the use of power machinery for a wide market for both producers' and consumers' goods, by means of a specialized working force with division of labour, the whole accompanied by accelerated urbanization'.[2]

The fact that towns and cities existed in different parts of the world before the era of the industrial revolution in Europe, and continue to exist at the present day in areas not yet affected by this revolution requires an explanation. This will become clearer after a review of the theory of urbanization as currently stated in the literature on the subject.

The functional specialization theory of urbanization

The fundamental idea in the theory of urbanization is that based on the specialization of functions among human communities through the division of labour. Functional specialization involves the narrowing of the range of activities or functions performed by an individual in a given time period with a view to increasing his skill or dexterity in the performance of these activities. The net effect of such specialization is to increase the total goods or services produced by the community within a given period of time.

Certain consequences stem from attempts at the specialization of functions among individuals. Two are particularly important in so far as they help to increase the productivity of the community. The first of these is the need to co-ordinate the activities of the numerous

Plate 1 Kano from Mount Dala (after Heinrich Barth, 1853)
Plate 2 The old town wall and gate of Zaria

Plate 3   The Central Mosque in Kano
Plate 4   A traditional two-storey house in Kano

specialized but interdependent producers. This often calls into existence new groups of specialists whose skill is shown in the achievement of a high level of co-ordination with as little friction or delay as possible. In terms of urbanization, the role of co-ordinators is performed by traders and administrators. The second consequence of specialization is that, given human ingenuity, the preoccupation with a narrowed range of operations is sure to give rise to the discovery of new and more productive ways of performing the same operations. Such technical specialization formed the basis of the industrial revolution in Britain in the nineteenth century. The greater facility for the co-ordination of technical processes made the factory the hall-mark of industrial development. Similarly, the greater ease of co-ordinating the production of goods, as well as significant 'external economies' that are gained in the provision of various services such as roads, water supply and electricity, led to the increasing concentration of factories in urban centres. Moreover, as transport improved, it became possible for urban centres to become more and more specialized in the industrial transformation of primary goods and be completely divorced from agriculture.

Specialization is the essence of urbanization, but by itself it need not give rise to urban centres. For the latter to happen, functional specialization must take place under certain well defined conditions. Without these conditions operating, there may be some functional specialization but there could be no urban centres. In examining the phenomenon of urbanization anywhere in the world, it is these limiting conditions that are crucial.

The limiting conditions

The three limiting conditions for the rise of urban centres can be stated in the following terms:

(a) For functional specialization to give rise to urban centres, there must be a surplus of food production with which to feed the class of specialists whose activities are now withdrawn from agriculture;

(b) For this surplus to be made available to the group of specialists, there must be a small group of people who are able to exercise some power over the group of food producers. This class also has to ensure stable and peaceful conditions in which both the food producers and the specialists can produce of their best; and

(c) For the work of the specialists to be facilitated and their needs for raw materials satisfied, there must be a class of traders and merchants.

In the following paragraphs, each of these limiting conditions will be explored in greater detail. It will be seen that where the conditions existed, urbanization flourished. Wherever one of them ceased to exist, there was an immediate decline in the vigour of the urbanization process, and in some cases a total eclipse of urban centres. Urbanization can therefore be seen as a process which seeks, through maximum specialization, to increase the output of goods and services in a community subject only to the three conditions enumerated above.

Perhaps the most obvious of the three conditions is that related to the availability of surplus food with which to feed the class of specialists. This presupposes that some relationship exists between urbanization on the one hand and, on the other, the fertility of the soil and the effectiveness of the technology available for exploiting this fertility. Indeed, it is the combination of the last two which decides the amount of surplus available. In the early history of urban evolution, when technology was largely primitive, we have to look for areas of exceedingly great fertility to account for the surplus of food crops. Such areas were, of course, limited to the alluvial plains of a few large rivers, notably the Nile, the Tigris-Euphrates, the Indus and the Yangtze-Kiang where soil fertility was kept perennially at a high level by the annual flood. With time, improvement in technology made it possible to exploit less fertile soils but on such a scale as to provide the required surplus. Thus the increasing urbanization of the United States of America in the last quarter of the nineteenth century and early this century is due largely to the application of advanced technology to moderately fertile soils to produce bountiful harvests.

The existence of a food surplus does not by itself imply that this will be handed over to the specialists or even bartered for their products. It could more easily be used to increase the population of the local community. It is for this purpose that, theoretically at least, we must postulate the existence of a power group able, as it were, to preside over the allocation of resources between the alternative ends of an increase in population or an increase in general welfare and income.

The role of the power group is crucial to the process of urbanization in more than one respect. Apart from exercising power over both the food producers and the specialists in the disposition of their output, it is their especial function to provide and maintain stable and peaceful conditions under which both groups can operate to the best advantage. Peaceful conditions, however, imply both the absence of disruptive internal strife and the creation of an image of strength sufficient to prevent rival communities from embarking on aggressive acts.

For the former purpose, the power class has had to devise methods of compelling subservience to their rule from the mass of the people. An important device has been the exploitation of the human fear of the hereafter. Over a large part of human history, the role of the priestly class or the divine representative has been important in providing the nucleus for the growth of urban centres. Similarly, the power to inflict bodily injury or to incarcerate through the use of organized agents or institutions have also been used to the same end.

To repel outside aggression, it has always been necessary to organize the males of the community into an army. Sometimes, all the adult males are involved, each being required to spend some years of his life in a people's militia or to be prepared to carry arms whenever he is required to do so. Sometimes there is a standing army—a group of specialists whose profession is to make war. This latter situation was rare in the past, for the economy was too fragile to support a class of unproductive specialists. Yet it was not unknown, particularly once the institution of slavery allowed non-members of a community to be impressed into its service. Indeed, for communities with ambition to dominate the resources of other groups, such standing armies became an important class.

The institution of a city army was thus an important concomitant of the rise of an urban centre. With time, the city which could develop this institution to a relatively higher level liquidated such institutions in neighbouring cities, provided its own 'pax' and created a nation or an empire. A national army then replaced a number of city armies and the presence or absence of stable conditions over the whole area became related to the vigilance and internal conditions of the conquering city.

Apart from guaranteeing peaceful conditions, the members of the power class play a more positive role in urbanization in so far as they determine the extent of functional specialization in the community. Their role in this respect stems from their interpretation of what are the desirable social goals for the community. This interpretation affects the rate of functional specialization through its effect on the prevailing economic attitudes, the level of technological consciousness and the direction of intellectual preoccupations in the community.

The goal of social aspirations has never been the same among different communities. Nor does it remain the same even within a single community over a long period of time. In one epoch it may be the spiritual survival of the community that is the major consideration predisposing to a social division of labour; in which case the priests would form the power class. They, in the name of the gods, would control and channel the production of the class of specialist craftsmen. However, as Gordon Childe observed, 'in so far as only "gods" and their favourite servants were in a position to purchase the products of the new industries, the effective demand for such products remained small'.[3] This restriction on the size of the market considerably weakens the urge to further specialization and in turn limits the productivity which is needed to stimulate a stronger tendency to urban agglomeration.

At another epoch the prevailing social goal may be the preservation of political or economic power in the hands of an oligarchy. The exclusive claims to power of such an oligarchy may be guaranteed not by 'divine rights' but by hereditary office, ownership of land, possession of the major means of production, or the acquisition of special skills. In this situation, a rigid stratification of society into guilds or castes results and specialization is constrained within the boundary of particular classes. This state of affairs is especially typified in ancient and medieval Europe and, in recent times, among many communities in Asia and Africa.

Nonetheless, beginning from the medieval period in Europe and continuing until the present there was a more pervasive social goal, namely, that of increasing the wealth of the community as a whole by ensuring to individuals freedom to increase their income and maximize the returns for their exertions. This economic basis to social action has had a far reaching effect not only on the progress of human history but also especially on the type of cities that developed. For people, once they are free of the restraining control of artificial social divisions, give free vent to their imaginative and inventive capabilities. And soon, from the professional or guild type of specialization in which a single individual mastered all the stages in the production of an article, society advanced to the other type of specialization based on the technical breakdown or elaboration of stages in the manufacturing of goods and involving, apart from human labour, the use of ancillary capital and machines.

The role of power groups in a community is thus seen to be fundamental not only for the genesis of urbanization but also for its direction and progress once generated. However the effectiveness of power groups constitutes only one element, albeit a most important one, in ensuring co-ordination and interdependence in the work of the specialist-producers. Also important is the role of the class of traders and merchants. The function of this class is more complex than is often imagined and needs, in the first place, to be distinguished from that of simple exchange involving no more than members of a single community.

The type of trading that constitutes a limiting condition for urbanization is an activity involving at least three processes. In the first place, there is the process of articulation whereby the surplus output of various productive units scattered over space is collected at a price in one or a few centres. Secondly, there is the process of distribution whereby goods already collected are made available at places where they are in greatest demand. Thirdly, there is the process of innovation whereby demand for new and formerly unknown commodities is generated in a community by various devices of advertisement.

These three processes impose certain obligations on the merchant class. The most obvious is their need to travel far and wide. Travelling was not always a pleasurable, safe and speedy activity so that for much of human history the work of a trader involved considerable hazards. Childe noted that in the early history of urbanization in Mesopotamia 'the conditions of commerce must have been exacting. Caravans must cross swamps, deserts and mountain ranges; flotillas had not only to thread their ways along the canal and tortuous river channels between shoals and marshes, but also brave the open waters of the Persian Gulf and perhaps also of the Arabian Sea. Both must traverse the territories of foreign tribes, who had to be either induced by bribes or forced by arms to permit passage and to supply water and other necessities.'[4] Even in the Middle Ages, Pirenne described the travelling merchants as comprising 'armed bands, the members of which equipped with bows and swords, encircled the horses and wagons loaded with bags, packs and casks.'[5]

To facilitate the work of collection in distant places, it was often necessary for the merchants to leave behind in those places some members of their community. This small group, in the interval between the departure and arrival of the caravan, bought and collected trading goods and generally kept a surveillance over the neighbourhood for novel commodities. The presence of such foreign elements in cities must have begun that process of ethnic heterogeneity which is so characteristic a feature of cities today, Speaking a foreign tongue, practising strange habits and keeping strange customs, the agencies of foreign merchants performed the vital role of predisposing city dwellers to tolerance of different ways of living.

Trading then provides a major life-blood for the existence of cities. It sets in motion a substantial flow of goods and services and by bringing these within easy reach of large sections of the populace increases the demand for them and motivates the acquisition of greater purchasing power. This leads to increased productivity and a greater tendency towards specialization. It can thus be assumed that the greater the flow of goods and services, the faster the rate of production as well as of urbanization. Any event that checks or hinders the pursuit of trade and commerce can therefore be expected to hamper the growth of cities.

The index of urbanization

Since neither the concept of specialization nor its limiting conditions are easily definable in quantitative terms, various attempts have been made to find an attribute or attributes which can be used as an index of urbanization to distinguish between communities which are urbanized and those which are not. Many of the indices so far suggested can be criticized largely on the basis of their being ethnocentric and they do not take account of all known cases of societies which were or are urbanized.

Gordon Childe insists, for instance, that the major attribute of an urbanizing society is its invention or adoption of writing. He equates 'city' with 'civilization' and defines the latter as 'the aggregation of large populations in cities; the differentiation within this of primary producers (fishers, farmers, etc.), full-time specialist artisans, merchants, officials, priests and rulers; an effective concentration of economic and political power; the use of conventional symbols for recording and transmitting information (writing) and equally conventional standards of weights and measures, of time and space leading to some mathematical and calendrical science'.[6]

Sjoberg, who supports Gordon Childe, makes the claim of writing more explicitly. He states emphatically that 'in addition to size, heterogeneity, public works and so on, writing is essential to the characterization of the city, implying as it does the existence of a highly specialized non-agricultural group that has the necessary leisure to develop such a

complex skill. Above all, the use of a writing system is the single firm
criterion for distinguishing the city, the nucleus of civilization, from
other types of early settlements.'[7] Moreover, as if to emphasize the
ethnocentric basis of this distinction, Sjoberg added that if the other
criteria, excluding writing, were to be applied in defining what is urban,
'we would falsely categorize as cities (*and this implies civilization*) some
of the large villages of, say, Neolithic Europe, or Africa and Polynesia,
or the Pueblo Indians and the Northwest Coast tribes'. Although he
admitted the complex social structure of traditional Dahomey, Ashanti
and Yoruba in Africa, all he can accept for them is a 'quasi-urban'
status, whatever that may mean.

Not all social scientists accept this arbitrary index for defining urban
development. Wheeler finds it a rather unsatisfactory criterion and
Louis Wirth ignores it in his definition of urbanism.[8] The present
writer finds it difficult to accept writing as an index precisely because
the literate group which is likely to invent it represents only one class of
specialists whose emergence in an urbanized society may or may not
be delayed.

A second index that is sometimes used to define an urban centre is the
absence of an agricultural group within the city. Dickinson, for instance,
defines an urban centre as a compact settlement engaged in non-
agricultural occupations.[9] What is missing in this definition is a time
perspective. Most urban centres began with a substantial proportion of
their inhabitants being farmers. However, as specialization increased
and transport improved, there was the tendency for urban centres to
concentrate more and more on secondary and tertiary activities and for
the farmers to find that greater efficiency requires that they should live
on their farms. Thus the absence of agricultural workers in cities represents only a very late development in the history of urbanization.
It can be used as a criterion not of urbanization in general but of a
particular stage of it. Pirenne puts the point clearly when he affirms that
'depending on time and place, sometimes commercial activity and
sometimes industrial activity is the dominant characteristic of a city
population. In antiquity, of course, a considerable section of the city
population was made up of landed proprietors, living either by the
cultivation of or by the revenue from the lands which they owned outside. But it remains nonetheless true that commensurately with the
development of cities, artisans and traders became more and more
numerous. The rural economy, older than the urban economy, con-

tinued to exist side by side with the latter; the one did not prevent the other from developing.'[10]

Other indices which have been suggested need not concern us here. These include, for instance, racial or ethnic composition of the population as a test of heterogeneity, and the level of impersonality of social relations.[11] What all this adds up to is the extreme difficulty of finding a single criterion to summarize the process of urbanization. It also emphasizes the complexity of the variants of the process in different places and at different times.

Conclusion

It has been necessary to review the theoretical basis of urbanization in order to facilitate understanding of the position in Nigeria. Urbanization is a continuing process, related to the increasing functional specialization in human society. As such, it is easy to conceive of communities at different stages of the process. The stage reached by any community has important repercussions on a whole set of social, economic and political relations in that community.

Nonetheless, there is nothing in the situation which makes the trend of the process uni-directional. Nothing constrains communities irrevocably on a path of increasing specialization. Indeed, as any of the limiting conditions enumerated above are relaxed, as the political situation becomes unstable or as trade declines, the rate of urbanization slackens. Most of the cities may decline, some may be deserted, while others may be destroyed completely in civil or international war. Again and again this fact is proved by the experience of Europe. It happened with the collapse of the Roman Empire and it happened again during the Thirty Years War.[12]

In West Africa the same is equally true. Four centuries of slave-trading by Arabs and various European nations destroyed the peace and stability which had been previously maintained in these areas by various indigenous empires. Vigorous trading activities in these empires in the medieval period had given rise to numerous towns and cities. Some of these towns and cities disappeared in the period of unstable conditions that followed; but many managed to linger on, no doubt with their activity greatly reduced. In Nigeria such centres include Kano, Zaria, Katsina, Ife and Ijebu-Ode which were still thriving at the beginning of the colonial régime. The colonial régime came to give new meaning to these centres and to inject advanced urban technologies, already developed elsewhere, into their traditional existence. The result was not always to the advantage of the old centres but its general implication in terms of greater volume of trade and faster transport was tremendous.

The study of urbanization in Nigeria, therefore, is an attempt to evaluate the impact of cultural contact between Nigeria and the rest of the world. With a few, though important exceptions, most urban centres in Nigeria are an amalgam of two contrasting levels of urbanization— a traditional, almost medieval, pre-industrial urbanization and an advanced, industrial urbanization. Both continue to exist side-by-side. The effects of this juxtaposition are not always predictable but an understanding of how this has happened remains of immense importance for any plan for economic and social advancement in the area.

References

1. Louis Wirth, 'Urbanism as a way of life', *American Journal of Sociology*, Vol. 44, No. 2, July 1938.
2. H. P. Fairchild (Ed.), *Dictionary of Sociology*, Ames, Iowa, 1955, p. 155.
3. V. Gordon Childe, *What happened in History*, London, 1964, p. 107.
4. Ibid., p. 105.
5. Henri Pirenne, *Medieval Cities*, Princeton, 1925, p. 85.
6. V. Gordon Childe, *Social Evolution*, London, 1951, p. 161.
7. Gideon Sjoberg, *The Pre-Industrial City*, Free Press of Glencoe, Illinois, 1960, p. 33.
8. M. Wheeler, 'The First Towns', *Antiquity*, Vol. 30, No. 119, September 1956, pp. 132-136 and Louis Wirth, op. cit.
9. R. E. Dickinson, *City Region and Regionalism*, London, 1947, p. 25.
10. H. Pirenne, op. cit., p. 94.
11. Horace Miner, *The Primitive City of Timbuktoo*, Princeton, 1953, 298 pp.
12. See C. V. Wedgwood, *The Thirty Years War*, London, 1938, pp. 512-520.

3 Pre-European Urbanization in Nigeria

a Northern Nigeria

The Federation of Nigeria occupies an area of 355,174 square miles and, according to the 1963 Census, it has a population of approximately 56 million people. Because of various problems connected with that Census, it has not been possible to identify what proportion of this population is urban. The 1952 Census, however, showed that of a total 31,168,000 people in the country, some 19 per cent or nearly 6 million lived in urban centres of 5,000 people and over. What was perhaps most striking was the wide variation of this proportion from region to region. In Northern Nigeria the proportion was 9 per cent, although for the Hausa area alone it rose to 12 per cent; in Eastern Nigeria it was 14 per cent, while in Western Nigeria it was as high as 49 per cent.

The background to the relatively impressive level of urban development in Nigeria is to be found in the contrasting environmental conditions within the country. Basically the country straddles two distinct natural regions. There is the southern forest zone which succeeds the stretch of swampy, mangrove vegetation inland from the coast. This forested area occupies only about one-third of the country. The remaining two-thirds are occupied by grasslands or savannas of varying characteristics. These include the tall, wiry grasses of the Guinea Savanna in the south, as well as the short, clumpy grasses of the Sahel Savanna close to the border of the Sahara Desert.

This extensive open grassland country provided the scene for the earliest urban development in Nigeria. Agriculturally, large parts of it are very fertile. Rainfall varies from about 20 to 40 inches, but most of it comes during a single season from May to October. As a result, although a wide range of crops can be grown, notably grains like sorghum and millet, only a single harvest can be had in a year. Fortunately, however, temperatures are never so low as to prevent cultivation of crops at other times of the year so that with the aid of water from wells or from rivers which are permanent or semi-permanent, other crops have been added to the staples. Most important of these has been rice, but vegetables, tobacco and a number of other market gardening crops like onions, tomatoes and beans are also raised by these methods.

The agricultural wealth of the Sudan grassland region has been an important factor in the development of its cities. The open nature of the countryside, offering great scope for unobstructed human movements and organization, has also been of decisive significance. Especially during the medieval period, these grassland areas became the scene of an extensive interregional and international commerce and witnessed the emergence of various kingdoms and empires providing peace and stability necessary for carrying on this commerce. This development affected the whole of the Western Sudan from the extreme west in the Cape Verde area eastward beyond Lake Chad and including much of the area of present-day Northern Nigeria. In order to appreciate the background to development in Nigeria, it is therefore necessary to describe briefly the medieval conditions in the Western Sudan as a whole.

Medieval urbanism in the Western Sudan

The medieval period witnessed an expansion of international trade which had ramifications throughout the area of the then known world. Recovering after five centuries from the vicissitudes and insecurity that had followed from the collapse of the Roman Empire, the Old World—especially those parts of it around the Mediterranean—gradually began to feel the stirrings of increased productivity and the need for wider exchange. From the Mediterranean ports of Naples, Venice, Genoa, Pisa, Marseilles and Castille ships went everywhere to the North African coast. Others on the Red Sea sailed across the Indian Ocean to places like Bombay, Poona and Cochin as well as to the East African coast. All these ships linked large parts of the Old World intimately together in trading relations that were unrivalled until long after the discovery of America. One major consequence of this tremendous and extensive revival of trade was the flowering of cities in different parts of the world. For Europe, Pirenne provided an impressive classic of the resultant urban development while the Asian component of this phenomenon has also received from historians fairly adequate treatment.[1] It is, however, only recently that the contribution of Africa, outside the Mediterranean areas, has started to be accorded any attention. It is now fairly certain that both West and East Africa were active participants in this revival of international trade in the medieval period. In both these areas, as was the case in Europe, trade provided the *raison d'être* for the rise of numerous cities.

The Mediterranean ports of the Maghreb of North Africa were the outlets for West Africa's contribution to this international commerce. According to Latrie, much of the commercial prosperity of the Arabs of Barbary at this time was due in no small measure to the trade with Italy on the one hand and with the West African Sudan on the other.[2] The trade goods from the Sudan included slaves, ivory, ebony, horses, hides and skins—especially the famed 'moroccan' leather which was derived from the Sokoto area of Northern Nigeria. But perhaps the most important of the commodities from the Sudan was gold which was particularly needed in Europe for its exchange value as well as its intrinsic preciousness. Mauny, in fact, asserts that 'the Sudan was one of the principal providers of gold to the European world right through the Middle Ages, up to the discovery of America'.[3]

Bovill emphasized that the foundation of the prosperity of the very first of the medieval empires of the Sudan—the Empire of Ghana— was this trade in gold.[4] Even after the eclipse of Ghana and the rise of the new Empire of Mali, gold continued to provide the major article of wealth in the Sudan. The King of Mali, Mansa Musa, was described as setting out in 1324 on a pilgrimage to Mecca across the desert preceded by 'five hundred slaves each carrying a staff of gold weighing 500 mithgal or about six pounds'.[5] The spectacular scale on which the journey was conducted caused such a sensation in Cairo and other places which witnessed the passage of this splendid caravan that the name of Musa became quickly familiar and renowned throughout a large part of the civilized world.

Much of the gold involved in this international commerce came from the more wooded regions to the south, from an area referred to in most medieval documents as Wangara. The situation of this area has not been satisfactorily located although it is increasingly being identified with the auriferous region of Bambuk and Boure which lies between the Faleme River and the Upper Niger within the northern Guinea Savanna. In exchange for this gold, traders from the north brought large quantities of salt. According to El Bekri, an Arab geographer of the eleventh century, the Ferawi, one of the tribes in the forest area, were so much in need of salt that they were prepared to exchange it for gold in equal measure.[6] The primary source of salt was the Sahara Desert. An important mining centre was Teghaza, a place owned by the town of Sidjilmassa in North Africa. This centre was constantly thronged with merchants, and work in the mines, which produced an enormous revenue, never ceased.[7] Other ancient salt-mining centres in the Sahara included Idjil (west of Teghaza), Hoggar, Ankalas (near Bilma), Abzar and Tamalma in the central Sahara. Apart from salt, other trade articles included a wide range of European manufactured goods, especially silver and copper which were in great demand in the Sudan where their bright colour made them popular, glass beads from most of the principal glass-makers of Venice, European cloth of various types, and cowries from the Indian Ocean.

This extensive international trade across the desert as well as the complementary interregional trade within the Sudan and between it and the forest areas to the south encouraged the rise of numerous cities (Fig. 2). In general, one can distinguish two broad zones of city development. There was a northern zone at the southern edge of the desert where the cities served the important functions of entrepôt of trade with North Africa and victualling stations for equipping the caravans for the journey across the desert. Such cities included, from west to east, Tekrur, Audoghast, Oualata, Kumbi, Timbuktu, Tirekka, Gao, Takedda, Tadmekka, Agades and Bilma. Not all these cities were contemporaneous but, whatever their date, they performed very similar functions. Kumbi, for instance, had virtually disappeared by the thirteenth century and was replaced by Oualata.

The southern zone of cities developed in connection with the interregional trade with the forest areas from where most of the gold, slaves, ivory and even maleguetta pepper were derived. Bovill noted the peculiar location of most of these cities close to the 12°N parallel. He mentioned only seven of them, but the list could easily be extended to include not only those which have disappeared but also numerous others which survived until the nineteenth century. From west to east, this southern group of cities includes Silla, Bamako, Segou, Djenne, Wagadugu, Fadan, Gurma, Gaya, Koukia, Jega, Katsina, Kano and Kukawa. Bovill observed that the latitudinal position of these cities approximately marks the southern limit of camel transport and the northern limit of the tsetse-fly.

This proliferation of city life emphasizes the vigorous participation of the Western Sudan in the world-wide commercial activities that characterized the medieval period. Although historians have often concentrated on the political conflicts that marked the rise and fall of the succession of empires of the Western Sudan during the period, it is important to stress that, behind the clashes of arms and soldiers, peace-

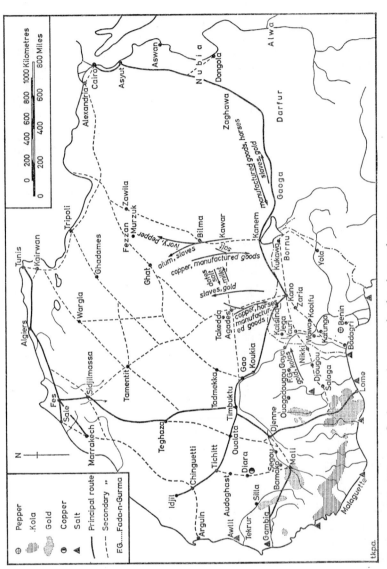

Figure 2   The Western Sudan: trade routes in the sixteenth century

ful trading went on. Moreover, for this reason, the cities and towns in general continued to flourish and to survive the changing fortunes of the successive empires. Indeed, Davidson struck what appears to be the right note when he stressed that the economic dimension, that is, the need to control the international trade and to provide the 'pax' necessary for this trade to thrive, cannot be discounted in an assessment of the succession of centres of power in the Sudan during this time.

The earliest of these Sudanese empires was Ghana, which was already a centralized state when the Arabs first mentioned it in A.D. 800. The second was Mali, which rose in the thirteenth century and persisted until the sixteenth century. A third was Songhai, whose power and prestige covered the fifteenth and sixteenth centuries, and whose area extended over much of the Hausa States of Northern Nigeria. The Songhai Empire achieved a measure of centralized control which was unparalleled in the history of the Sudan. It was organized into provinces, each with a governor in charge. Cities of importance had mayors put also in charge of them. A standing army was established and an elaborate code of court etiquette defined the precedence, uniform and privileges of the numerous officers of state. The resulting security and stability, as was to be expected, stimulated trade and prosperity to a new height. Furthermore, as if to demonstrate this fact again to the rest of the world, the ruler of the Songhai Empire, Askia the Great, set out in 1495 on another spectacular pilgrimage to Mecca. His escort consisted of 500 cavalry and 1,000 infantry, and he carried with him some 300,000 pieces of gold from the national treasury.

Unfortunately the order and stability which was created did not last more than a century when it received a catastrophic blow from external aggression. In 1591 the Moroccan army of El Mansur emerged from the Sahara armed with firearms, captured Gao and Timbuktu, scattered the Songhai army and ruined the state. In the word of Es Sadi, an eye-witness chronicler of these unhappy events 'security gave place to danger, wealth to poverty, distress and calamities, and violence succeeded tranquillity. Everywhere men destroyed each other; in every place and in every direction there was plundering, and war spared neither life nor property nor persons. Disorder was general and spread everywhere, rising to the highest degree of intensity.'[8] By 1600, the great days of the Sudan was over and Northern Nigeria was left to chart its own historical course. Nonetheless, much in its present-day urban characteristics can be understood only in terms of this involvement with the rest of the

Western Sudan both politically and economically during the medieval period.

Pre-nineteenth century urban development in Northern Nigeria

Although Northern Nigeria derived some of its economic inspiration from contacts with the Empire of Songhai in the west, it was also strongly influenced by the Kanem Empire in the east. The rise of this latter empire had been due to incursions of semi-nomadic groups of the Beni-Sef (or Sefawa) who set up a small state east of Lake Chad sometime in the eighth century. This small state grew in importance with the centuries. At its apogee in the early thirteenth century, it stretched from Fezzan in the north to Dikwa in the south while to the west it included most of Hausaland.

Throughout most of the period, the centre of power of the Kanem Empire lay outside the present area of Nigeria. Certain events not unconnected with the large size of the empire gradually led to a westward shift of the centre and to the emergence of the powerful kingdom of Bornu. These events arose because of the need to have provincial governors to administer the far-flung districts of the empire. Because most of these governors were chosen from among members of the royal family, and placed in centres sufficiently remote to provide a safe basis for organizing rebellion, much of the history of Kanem in the thirteenth and fourteenth centuries was taken up by revolts and internal bitter struggle for the control of the empire by members of the royal house. This so weakened Kanem that it was easy for another neighbouring group of nomads, the Bulala, to expel the Sefawa dynasty about 1389 and establish their own control.

The Sefawa were then forced to move south-west into Bornu and over the next century to build up a new state in this area. By the middle of the fifteenth century, this state was sufficiently powerful to exact tribute from the city-state of Kano with which it carried on extensive trade. Bornu also achieved a tremendous revival of prosperity, and by the late sixteenth century its rulers succeeded in expanding its borders southwards and eastwards to include the Marghi, the Gamergum, the Mandara and the Wadai. Over all parts of the new empire, Koranic law was extended and brick mosques appeared in a number of places. Provincial administration was entrusted to slaves or people of humble origin, so preventing the internecine rivalry that marked the end of the first Sefawa rule over Kanem. The greatness of Bornu, however, only

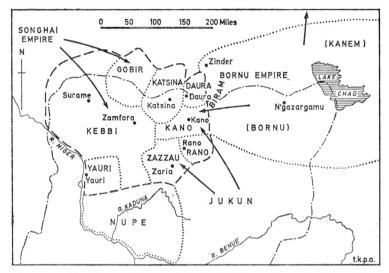

Figure 3   The Hausa States and their neighbours from the sixteenth to the nineteenth century

outlived that of Songhai by a few decades and the period up to the end of the eighteenth century was marked by inactivity and decline.

Meanwhile the Hausa States were undergoing an equally chequered history. The origin of these states is lost in obscurity, although it is clear from oral tradition and the few extant chronicles that they were due to the activities of immigrant groups some time between A.D. 1000 and 1200. The story is told of a certain Bayajidda (Abuyazidu), son of Abdulahi, King of Baghdad, who, after quarrelling with his father, journeyed to Bornu, and thence to Daura where he slew a snake that used to prevent the local people from drawing water from a well. The Queen of Daura then married Bayajidda and had a son called Bawo. When his father died, Bawo ascended his throne and had six sons who became the kings of Kano, Zazzau (Zaria), Gobir, Katsina, Rano and Biram (Fig. 3). Together with Daura, these states were known as the *Hausa Bokwoi* or the Seven Hausa States in contradistinction to the *Banza Bokwoi* or the seven 'bastard' Hausa States which were probably states that came under Hausa influence. The latter included Zamfara, Nupe, Gwari, Yauri and Kororofa.

Although various versions of this legend exist, they all serve to underline the great cultural homogeneity of the Hausa States. The tradition also exists that each of the states had specific functions connected with the growth and security of all the states. Thus Gobir, which is located on the fringes of the desert, served as the northern outpost of Hausaland, guarding it against attackers from the desert, especially the Tuaregs. Zaria, to the south, was the procurer of slaves; Kano and Katsina were the trading states; Rano was the industrial centre while Daura remained the spiritual home of the Hausa.

The involvement of both Bornu and the Hausa States in the international commerce across the desert appears to have been somewhat later than in areas farther west. When El Edrisi visited Njimi, capital of Kanem, in the middle of the twelfth century, for instance, he found it a very small town, with little industry and trade and its population very miserable.[9] By 1352, however, when Ibn Battuta visited this area, we learn that '. . . copper is exported from Tagadda . . . to the country of Barnu, which is forty days' journey from Tagadda. The people of Barnu are Muslims, and have a king called Idris. . . . From this country come excellent slave-girls, eunuchs, and fabrics dyed with saffron.'[10] From this it can be inferred that by this date, Bornu (i.e. Kanem) was already involved in the international trade. Leo Africanus, who visited the area between 1512-14, also noted that 'the King of Bornu sent for the merchants of Barbary and willed them to bring him great store of horses: for in this country they use to exchange horses for slaves and to give fifteen, and sometimes twenty slaves for one horse. And by this means there abundance of horses brought.'[11] This trade in slaves was so remunerative that 'the King's spurs, his bridles, platters, dishes, pots and other vessels wherein his meat and drinks are brought to the table, are all of pure gold: yea, and the chains of his dogs and hounds are of gold also'.[12]

As against this emphasis on slaves, the medieval foreign trade of the Hausa States was much diversified. As with the situation in Bornu, however, this trade seems to have developed late in the medieval period, probably only from the early fifteenth century. Ibn Battuta made no mention of the Hausa States at all in the narrative of his travels, although his reference to Kubar, another place to which copper was exported from Tagadda, has been interpreted to mean Gobir.[13] The *Kano Chronicle*, however, records that in the reign of Yakubu (1452-63) 'the Asbenawa (people from Asben to the north) came to Gobir, and salt became common in Hausaland. In the following year, merchants from Gwanja began coming to Katsina; Beriberi came in large numbers, and a colony of Arabs arrived. Some of the Arabs settled in Kano and some in Katsina.'[14] The *Chronicle* further records a considerable Fulani and Wangara immigration from Mali, which was then in decline. The immigrants, many of whom moved on to Bornu, were said to have brought many books with them.

It is thus not improbable that this record marked the beginning of the international commercial relation of the Hausa States and North Africa. By the time of the visit of Leo Africanus, we get some fairly detailed information of economic activities in this region. Journeying through Hausaland from west to east, he came first to Gobir.

> 'Here', he noted, 'are great stores of artificers and linen weavers; and here are such shoes made as the ancient Romans were wont to wear, the greatest part whereof is carried to Timbuktu and Gao. In this region there is a certain great "village" containing almost six thousand families, being inhabited with all kinds of merchants, and here was in times past the court of a certain king, who in my time was slain by Izchia, the king of Timbuktu. . . .'[15]

Of the other Hausa states which he visited, namely Zamfara, Katsina, Kano and Zegzeg (Zaria), he depicted their desolate state owing to recent invasion by the army of Songhai and the crushing burden of tribute imposed on the people. In spite of this, many of their cities seemed to have maintained some measure of economic prosperity. Kano, for instance, was described as a city whose 'inhabitants are rich merchants and most civil people. Their king was in times past of great puissance and had mighty troops of horsemen at his command.' Of Zegzeg, Leo Africanus remarked that 'the inhabitants are rich and have great traffic into other nations'.

International trade from this area was carried on along two major caravan routes. One ran through Bilma, Murzuk and Fezzan to Tripoli; the other went through Agades and Ghadames to Kairwan (see Fig. 2). Transport itself depended on camels across the deserts though within the Sudan region this was supplemented by other draught animals, notably asses, horses and bullocks. According to Mauny, the average distance which a camel can cover per marching day is between thirty and forty miles so that the journey across the desert took over a month.[16]

Within the Sudan itself, these caravan routes broke up into innumerable secondary routes serving interregional trade and, in some cases, leading southwards to the Guinea Coast. This interregional trade was carried on in all directions. From the Kano-Katsina area, handicraft goods, notably dyed cloths, leather goods and shoes, were carried westward to Gao, Timbuktu and beyond. In exchange for these came metals such as copper from Takedda which appeared to have been re-exported southward to the Yoruba country and Benin. Southward and southwestward through Nikki, Yendi, Salaga and Kintampo, were sent salt as well as commodities imported from the North African coast in return for gold, kolanuts, ivory and spices.

Although this extensive interregional and international commerce called into being a number of cities in Northern Nigeria, we have rather limited information about them. Leo Africanus only mentioned the major cities such as Katsina, Kano, Zegzeg (Zazzau) and Katsina-Lake. The *Kano Chronicle*, however, gave some indication of city-forming activities going on at this time. In the reign of Abdulahi Burja (1438-52) roads are said to have been opened from Bornu to Gwanja and large numbers of Beriberi moved to settle in the country.[17] It was also at this time that camels are said to have been introduced into Hausaland. By the end of the seventeenth century, Kano, worn out by a century of inter-necine wars as well as by the Kororofan invasion of 1653, was replaced in importance by Katsina which, in particular, had profited by the collapse of the Songhai Empire. With the fall of the Songhai Empire, the prosperity and learning of its capital were diverted to Katsina. The leather-working trade for which Agades was famous was introduced to Katsina by the Songhais. Citizens of Katsina became renowned for their manners and courtesy, her schools for their learning, her administration and judiciary for their wisdom.[18] Before the ruin wrought on her early in the nineteenth century, Katsina was the most important commercial centre in Hausaland and caravans converged on her from all directions.

Urbanization in Northern Nigeria in the nineteenth century

The nineteenth century opened with the estrangement between the Sarkin Gobir and his former Fulani tutor, Uthman dan Fodio, which was to lead to the Fulani *Jihad* from 1804 to about 1810. Within that short space of time virtually all the Hausa States, Nupe, Adamawa and some parts of Bornu came under the rule of Fulani emirs. According to Hogben, this replacement of hereditary chiefs by Fulani usurpers did wholesale damage to the country.[19] Books, records, towns, houses, institutions and ancient customs were wantonly destroyed. Be this as it may, the need for strategic locations on the part of the Fulani led to the foundation of a number of new towns. Among these was Sokoto which, until 1805, was a tiny hamlet but whose strong natural advantages were so obvious that the Fulani built it up as their major centre. In 1809 they built the first wall round it which was succeeded by a second wall in 1818. Other towns owing their origin to the Fulani include Gwandu (which was walled round three years before Sokoto), Gombe and Katagum in the western frontier districts of Bornu, and Wurno, twenty miles north of Sokoto, which became a second capital of the Fulani.

Soon after the *Jihad* began, European explorers started to arrive from whom we get some more detailed description of economic and urban life in Northern Nigeria. After the disastrous termination of Mungo Park's second journey down the Niger at Bussa in 1805, the next major British attempt at penetration into Northern Nigeria was that of Denham, Clapperton and Oudney in 1821. This was followed in 1826 by the exploration of Clapperton and Lander; by that of the Lander brothers in 1829; and by that of Heinrich Barth in 1851.

The journals of Denham, Clapperton and Oudney emphasized not only the amount of destruction to urban life which the *Jihad* had occasioned but also the vigour with which the international commerce was still carried on. Katsina, for instance, was found mostly in ruins, with its principal commerce being carried on at Kano since the Fulani conquest. Yet there were still two daily markets being held in different parts of the town: one to the north, the other to the south.[20] The southern market was chiefly attended by merchants of Ghadames and Tuat; the one to the north by Tuaregs. The Ghadames and Tuat merchants brought raw silk, cotton and woollen cloths, beads, and a little cochineal, which they sold for cowries. These were sent to their agents at Kano to purchase blue *tobes* and *turkadees* which were conveyed across the country to supply the fair at Gharaat. A *tobe* is a cotton cloth woven and dyed in blue, while a *turkadee* is an oblong piece of dress of dark blue colour worn by women. At Gharaat any commodities which were not sold were sent to Timbuktu in exchange for civet, gold and slaves. Tanned bullocks' hides also were frequently carried to Fezzan and Tripoli.

Of the transportational organization for this trade we also learn that merchants from Ghadames and Tuat kept no camels of their own but hired them from the Tuaregs. The latter carried their goods across the desert to Katsina at the rate of ten dollars a load, and likewise conveyed slaves at twenty-five dollars a head.[21] With this revenue and the produce of the salt they brought with them, the Tuaregs bought grains and other necessaries to serve them during their sojourn in the desert. How large the caravans were, is not easy to say. Clapperton mentioned a caravan of nearly 3,000 camels arriving in Kano in 1824. Barth, nearly thirty years later, estimated that the salt-caravan to Katsina was at least about 2,500 camels strong. This comprised different divisions or troops of not more than 200 camels each. The whole of the salt they carried he computed as being, at the utmost, worth one hundred millions of *kurdi*, or about £8,000 sterling at the time.[22]

Another measure of the international trade at the time can be derived from the prevalence of the use of imported sword blades among the cavalries of the various Hausa States. Clapperton first noticed these sword blades in the cavalry of the Emir of Kano. According to him,

> 'the swords are broad, straight, and long, but require no particular description, as, by a vicissitude somewhat singular, they are the very blades formerly wielded by the knights of Malta. These swords are sent from Malta to Bengazee, in the state of Tripoli, where they are exchanged for bullocks. They are afterwards carried across the desert to Bornou, thence to Hausa, and at last remounted at Kano, for the use of the inhabitants of almost all central Africa.'[23]

A few years later at Rabbah, a town nearly three hundred miles south from Kano, Laird was to notice the same type of sword imported through the Arabs via Tripoli, used by the king's army, which comprised 5,000 cavalry and 20,000 infantry.[24] This southerly penetration of the Saharan trade is further attested to by the fact that Laird's stay in Rabbah coincided with the presence of *kafilas* (or caravans) of merchants, most of whom were Arabs from Tripoli, Sokoto, Kano and the Hausa country. Barth, in fact, estimated that something like 50,000 of these sword blades were annually imported into Kano.[25]

Nowhere, however, was the importance of this international commerce better demonstrated than at Kano. Fig. 4 shows cartographically the very extensive nature of the European sources of imports into Kano as well as their relative importance estimated in cowrie-value by Barth in 1851. Indeed Barth made a very detailed description from which it has been possible to construct Table 2 to show the variety of imports, their sources and other remarks about them. The approximate total value of 488 million cowrie worked out at about £50,000 at that date.[26] This figure took no account of imports such as salt from the desert region and of the proportion of all imports that went to some of the other major centres such as Katsina, Sokoto and Kukawa. It also ignored some of

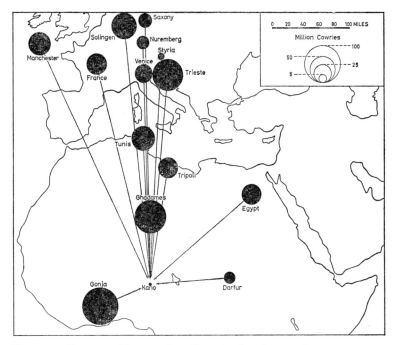

Figure 4   Sources of imports into Kano in the nineteenth century

the sizeable re-exports that filtered southward into Nupe, Yoruba and Gonja in exchange for the imports from these areas.

Nonetheless, even as late as 1896, the greater part of European goods in the Kano market came across the desert. According to Robinson, the caravans which came from the north brought about 12,000 camel-loads of goods annually, consisting of copper (chiefly in the form of manufactured articles), sugar, pepper, gunpowder, needles, cloves, white cloth turbans, red silk burnouses, Arab woollen dresses, red Sudanese caps, mirrors, red coral beads, etc.[27] The time occupied between Kano and Tripoli varied from three to nine months, the distance being about 1,800 miles. The routes that were used in the medieval period continued to be followed even at this date.

How profitable this trade was, particularly from the point of view of the North African merchants, can be inferred from a comment of Denham. According to him, the usual calculation of a Moorish merchant was that a camel-load of merchandise bought at Murzuk for 160 dollars

TABLE 2   IMPORTS OF KANO, 1851

	Money value (in million cowries)	Sources	Remarks
1. CALICOS	40	MANCHESTER	PART DYED AND RE-EXPORTED TO GHADAMES
2. MUSLINS	40	,,	—
3. COARSE SILK	70	TRIPOLI	USED FOR ORNAMENTING ROBES, SANDALS, ETC.
4. WOOLLEN CLOTH (RED AND GREEN)	15	SAXONY	GOING OUT OF FASHION
5. BEADS	50	VENICE AND TRIESTE	LOW PRICE, REDUCED SUPPLY
6. SUGAR	12	FRANCE	IN SMALL LOAVES OF $2\frac{1}{2}$ LB. EACH
7. COMMON PAPER	5	NUREMBERG	USED FOR WRAPPING
8. NEEDLES AND LOOKING-GLASSES	8	NUREMBERG	CHEAP
9. SWORD-BLADES	50	SOLINGEN	RE-EXPORTED AFTER BLADES ARE SET
10. COMMON RAZORS	2-3	STYRIA	CHEAP
11. FRENCH SILKS	20	FRANCE	RE-EXPORTED TO YORUBALAND AND GONJA
12. ARTICLES OF ARAB DRESS	50	TUNIS AND EGYPT	—
13. WHITE SHAWLS	10	EGYPT	—
14. FRANKINCENSE AND SPICES	15	—	—
15. ROSE OIL	40	—	EXPENSIVE, MAINLY FOR UPPER CLASS
16. TIN, ETC.	10	—	
17. COPPER AND ZINC	15-20	TRIPOLI AND DARFUR	
18. SILVER	SMALL AMOUNT		SILVERSMITHS QUITE ACTIVE
19. GOLD	SMALL AMOUNT		GENERAL STANDARD MITHKAL=4,000 KUNDI

TOTAL approx. 488 million cowries

would make a return in trading with Bornu of 500 dollars after paying all expenses. People in Fezzan sent three camel loads in charge of one man and, after paying all the expenses out of the profits, would give him a third of the remainder for his labour.

The goods that were exchanged for these imports were also numerous and varied. Curiously enough, one of these, especially from Bornu, was the Koran, copies of which sold in North Africa for 40 to 50 dollars each. Denham, in 1823, noticed that in the Bornu towns were many *hajis*, who had made the pilgrimage to Mecca, and excelled in writing the Arabic characters, as well as teaching the art to others.[28] The most important exports to the north, however, remained slaves. Tripoli continued to be the most important centre to which slaves were sent. Denham in 1823 pointed out that the number of *kafilas* between Tripoli and Bornu in the preceding five years had greatly exceeded any former period.[29] Later, in 1851, Barth pointed out that it was extremely difficult to say how many slaves were exported, as a greater number were carried away by small caravans to Bornu and Nupe than on the North African route. Altogether he estimated that about 5,000 slaves were exported annually from Kano. He believed that the abolition of slave trade in Tripoli at about that time might have affected the size of export. However, even in 1896, Robinson still found that there were usually as many as 500 slaves at a time on sale in the Kano market, although he gave no indication what proportion of these were exported.[30] Other exports from Northern Nigeria across the desert included ostrich skins and hides, including 'moroccan' leather, especially from the red goats of the Sokoto area, and ivory.

Compared with the international commerce to North Africa, it appears that the trade to other parts of West Africa, both the Sudan and the forest regions, was more important. The exports from Northern Nigeria to these regions consisted predominantly of craft products, minerals and agricultural crops. In these respects, one must take note of regional specialization within the north. The Bornu country was not particularly rich in craft wares except for a coarse type of dress consisting of stripes of deep indigo colour, or stripes of it alternating with white. But it was the major exporter of rock salt known as *trona* or *natron* and obtained around Lake Chad. Barth in 1851 met a natron caravan from Kukawa and counted as many as five hundred loads of natron.[31] He estimated that in any one year probably some 20,000 loads at the very least, worth 10 million cowries, passed through the Kano market which was the major centre for redistributing this commodity to Nupe and Yorubaland.[32]

The Kano area, besides, was the great manufactory for much of the north. Its manufactures consisted in particular of textile and leather goods. The textile was provided in different forms and styles. Barth mentions the *tobe* (or *riga*); the *turkedi*, which is an oblong piece of dress of dark-blue colour worn by the women; the *zenne*, which is plaid and is of various colours; and the *rawani baki* or black litham.[33] These manufactures had a very extensive market spreading 'to the north as far as Murzuk, Ghat, and even Tripoli; to the west not only to Timbuktu, but in some degree even as far as the shores of the Atlantic, the very inhabitants of Arguin dressing in the cloth woven and dyed in Kano; to the east, all over Bornu, although there it came in contact with the native industry of the country; and to the south it maintained a rivalry with the native industry of the Igbira and Igbo, while toward the southeast it invaded the whole of Adamawa, and was only limited by the nakedness of the pagan *sans-culottes*, who do not wear clothing'.[34] Barth put the export to Timbuktu alone at the least at 300 camel-loads annually, worth 60 million cowries. He estimated the whole produce of this manufacture, as far as is sold abroad, at about 300 million cowries. Even as late as 1896, Robinson still asserted that Kano clothed more than half the population of the Central Sudan. 'Any European who will take the trouble to ask for it, will find no difficulty in purchasing Kano-made cloth at towns on the coast as widely separated from one another as Alexandria, Tripoli, Tunis or Lagos.'[35]

Of the leather goods, the manufacture of sandals was perhaps the most important. Barth reports that 'the sandals are made with great neatness, and like the cloth, are exported to an immense distance. . . . It is very curious that the shoes made here by Arab shoemakers, of Sudan leather, and called *belgh'a* are exported in great quantities to North Africa.'[36] He estimated the total value of trade in leather goods at 15 million cowries.

Other parts of Northern Nigeria had their own lines of craft specialization. Katsina, like Kano, was noted for the manufacture of leather goods and the export of hides, skin and dried beef.[37] In Eastern Bornu, especially in the Logone area, Denham found that 'almost every house has its rude machinery for weaving, and the finer and closer linen is here produced; the width, however, is invariably the same as the Bornu *gubka*, not exceeding six or seven inches'.[38] In the Nupe country, large

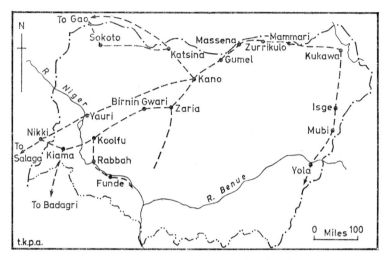

Figure 5   Trade routes in Northern Nigeria in the nineteenth century

black *tobes* or *tobes* of mixed silk and cotton were produced and a considerable trade was carried on in this commodity with Kano.

In exchange for the manufactures from the northern cities, the forested southern country sent various agricultural products, the most important of which was the kolanut. Barth noted that this commodity formed an important article of transit which brought considerable profit to the northern traders, from the fact that large sums of money were expended by the natives on this luxury which had become to them as necessary as coffee or tea to the Europeans. Different kinds of nut were imported, and Barth estimated the import into Kano alone as being certainly more than five hundred ass-loads every year. Each ass-load, if safely brought to the market—for kolanut is a very delicate article and very liable to spoil—could be sold for as much as 200,000 cowries, thus giving an average annual value of 80 to 100 million cowries. Most of the kolanut brought to Kano in the nineteenth century came from the Gonja country of modern Ghana. The kolanut from this area was of a uniformly red colour but was preferred because it kept better than any other. According to Robinson, at Gonja the average nut cost 5 cowries; at Say, on the Middle Niger, 70 to 80; at Sokoto, 100; at Kano, 140 to 250; at Kuka, on Lake Chad, 250 to 300 cowries.[39]

Fig. 5 gives some idea of the major routes of this interregional trade.

Much of this was carried on by caravans using bullocks, asses and mules rather than camels. Some of the traders, especially the petty ones, carried their goods on their head. According to Denham, this was more true of Hausa than of Bornu traders and certainly so of Nupe and other southern traders.[40] A concomitant of this long distance trade was the need to pay tolls at the major market towns. Clapperton noted that at the town of Wazo, or Wazawo, the first town in the province of Kontagora, the merchants had to pay 250 cowries for every loaded ass, bullock, horse or mule.[41] At Rajadawa, in the province of Yauri, the toll was 500 cowries for every loaded bullock and 300 for every loaded ass.[42] At Zaria, one-twentieth of the value of a merchant's goods was exacted as a duty.[43]

Both the needs of the extensive trading activities over the whole country and of the taxes and tributes required by the ruling aristocracy emphasized the important role of a commonly accepted currency over a large part of the country. Although there were a number of local currencies, the most common and widespread was the cowry which was imported through Cairo from the East. As early as 1353, Ibn Battuta, in describing Gao on the Niger, had noted that 'the buying and selling of its inhabitants is done with cowry shells and the same is the case in Malli'.[44] There appeared, however, to be areas such as Bornu where its acceptance was delayed owing to the strength of the local currency. Thus Denham had noticed that, coming from Bornu, cowrie became a currency only from Katagum which was a frontier town between Bornu and Kano.[45] Barth also pointed out the great increase in the import of cowries especially since 1848 owing to its introduction as currency into Bornu.[46]

Irrespective of the variety of local currencies, however, there was always an exchange rate established against cowries. Gold, for instance, was also a standard currency, and in 1851 an exchange rate of 4,000 cowries to a *mithkal* of gold (approx. $\frac{1}{8}$ oz.) was usually maintained in Kano. Cowries also exchanged against the Maria Theresa dollars at 2,500 cowries to one dollar in 1851.[47] Currencies of only local significance included the *rottala* or *rottl*, which was a copper currency exchanging ten to the dollar. In Bornu there was the *gubbuk*, a strip of cotton about three inches wide and a yard in length, three, four or five of which, according to texture, exchanged for one *rottala*.[48] In the Logone area (around Lake Chad) a metal currency was in use. This consisted of thin plates of iron, something in the shape of a horseshoe, made into parcels of ten and twelve, according to the weight, thirty of which parcels were equal in value to a dollar or ten *rottala*.

Trading activities in many of the cities were also generally regulated with the greatest care and strictly and impartially enforced. Especially for markets involved in long-distance trading, it was usual for much of the buying and selling in the market to be conducted through a broker or *mai dilali* who received a percentage of the price paid from the buyer or the seller in recognition of his services. Denham, in 1823, described the nature of the obligations of a *dilali*. Writing about the market in Kano, he pointed out that:

> 'If a *tobe* or *turkadee*, purchased here, is carried to Bornou or any other distant place, without being opened, and is there discovered to be of inferior quality, it is immediately sent back as a matter of course—the name of the *dylala*, or broker, being written inside every parcel. In this case the *dylala* must find out the seller, who, by the laws of Kano, is forthwith obliged to refund the purchase money.'[49]

How large were these trading centres? To this question no definitive answer can be given. An attempt has been made here to provide a list of a sample of towns whose populations were estimated by the various explorers who went through them. Some of these towns no longer exist and some have been difficult to identify. A very large number were simply described as small, medium sized, or large. Whatever the situation, the table emphasizes that some of the towns were of considerable size. Most of the major towns of the north today all had a population of about 30,000 early in the nineteenth century. The figure of 120,000 for Sokoto given by Lander may appear somewhat exaggerated. However, one should bear in mind that Sokoto was at this time the capital of the victorious Fulani army and was likely to have attracted a large number of those interested in seeking their fortune through pillage or distinguishing themselves in warfare, as well as their numerous slaves. We find later that Ibadan, which in Yorubaland rose to much the same position as Sokoto in the nineteenth century, was estimated by a number of independent visitors around 1850 as having a population of about 100,000.

As would be expected, the population of the cities tended to be heterogeneous and socially stratified. Heterogeneity, however, probably increased with increasing trading function. Barth found in Kano not only that the population was ethnically heterogeneous but also that separate quarters were reserved for traders from different parts of the

TABLE 3   SAMPLE OF ESTIMATES OF POPULATION OF CITIES IN NORTHERN
NIGERIA, 1820-55

Bornu

1. NEW BIRNIE	10,000	(D)	6. UJE MAIDUGURI	6,000	(B)
2. ARGONOU	30,000	(D)	7. UJE MABANI	8,000	(B)
3. DEEGOA	30,000	(D)	8. YOLA	12,000	(B)
4. BORZARI	8,000	(B)	9. DIKWA	25,000	(B)
5. ZURRIKULO	8,000	(B)			

Hausaland

1. KATAGUM	7,000	(D)	5. BAEBAEGIE	20-25,000	(C)
2. KANO	30-40,000	(D)	6. SOKOTO	120,000	(L)
KANO	30,000	(B)	7. KATSENA	7-8,000	(B)
3. QUARRA	5-6,000	(D)	8. GERKI	15,000	(B)
4. ZARIA	40-50,000	(C)	9. GUMMEL	10,000	(B)

Borgu-Nupe

1. KIAMA	30,000	(C)	4. KOOLFU	12-15,000	(C)
2. WAWA	18-20,000	(C)	KOOLFU	15-16,000	(L)
WAWA	20,000	(L)	5. RAJADAWA	6-7,000	(C)
3. TABRA	18-20,000	(C)	6. WOMBA	10-12,000	(C)
TABRA	18,000	(L)			

D = DENHAM 1822-24   C = CLAPPERTON 1825-27

L = LANDER 1825-27   B = BARTH 1851-55

Sudan.[50] Thus the area around Dala (Plate 1), the oldest quarter of the
town, and which, in commercial respects was the most important one,
was the residence of almost all the Arab and Berber (principally
Ghadasiye) merchants. There was also Agadesawa, the quarter largely
occupied by people from Agades, as well as Yaalewa and Marmara,
which were largely for the Fulani.

Apart from heterogeneity based on ethnic origin, there was also
heterogeneity based on occupation and reflected clearly in the guild
system or institutionalized occupational groupings. Smith points out
that in Zaria occupational categories were sharply distinguished in the
complex exchange economy of the Hausas and that in terms of the
arziki (the good fortune and social recognition associated with each
occupational category) it was possible to evaluate and rank occupations
socially.[51] He lists, below the aristocracy, ten occupational categories
in descending order of social prestige. These are:

Mallams or Koranic scholars
Attajiras—successful merchants

Masu-sana'a—craftsmen other than those mentioned below
Yan kasuwa—smaller traders
Dillalai—brokers
Manoma—farmers with unimportant subsidiary occupations
Makira—blacksmiths
Maharba—hunters
Maroka and *Makada*—musicians, drummers and eulogists
Mahauta—butchers.

Each of these occupational classes in the past had its titled head. Thus there was the *Sarkin Marina* or Chief of Dyers, *Sarkin Makera*, Chief of Blacksmiths and so forth who appointed other title-holders drawn from the members of their occupations. Usually it was to this titled head that the ruler of the city or kingdom gave bulk orders for craft products such as farm tools, war equipment, metal wares, leather goods and clothing. He, in turn, subdivided the orders among the available workers. A good deal of responsibility attached to the titles. As Smith notes, craft-heads of the capital city were required to tour the kingdom at the tax season and collect the allotted tax of their particular crafts from the local heads.[52] These local craft-heads, in their turn, despatched their titled assistants throughout the area for which they were responsible to collect the tax from each exponent of their particular craft.

Thus, by the nineteenth century, Northern Nigerian cities already possessed a high degree of social complexity and physical distinctiveness, setting them apart from purely rural communities (Fig. 6). The use of clay for house-building was the hall-mark of urban construction as distinct from the thatch buildings of the rural areas. The transition from urban to rural surroundings was clearly emphasized by the presence of the town wall (Plate 2). Generally town walls were anything from 20 to 40 feet in height and about 10 to 20 feet in width. Usually their shape was squarish to rectangular. At strategic points along their length, there were high towers containing the city gates. The responsibility for keeping the walls in good repair usually fell on quarter chiefs who looked after that portion of the walls passing by their quarter. Most cities in the north had only a single town-wall although a few had two. Usually at the city gates toll collectors were to be found.

The roads from the gates were often very broad, for they served, in particular, as ceremonial thoroughfares for the annual festivities. All of them converged on the centre where were concentrated all the major

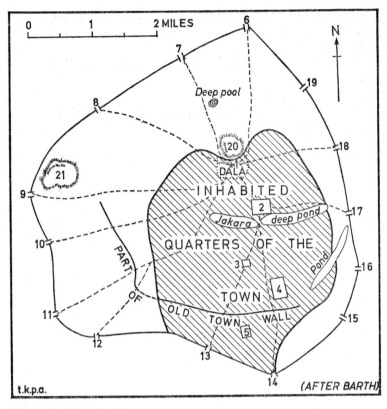

Figure 6   Kano in 1851

institutions and facilities in the city. Dominating everything in the centre of the city was the palace of the city head. This covered an extensive area of land and was in many cases walled round. Even in a relatively small town like Katagum (1823 population approx. 7,000), the palace of the governor was described as 'a large square, surrounded by a wall of red clay, at least thirty feet high, and divided by lower walls into four principal quarters: besides several flat-roofed houses of clay, it contained a number of *coozies* (huts), for the most part ranged in a single row, just within the great walls. These are principally for the slaves and guards attached to the governor's establishment. Near the eastern gate there was a sort of council or audience hall, from which a passage led to the women's apartment on the north side of the square. The

Plate 5   A modern view of Kano
Plate 6   Street scene in Enugu

flat roofs or huts with thatched conical roofs mixed together. The clay houses were said to reflect Arab influence because of their flat roofs (Plate 5). Barth complained that these houses 'are built in a most uncomfortable style, with no other purposes than that of obtaining the greatest possible privacy for domestic life, without any attempt to provide for the influx of fresh air and light'.[58] Barth, of course, was in Kano in the month of March when the weather was particularly hot and sticky and he might well complain of the lack of an influx of fresh air. At any rate, he himself admitted that there were a number of other houses built in somewhat better taste and with much wider courtyards.

For most urban centres it was usual for the spread of houses to terminate some distance from the town wall. The space between was left wild during peace time but could become cultivated when strife was imminent. The unused space varied as between towns and reflected not only the growth of the city but also the depredations which the city had suffered. Thus, although the walls of Katsina in 1851 still had a circumference of between thirteen and fourteen miles, much of the city had been destroyed, and the inhabited part restricted to the north-western area within the walls.[59]

Conclusion

By the time of the European penetration, Northern Nigeria had certainly evolved its own system of cities, good number of which derived from the medieval period. In spite of the vagaries of their political fortunes, the relative stability of the various kingdoms served to maintain some semblance of order and peace necessary for their survival. Even the Fulani *Jihad* of the nineteenth century left its mark not by the wholesale destruction of cities (though a good number of the smaller ones were virtually wiped out) but by altering the relative importance of the cities. Only in the area much farther south, in what was marchland between Hausaland and Nupe, in places with less defined and cohesive political consciousness, did the instability of the nineteenth century leave a fairly permanent mark on the towns.

If the records are to be believed, Sokoto had emerged by the end of the nineteenth century as the most populous city in Northern Nigeria, more because of its political importance than its commercial functions. Below it were the metropolitan centres, the headquarters of the various emirates whose population by the early twentieth century varied between 30,000 and 60,000. Some of these, like Kano and Kukawa, were major trade termini and were important craft centres, their craft goods entering into general inter-regional commerce and, equally important, serving the needs of the royal court and the aristocracy. Below these were the trade centres, places which were critically located on the various trade routes. There were, for instance, Koolfu in Nupe, Gummel between Bornu and Kano, and Baebaegie between Kano and Zaria. Below these again were the numerous small towns serving local trade purposes and providing craft goods for local consumption.

Irrespective of their position in the hierarchy, these towns served the purposes of trade and craft, and were important in the pattern of administrative organization linking the most remote parts of the kingdom to the capital city. Moreover, we have seen how, among the craft guilds, this framework underlined the structure of their organization. It also served as the means of diffusing culture and social etiquette among the common people. The mosque which featured in every town was the centre for much of this cultural activity. Furthermore, the mallams, in their concern for the propagation of their faith, were active agents of literacy and education. The art of writing which they taught was, for instance, turned to good effect in the fact that brokers in markets were expected to record their names on goods that they were instrumental in purchasing, so that they could be returned if found unsatisfactory.

Viewed from the vantage point of our own times, these pre-European towns were not particularly impressive either in their size, their buildings or their layout. However, in their own time, their physical distinctiveness from the ordinary rural settlements were not lost on the foreign visitors. Moreover, their number appeared great and the distances separating one from the other somewhat regular. Between Kiama and Kano, for instance, Clapperton in 1827 counted on his route twenty-eight towns. This was over a distance of approximately 320 miles, giving an average distance apart of 12 miles (Fig. 7). Similarly Barth, between 1851 and 1854, listed some thirty-seven towns between Kukawa and Kano, a distance of 350 miles, and another twenty-eight between Kano and Sokoto, a distance of 230 miles. These gave average distances apart of 10 and 8 miles respectively. The figures of average distances apart conceal the close spacing of towns in areas of high population density especially in the area within some fifty miles radius of Kano.

This close spacing of relatively small towns was not, of course, peculiar to the pre-industrial conditions of these areas. A similar situa-

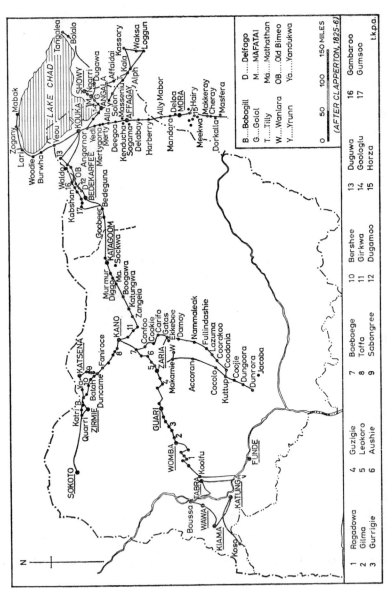

Figure 7   Northern Nigerian towns (after Clapperton)

tion was described for the purely agricultural counties of East Anglia in England before the modern period as well as for Germany in the medieval period.[60] The close spacing represented an adjustment to the undeveloped transport system which made it necessary for towns serving as market centres for surrounding rural areas to be not much more than about eight miles apart. Dickinson, for instance, referred to Saxton's map of East Anglia in the sixteenth century which showed that market towns were distributed in such a way that they served a trade area of some four-mile radius. Indeed he emphasized that, in accordance with an old law, no market town could be established within $6\frac{2}{3}$ miles of an existing legal market.

Clapperton also appears to have used the designations 'town' and 'city' to differentiate between a low and a higher order of urban settlements. Equally interesting therefore was the spacing apart of these higher order centres. Between Kiama and Kano, where he had noted twenty-eight urban settlements as a whole, eight of these (Kiama, Wawa, Bussa, Tabra, Womba, Guari, Zaria and Kano) were each designated a 'city'. The distances apart of these cities were much greater but surprisingly fairly even, varying only between 32 and 67 miles. In areas of lower densities of population, the same relative evenness of spacing was found among the settlements designated 'cities', although their distances apart were somewhat greater. Thus between Kano and Kukawa were found Katagum and Bedekarfee, each 134, 115 and 110 miles distant from its neighbour respectively. Between Kukawa and Masfera to the south were Affagay and Mora, 91, 96 and 75 miles apart. From Kano to Sokoto were Katsina and Zirmie, 96, 60, 96 miles apart respectively.

This discussion of the size and spacing of Northern Nigerian urban settlements emphasizes the existence of an urban hierarchy in this area in the pre-European period. It was a hierarchy reflecting the prevailing economic conditions and the dependence on animate means of transport such as camels, asses, donkeys and human beings. It is these aspects of economic life—the relatively low volume of production, the comparatively low average per capita income and the relatively undeveloped state of transport—that were the matrix within which the towns and cities were formed. When these conditions were drastically altered in the era of colonial administration, significant departures from the patterns of the nineteenth century occurred.

References

1. See Henri Pirenne, *Medieval Cities, their origins and the renewal of trade*, Princeton, 1925.
2. Mas Latrie, *Relations et Commerce de l'Afrique Septentrionale en Maghreb avec les Nations Chrétiennes du Moyen Age*, Paris, 1886, p. 22.
3. Raymond Mauny, *Tableau Géographique de L'Ouest Africain au Moyen Age*, IFAN, Dakar, 1961. See Basil Davidson, *Old Africa Rediscovered*, London, 1959, p. 84.
4. E. W. Bovill, *The Golden Trade of the Moors*, London, 1958, p. 82.
5. Ibid., p. 88.
6. El Bekri, *Description de l'Afrique Septentrionale*, trans. by de Slane (Algiers, 1913), pp. 327-331. See also E. W. Bovill, op. cit., p. 84.
7. Ibid., p. 322.
8. Abderrahman-es-Sadi et Timboukti, *Tarikh-es-Soudan*, trans. by O. Houdas (Paris, 1900), p. 223.
9. El Edrisi, *Description de l'Afrique et de l'Espagne*, trans. by R. Dozy and M. J. de Goeje, Leyden, 1866, p. 15.
10. Ibn Battuta, *Travels in Asia and Africa 1325-1354*, trans. by H. A. R. Gibb, London, 1929, p. 336. The notes in the translation points out that Barnu here should be interpreted as Kanem and not the present day area of Bornu in Nigeria.
11. Leo Africanus, *The History and Description of Africa*, trans. by J. Pory, 1600, London, 1896, Vol. 3, p. 833.
12. Ibid., p. 834.
13. See Ibn Battuta, op. cit., p. 382, footnote 36.
14. See J. A. Burdon, *Northern Nigeria: Historical Notes on Certain Emirates and Tribes*, London, 1909, p. 32.
15. Leo Africanus, op. cit., p. 828.
16. Raymond Mauny, op. cit., p. 394.
17. J. A. Burdon, op. cit., p. 31.
18. S. J. Hogben and A. H. M. Kirk-Greene, *The Emirates of Northern Nigeria*, London, 1966, pp. 165-166.
19. Ibid., p. 113, footnote.
20. D. Denham, H. Clapperton and N. Oudney, *Narrative of Travels and Discoveries in Northern and Central Africa in the years 1822, 1823 and 1824*, London, 1828, Vol. 2, p. 391.
21. Ibid., p. 392
22. Heinrich Barth, *Travels and Discoveries in North and Central Africa 1849-1855*, London, Centenary Edition, 1965, Vol. 1, p. 453.
23. D. Denham *et al.*, op. cit., Vol. 2, p. 276.
24. M. Laird and R. A. K. Oldfield, *Narrative of an Expedition into the Interior of Africa, in 1832, 1833, and 1834*, London, 1937, Vol. 2, p. 87.
25. H. Barth, op. cit., Vol. 1, p. 519.
26. Barth (op. cit., p. 522) estimated that 2,500 cowries are equal to one Spanish or Austrian dollar at the time. Denham and Clapper-

ton (op. cit., p. 286), a few years earlier had estimated that the dollar was equivalent to five shillings. This would mean that a pound sterling was worth roughly 10,000 cowries.

27. C. H. Robinson, *Hausaland or Fifteen Hundred Miles through the Central Sudan*, London, 1896, p. 119.
28. D. Denham *et al.*, op. cit., Vol. 2, p. 189.
29. Ibid., Vol. 1, pp. 406 and 288.
30. C. H. Robinson, op. cit., p. 120.
31. H. Barth, op. cit., Vol. 1, p. 533.
32. Ibid., p. 515.
33. Ibid., p. 510.
34. Ibid., p. 511.
35. C. H. Robinson, op. cit., p. 113.
36. H. Barth, op. cit., vol. 1, p. 513-514.
37. D. Denham *et al.*, op. cit., Vol. 2, pp. 392.
38. Ibid., p. 31.
39. C. H. Robinson, op. cit., p. 117.
40. D. Denham *et al.*, op. cit., Vol. 2, p. 219.
41. H. Clapperton, *Journal of a Second Expedition into the Interior of Africa*, London, 1829, p. 147.
42. Ibid., p. 146.
43. Ibid., p. 159.
43. Ibid., p. 159.
44. Ibn Battuta, op. cit., p. 334.
45. Ibid., p. 247.
46. H. Barth. op. cit., Vol. 1, p. 522.
47. This coin was made in Vienna and Trieste, and to be acceptable it usually bore the date 1780. It was manufactured exclusively for export to West Africa.
48. D. Denham *et al.*, op. cit., Vol. 2, p. 176.
49. Ibid., p. 287.
50. H. Barth, op. cit., pp. 137-8.
51. M. G. Smith, *The Economy of Hausa Communities of Zaria*, Colonial Research Studies, No. 16, London, 1955, p. 15.
52. Ibid., p. 98.
53. D. Denham *et al.*, op. cit., Vol. 2, p. 251.
54. R. Lander, *Records of Captain Clapperton's Last Expedition to Africa*, London, 1830, Vol. 1, p. 277.
55. H. Barth, op. cit., Vol. 1, p. 507.
56. Ibid., Vol. 2, p. 52.
57. D. Denham *et al.*, op. cit., Vol. 2, p. 284.
58. H. Barth *et al.*, op. cit., Vol. 1, p. 509.
59. Ibid., p. 476.
60. See R. E. Dickinson, 'The distribution and functions of the smaller urban settlements of East Anglia', *Geography*, Vol. 17, 1932, pp. 19-31; and 'The development and distribution of the medieval German town', *Geography*, Vol. 27, 1942, pp. 9-20 and 47-53.

4 Pre-European Urbanization in Nigeria

b Yoruba Towns

To what extent can the Yoruba urbanism of the southern forest belt be regarded as a direct descendant of, or as related to the Sudan medieval urbanism? This is a tantalizing question to which no conclusive answer can be given at present. Certain facts, however, are very suggestive of some relations and it may be worthwhile amplifying them at this stage.

It has already been stated that the flowering of the Ghana Empire took place some time between the eighth and tenth century A.D. and that to a large extent its dominance was reputed to be based on the knowledge of iron-working. It is therefore highly significant that while there is little dispute about the Yoruba having migrated into their present region from a north-easternly direction, the period suggested for this was some time between the seventh and tenth century, and their ability to dominate the aborigines whom they met in the area was attributed to their iron-smelting capabilities![1] This is not to say that their knowledge of iron-smelting was derived from Ghana. The latter was too far west to have been a direct influence. However, it lay within a region where considerable movement of men and ideas was going on, and it was not unlikely that the Yoruba knowledge of iron-smelting came from being for a time part of this movement. Johnson, for instance, asserted that the Yorubas were blood relations of the Gogobiri and the Kukawas, the latter being the people of Kanem and Bornu to the north-east.[2] Later he mentioned that one of the items inherited from Oduduwa, the progenitor of the Yoruba, by Oranyan, the most powerful and prosperous of his sons, comprised 21 pieces of iron.[3]

Whatever the nature of the connection with the Sudan during this early period, there is some evidence that trade relations had developed long before the British came. Sultan Bello of Sokoto, in one of his major historical works, from which Captain Clapperton made copious extracts early in the nineteenth century, indicated major trade relations with the Yorubas. According to him, 'Yoruba is an extensive province containing rivers, forests, sands and mountains, as also a great many wonderful and extraordinary things. . . . By the side of this province there is an anchorage or harbour for the ships of the Christians, who used to go there and purchase slaves. These slaves were exported from our country and sold to the people of Yarba, who resold them to the Christians.'[4]

What the Yorubas traded in the north in exchange for the slaves is not known. When the European explorers began to move into the country from the 1820s onward, we get more information about the extensiveness of the trade relation between Yorubaland and the Sudan. Clapperton noted in the market at Katunga (Old Oyo) that 'trona, or natron is brought here from Bornou and sold to all parts of the coasts where it is much in request to mix with snuff and also as medicine'.[5] The Lander brothers in 1832 provided more information about the penetration of this trade. At Mowo, a coastal town near Badagri, they found 'trona (a vegetable alkali) and other articles brought hither from the borders of the desert of Zaarha (Sahara) through the medium of wandering Arabs'.[6] Near Jaguta (a town about twelve miles east-south-east of Igboho) they met 'a party of Nouffie (Nupe) traders from Coulfo with asses carrying trona for the Gonja market. These asses were the first beasts we had observed employed in carrying burdens.'[7] They described Bumbum, near Kishi, as 'a lively little walled town, a great thoroughfare for fatakies (caravans) of merchants, trading from Hausa, Borgu and other countries to Gonja; and consequently a vast quantity of land is cultivated in its vicinity with corn and yams to supply them with provisions'.[8] Of Kishi itself, they noted that 'a great number of emigrants from different countries reside here: there are not a few from Borgoo, Nouffie, Hausa, and two or three Tuaricks from the borders of the Great Desert'.[9]

One other point needs to be made concerning the contacts between the Sudan and the Yoruba country before the period of active European penetration. This is in connection with the currency of trade. We have noticed in the previous chapter that although gold was used for the larger purchases in the medieval Sudanese empires, cowries performed the same function for smaller ones. In Yoruba country, evidence points to an age-long use of cowries as a medium of exchange. The mythological history that dealt with the division of the inheritance of Oduduwa by his sons noted that whilst Oranyan inherited the land, its iron content and a cock, the Oba of Benin inherited the money which consisted of cowries.[10] The existence of a common currency between Northern

Nigeria and Yorubaland would surely facilitate trade relations between the two areas.

The origin of Yoruba towns

Nonetheless, in spite of possible connections and contacts with the Sudan from early times, the impression must not be created that Yoruba towns owed their origin to the same cause, namely, the thriving trade across the Sahara to North Africa. The Yoruba, as already indicated, were an immigrant group who moved into the south-western part of present-day Nigeria from the north-east some time between the seventh and tenth centuries. According to Biokabu, this movement was in a series of waves.[11] The earliest of this under Oduduwa, the progenitor of the people, probably led to the founding of Ile-Ife, to which town even today most other Yoruba towns trace their origin. From Ile-Ife, there occurred a dispersion of sons of Oduduwa to found their own cities and carve out kingdoms for themselves. Of these, according to Johnson, three went west to found the kingdoms of Ketu, Sabe and Popo; one went to the south to found the kingdom of Owu; another to the east to found the kingdom of Benin; and two went north to found the kingdoms of Ila and Oyo. The last-named kingdom was to become the most important and most extensive of them all.

However, Biobaku believes that the Oyo kingdom was rather the product of a second wave of migration which came to centre on Old Oyo (or Katunga) from where a similar dispersion of founders of cities and minor kingdoms took place. Johnson himself noted that 'as Oranyan (the founder of Oyo) and his army, as well as his brothers pushed on their conquests in every direction, the princes and the warlords were stationed in various parts to hold the country, and from them sprang the many provincial kings of various ranks and grades now existing'.[12]

One fact stands out from all this consideration, namely, that Yoruba towns arose largely as a form of 'colonial settlements' among indigenous, more backward and perhaps hostile peoples. They were not products of indifferent growth but were a conscious attempt to dominate and control the unorganized mass of aborigines found in the region. Present in the history of many of the towns are references to numerous hamlets and villages being forced to break up and move into the town. This method of founding towns seemed to have been elevated to the status of a tradition. Indeed, as late as the early nineteenth century, when the present Oyo was to be founded, Johnson remarked that

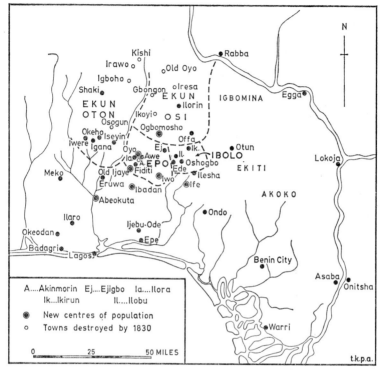

Figure 8   Metropolitan provinces of Old Oyo (after Johnson)

several of the surrounding towns and villages within 10 to 20 miles of
the new city were depopulated and their inhabitants forced to move
into the new town.[13]

The role of towns for purposes of colonial domination or imposition is,
of course, not peculiar to the Yoruba. Alexander the Great had used
towns in much the same way in his excursion into the Middle East, and
so had the Romans at a much later date.[14] The Germans also in the
Middle Ages made towns serve an important colonizing role in their
eastward movement into the Slav country.[15] The English did likewise
in their planned colonization of Northern Ireland in the seventeenth
century.[16] Thus, as Smailes remarked, 'it is hardly an exaggeration to
regard the town as the normal settlement form of imperial expansion
and intrusion of civilized people into territories already occupied by
societies engaged in practising a less advanced economy. The incomers

find security in concentration and collect in towns for their mutual protection. Their urban character further expresses their role as administrators, traders or military pensioners.'[17]

Yoruba towns therefore were basically administrative centres and over the centuries they had evolved an elaborate power structure and a hierarchical system of administration both at the city level and the level of a kingdom. The similarity in the institutional characteristics of the political system remained a major element in the consciousness of the Yoruba as a nation and in their belief of descent from a common ancesrtal stock. The spatial organization of this system found expression in the sub-division of the kingdoms into provinces or districts. The Oyo kingdom or empire, which became the largest, consisted, for instance, of four provinces (Fig. 8).[18] The Western province included all the towns to the west of the River Ogun down to Iberekodo. The chief town here used to be Igana while other important ones included Shaki, Okeho, Iseyin, Iwawun, Eruwa and Iberekodo. The Eastern Province, which was also the Metropolitan Province and included Oyo (Old Oyo), the metropolitan capital itself, had its own provincial capital at Ikoyi. It included other large cities such as Kishi, Igboho, Ilorin, Irawo, Iwere and Ogbomosho. Then there was the Ibolo Province to the southeast as far as Ede with Iresa as the chief centre. Other important towns were Ikirun, Ilobi, Ede and Ejigbo. Finally, there was the Epo province to the south-west with its chief town at Idode and other major centres including Iwo, Ilora, Akinmorin, Fiditi and Awe. Similar provincial arrangements are found among the Egba, the Ijebu and to a lesser extent the Ekiti.

If administration was the major reason for the existence of many of these towns and cities, they were, in this respect, not much different from many towns and cities of the medieval period elsewhere in the world. Ibn Khaldun, who lived in Spain and North Africa, writing about 1375, placed primary emphasis on the fact that cities were centres of government and political power.[19] He noted that, partly because of this, they soon exhibited economic patterns significantly different from those of the surrounding countryside. Since the proceeds of taxation were accumulated in the cities, and since governmental and educational functions were concentrated here, new patterns of demand arose. These tended to affect, in turn, the patterns of production and supply, bringing about profound economic differences between country and city.

In short, we find that whatever the nature of origin of towns and cities, their continued survival depended on trade. And trade in turn resulted from the production of agricultural surpluses which could be traded against the products of craft manufactures or personal services in the cities and towns. Unequal distribution of natural resources was soon capitalized upon and specialized centres of production emerged. Considerable movements of peoples and goods became a major factor linking the towns and determining the nature of their interaction one with the other as well as of their co-existence in the days before the emergence of powerful national states.

The trading activities of Yoruba towns

Trade based on agriculture and craft production was thus a major element in the survival of Yoruba towns. Although evidence for this is not abundant until the nineteenth century, there is fragmentary information to show that, at least for the coastal parts of Yorubaland, trade had been the normal order from much earlier times. In the sixteenth century Pereira commented on the coastal trade in slaves from the Ijebu kingdom. He noted that 'twelve or thirteen leagues up this river is a very large city called Geebuu, surrounded by a great moat. The ruler of this country in our time is called Agusale, and the trade is mainly in slaves (who are sold for twelve or fifteen brass bracelets each) but there is some ivory.'[20] By the eighteenth century, statements about the coastal trade of the Ijebu placed greater emphasis on the traffic in craft products. John Barbot, writing in 1732, noted that 'the Portuguese geographers placed Cuidade de Jebu, or City of Jebu, several leagues inland of this river (the Rio Lagos) . . . the village Almata, on the east point of Rio Lagos, and not far from it and east again the town of Curamo where good fine cloths are made and sold by the natives to foreigners, who have a good vent for them at the Gold Coast, especially the Hollanders, who carry thence great quantities, which they turn to a good account.'[21]

By the nineteenth century we have much more detailed accounts both of the coastal and of the interior trade of Yoruba country. The major body of documents for this account comprises the numerous journals and letters of Christian missionaries who began to penetrate the Yoruba country from 1842 onwards, the reports and maps from the British Foreign Office and later the Colonial Office, and the publications of explorers, notably Captain John Adams, Hugh Clapperton, Richard Lander and Sir R. F. Burton. All this material has facilitated a reconstruction of the economic activities of Yoruba towns, of their trade routes and trade organization, their population and social characteristics, and the physical structure of many of the towns and cities.

Trade in Yoruba country was carried on at two basic levels. First, there was local trade involving exchange between the residents of a town and its surrounding rural area. This found expression in daily morning or daily evening markets where agricultural products were usually exchanged for craft products and imported goods. Second, there was the regional trade involving periodic markets (Plate 8) which were held at specific intervals and whose main purpose seemed to be to replenish the stocks of traders in the daily markets.

Broadly it is possible to distinguish three types of periodic market corresponding to three tiers of regional organization. First, there was what might be called the *provincial periodic market*. This was usually held every fourth day and was attended by people living not too far away in the same province or the same kingdom, where this was not too big. The interval indicated that people did not have to travel to and from the market for longer than a day. References to this type of market in the nineteenth century are numerous. In Awori country some of the better known markets included Badagri, Bese, Ipokia, Igbessa, Mowo, Ibawe, Ebute Metta, Mushin, Isheri, Otta, Iworo, Ojo, Itele and Ajilete. In Egbado there were Ado, Afanyin, Oke-Odan and Ilaro; in Egba were Awoyade, Alowaga, Iro, Sala, Osielle and Abeokuta. In Ijebu there were Iperu, Ejinrin, Ikorodu, Ipara, Atijere, Shagamu, Oru and Ijebu-Ode. In Ife and Ekiti we find Apomu, Itagumodi, Isoya, Apimido, Odo and Otun, while in Oyo there are references to Jaguta, Iberekodo, Eruwa, Ijaiye, Koso, Iseyin, Shaki, Iganna, Ibaja, Kishi, Ogodo, Iwo, Ogbomosho, Ibadan, Oyo and Ilorin.

Some of these markets, apart from participating in provincial trade, belonged to a second tier of what might be called *inter-kingdom periodic markets*. This meant that they also engaged in trade involving people coming from other kingdoms. Because the distances to be covered was often greater in such cases, it appeared that inter-kingdom markets were usually held every eight days. Since, however, this interval was simply a multiple of four, it was not always so clear that the level of trade was different on each occasion. The people themselves made a distinction, however, calling the purely provincial marketing the 'small' market and the inter-kingdom marketing the 'large' market. Thus Haddon-Smith commented on Otta that 'there are two markets held, a small one every five days and a large one every 9 days, when a large amount of produce arrives'.[22]

Some of the inter-kingdom markets did not perform the functions of provincial markets and were held only once in eight days. Such markets were usually located in small frontier towns and their neutral status was guaranteed by the various kingdoms trading at this centre. An illustration of the nature of the establishment of this type of market is provided by the case of Iberekodo and Eruwa. In May 1874 Foster described Iberekodo as the place where the Egba and the Yoruba generally had a market every 9 days. Then on 27th November he wrote that 'they went by the new road to Eruwa as the Berekodo road was shut by the joint order of the Alafin of Oyo, the King of Iseyin, Ogundipe of Abeokuta and the Kakanfo of Ibadan'.[23] The accusation against Iberekodo was that a rich woman of the place, by name Adeyanju, was habitually stealing strangers' slaves and she of late stole one of the Aseyin's slaves. The secret was known, so the Aseyin asked the other powers to join him to shut the Iberekodo market. A few years after, we learn the other side of the story, namely the establishment of a new inter-kingdom periodic market at Eruwa. 'Eruwa', Johnson remarked in February 1878, 'is not a very large place. But it is an important market town, visited every ninth day by traders from Abeokuta, Ibadan, Oyo, Ilorin, Iseyin, Bariba, Shaki and many small towns nearby. There are trees at the market place planted by the Oyo king, the Ibadan governor and one of the Abeokuta chiefs to signify their common interest in it and their willingness to protect it.'[24]

Whether this or another type of formality was gone through in the establishment of other inter-kingdom markets is not clear, but it can hardly be doubted that some form of guarantee of safety for traders would be demanded by the existence of such markets. Apomu, for instance, was one of the most famous of the inter-kingdom market towns where Oyo, Ife, Owu and Ijebu met for trade. It was situated in Ife territory, and within the border of the Olowu's dominion. In the early nineteenth century, for instance, it was necessary for the Alafin of Oyo to send to both the Olowu and the Owoni of Ife to keep a strict watch and check the growing practice of kidnapping Oyo traders who came to this market from a considerable distance. The Owoni and the Olowu in turn sent strict orders to the Bale of Apomu to be on the watch and arrest any offender.[25] In spite of this, it is significant that the incident which was to plunge the whole of Yorubaland into chaos for most of the nineteenth century took place as a result of a dispute at this market.

Some of the larger metropolitan centres constituted a third tier of regional trading activities, serving as terminals of numerous long-distance trade routes both from other Yoruba centres as well as from areas outside Yorubaland. Hinderer, for instance, noted that two large caravans of traders come to Ibadan from Ijebu every month. He also remarked that 'traders from Kano were pretty well in the centre of Yoruba country'.[26]

Craft specialization in Yoruba towns

Apart from trade, craft specialization was important for the economic life of the towns. We have already noticed that, by the early eighteenth century, the export of locally woven cloth was taking place from Ijebuland to the Gold Coast through the intermediary of the Dutch.[27] Clapperton, the first European to penetrate Yoruba country, described the weaving industry in the small town of Ijanna in the following terms: 'We found several looms working. In one house, we saw eight or ten—in fact, a regular manufactory. Their cloth is good in texture, and some are very fine. We later visited several manufactories of cloth and three dye-houses with upwards of twenty vats or large earthen pots in each and all in full work. The indigo here is of excellent quality and forms a most beautiful and durable dye.'[28] Townsend also noted that 'a large number of people (in Ijaiye) are engaged in weaving cloth'.[29] At Erunmu, near Ibadan, Kefer found 'the Bale's wife and children spinning cotton which, the Bale said, they sold to Ibadan weavers'.[30] At Lalupon he found that 'clothes are dyed and indigo prepared for use and to sell'. Ogbomosho was described as a town of '40,000 people who live mostly by the produce of their fields and the manufacture of cloth'.[31]

Iron-working, iron-smelting and blacksmithery constituted another major group of crafts. Iron ore was extracted from mines scattered all over the country. Ewart described an iron ore mine near Ajilete in Egbado as consisting of 'large numbers of holes 8 feet in diameter, now filled up, but formerly sunk to a depth of 50 and 60 feet, out of which excellent iron ore was taken and used for making axes, hoes, etc. The iron is said to have been very hard and lasting, but when iron hoops and axes were brought into the country from Europe, they were found to be much cheaper, though not so good, than the native manufactures; consequently this industry discontinued 40 or 50 years since, and there are now no furnaces for smelting iron in Ilaro, though similar iron is said to have been found and used in Ilobi twelve years since.'[32]

Blacksmiths smelting iron and fashioning agricultural implements, domestic utensils or implements of war were to be found in almost all Yoruba towns. They were closely associated with the guild of hunters and formed one of the most important guilds in the town. As the state of civil disorder became more general in the nineteenth century, the importance of blacksmiths increased tremendously. Ibadan, for instance, was said to contain at this time several iron-smelters and blacksmiths, no doubt fashioning guns for the frequent wars in which the city was engaged.

Carving was another major craft that occupied most of the male population of a town and provided important articles of trade. Clapperton noticed, for instance, that the 'inhabitants of Ijanna are very industrious and are great carvers. Their doors, drums and everything of wood is carved'.[33] At Katunga he observed that the people 'are fond of ornamenting their doors, and the posts which support their verandas with carving; and they have also statues or figures of men and women, standing in their courtyards'.[34] A few years later Townsend made the following observations about a caravan of traders met on the road from Abeokuta to Ijaiye carrying, among other things, loads of calabashes. 'Many of the calabashes', he remarked, 'will be cleaned and carved in Ijaiye and purchased for the Abeokuta and Lagos markets and probably some of them will find their way to Sierra Leone.'[35]

Another notable craft product of trade was beads. These were important not only for the making of crowns and coronets for the numerous Obas of cities and towns but also as part of the fineries of the womenfolk. There seems to have been a high degree of specialization in its production and, according to Hinderer, the two most important places for its production were Ede and Ife. Indeed he noted that Ede 'was once the richest town in the Yoruba country, perhaps owing to a kind of precious bead which was found there as well as in Ife'.[36] Earlier, in 1832, the Landers had emphasized how important beads were as trade articles. At the Oyo market they had noticed 'a great variety of beads, both of native and European manufacture, amongst the former of which we recognized the famous Agra bead which, at Cape Coast Castle, Accra, and other places, is sold for its weight in gold, and which has vainly been attempted to be imitated by the Italians and our own countrymen'.[37]

Most of the crafts described above were engaged in largely by men and there were many other crafts besides. There were brass and coppersmiths, workers in leather, makers of musical instruments, herbalists and carpenters, as well as builders.

Like the men, women also participated in craft production for trade. Much of the spinning of cotton was done by them and nearly all the dyeing of cloths. They shared with the men the weaving of cloth although they employed a different type of loom and were seldom found as groups or in a manufactory. Food-processing, particularly the making of oil, the conversion of yam to flour and the making of soap were essentially female crafts. Equally important was their specialization in the craft of pottery. Tokpo was an important centre for this craft, although there were numerous other centres all over Yorubaland. Gollmer noted that the pots made at Tokpo 'answer many purposes but are principally used in making salt, palm oil, nut oil, soap and for conveying fluids as water, palm-wine and oil. The dishes, some of which are very neat indeed, answer all purpose of earthen-ware.'[38]

One of the more fascinating crafts of the women was the manufacture of salt from sea-water. Just as salt had been an important staple in the trans-Saharan trade, it no doubt constituted an equally important trade commodity in Yoruba country. Johnson noted that salt was introduced into the Yoruba country during the reign of the Alafin Obalokun some time in the fifteenth century.[39] Before then the article used for salt was an insipid rock salt known as *Obu*. The new salt was first called *Dunmomo* and later took its present name *Iyo*. It is not clear where this new salt came from, but it is fairly certain that at least by the early nineteenth century the coastal areas were exporting large amounts of salt into the interior markets.

Both Martin and Gollmer describe one of the centres for the manufacturing of salt at Ajido on the coastal lagoon. According to Martin, 'the whole process reflects credit on the inhabitants of this town. Scattered over the beach for about a mile in length are a great number of wicker baskets.[40] These baskets, according to Gollmer, were

'about $2\frac{1}{2}$ feet in diameter and $3\frac{1}{2}$ feet above ground and about 2 feet deep in the ground, which are filled with sand. About 3 feet distant there is a pot (containing about 3-5 gallons) buried up to the neck in the ground into which the salt water, after having passed through the sand in the basket, runs, by means of a pipe, or hollow piece of wood. From these pots, the strained salt water is conveyed to ponds under sheds close by. When the ponds are full, the oven is kindled and the water sufficiently boiled in small pots, containing about 2 gallons. The oven is a circular hole in the ground, about 5 feet in diameter and about 4 feet in depth over which there are nicely constructed arches built of clay, which admit about 10 of these smaller pots; two holes in the centre of the hearth serve as chimney. There are other ovens on a larger scale. Many people along this coast derived formerly their livelihood from this employment, but the repeated attacks of Dahomians have turned many away from their employment and obliged them to retire beyond the river and to give up to a great degree the manufacture of this valuable commodity'.[41]

Another centre of salt manufacture was at Arugbo, farther to the east on the lagoon. From this place the people of Ibadan were said to have obtained their salt when the roads of the Egbas and Ijebus were closed against them during the Ijaiye War of 1862-65.[42]

It has been necessary to go into this detail with regard to craft production entering traditional trade for two reasons: first, to emphasize the large number of people for whom craft production for trade must have provided employment in the past; and secondly, to make patent the illogicality of assuming that, because many Yoruba towns are today occupied by a majority of farmers, this majority has always been so numerically important in the past. As was seen in the case of salt manufacturing, there is little doubt that the effect of the civil disorder of the nineteenth century in particular, by creating general instability, probably forced more people from craft to agriculture, if only to assure at least a subsistence level of living. More important, however, for the decline of local crafts was the penetration into the country of cheap, manufactured articles from the factories of Europe. For two of the basic industries of these towns—iron-smelting and weaving—the effect was almost catastrophic. We have noted the closing down of iron-mines even by 1850 owing to this fact. Similarly, there is the paralysis which crippled the traditional weaving industry once cheaper textiles from Lancashire began to flood the local markets. Nonetheless, even in the twentieth century, these craft goods continued to be important items of internal exchange and, along with agricultural produce, they were distributed extensively throughout the length and breadth of Yorubaland.

Trade routes and organization

Traditionally, these extensive trade activities within Yorubaland were channelled along certain major routes (Fig. 9). Of these, four generally north-south routes can be identified. One ran from Badagri on the coast

Figure 9   Major trade routes in Yorubaland in the nineteenth century

through Ilaro, Eruwa to Koso and on to Northern Nigeria. At Koso, this road was joined by one coming from Cape Coast in present-day Ghana. A second trade route started from Lagos and passed through Otta to Abeokuta, Iseyin and Ilorin to the north. A third route went from Ikorodu through the Remo towns of Shagamu, Iperu and Ipara to Ibadan. From Ibadan it continued northward through Oyo and Ogbomosho to Ilorin. According to Johnson, this road, at least the stretch of it between Ogbomosho and Ilorin, used to be called the Pakaba Road.[43] The fourth of the main north-south routes also started from the lagoon ports of Atijere and Igbobini and passed through Ondo, Ilesha, Okemessi, and Ibaja to Ilorin.

East-west routes, on the other hand, do not appear to have provided major avenues of trade, for they served mainly to link together towns and cities on major routeways or within the kingdom. Within Ijesha-land, for instance, Johnson mentioned the Erinmo Road, the Iwaye Road and the Efon Aye Road which linked together a number of the Ijesha towns.[44]

What was the character of these roads? To this there can be no simple answer. In some areas the roads were relatively wide and well kept; in others they were no more than footpaths strewn with a lot of obstructions. Crowther in 1845 described the road from Ipokia near Badagri as a fine road which would admit four persons riding abreast for some distance. This road was cleared and put under repair once a year. Crowther went on to comment that 'these fine roads are fine specimens of what they used to be at one time in the Yoruba country'.[45]

Descriptions of roads in Ijebu country, where the upheavals of the early nineteenth century hardly left any serious scars, seem to confirm this statement. Both the Rev. D. Hinderer and Dr Irving were the very first Europeans to pass through Ijebu country in 1855. As they passed from the Ibadan farms into the Remo district of Ijebuland, Hinderer noted: 'a large and beautiful avenue road indicates now our approach to the town and the tall bare *Oro* trees bereft of their branches told beyond all doubt that we were near our expected Ipara. . . . From there (Ipara) to Iperu, we had again our wide beautiful avenue road and fully an hour and half ride to that town. . . . (From Iperu to Offin) our usual avenue road was not so good.'[46] Irving, in his journal, has described this road as 'the most beautiful in Africa . . . so tempting did the road appear (from Ode-Remo) that we could not resist putting spurs to our horses and having a good canter to the end.'[47]

One of the major obstructions along these roads were the rivers and across them were often thrown wooden bridges of various descriptions. One over the River Yewa close to Ilaro was described as '. . . about 100 feet long and about 3 feet above water at flood. It is constructed of about 500 sticks; two rows of forked sticks (instead of piles) are driven into the bed of the river, one stick opposite the other, and about 3 feet apart both ways.'[48] The bridge over the River Owiwi, west of Abeokuta, was described in similar terms. It was said to be 'a very good bridge formed of planks of about 4 inches thick, supported by posts with a hand rail on each side'.[49]

Not all streams and rivers were crossed by bridges. The larger streams in particular were crossed by means of ferries. There appears to have been a difference between the inland Oyo people and the coastal Egba and Ijebu in their ferries. The Oyos depended on huge calabashes; the coastal peoples on canoes. Townsend described the novel experience of crossing the Ogun River near Iseyin by means of calabashes:

'I arrived first and hastened to the water's edge to see this singular mode of crossing a river. There being many persons on the opposite bank waiting to come over I had an opportunity at once of seeing it. The calabashes used are very large. They appear to be two large halves of different calabashes cemented together and watertight. On this is placed the traveller's load which he holds steadily until he gets into deep water. He (the waterman) then places the traveller on the side opposite to him and each holds by the other's arm near the shoulder embracing the calabash between them which is sufficiently light to float them safely over. The waterman paddles with his feet. The picture of these two persons sunk to their waist in the water with a heavy load between them moving steadily along without any visible moving power is singular.'[50]

Hinderer described having to cross the Oba River near Iwo by the same means in 1858.[51] Here, according to Allen, there were 'twelve men whose business it is to cross people and loads for their daily earnings, and there were some women who were selling food for passengers'.[52] Campbell emphasized that the Oyos 'not only prefer the use of cala-bashes, but will have nothing whatever to do with canoes and affect to despise those who use them. Not infrequently I heard the term *Agayen* reproachfully applied by the people of the interior towns to my inter-preter and other persons from places on or near the sea-coast. The word simply means canoe-men.'[53]

One possible reason for this state of affairs was the fact that the rivers of Yorubaland were in general not navigable. Apart from east-west movement along the lagoon, the only other navigable water here was the lower Ogun River, south of Abeokuta. Marsh conveys some idea of the importance of this river in the trade between Lagos and Abeokuta. At Isheri, a rural market on the Ogun River, he found in 1845 more than 400 small canoes from Abeokuta and about 100 large ones from Lagos.[54] Gollmer also in 1854 remarked that 'about 280 Abeokuta canoes re-turned home (from Lagos). . . . It is astonishing how much trade in-creased between this and Abeokuta since the free navigation of the Ogun.'[55]

The organization of trade between Yoruba cities in the nineteenth century was carried on through the system of caravans, usually on foot. The trade caravans from a big city initially collected at small villages some 8 to 10 miles from the city. Such a village was referred to as a *caravansary*. One of the best known of the caravansaries was that for caravans from Abeokuta trading to Ibadan located at the village of Atadi, nine miles from Abeokuta. Hinderer noted in his Journal of June 1851 as follows:

> 'Atadi—a caravansary for traders to Ibadan. Both sexes. Has to wait for the women if *Oro* or such religious occasions prevents their leaving Abeokuta on particular days. Numbered at least 4,000, but this number regarded as a little unusual. Their presence caused price of provisions to rise at Atadi. Caravans made up of rough soldiers and impatient traders.'[56]

On the Badagry and Lagos road, Abeokuta had another caravansary at Awoyade. Badagry had one at Mowo for traders going to Abeokuta. In the Oyo Area, Fiditi was described as a caravansary for traders from Ibadan through Oyo to Ilorin, while Kuta was the caravansary for traders from Iwo to Oshogbo.[57]

Because of the need to wait at the caravansaries and at specific halts on the route, caravan journeys often took twice as long as the normal walking time. Abeokuta, for instance, was said to be six days from Ilorin, but the caravans generally took twelve days, resting one day and travelling the next.[58] Some idea of caravan distances was given by Millson in 1890. According to him 'by the Ijebu route, Lagos is only seven days distant from Ibadan, ten days from Oyo, fourteen from Ikirun and twenty-one from the Niger. . . . Caravans take twenty-one days to reach Oke-Mesi from Lagos, twenty-nine days to reach Ilorin, and thirty-three days to reach the Niger.'[59]

As in Northern Nigeria, traders had to pay toll to enter a town or sometimes a kingdom. Between Lagos and Abeokuta there were three toll gates: one at the town of Otta, the second at Papalanto, the frontier post between the Otta and the Egba, and the third at Awoyade, the caravansary for Abeokuta.[60] The tolls paid at Otta were listed in 1888 as follows[61]:

From strangers with load from interior to Lagos or vice versa	7½ strings of cowries	
From strangers without load to or from interior	5	„
For every horse from the interior	25	„
For every cow from the interior	25	„
For every sheep or goat from the interior	10	„

Townsend in 1853 also discovered that there were three toll gates between Abeokuta and Ijaiye and three others between Ijaiye and Oyo. He noted that toll gates were found everywhere in Yorubaland in this proportion. He was nevertheless surprised that 'notwithstanding these sore hindrances to trade there is a great internal traffic'.[62] In the Badagri area, the town of Pokia was said to have a toll house at its northern gate. Here, according to Crowther, 'custom is paid by all trading passengers, from 5-10 cowries each person having load or live-stock and 200 cowries for every slave'.[63] The Ijebu had their major toll gate at the town of Oru for all traders from the interior travelling to Lagos.

Apart from tolls at town gates, traders had to pay something of a turnpike charge to the armed group which led each caravan. At Bidjie on the road from Badagry, Lander in 1828 noted that 'turnpikes are as common from Badagry to this place as on any public road in England. Instead of horses, carriages, etc., people carrying burden alone are taxed.'[64] Hinderer in 1851 described a similar turnpike on the road from Abeokuta to Ibadan:

'At the entrance of our resting place the soldiers conducting (or pre-tending to conduct) the caravan have a sort of turnpike where they exact money from the traders. Until late in the night the forest echoed with the dreadful noise they made and several times during the evening fighting threatened to break out among them.'[65]

This general condition of trading emphasizes that it was not a hap-hazard occupation in which any person might engage. The vicissitudes of the trader's life, the innumerable tolls he had to pay as well as the somewhat arbitrary turnpike charges—all these set the entry conditions into the business. No doubt profits from trading must have been rela-tively large to cover the various expenses of trading. And these expenses, especially that of tolls, provided part of the revenue for the maintenance of the administrative and political élite in the towns.

Size and social characteristics of Yoruba towns

How large, it may be asked, were these pre-European Yoruba towns? Travellers through the area in the nineteenth century described most of the towns by such epithets as 'large' or 'small'. However, estimates of the population of some of the towns were attempted at various times. Table 4 shows the various estimates for some 32 towns grouped into four size categories. It showed that, by the middle of the nineteenth

TABLE 4   ESTIMATES OF THE POPULATION OF YORUBA TOWNS IN THE NINETEENTH
CENTURY

A. Towns with population of over 40,000

IBADAN	100,000	(Hinderer, 1851)	ABEOKUTA	60,000 (Hinderer, 1851)
	70,000	(Bowen, 1856)		60,000 (Macaulay, 1853)
	100,000	(J. Johnson, 1878)		60,000 (Bowen, 1856)
	120,000	(Millson, 1891)		100,000 (Campbell, 1861)
ILORIN	70,000	(Mann, 1853)		100,000 (Maser, 1867)
	70,000	(Bowen, 1856)	OSHOGBO	60,000 (Moloney, 1890)
IWO	20,000	(Bowen, 1856)	EDE	20,000 (Bowen, 1856)
	50,000	(Millson, 1890)		50,000 (Moloney, 1890)
	60,000	(Moloney, 1890)		

B. Towns with a population of 20-40,000

LAGOS	20,000 (Bowen, 1856)		IJEBU-ODE	35,000 (Moloney, 1890)
	30,000 (Campbell, 1861)			40,000 (quoted)
	40,000 (Freeman, 1864)			13,000 (Millson, 1891)
OYO	25,000 (Bowen, 1856)		OGBOMOSHO	25,000 (Bowen, 1856)
	40,000 (J. Johnson, 1878)			40,000 (Mann, 1855)
IJAIYE	40,000 (Mann, 1853)			30,000 (Chausse, 1883)
	30,000 (Maser, 1867)		ISEHIN	15,000 (Townsend, 1852)
KOSO	20,000 (Clapperton, 1825)			24,000 (Mann, 1853)
EPE	20,000 (Braithwaite, 1877)			20,000 (Bowen, 1856)
			OKE-ODAN	30,000 (Marsh, 1845)
				24,000 (Nicholson, 1863)
			ADDO	20,000 (Faulkner, 1879)

C. Towns with a population of 10-20,000

IGANNA	8-10,000 (Clapperton, 1825)		ILARO	15,000 (District Comm.
	5-6,000 (J. Johnson, 1878)			1887)
AWAYE	10,000 (Mann, 1853)			5,000 (Ewart, 1890)
APOMU	8-10,000 (Hinderer, 1851)		OKEHO	12,000 (Doherty, 1875)
				6,000 (J. Johnson, 1878)
			ONDO	15,000 (Chausse, 1883)

D. Towns with a population of under 10,000

BADAGRI	5-6,000 (Gollmer, 1846)		IPOKIA	4,000 (Gollmer, 1846)
	5,000 (Freeman, 1864)			2,000 (Crowther, 1846)
	3,000 (Moloney, 1890)			4,000 (Pearce, 1860)
IKORODU	6-8,000 (Gollmer, 1854)			1,500 (Faulkner, 1874)
OTTA	3,000 (King, 1850)		IPERU	6,000 (J. Johnson, 1878)
	2,000 (Faulkner, 1879)		ORU	4-5,000 (Millson, 1891)
FIDITI	6-7,000 (Chausse, 1883)		IPARA	1,000 (Hinderer, 1851)
IBOKUN	5-7,000 (Hinderer, 1851)			900-1,000 (Irving, 1851)
			AWE	2,000 (Meakin, 1871)

century, three Yoruba cities were at least close to the 100,000 mark and a few others were certainly of considerable size. This situation is a peculiarly nineteenth century development and is related to the historical events which shook the whole of Yorubaland in that century.

The remote cause for the upheaval was the rising profitability of the slave-trade towards the end of the eighteenth century. The increasing incidence of the kidnapping of people for sale at Apomu market in the Owu district had led the Alafin of Oyo to send to the Olowu of Owu to exert himself to check this practice. According to Johnson, the Olowu, in carrying out his orders, punished several towns especially those in Ife territory.[66] This so incensed the Ife that they declared war against Owu about 1807. Later, over a trifling incident at the Apomu market involving an Ijebu and an Owu, the Ijebu, the major slave-exporting group, sided with the Ife and together they laid siege to Owu city. The defenders of this city successfully fended off the assaults of their enemies for almost seven years and on occasions carried out successful sorties against them.

What eventually turned the scale against the Owu were certain other happenings in Northern Yorubaland. Here Afonja, the Commander of the Yoruba army, had revolted against his sovereign, the Alafin of Oyo and had established a rival capital at Ilorin. Faced with the prospect of a joint assault by the loyal Oyo forces, Afonja had solicited the help of the Fulani fresh from their victorious *Jihad* against the Hausa States. In the encounter the Yoruba army was defeated. The Fulani and their Hausa soldiers then proceeded systematically to lay siege to most of the Oyo towns, many of which were in the end either deserted or destroyed. Large numbers of refugees from these towns flocked to the banner of the armies laying siege to Owu. Together they again renewed the assault on the city whose stalwart defenders, after the strain and privations of seven years, could no longer maintain the struggle. Owu was defeated, its people harried and dispersed, and the city itself razed to the ground.

After a short respite, the allied army of Ijebu, Ife and Oyo turned on the Egba who were neighbours of the Owu people and had helped the latter during the years of siege. Systematically they set about destroying their numerous small towns. By 1830, what remained of the population of the various Egba towns came together to found the new settlement of Abeokuta which, as the table above showed, was already very large by 1851.

Meanwhile the allied army itself had come to settle down in one of the

Egba towns which had by chance escaped being set ablaze when its people were conquered and dispersed. This was Ibadan. No sooner had the army settled here than it began to exert a strong attractive force on all and sundry throughout the length and breadth of Yorubaland. Craftsmen of varying specialisms, traders in different commodities, young men with nothing but their determination to survive and succeed, women attracted by the excitement of life in a large military establishment and slaves of both sexes all began to converge on Ibadan. Over the years, Ibadan came to carve out its own area of influence and to emerge by 1865 as the sigle, most important city in Yorubaland.

Some of the refugees from cities in the northern area of the Yoruba country went on to swell the population of other cities farther south. The capital of the Yoruba country which Clapperton and Lander visited in the 1820s was deserted about 1837 and refounded in an area much farther south in what is now Oyo (formerly Ago-Oja).[67] Ogbomosho received an influx of population notably from Ikoyi, which used to be some seven miles to the north-west.[68] A whole colony of northern Oyo refugees settled close by Ife in a quarter which became known as Modakeke. Many other centres, such as Shagamu in Ijebu-Remo, grew as a result of the amalgamation of a number of relatively smaller communities seeking safety and security in numbers.

All in all, the nineteenth century was the period of town coalescence and growth in response to the need of defence and security. This development, however, was largely confined to an east-west belt running from Ilesha in the east, westward through Ife, Oshogbo, Iwo and Ibadan to Abeokuta. Elsewhere, especially in the north-east and south-east forested areas, where the threat to life and property was not so acute, most metropolitan centres of kingdoms (Ijebu-Ode, Ondo and Owo) were no more than 25,000 to 40,000 in population and many of the other towns had a population of considerably less than 20,000.

The urban population, even though small by present standards, was characterized by its relatively greater heterogeneity. Heterogeneity was due not only to ethnic differences but also to occupation, social status and religion. Ethnic heterogeneity resulted largely from the needs of trade which encouraged people to travel far and wide. It was also encouraged by slavery and the slave-trade whereby a large number of non-Yorubas, notably Hausas and tribes from the Middle Belt, were kept as household slaves in most Yoruba compounds. Occupational differences provided a basis for social stratification related largely to the ways in which traditional skills were jealously guarded. These skills were handed down largely within the framework of specific lineages. Lineage membership also determined social status in the towns. Certain lineages, especially those from among whom the city rulers were chosen and those which were large land-owning groups, were generally treated with some deference. Cutting across the lineage was status identification based on age-classes. Among the Yoruba, people were grouped into age-classes at four- or five-yearly intervals. A member of a class below was generally expected to show deference to anyone in the groups above him. Sometimes, as among the Ijebu and Ekiti, these classes were banded into broader groups which were saddled with specific responsibilities in the administration and defence of the town. Wealth was also a factor making for social heterogeneity especially as it obliged many people to pay deferential attention to members of wealthy lineages.

From the end of the eighteenth century, but especially since the early nineteenth century, a new factor making for increasing heterogeneity in the population was Islam. It is not known for certain when Moslem influence began to penetrate into Yorubaland. Adams mentioned that traces of Islam were already evident at Ardrah on the coast just west of Yorubaland in the 1790s, while Moloney noted that 'Mohammedanism was introduced into Lagos about 1816; in the reign of Oshiloku, who was the eighth king, there were many sheikhs of the Ulema in Lagos'.[69] In 1830 Lander found at Ilaro that a chapter of the Koran was being repeated to the Chief by a *mallam*, to which both he and his people seemed to pay great respect and attention.[70] Moreover, as in Northern Nigeria, schools were established at Ilaro for the avowed purpose of teaching the rudiments of Islam.

The point about Islam in Yoruba towns at this time was that it was becoming the religion of an *élite* which tried to exercise considerable influence both in the royal court and in town affairs. In Ibadan, Hinderer noted in 1851 that 'the predominant part of the inhabitants are heathen though the large number of Mohammedans also are by no means without influence, especially as their warlike disposition seems to suit the chiefs as well'.[71] The Oba of Ede was by 1858 already a Moslem, and through his influence that religion was gaining ground among the populace.[72] Meakin, writing to the Secretary of the Church Missionary Society in 1859, commented that Iwo was by then a stronghold of Islam.[73] In Lagos, in 1863, Burton also remarked that the city contained 'some 800 Moslems, though not yet 2,000, as it is reported. Though few, they have already risen to political importance; in 1851 our bravest and most active opponents were those wearing the turbans.'[74] In Oyo by 1878 Islam could boast of twelve or more mosques.[75] By 1883, in Iseyin, the Catholic missionaries, Fathers Chausse and Holley, mentioned that there were two quarters occupied exclusively by Moslems who were striving to exercise great influence in the country.[76]

Traditional administration of Yoruba towns

It is obvious that the administration of such a heterogenous population required considerable skill and organization. Among the Yoruba, the major institution of urban administration was that of the Oba. An Oba was a crowned head who exercised jurisdiction over the affairs of a town and its tributary settlements. The latter may consist of other towns apart from the more usual villages. The crucial symbol of urban status was the crown. Since the crown conferred a measure of independence on the ruler and, therefore, the people of a town, it is easy to appreciate why, when a settlement felt it had grown large and important enough to be a town, the external symbolic manifestation was the agitation that its ruler should wear a crown.

This question of the crown provides the best evidence of the fact that most Yoruba towns grew up as colonies of an immigrant group based originally at Ife. There is a general consensus of opinion that all crowns derived from Ife and that no Oba in Yorubaland could be regarded as properly installed until his staff of office had been issued from Ife. In a celebrated instance in which the ruler of Epe in 1902 had crowned himself, the British Government had sought the opinion of the Oni of Ife. He had asserted that 'no one on the face of the earth has power to give the Elepe of Epe a crown unless the Oni of Ife. . . .'[77] Although the Oni listed some 22 Obas who had been given crowns by him, it is not quite clear under what circumstances the Oni was willing to bestow the crowns.

In spite of the symbolic importance of the crowned head and his major role as spiritual leader, the traditional administration of Yoruba towns was in general hierarchical and democratic. It combined representation on the basis of residential quarters with that of special interests. Each quarter had a chief through whom the views of the people were conveyed to the town's authority. Apart from quarter chiefs, there were guild heads who, in some towns, were represented on the town's council of chiefs. There were also heads of age-sets who might be represented in the administration of the town. Moreover, there was the *Iyalode*, a female chief who represented in the council the interests of all women in the town, especially those relating to their trade. She also had under her a hierarchy of subordinate female chiefs.

More important for policy-making than this wide council was an inner council of elders known as the *Ogboni* or *Osugbo* (in Ijebu). This council, in anthropological literature, was regarded as a cult society because of the secrecy that surrounded much of their activities. In essence, however, they functioned as a privy council or cabinet to keep a check on the powers of the Oba. In most Yoruba towns, their lodge house was found not very far from the palace. Usually, as in all constitutional situations, the extent of their importance depended on the personality of the Oba at any particular time. Thus, in areas such as in Oyo, where the powers of the Alafin overshadowed everybody else's, the Ogboni was less prominent as a political institution. In other places, such as in Ijebu, their power even today is very great.

The position of immigrant communities in the administration of Yoruba towns was one that had been hallowed by age. As soon as an immigrant group became sufficiently numerous in a town, it was encouraged by the town's authority to appoint a head or representative who could be invited to the council of chiefs when matters affecting his group were being discussed. He was also expected to call on the Oba of the town periodically to pay his respects. Because of the tendency of immigrants from different parts of the country to concentrate in particular areas of a city, the head of such a group became more or less a quarter chief. This principle of representation applied equally to other Yoruba who were strangers to the town as well as to the non-Yoruba. It was also extended to groups differentiated by any other factor such as religion. Thus the Moslems had a chief of their own and this practice now applies to the Christians.

The physical structure of Yoruba towns

Irrespective of the way they developed, most Yoruba towns approximated to a given town-plan. The most salient physical elements in this plan were those related to the administrative, the trading and the defence functions of the town. Centrally placed within most Yoruba towns was the palace of the Oba, the head of the city administration and the symbol of its urban status. So important was the palace that its grounds, in general, occupied an extensive area of land. The palace grounds, apart from containing the palace, also provided ample open space for recreation and for public religious or social occasions (Plate 9). In modern times, much of this space has been subdivided and used for building various offices of the local or regional administration such as the Tax Office, the Council Office, the Central Police Station and the Post Office.

Some impression of the magnitude of the palace grounds can be gleaned from the description given by nineteenth century travellers. Of the palace grounds in Old Oyo (Katunga), Clapperton in 1825 noted that it covered 'about a square mile . . . having two large parks one in front, and another facing the north.'[78] Of those in Iwo and Ede, there is the comment of Hinderer in 1858:

'The King's compound (in Iwo) is quite a palace in native style, with those curious kind of towers peculiar to the Oyo palace. But the *agbala* (the palace ground), an extensive garden adjoining to it, containing a variety of lofty and wide spreading trees was something quite new to me in this country, and the King's special *Oris*, a grove close by with its gigantic trees is something imposing. . . . (In Ede), the King's palace is the picture of neatness of a native building, and his *agbala* behind which is very large, would be a fine park if the walls were not in ruins.'[79]

The palace itself was usually an impressive building enclosed by a very high wall. That at Ife, according to Frobenius in 1911, was the most impressive sight in the town, its massive walls being visible from whatever quarter one approached the town. 'Its front', he went on to say, 'especially with the fine open square on which it stands, makes an imposing effect in spite of all its ruin. . . . The walls are mighty, over a yard at the base and some eighteen feet high.'[80] Inside the wall, the palace was a veritable labyrinth of rooms and courtyards whose historical or functional significance has been adequately indicated in the study of *Yoruba Palaces* by G. J. A. Ojo.[81]

Opposite the palace was the most important market in the city. This joint location of palace and market in the centre of Yoruba towns was, according to Johnson, 'a rule without an exception and hence the term *Oloja* (one having a market) used as a generic term or title of all chief rulers of a town be he a King or a Bale'.[82] Other smaller markets found elsewhere within the town were closely associated with the residences of minor chiefs. Close by the central market was found the fetish temple or the principal mosque of the town. The fetish temple at Ogbomosho was described as 'the most remarkable in Yoruba with a door, ornate with figures in relief which give it a very striking appearance.'[83]

From the palace, market and religious places in the centre, roads radiated to every part of the town and to neighbouring towns. Those that served as major thoroughfares were usually wide and impressive since, apart from traders and others using them, they had to carry large crowds of dancers and processions. Townsend commented on Ijaiye in 1852 (it was destroyed ten years later) that 'many of the streets are broad and straight and a spacious market place in the centre of the town is the best I have seen in Africa, not excluding Sierra Leone'.[84] Chausse and Holley noted in 1883 that the roads in Ilesha 'were formerly broad but are now no more than narrow lanes where men may walk only in single file. In a word, the war has made of a fine town an immense field of devastation and misery.'[85] This comment on the effect of wars on the streets in Ilesha has significance for the whole question of the layout of Yoruba towns.

Today most of the important Yoruba towns such as Ibadan, Oyo, Oshogbo, Abeokuta, Iwo and Ede show no discernible town plan, and their streets are narrow and winding. From this it has often been mistakenly inferred that Yoruba towns had no plan or layout. Traditionally, however, Yoruba towns were planned. Since most of them, as had been indicated earlier on, were something of a colonial creation, they copied the layout of the major centres of Ife or Oyo. Johnson, in fact, pointed out that Ilesha was consciously laid out on the same plan as that of Old Oyo.[86] Plate 9 shows the plan of Ilesha which is very similar to what one finds in Ile-Ife, Ondo, Akure, Ijebu-Ode, Iperu and a number of other towns in the north-east and south-east of Yorubaland. This plan shows the palace, the principal market and the main grove or temple in the centre, two main roads, relatively broad, about 30 feet wide, running virtually across the town and crossing at its centre and a number of rectilinear, narrower roads leading away from these main roads.

It is this plan which was destroyed or completely forgotten in the hectic struggle for survival in the nineteenth century. As Johnson remarked:

'It must strike the most casual observer who has travelled over the Yoruba country that those portions of the country which are supposed to be more backward in intelligence, viz. the Ijesa, Ekiti, Ife and other provinces, have better streets than the more intelligent ones. Old men attribute this fact to the effect of the intertribal wars. For instance, in the case of Abeokuta, however well laid may have been the streets of the original farm villas, when the refugees began to flock in, attention could scarcely be paid to the alignment of the houses; each one simply tried to find out the whereabouts of the members of his township, and thus they grouped themselves by their families in every available space around the chief of their town. The same may be said of all the towns of Yoruba proper which have suffered from the vicissitudes of war. In later years the people seem to have lost altogether the art of laying out and naming streets as is the case in Ijesa and Ekiti towns.'[87]

Surrounding the Yoruba town was usually a wall with a deep trench on the outside. According to Johnson, towns in the plain which were greatly exposed to sudden attacks or had to withstand long sieges had a second or outer wall enclosing a large area used for farming during a siege.[88] This wall was called *Odi Amola* ('wall of safety'); but sometimes it was called *Odi Amonu* ('wall of ruin') depending on whether the wall had been to the townspeople the means of safety or had been unavailing for the purpose. Towns like Gboho, in the extreme north of Yorubaland, had three walls. Others like Kishi, Koso, Ilesha and Ife had two. Many others had only one. The walls were usually over 15 feet high and probably equally broad at the base. With a ditch equally as deep, the town wall provided a good defence against invaders. In general, the walls were built of clay dug from the trench. In the stony districts to the north-west, some towns, notably Oke Amo and Ilessan, had their walls built of stones.[89]

The increasing use of firearms in the nineteenth century occasioned a revolution in the construction of the Yoruba town wall. Before this time, the town wall simply served to keep the enemy out until famine served to disperse them. Both sides of the siege tried to starve the other out, the besieged town trying as often as possible to resolve the issue by making sorties against the enemy. With firearms it was possible to engage the enemy from the safety of the town wall. This meant that town walls had to be of moderate thickness to allow for holes through which to fire guns. The result was that town walls came to be constructed such that their thickness was scarcely more than two to three feet, although their heights remained between fifteen and twenty feet. This was the type of wall built around Abeokuta and also the second wall (the Ibikunle Wall) constructed around Ibadan in 1858.

The circumference of the walls, of course, gave no indication of the built-up extent of the towns since they enclosed a substantial unbuilt area. The circumference of the town wall of Old Oyo is said to have been about 15 miles[90]; that of Ibadan 18 miles[91]; Gboho's triple wall had a circumference of nearly 20 miles[92]; while the wall around Abeokuta was said to be about 23 miles.[93]

Through the town wall roads led to neighbouring towns. At such points along the wall were to be found massive wooden gates where toll collectors sat. These gates were named after the most important towns to which they led. Each of the gates was in charge of a chief who was responsible for maintaining order along the highways leading through the gate.[94] Gollmer described one of the gates into Ketu as 'a wide and lofty double entrance (closed by two huge carved gates 8 ft. 6 in. long and 8ft. 6 in. wide each, and formed of country board, made to lap over and nailed together)'.[95] Old Oyo had ten gates leading into it.[96] Most towns had at least four gates. Sometimes, as in the Ijebu-Remo towns, these gates were surmounted by two towers on both sides. Irving described the towers by the town gate of Ode in Remo as 'a two-storied, square, vermilion-coloured tower, thatched, and loopholed for musketry'.[97]

Within the town wall the town was organized into quarters. In the planned Yoruba town, each street branching off the main roads of the town constituted a quarter. The quarter comprised a number of compounds housing members of one or more extended families on both sides of the street. The Yoruba compound, unlike that of the Hausa or Nupe, was an enclosed space, generally in the form of a square, bounded by a mud wall about seven feet high. There was only a single entrance to it which, for the nobilities, was topped by a gabled roof (kobi) to allow the easy entry of men on horses. Inside, the compound was divided into numerous rooms housing a number of related families. Until the early twentieth century, most of the compounds were roofed with thatch. The smallest compound might cover about half an acre of land; the compounds of chiefs covered several acres.

What the sanitary arrangements in the towns were is not clear, although they could hardly have been anything but primitive. Johnson noted that 'near every large thoroughfare or a market place is a spot selected as a dust heap for the disposal of all sorts of refuse and sweepings in the neighbourhood, and, at intervals, fire is set to the pile of rubbish'.[98] Here and there about the town, leafy groves were left standing for the disposal of sewage. Important chiefs had a large area of land enclosed within their compounds within which selected spots were used for sanitary purposes. Usually the work of keeping the compounds and their frontage clean and tidy fell on the domestic slaves as well as on the women and children. The general upkeep of the town was undertaken on the basis of each quarter looking after its own portion of the town. Where the administration was efficient, a very clean town was preserved. Clapperton, for instance, commented on the cleanliness of the town of Ilaro.[99] Usually towns with important trading functions were some of the dirtiest in the country.

Drinking water was usually procured from wells or from nearby streams. The town of Ketu, near which there was no stream or river, was said to possess an ingenious system of water supply from subterranean cisterns. According to Gollmer, 'there is no compound or house in Ketu which does not possess from three to a dozen artificial subterranean cisterns or tanks, some of great depth and extent and full of water. The tank is covered in by a ceiling of strong beams and earth, a small aperture being only allowed for the water to flow into, and to be drawn out, and this is generally covered over with a pot, so that one may walk over or stand on a tank of water without knowing it.'[100]

In general the socio-economic structure of the towns showed a tendency for the wealthier and more notable families to be located near the centre of town in relatively large and spacious compounds while the poorer and less well-known families were pushed towards the margin in generally much smaller compounds. This situation was primarily a function of the length of stay of families in a town and the relation of this fact to the ownership of land. Nonetheless, apart from the central district which contained the palace, the market and the religious places, no clear areal differentiation was obvious. Craft activities were carried on within the compounds or, in certain cases such as pottery-making, close to the stream or on an open patch behind a compound.

Conclusion

Such then is the picture of Yoruba urbanization up to the time of the European penetration at the end of the nineteenth century. It was an urbanization based largely in the open grassland area where human movement and contacts were easy and frequent. Johnson emphasized that, before the period of the revolutionary and intertribal wars, the bulk of the Yoruba people lived in the towns of the plain, the towns in the forest lands being small and unimportant, except for the town of Owu.[101] It has been shown that these towns, irrespective of their colonial-type origin, performed important trading and administrative functions for wide areas around them. Theoretically, therefore, we should expect their spatial distribution to show evidence of some ordering process. Unfortunately the nature of the documentary material which we have used so far does not allow this fact to be easily demonstrated. Nevertheless Clapperton, whose journey in 1825 from Badagri to Old Oyo (Katunga) was through the western grassy area of Yorubaland, indicated five major centres between the two places. These were Ijanna, Assoudo, Duffo, Shaki and Koso. Over a distance of about 237 miles the spacing of these centres gave a distance apart of nearly 40 miles.

Between the date of Clapperton's journey and the present century there is no evidence of a shift in the location of the major Yoruba towns. It is thus instructive to find that the distance apart of these towns varies generally between 30 and 50 miles. Thus the distance of Ibadan from its six nearest neighbours are 30 miles (Iwo), 33 miles (Oyo), 43 miles (Ijebu-Ode), 44 miles (Abeokuta), 44 miles (Shagamu) and 44 miles (Ede). Eastward from Ibadan towns are the following distances apart: Ibadan to Ife (49); Ife to Ondo (34), Ondo to Akure (30), Akure to Owo (30), and Akure to Ado-Ekiti (30). Northward from Ibadan, we have Ibadan to Oyo (33), Oyo to Ogbomosho (30), Ogbomosho to Ilorin (33). Where this fairly regular distance apart is seriously reduced, some other ordering process, notably political or administrative, is usually found to be involved. A good example is the situation of Oshogbo and Ede, both important centres but only 9 miles apart. According to Johnson, both settlements were frontier towns of Ijeshas and Oyos respectively set up to protect the traders of the two kingdoms.[102] Ede was founded in the reign of Alafin Kori to check the frequent incidence of Ijeshas kidnapping Oyo traders on their way to the Apomu market. 'The Owa of Ilesa,' Johnson claimed, 'imitating the same appointment, posted an opposition kinglet at Oshogbo named Ataoja.'

The ordering process behind the pattern of distribution of Yoruba towns is thus clearly trade and administration in a pre-industrial, pre-European context. It was a process which found its best expression in the open grassland country of the northern half of Yorubaland. In the present century, when the productive centre of gravity has shifted to the forest belt with its cocoa, kolanuts, timber and rubber; when strong international relationships are now coming from the southern coast and not from across the desert; and when the major lines of modern transport were initially displaced to the western edge of the area of Yoruba urban development, we may expect to find significant changes in the character of Yoruba towns.

References

1. S. O. Biobaku, *The Origin of the Yoruba*, Federal Information Service, Lagos, 1955, p. 21.
2. S. Johnson, *The History of the Yorubas*, London, 1921, p. 3.
3. Ibid., p. 9.
4. From a translation of an Arabic MS. extracted from a larger work by Sultan Mohammed Bello of Sokoto, Appendix XII in D. Denham, H. Clapperton and N. Oudney, *Narrative of Travels and Discoveries in Northern and Central Africa, 1822-24*, London, 1828, Vol. 2, p. 454.
5. Hugh Clapperton, *Journal of a Second Expedition into the Interior of Africa*, London, 1829, p. 59.
6. Richard and John Lander, *Journal of an Expedition to explore the Course and Termination of the Niger*, London, 1838, Vol. 1, p. 45.
7. Ibid., p. 116.
8. Ibid., p. 153.
9. Ibid., p. 154.
10. S. Johnson, p. 8 This may point to the fact that the cowries were imported to Yorubaland through Benin.
11. S. Biobaku, op. cit., pp. 21-22.
12. S. Johnson, op. cit., p. 15.
13. Ibid., p. 281.
14. See M. Rostovtzeff, *The Social and Economic History of the Hellenistic World*, Oxford, 1941, pp. 130-133. Rostovtzeff disagrees with Plutarch that Alexander founded as many as 75 colonial towns in the Middle East; also, by the same author, *The Social and Economic History of the Roman Empire*, Oxford, 1957, pp. 83-84.
15. See J. W. Thompson, *Economic and Social History of the Middle Ages (300-1300)*, Vol. 2, New York, pp. 536-538.
16. T. W. Freeman, *Ireland, a General and Regional Geography*, London, 1950, pp. 92-94.
17. A. E. Smailes, *A Geography of Towns*, London, 1953, p. 75.
18. S. Johnson, op. cit., pp. 12-25.
19. Ibn Khaldun, *Protegomenes* (written between 1375 and 1378), edited and translated by M. G. de Slane, Paris, 1936, Vol. 2, pp. 238-41, 277-82, 294-313.
20. Duarte Pacheco Pereira, *Esmeraldo de Situ Orbis, 1505-1508*, translated and edited by G. H. T. Kimble for the Hakluyt Society, London, 1937, p. 123.
21. John Barbot, *A description of the Coasts of North and South Guinea*, Book 4, London, 1732, p. 354.

22. Letter from Assistant Inspector Haddon-Smith to the Governor, 24 June 1890, C.O. 806/334, No. 38, encl. 14. The intervals given follow the common reckoning among the Yoruba who count the day of the market as included in the interval. Thus a market which is held on a Monday and again on the following Friday is regarded as a five-day (instead of a four-day) market.

23. A. F. Foster, Journal, CA2/040, November 1874—June 1875.

24. J. Johnson, Journal, CMS CA2/056, February 1878.

25. S. Johnson, op. cit., p. 188.

26. D. Hinderer, Journal, CMS CA2/049, March 1855 and September 1851.

27. J. Barbot, op. cit., p. 354.

28. H. Clapperton, op. cit., pp. 14-15.

29. H. Townsend, Journal, CMS CA2/085, letter August 1852.

30. J. T. Kefer, Journal, CMS CA2/059, March 1853.

31. A. C. Mann, Journal, CMS CA2/066, July-September 1855.

32. Report of a Visit to Ilaro by Major W. H. Ewart, C.O. 806/334, No. 40, Enc. 1, 28th August 1890.

33. H. Clapperton, op. cit., p. 13.

34. Ibid., p. 48.

35. H. Townsend, Journal, CMS CA2/085, September 1853.

36. D. Hinderer, Journal, CMS CA2/049, December 1858.

37. R. and J. Lander, op. cit., p. 136.

38. C. A. Gollmer, Journal CMS CA2/043, September 1845.

39. S. Johnson, op. cit., p. 168.

40. J. Martin, letter to the Secretary, Methodist Mission, 5 September 1846.

41. C. A. Gollmer, Journal, CMS CA2/043, March 1846.

42. J. A. Maser, Journal, CMS CA2/068, December 1873.

43. S. Johnson, op. cit., p. 267.

44. Ibid., p. 311.

45. S. Crowther, Journal, CMS Archives, CA2/031, December 1845.

46. David Hinderer, Journals, CMS Archives, CA2/049, March 1855.

47. Dr Irving, 'Journal of Journey into Ijebu Country', *CMS. Intelligencer*, Vol. 7, 1856, pp. 117-118.

48. Rev. C. A. Gollmer, Journals, CMS Archives, CA3/043, September 1859.

49. Rev. H. Townsend, Journals, CMS Archives, CA2/085, March 1847.

50. Rev. H. Townsend, CMS Archives, CA2/085, September 1853.

51. Rev. D. Hinderer, Journals, CMS Archives, CA2/049, December 1858.

52. Rev. W. S. Allen, Journals, CMS Archives, CA2/019, February 1872.

53. R. Campbell, *A pilgrimage to my motherland: an account of a journey among the Egbas and Yorubas of Central Africa 1869-60*, 1861, p. 25.

54. William Marsh, Journals, CMS Archives, CA2/067, 11 June 1845.
55. Rev. C. A. Gollmer, Journals, CMS Archives, CA2/043, March 1854.
56. Rev. D. Hinderer, Journals, CMS Archives, CA2/049, June 1851.
57. For Fiditi, see J. Johnson, CA2/056, February 1878; for Kuta, see W. S. Allen, CA2/019, July-December 1869.
58. D. Hinderer, Journals, CMS Archives, CA2/049, September 1849.
59. Letter from Mr Alvan Millson to Hon. Ag. Colonial Secretary, 26 April 1890, C.O. 806/334, p. 132, No. 31, Enc. 8.
60. Rev. J. A. Maser, Letter to Rev. H. Venn, 5 February 1854, CMS Archives, CA2/068.
61. Gov. Moloney's Interview with Otta Representatives, 2 June 1888, C.O. 806/299, p. 63 No. 31, Enc. 1.
62. Rev. H. Townsend, Journals, CMS Archives, CA2/085 September 1853.
63. Rev. S. Crowther, Journals, CMS Archives, CA2/031, December 1845.
64. Richard and John Lander, op. cit., p. 68.
65. Rev. D. Hinderer, Journals, CMS Archives, CA2/049, June 1851.
66. S. Johnson, op. cit., pp. 206-207.
67. Rev. J. Johnson, Journals, CMS Archives, CA2/056, February 1878.
68. Rev. Adolphus C. Mann, Journals, CMS Archives, CA2/066, July-September 1855.
69. Capt. John Adams, *Sketches taken during ten voyages to Africa between the years 1786 and 1800*, London, 1823, p. 79; also Sir Alfred Moloney, 'Notes on the Yoruba and the Colony and Protectorate of Lagos, West Africa', *Proceedings of the Royal Geographical Society*, 1890, p. 599.
70. R. and J. Lander, op. cit., p. 77.
71. Rev. D. Hinderer, Journals, CMS Archives, CA2/049, June 1851.
72. Rev. D. Hinderer, Journals, CMS Archives, CA2/049, December 1858.
73. G. Meakin, Letter to the Secretary of the Church Missionary Society, CMS Archives, CA2/069, 29 January 1859.
74. R. F. Burton, *Wanderings in West Africa*, London, 1863, p. 225. The reference to 1851 was to the time of the bombardment of Lagos.
75. Rev. J. Johnson, Journals, CMS Archives, CA2/056, February 1878.
76. J. B. Chausse and Father Holley, 'Abeokuta', *Les Missions Catholiques*, Tome 17, Lyons, 1885.
77. 'Native Crowns', *Journals of the African Society*, No. 7, April 1903, p. 313.
78. H. Clapperton, op. cit., p. 58.
79. Rev. D. Hinderer, op. cit., December 1858.
80. Leo Frobenius, *The Voice of Africa*, London, 1913, p. 276.
81. G. J. A. Ojo, *Yoruba Palaces*, London, 1966.

82. S. Johnson, op. cit., p. 91.
83. J. B. Chausse and Father Holley, op. cit.
84. Rev. H. Townsend, Journal, CMS Archives, CA2/085, 30 August 1852.
85. J. B. Chausse and Father Holley, op. cit.
86. S. Johnson, op. cit., p. 22.
87. Ibid., p. 93.
88. Ibid., p. 91.
89. Rev. Henry Townsend, Journal, CMS Archives, CA2/085, July 1856; and S. W. Doherty, Journal, CMS Archives, CA2/035, April-June 1876.
90. See H. Clapperton, op. cit., p. 58.
91. Alvan Millson, op. cit., note 59.
92. R. and J. Lander, op. cit., p. 110.
93. R. Campbell, op. cit., p. 32.
94. S. Johnson, op. cit., p. 92.
95. Rev. C. A. Gollmer, Journal, CMS Archives, CA2/043, March 1854.
96. H. Clapperton, op. cit., p. 58.
97. Dr Irving, op. cit., p. 117.
98. S. Johnson, op. cit., p. 92.
99. H. Clapperton, op. cit., p. 8.
100. Rev. C. A. Gollmer, Journals, CMS Archives, CA2/043, September 1859.
101. S. Johnson, op. cit., p. 93.
102. Ibid., p. 156.

5 Modern Revival of Urbanization

The prelude to British administration

The British bombardment of Lagos of 1851 marked the beginning of the end of pre-European urbanization in Nigeria. The event itself had been foreshadowed as early as 1807. In that year the British Parliament had passed the momentous Act freeing all slaves that set foot on British soil. In the succeeding years, various other decisions were taken which were logical extensions of the Act of 1807. First, attempts were made to stop the slave-trade as a whole. Several European nations signed treaties renouncing their further participation in the trade, and agreed that the British Naval Squadron could search any ship flying their flags and carrying slaves from the West African shores. Secondly, Freetown (now in Sierra Leone) was established for the trial of the captains of such ships that were caught, and for the free settlement of the slaves found on board. Here Christian missionaries helped in rehabilitating the freed slaves, educating them in the English language and equipping them with some skills. Thirdly, encouraged by the demands of the new industrial revolution sweeping across Europe in the early part of the nineteenth century, attempts were made to stimulate the growth of legitimate commerce in the produce of the West African hinterland. Palm produce was the crop of major demand at the time, and it was hoped that African slave-dealers would be attracted away from their nefarious traffic to the more humane exchanges in agricultural produce.

However, risks surrounding the slave-trade only made it more profitable. Areas which could provide an effective hide-out against the vigilance of the British Naval Squadron continued the trade. Lagos, because of its situation close to a maze of lagoon waterways and the difficulty of entry into the lagoon, became a most important stronghold of the slave-trade. It was to put an effective end to the trade in this area that the town was bombarded and occupied by the British in 1851. The occupation of Lagos brought peace and security to the town and its immediate environs. It also encouraged the coming of European merchants. By 1852, there were five of them. Two more arrived in 1853, and within a decade there were several others.[1] The activity of European traders in legitimate commerce soon extended to two other

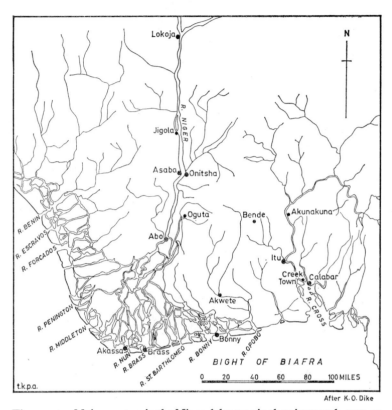

After K.O. Dike

Figure 10   Major centres in the Niger delta area in the nineteenth century

areas in Nigeria. These were in the Niger delta and along the Lower Niger River.

In the Niger delta, the vigilance of the British Naval Squadron had brought an early end to the slave-trade. This area, comprising Ibo and Ibibio land, had no ancient tradition of urbanism. The needs of the trans-Atlantic trade in slaves had, however, led to the emergence of a number of towns at the mouths of the numerous distributaries of the Niger delta (Fig. 10). According to Dike, most of these towns grew up between 1450 and 1800 and involved all the tribes within the delta hinterland.[2] Bonny, the most important of them, was by the 1830s already paying increasing attention to the trade in the natural produce of its area. Hope Waddell, writing in 1846, noted that 'by its safe and extensive anchorage, its proximity to the sea, and connection with the great rivers of Central Africa, Bonny is now the principal seat of the palm oil trade as it was formerly of the slave-trade'.³ Other centres which were changing their commercial complexion in the delta during this period included Old Calabar at the mouth of the Cross River, New Calabar (Kalabari) and Brass. Each of these towns occupied island sites dominating the mouths of the rivers and, except for trade relations with interior centres, they were isolated from one another by wide tracts of swampy land.

Along the Lower Niger were also found a number of urban centres which had grown up as a result of the trade in slaves. In Ibo country, Abo was reckoned perhaps the most important of these places because of its strategic importance at the head of the three great outlets of the Niger—the Benin, the Bonny and the Nun. By the 1830s this town was already turning to trade in commodities of 'legitimate' commerce. Laird, in 1832, described its people as 'industrious in growing yams, immense quantities being sent down to the coast and up the river. They carry on an extensive trade in palm oil and slaves: traders from Bonny, Benin and Brass are constantly at Eboe purchasing palm oil.'⁴ North of Abo, the Niger was even more important as an avenue for legitimate commerce. Laird noted that 'the intercourse and trade between the towns on the banks is very great (I was surprised to learn from Dr Briggs that there appeared to be twice as much traffic going forward here as in the upper parts of the Rhine) the whole population on the Niger being eminently of a commercial character, men, women and children carrying on trade'.⁵ Laird also commented on the trade specialization between the sexes in this area, remarking that the traffic in slaves, cloth and ivory was confined to the men; everything else being left to the other sex, who, he confessed, were far more difficult to deal with.

Establishment of direct trading relations between European merchants and the interior areas along the Lower Niger had to wait until after 1854. In that year Baikie sailed as far as Yola on the River Benue, a distance of over 900 miles from the coast, and demonstrated that with the use of quinine as a prophylactic against malaria it was possible for Europeans to survive anywhere in the interior of Africa. Soon factories or trading posts were established at Abo, Onitsha and Lokoja. Although attempts were made to extend direct trade relations beyond the confines of these posts, most of them met with sharp opposition from the local inhabitants. Indeed the Traders' Period, as McPhee called this time, was marked by the commercial penetration of the interior essentially through the work of African middleman serving as agents of European firms on the coast.[6] It was they who established stores in the interior on the basis of credit goods advanced to them by their European principals on the coast. They kept up regular communications with the latter, and invariably had to rely on the extensive use of native carriers to move commodities to the coast and bring inland the assortment of imported goods.

What the effect of this trading arrangement was on the urban development in Nigeria is not clear. Since, however, the African agent had to seek existing centres of commerce if his own operations were to be profitable, it was certain that the tendency was for trade at this stage to emphasize the relative traditional importance of various urban centres. Thus, especially in Yorubaland, places like Abeokuta, Ibadan and Ijebu-Ode came to feature prominently in the commercial relations of the period.

However, trade without the guarantee of political stability or security was still largely a risky proposition. Again and again in the records of the period there were innumerable references to the vicissitudes of the traders and frequent stoppages of trade.[7] Within Yorubaland, for instance, the intertribal warfare and the Fulani threat meant that conditions were far from stable almost throughout the nineteenth century. In the Niger delta, in spite of consular rule, local potentates could still impose arbitrary conditions and compel traders to take sides in their internal power rivalry.

To add to the precariousness of trade from the point of view of the British, there was increasing competition from other European merchants, notably those of France. Within their own group there was also bitter rivalry and cut-throat competition. This had arisen as a result of the introduction of a regular mail service between Liverpool and West Africa based on a fleet of steamers owned by MacGregor Laird and subsidized by the British Government. This service cheapened transportation costs so drastically that it enabled a large number of small traders to come out to Nigeria, who would otherwise have been unable to do so since they would never have had the capital to finance a ship. These small traders found that they could undercut the prices of the older established and highly monopolistic firms.

The Berlin Conference of 1884, which was designed to resolve the conflicting claims of European powers in Africa, conceded both the Lagos region and the Niger delta to the British, and accepted that their sphere of influence extended for an indeterminate distance inland. In the next decade, largely through the continued vigilance of the Royal Niger Company, much of the present area of Nigeria was secured for Britain. The closing years of the nineteenth century saw the definition of boundaries with the French, and on 1 January 1900 the British Government assumed full control of the administration of both Northern and Southern Nigeria.

The colonial administration and the institution of township status

The next sixty years of British rule in Nigeria were to have remarkable effects on urban growth and development in the country. It was a period of far-reaching changes in the general economic conditions of the country. Initially the major pre-occupation was the creation of peaceful conditions and orderly government, without which economic activities could hardly flourish. It was to Lord Lugard that Britain owed the introduction of a system of administration in Nigeria at only minimal cost to the colonial government. This was the system of indirect rule whose basic aim has been described as 'the development of an African society able to participate in the life of the modern world as a community in its own right'.[8] Lord Lugard found in Northern Nigeria a series of Moslem emirates formed from former Hausa States as a result of conquest by invading Fulanis. Economic development had reached a point of considerable specialization, and an elaborate series of taxes on the produce of the land, on cattle and on the practice of various trades, were collected by the nominees of the emirs.[9] Justice was administered by *Alkalis* learned in Koranic law. In short, as Mair pointed out, there was already in existence 'an organization which needed but little adaptation for the performance of the tasks required by a European government, and a personnel closely acquainted with the circumstances of the native population, and more numerous than any staff that a British administration could hope to provide'.[10] What Lugard did was simply to utilize the services of these officials in the development of a native administration based on British principles of county or provincial local government.

After the amalgamation in 1914 of the Northern and Southern Provinces of Nigeria to form a single country, the system was extended to the Southern Provinces. It was relatively easy to transplant the system to the Yoruba areas where existing kingdoms provided some basis of organization. The position was less satisfactory east of the Niger, where no administrative organization larger than the village or the coastal town ever existed.

While this form of provincial administration provided the basis for the maintenance of law and order, it was necessary for economic effectiveness to attempt improvements and modernization on a more restricted basis. Existing concentrations of population provided the means of doing this. In 1917 government passed the Township Ordinance which provided for the creation, constitution and administration of all towns and municipalities in Nigeria with the exception of those native towns where the population was sufficiently homogeneous for it to be administered by a Native Administration. Three categories of townships were constituted and designated first, second and third. A first-class township was administered by a Town Council; second and third-class townships were administered by officers appointed by the Governor, and assisted, in the case of the second-class township, by an Advisory Board. First and second-class townships had their own annual estimates of revenue and expenditure; in the case of third-class townships the revenue was paid into the Government Treasury.

The Township Ordinance operated until the end of the Second World War. After that it was overtaken by the series of constitutional changes which marked the post-war period. Throughout the period of its operation, Lagos was the only first-class township in the country. It had a council which consisted of ten members, only three of whom were elected. The rest were nominated by the governor. Second-class townships consisted principally of large centres of trade and numbered eighteen in 1919.[11] As the following list shows, twelve of these were in the Southern Provinces and six in the Northern Provinces. An inspection of the list shows that these were centres either along the railway line or on the coast, so that they represented places where European traders had set up stores. They were not particularly distinguished by the size of their population nor their traditional importance as is evidenced by the absence of many of the larger Yoruba towns. The list itself did not remain unchanged for very long. In 1924, for instance, Aba was downgraded to a third-class township only to re-appear again as a second-class township in 1925. In the latter year, Abeokuta disappeared permanently from the list and its place was taken by Oron. In the Northern Provinces, Minna also was dropped from the list in 1927. It is not clear what criteria of inclusion or exclusion were used, but by 1936 the number of second-class townships had decreased to twelve, comprising seven in the Southern Provinces (Aba, Calabar, Enugu, Onitsha, Port Harcourt, Sapele and Warri), and five in the north. All the Yoruba towns had been removed, although the ten largest among them were listed separately.

TABLE 5   LIST OF SECOND-CLASS TOWNSHIPS, 1919

Southern Provinces		Northern Provinces
ABA	ITU	ILORIN
ABEOKUTA	ONITSHA	KADUNA
CALABAR	OPOKO	KANO
ENUGU NGWO	PORT HARCOURT	LOKOJA
FORCADOS	SAPELE	MINNA
IBADAN	WARRI	ZARIA

Third-class townships in the 1919 *Handbook* numbered fifty. Thirty-eight were in the Southern Provinces and twelve in the Northern Provinces. They were described as 'government stations, with a small but mixed native population'.[12] The following places were listed.

TABLE 6   LIST OF THIRD-CLASS TOWNSHIPS, 1919

Southern Provinces

ABA	ASABA	EKET	KOKO	ONDO
ABAK	AWKA	EPE	KWALE	ORON
ABAKALIKI	BADAGRI	IFE	OBUBRA	OWERRI
ADO	BENIN	IJEBU-ODE	OBUDU	UBIAJA
AFIKPO	BONNY	IKOM	OGOJA	UYO
AGBOR	BRASS	IKORODU	OGWASHI	UZUAKOLI
AHOADA	BURUTU	IKOT-EKPENE	OKIGWI	
AROCHUKU	DEGEMA	ILARO	OMOHIA	

Northern Provinces

ABIUSI	BAUCHI	JEBBA	OFFA
ANKPA	BIDA	KONTAGORA	SOKOTO
BARO	IBI	MAIDUGURI	ZUNGERU

A close examination of the list reveals that, while the definition appears appropriate for most of the centres, especially those from the Eastern Region, which numbered twenty-two, they were inappropriate for places like Ife, Ijebu-Ode, Benin and Sokoto, which were old and large centres of population. As with the second-class townships, there were frequent variations in the composition of the list. By 1924, for instance, there was no further mention of third-class townships in Northern Nigeria. By 1936 their number in the south had decreased to thirty-six.

Six centres (Ado, Awka, Idah, Kwale, Okwoga and Ondo) had disappeared from the list, while their places had been taken by Forcados
and Itu (down-graded) as well as Agege and Ejinrin.

The location of modern urban utilities

Township status seems initially to have guided the distribution of
governmental amenities. The *Handbook* of 1917 noted that 'government medical officers are posted to various stations, and there are
European hospitals at Calabar, Kaduna, Kano, Lagos, Lokoja, Onitsha
and Warri at which European Nursing Sisters are stationed'.[13] These
were all either first or second-class townships, while the *Handbook* of
1924 showed that the utility had been extended to Jos and Port Harcourt
as of that date.[14] In that year, we also learn that there were hospitals for
Africans at Calabar, Ikot-Ekpene, Ilorin, Kaduna, Kano, Lagos,
Lokoja, Minna, Onitsha, Port Harcourt, Warri and Zaria—some of
which places were third-class townships. By 1929 the list of places with
African hospitals had lengthened to include many more third-class
townships, notably Aba, Abakaliki, Ado-Ekiti, Agbor, Bauchi, Benin,
Degema, Ibi, Ijebu-Ode, Maiduguri, Ogoja, Okigwi, Owerri and
Sokoto. The *Handbook* of 1936 noted that by then there were twelve
European hospitals and fifty-six African hospitals in the country.

The same principle of township status seemed to have underlined the
provision of other public utilities like water supply and electricity. For
many years Lagos, as a first-class township, was the only centre with a
piped water supply. The Lagos Waterworks were completed in 1914
on the Iju River, at a point seventeen miles away from the town. The
available supply up to 1939 was about $4\frac{1}{2}$ million gallons in the dry
season, rising to 8 million gallons a day during the rains. Consumption
even at that date was no more than 3 million gallons in the dry and
$2\frac{1}{3}$ million gallons in the rainy season. By 1927 a number of the second-
class townships were being supplied with water. The Enugu Water
Works was completed in 1927 with a capacity of $\frac{1}{2}$ million gallons a day,
and at a capital cost of £40,000. Onitsha, Aba, Kaduna and Kano had
their water schemes completed by 1929, while small schemes were
established at Lokoja, Port Harcourt, Calabar, Abeokuta and Benin.
By 1932, twelve centres (Lagos, Agege, Aba, Benin, Calabar, Enugu,
Onitsha, Port Harcourt, Abeokuta, Ijebu-Ode, Kaduna, Oyo and Kano),
nine of which were either first or second-class townships, had efficient
water supply systems. Eight other centres, mostly third-class townships,

TABLE 7 WATER SUPPLY SYSTEMS, 1950 (CAPACITY IN '000 GALLONS DAILY)

Class	Western	Eastern	Northern
FIRST	LAGOS (5,153)		
SECOND	ABEOKUTA (620)	ENUGU (668)	KANO (726)
	WARRI (112)	ONITSHA (498)	KADUNA (499)
	IBADAN (1,407)	ABA (438)	ZARIA (361)
		P. HARCOURT (376)	JOS (176)
THIRD	BENIN (236)	CALABAR (272)	SOKOTO (500)
	IFE (214)		
	IJEBU-ODE (185)		
UNCLASSIFIED	OGBOMOSHO (137)		ILORIN (600)

Source: Nigeria, Handbook of Commerce and Industry, Lagos, 1954, p. 45

had smaller schemes. Except in Lagos, however, no water rate was paid initially in many of these centres. In the former place, a general water rate began to be levied in 1916 in respect of all tenements within certain areas of the township.

By 1950 there were nineteen major schemes in the country whose capacity and relation to the 1917 township classification is shown in Table 7.

The provision of electricity services followed much the same pattern. Lagos was first lighted by electricity in 1896 from a small central power

TABLE 8 ELECTRICITY INSTALLATIONS, 1950 (CLASSIFIED BY 1917 TOWNSHIP STATUS)

Class	Western	Eastern	Northern
FIRST	LAGOS		
SECOND	ABEOKUTA	ENUGU	KADUNA
	WARRI	PORT HARCOURT	KANO
	SAPELE	CALABAR	ZARIA
	IBADAN	ABA	JOS
THIRD		ABAKALIKI	MAIDUGURI
			SOKOTO
UNCLASSIFIED			KATSINA
			YOLA
			VOM
			BUKURU

Source: Nigeria, Handbook of Commerce and Industry, 1952, Lagos, 1952, pp. 87-88.

station operated by the electricity branch of the Public Works Department. The discovery of coal at Udi in 1916 led to the construction in 1923 of a more modern power station having a plant capacity of 3,000 kW. Since then, electricity installations were gradually extended to other second-class townships in the country. Power stations was opened in Port Harcourt, Enugu and Kaduna in 1929. Native Administrations in Abeokuta and Kano operated their own electricity plants. The plant in Abeokuta was completed in 1928 and replaced by a new power station in 1935. The Kano power station was completed in 1930. By 1950, twenty towns had electricity installations in Nigeria, and although by then the distinction into grades of township was no longer in operation, no less than twelve of these centres were either first or second-class townships. In that year, all electricity installations were brought under the unified control of the Electricity Corporation of Nigeria.

The division of Nigerian towns into grades as well as the effect of this on the location of infrastructural development serve to underline the fact of increasing differentiation among the towns. By 1950, it had become less easy to characterize the towns simply as 'African'. The variation covered by this term was just as significant as the distinction it tried to establish from towns of other races or continents. The characterization of Nigerian towns, therefore, can best be appreciated if treated from three viewpoints which take account of the tremendous changes that took place during the colonial period. These viewpoints relate to the physical forms of Nigerian cities: the nature of their economic activities and the social and demographic characteristics of their population.

Modernization of the physical structure of Nigerian towns

A basic distinction among Nigerian towns is that between northern and southern towns. This is a distinction related to the design and architecture of the houses and derives in part from the influence of climate as well as of history. Traditional houses in most Nigerian towns were built wholly or partly of mud. In most of the southern parts of the country the mud walls of houses were rectangular in ground plan. In the north, while such a plan is found, it is also possible to find houses with round walls. Moreover, some traditional mud houses in Northern Nigeria are two-storeyed, a feature which represents modern innovation in the south. Barth in 1851 noted that almost all the houses in Kano had very irregular upper storeys on different levels and very badly aired. He observed that many Arabs tended to sleep on the terrace-like roofs of the houses.[15]

Everywhere a characteristic of the traditional Nigerian house is the absence or inadequacy of ventilation. Various reasons have been put forward to account for this. One possible reason is that the state of the arts of the people was not sufficiently developed to resolve the problem of fitting windows in houses. On the other hand, it has been suggested that the thick walls of traditional houses were poor conductors of heat, and most houses, in spite of the absence of windows, were relatively cool. Moreover, the existence of windows exposed the privacy of home life to prying eyes. In an age of strong community control, it may be that the windowless house was a protection against public disapproval of private irregular behaviour.

Everywhere the roofs of the houses were constructed of thatch, but quite early in the development of Northern Nigerian towns, the thatched roof was replaced by the flat, mud roof (see Plate 5). This has given most towns in the north a distinctive appearance reminiscent of cities in North Africa. While the flat roof has survived in northern towns, the thatched roof has virtually disappeared from the southern towns. Its disappearance was consequent on the fire hazards to which it made a town frequently liable. Payne, for instance, calculated that between 1859 and 1892 there were as many as forty major outbreaks of fire in Lagos.[16] One of the most disastrous was that of 1877. An eye-witness described it as astonishing even to the people of Lagos themselves, much as they were accustomed to witnessing such annual ravages.[17] The casualties involved two churches, one chapel, three mosques, between 1,000 and 2,000 houses, much property, and seven lives.

Traditional houses in Nigeria are more correctly referred to as 'compounds'. A compound (Plate 10) housed an extended family, comprising a man's immediate, though polygamous, family, the families of his grown-up male children and sometimes the families of his brothers as well as the slaves belonging to each of these families. A compound could thus be a very elaborate building containing many rooms and sometimes occupying several acres.

The basic unit of traditional residential organization in Nigerian towns, however, was the 'quarter'. A quarter consisted of groups of compounds occupied by members of one or more extended families. Each quarter was centred around a chief who performed social and jurisdictional functions within the limits of the quarter. Usually the chief was a descendant of one of the oldest families in the town. Old Lagos, for instance, had as many as twenty-two quarters; Ibadan had over seventy quarters, while the 1952 Census listed as many as ninety-three quarters in Abeokuta. Barth also listed some seventy-four quarters in Kano in 1851.

In the last hundred years, Nigerian cities have undergone tremendous changes in every aspect of their construction and physical organization. Many of these changes had their origin in Lagos and have gradually diffused inland from the coast. One of these was the replacement of the mud wall by baked-brick wall. As early as 1859, a certain Mattieu de Cruz established a brick kiln in Lagos at Ebute Metta.[18] Another kiln was established in 1863 by the American Baptist Mission. These examples were soon followed by other missionary bodies and finally by the government in 1896. The result was that not only public buildings, but also numerous private houses began to be built of bricks. Even by 1865 Eales reported that in Lagos 'the European merchants have very fine brick houses; there were some that would not disgrace the best part of London, houses that cost £2,000 in the building'.[19]

In the succeeding years, brick walls were gradually displaced by those built of cement blocks. Cement, however, can be used not only to produce blocks, but also to plaster mud and brick houses. In this way, the latter are given a better protection against the elements of climate and a longer lease of life. Houses in present-day Nigerian towns thus vary from purely mud houses, mud houses with cement plaster, and brick houses with cement plaster to houses built of cement blocks. Generally the rate of change has been quicker in the southern than in the northern towns. In the latter, one often notices that, while houses in the traditional city (the *birni*) are still largely of mud, in the southerners' quarters (*sabon gari*) of the city, they are of more diverse materials.

The roofing material for houses has also been affected by great changes. As with the building material, the direction of change has been from Lagos inland, the effect being hardly felt in the traditional city of the north. The background to this change, as already stated, was the incessant hazard of fire which was becoming a real threat to the commercial life of Lagos in the mid-nineteenth century. As early as 1862, the European merchants in Lagos sent a letter to the British Governor advocating, 'first, that native houses throughout the town be within a given time covered with some less combustible material than is now used, and we recommend the bamboo mat as made at Calabar (Plate 7);

secondly, that all houses between the water side and the next street running parallel should be covered with slates, tiles, shingles or felt'.[20] Nothing was done at the time, but in 1877 it was proposed that the houses of the poorer people should be covered with corrugated iron, and that they should be made to pay the cost of it to the government by easy instalments.[21] The suggestion was turned down by the Governor-General of the colony who was then resident in Freetown, Sierra Leone. Later, however, towards the end of the century, corrugated iron had become very popular roofing material and with time it came to give to most Nigerian towns the appearance of an extensive, rusty-brown junk-spread.

The introduction of both cement and corrugated iron sheets into the building technology of the country had far-reaching consequences. Both were imported articles and to purchase them meant accumulating capital for the purpose. Fortunately by the end of the nineteenth century legitimate commerce had made great strides. Increasingly varied exports of palm oil, palm kernel, cocoa, groundnuts and cotton had served to put substantial sums of money in the hands of many individuals. However, the economic progress of individuals did not mean uniform progress among all members of an extended family. Differences in income and wealth began to give rise to differences in tastes, standards of living and expectations. The effect of this development was felt on kinship ties and family authority. It was more visibly reflected in the strains and stresses which were imposed on the form and design of the compounds. As with the enclosure movement in British agriculture in the nineteenth century, the 'improving' members of the family were anxious to break up the compound and to enclose and improve their portion of it. The disintegration of the compound into a number of houses containing a unit family is thus a feature of Nigerian towns in the last sixty years.

The disappearance of the family compound was hastened by the emergence of an architectural design which was more aesthetically exciting. This design, known as the Brazilian-style (Plate 12), was introduced into the country by ex-slaves returning from Brazil. It involved the use of numerous ornamental frills to doorways, windows, pillars, balconies and verandas, as well as the application of bright colours to the house. Its layout consisted simply of a central corridor on to which rooms opened on both sides. This design has been in vogue for nearly a century, and is particularly dominant in the Yoruba country. Its popularity, however, is being increasingly challenged by new developments in the country, especially since 1956.

With the disappearance of the compound went many other forms of town organization. The 'quarter system' is remembered only through the fact of the existence of a chief, but it has today little functional significance. The functions of the quarter chief himself have been taken over by numerous other bodies: his representational role by the elected local councillor, his ritual role by the various churches and mosques, and his jurisdictional role by the courts. The quarter itself has been submerged in the new electoral wards which form the basis of modern political organization in the towns.

Changes in the form and layout of the city itself are more complex, and are exemplified in the second half of this book. In general, however, increasing exposure to modern Western technology and economic institutions has resulted in a greater demand for wide, straight roads and for buildings of multi-storey dimensions serving other than residential functions (Plate 6). Furthermore, the vehicular traffic which these functions generate has brought with it new problems and given new meaning and importance to different parts of the city. The result is that specialized areas are beginning to emerge in Nigerian cities. Their control and regulation pose challenging problems to city administrators throughout the country.

Changes in the urban economic base

Just as the physical structure of Nigerian cities underwent tremendous changes during the colonial period, so also did their economic base. One major area of such change was in the production of craft goods such as textiles, leather, earthenware, metal wares and various implements of war and agriculture. The production of these goods traditionally engaged a sizeable proportion of the urban population. However, beginning from the middle of the nineteenth century and especially during the colonial period, traditional handicrafts were seriously undermined by the effective penetration of cheaper, mass-produced substitutes from the factories of Europe. The result was that many traditional textile workers were deprived of their means of livelihood, numerous smithies closed down, soap makers, leatherworkers, calabash decorators, bead makers and numerous other craftsmen were forced out of their traditional occupation. For some, a solution was found by engaging in the modern equivalent of traditional crafts. Thus a blacksmith might become a tinker, bicycle repairer or mechanic; a woodworker could become a carpenter, and a weaver might become a tailor. For some, trading in the various commodities demanded by the European markets provided new employment opportunities. But for the large majority, a return to the land was perhaps the safest and most certain of opportunities.

No measure of this continuous change in the economic base of Nigerian towns exists. However, the 1952 Census which provided information about the occupational distribution of the city population may serve as an indicator of the position among towns in the different regions of the country and in different sized groups. The Census of 1952 defined a town as 'a compact settlement with a population of at least 5,000'.[22] On this basis, it identified 329 urban centres within the present area of the country (Fig. 11 and Appendix 1). For each of these centres, the Census distinguished five major classes of occupation for the male population and two for the female population. The definition of each of these classes is shown in the table below.

TABLE 9   1952 CENSUS DEFINITION OF OCCUPATIONAL CLASSES

Class	Definition
AGRICULTURAL	INCLUDES FARMERS, FISHERMEN, LUMBERMEN, WOOD-CUTTERS, HUNTERS AND RELATED WORKERS.
CRAFTSMEN	INCLUDES ARTISANS, PRODUCTION PROCESS WORKERS AND LABOURERS.
TRADING AND CLERICAL	INCLUDES SALES WORKERS, TRADERS, CLERKS, ACCOUNTANTS, BANKERS, POSTMEN, SECRETARIES AND RELATED WORKERS.
ADMINISTRATIVE AND PROFESSIONAL	INCLUDES ADMINISTRATORS, PUBLIC SERVICE OFFICIALS, MANAGERS, TEACHERS, JUDGES, LAWYERS, ENGINEERS, ARCHITECTS, RELIGIOUS WORKERS, ETC.
OTHER OCCUPATIONS	INCLUDES WORKERS SUCH AS DRIVERS, LORRYMEN, STEWARDS, OTHER DOMESTIC WORKERS, DOCK WORKERS, MINERS, QUARRY WORKERS, ETC.

Figures are given for the male population in respect of each class but for the female only in respect of agricultural, trading and clerical workers. However, these figures are not in the published bulletins of the 1952 Census and have had to be extracted from the original data cards in the Federal Department of Statistics in Lagos. Unfortunately these cards have not received the care they deserve and a number of them are al-

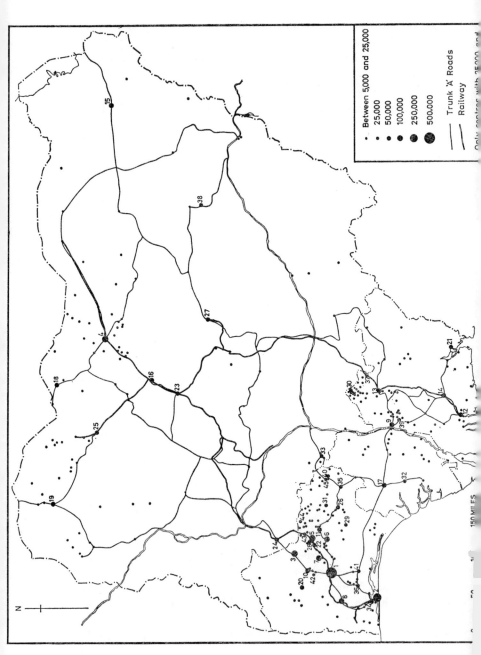

Figure 11   Urban centres by rank, 1952

ready missing. Thus out of a total of 329 towns, thirty-six had no cards. Twelve of these towns are in Northern Nigeria, sixteen in Eastern Nigeria and eight in Western Nigeria. Western Nigeria in this Census included Lagos and the Mid-West. The following table shows the position as between the regions and as between the various size groups. It represents, as it were, the 'non-response' situation for this investigation.

TABLE 10   ANALYSIS OF TOWNS (BY SIZE) FOR WHICH DATA IS AVAILABLE

	North		East		West		Total		Grand total
	A.	N.A.	A.	N.A.	A.	N.A.	A.	N.A.	
Over 80,000	1	—	—	—	7	—	8	—	8
40-80,000	7	—	3	2	5	—	15	2	17
20-40,000	4	1	5	—	19	2	28	3	31
10-20,000	24	4	13	6	25	1	62	11	73
5-10,000	67	7	42	8	71	5	180	20	200
TOTAL	103	12	63	16	127	8	293	36	329

A.   =   *Available*
N.A.   =   *Not available*

The table is revealing in a number of ways. The 'non-responses' at the national level appear less likely to significantly distort the picture, although at the regional level the position is particularly serious in the case of the Eastern Region where the 'non-responses' account for about 20 per cent of the total number of towns. Moreover, for the different size-classes, the position may be particularly serious for towns in the 10,000 to 20,000 range where non-responses are as high as 15 per cent (a figure which rises to over 30 per cent in Eastern Nigeria). In Eastern Nigeria also, the returns for towns in the range 40,000 to 80,000 also show 'non-responses' of 40 per cent compared with a national figure of only 12 per cent. Subsequent tables, however, take no account of the non-responses but have tried to provide descriptive statistical information for the various classes of town in the different regions of the country.

One of the first economic variables examined is the position of the agricultural and non-agricultural occupations in the population of the towns. Tables 11 and 12 indicate the position not only as between different sizes of towns but also the three regions of the country. Table 11 emphasizes in the first place that while, for the male population, the Northern Region is the most agricultural of the three regions, its towns, except for the very small ones (5,000-10,000) are the least agricultural; secondly, that in all three regions the agricultural element in the male urban population tends to increase with decreasing size; thirdly, that the large towns (40,000-80,000) of Eastern Nigeria have the lowest proportion of male population in agriculture, but below this class the agricultural workers bulk very large in the male population; fourthly, that in the Western Region, towns of all sizes are shown as having a substantial proportion of their male population working in agriculture. This last situation probably reflects the fact that cocoa cultivation permits the existence of absentee landowners who live in towns, hire labourers on their cocoa farms and pay only periodic visits to the farms during the year.

TABLE 11   NIGERIAN TOWNS: PERCENTAGE OF AGRICULTURAL POPULATION

National—Male 42·7%; Female 32·1%

REGIONS	NORTHERN		EASTERN		WESTERN	
	Male	*Female*	*Male*	*Female*	*Male*	*Female*
REGIONAL AVERAGE	47·1	24·0	37·4	46·6	36·9	37·7
Towns with pop.						
Over 80,000	8·3	11·7	—	—	21·5	22·2
40-80,000	17·6	3·6	2·0	2·2	30·9	26·8
20-40,000	28·6	10·0	41·3	49·6	32·6	33·3
10-20,000	34·1	8·2	38·7	48·7	36·7	37·2
5-10,000	40·6	14·1	38·8	46·4	39·5	37·3

The position among the female population is in many ways the very opposite of that of the males. Females in Northern Nigeria are less involved in agriculture than in the other regions—a fact no doubt due to the strong Islamic influence in the north. This is even more so in the towns where in nearly all size-classes the mean percentage is about half that of the region. In Eastern Nigeria, apart from the large towns where the agricultural females are as few as agricultural males, towns in the other classes show a large female agricultural population. In fact the mean percentage values for towns in both the 10,000 to 20,000 and the 20,000 to 40,000 classes are greater than the regional mean and the male average.

Table 12 refers to the non-agricultural population. When compared with the previous table, it shows that, at the national level, both for male and female, the ratio of non-agricultural to agricultural is about 1-4.

This means that for the whole country there are four times as many farmers as there are non-farmers in the population. Generally, with regard to the regions, it is found that the greater this ratio, the more economically advanced is the region. For the male population it is 1:5 for Northern Nigeria, 1:3 in Eastern Nigeria and 1:2 in Western Nigeria. For the female population it is about 1:3 in the North, 1:12 in the East and 1:3 in the West.

In Northern Nigeria the non-agricultural male and female population shows a very clear tendency to increase as the size of the towns increases. The ratio of male to female in non-agricultural occupations seems to be of the order of 2:1, except in the case of the smallest town. In the East a different pattern is evident. In the first place, the largest towns stand out clearly as having a large proportion of their male and female population in non-agricultural occupation in a ratio again of nearly 2:1. In the second place, for towns below the largest, there appears to be an inverse relation between size and non-agricultural population such that the smaller the town, the less agricultural it is. This situation calls attention to the fact that, in Eastern Nigeria, there exist a number of placcs whose occupational characteristics are such as to exclude them from being considered urban at all. In Western Nigeria the proportion of male and female non-agricultural population shows a gradual decrease with decreasing size. Unlike in the other regions, howver, the ratio of male to female in non-agricultural occupation is virtuaey 1:1 in nearly all size-classes of town.

Among the male population a further breakdown of the non-agricultural occupations was carried out in order to show the pattern of specialization among different sizes of town. Table 13 shows the posi-

TABLE 12   NIGERIAN   TOWNS: PERCENTAGE   OF   NON-AGRICULTURAL
POPULATION
National—Male 11·6%; Female 9·2%

	NORTHERN		EASTERN		WESTERN	
	Male	Female	Male	Female	Male	Female
REGIONAL AVERAGE	9·6	9·7	11·9	3·9	16·6	14·1
Towns with pop.						
Over 80,000	56·3	26·8	—	—	28·6	20·9
40–80,000	39·1	13·9	54·2	23·8	21·2	20·3
20–40,000	33·1	12·6	8·1	3·0	21·2	17·0
10–20,000	22·9	10·5	10·4	3·9	14·0	12·9
5–10,000	17·9	19·5	12·3	5·4	14·2	15·9

TABLE 13   OCCUPATIONAL DISTRIBUTION BY SIZE OF TOWNS

(Mean percentage for size-classes)

	NORTHERN NIGERIA					EASTERN NIGERIA					WESTERN NIGERIA				
	I	II	III	IV	V	I	II	III	IV	V	I	II	III	IV	V
NATIONAL %	3·3	3·1	1·5	44·4	44·4	3·3	3·1	1·5	3·7	44·4	3·3	3·1	1·5	3·7	44·4
REGIONAL %	3·5	1·8	1·3	3·0	43·3	2·2	4·2	1·5	4·0	45·5	4·1	5·3	2·2	5·0	46·5
Towns with pop.															
Over 80,000	14·45	17·43	8·71	15·94	35·17	—	—	—	—	—	7·17	9·57	4·09	7·79	49·89
40–80,000	9·53	8·69	8·05	13·36	41·98	7·20	23·36	6·53	17·16	43·79	5·65	6·70	3·12	5·70	47·97
20–40,000	6·30	11·20	3·93	11·37	38·66	1·49	2·97	1·03	2·62	50·55	5·41	6·86	2·83	6·16	46·13
10–20,000	7·88	5·01	3·30	7·13	42·48	2·45	2·79	1·35	3·78	50·95	3·81	5·36	1·61	3·58	48·00
5–10,000	6·31	4·66	2·31	4·57	40·80	2·35	5·02	1·56	3·47	48·85	3·65	4·35	1·46	4·66	47·10
GRAND MEAN	6·98	5·39	3·05	6·14	41·13	2·53	5·27	1·71	4·12	49·18	4·42	5·30	1·91	4·88	47·32

I: *Crafts*
II: *Trading*
III: *Admin/Professional*
IV: *Other Occupations*
V: *Other Males*

tion for the three regions with respect to the four categories into which the 1952 Census divided the non-agricultural population. The fifth category—Other Males—has been included to give some indication of the extent to which the male population is engaged in economic activity. It is a residuum comprising unemployed adult-males, children and the aged.

A quick comparison of the national and regional figures provides a useful background to the study of the urban situation. At the national level both craft and trading are of about equal importance (3·3 per cent and 3·1 per cent respectively), with craft, in fact, having a slight advantage over trading. Administration and the professions account nationally for about half the number employed either in craft or trading (1·5 per cent) while other occupations cover the largest proportion of the non-agricultural workers (3·7). Among the regions it is noticeable that while craft occupation is proportionally above the national average in the North and the West, it is much lower in the East. By contrast the West and the East are above the national average with respect to trading while the North is grossly below—a pattern also depicted in the case of other occupations. For the administrative and professional occupations, the West is clearly above the national average while the East has the same proportion and the North has less. All in all, the table shows that for all categories of non-agricultural occupations the Western Region has more than the national average; the East has a higher proportion for trading and other occupations, and the North only in the crafts.

When we turn to the towns still further interesting facts are revealed. As we would expect, for virtually all size-classes of towns, the trading function is the most important. The only exceptions are the smaller towns of Northern Nigeria and the seven moderately large cities (40,000 to 80,000) in the same region where craft is proportionally more important. The case of the latter group of cities is perhaps worth some comment. The seven cities are Yerwa, Zaria, Katsina, Sokoto, Kaduna, Ilorin and Gusau. Inspection of the data shows that the mean value for this class of centre has been affected largely by the position in the major traditional Northern cities of Zaria, Sokoto and Ilorin where the crafts still account for a relatively high proportion of the occupied non-agricultural males.

Furthermore, among towns in the North and West, the difference in the proportion of trading and craft population is not very great. In the larger towns of Eastern Nigeria, however, the trading element clearly predominates and constitutes nearly a quarter of the total male popula-- tion. In the same region the average proportion of the trading and craft elements in the population of towns in the range 10,000 to 40,000 is so low as to emphasize the doubts already entertained as to their urban character. Indeed these are the only proportions which are lower than the national average.

The administrative and professional workers, as one would expect, represent a much smaller proportion of the non-agricultural population. Again, there appears to be some direct variation with size, the only exception being in Eastern Nigeria. The position in the category 'Other Occupations' tells much the same story as the others except that this category of occupations tends to be more important in Northern Nigerian towns and in the larger towns of Eastern Nigeria than it is in the West. Furthermore, except in the North, the relation of this variable to size is not obvious.

Lastly, there is the residual 'Other Males' category which is character- ized by its relatively low variation between different categories of towns and the general pattern of distribution is not too clear. Generally it can be said that the residual male population tends to be lower in the northern cities than in the southern. Except in Western Nigeria, the larger cities also tend to have a lower residual male population. This phenomenon may indicate a generally earlier age of involvement in economic activity in the North than elsewhere in the country—a situa- tion which is plausible given the fact that relatively fewer children are sent to schools in the North. This fact, however, must not be over- stressed since a high percentage of 'other males' need not imply that most children are in the school.

To conclude on the issue of the economic characteristics of Nigerian towns, four points need to be emphasized. First, in general throughout the period of the colonial régime, Nigerian towns remained essentially centres of trade and commerce as they had always been. Secondly, in the Northern and Western Regions of the country where there is a longer tradition of urbanization, craft activities were almost as important as trading—an indication of the survival of some traditional skills in these centres. Thirdly, by and large opportunities for employment in non-agricultural activities tended to increase as a town grew in size. Lastly, in Eastern Nigeria there were indications that some places listed as urban in the medium-size category hardly performed urban functions.

Changes in the socio-demographic characteristics of Nigerian towns

There can be no doubt that whereas the colonial period undermined in a serious way the crafts of traditional Nigerian cities, its general economic impact was one of a gradual increase in per capita income and of rising social expectations. We have already seen that modern urban facilities—especially water supply, electricity and hospitals—were concentrated in a number of centres identified as townships during the first quarter of the century. To these facilities must be added schools, both primary and secondary, as well as dispensaries, maternity homes, improved roads and housing. The presence of such utilities would naturally serve to attract a number of modern businesses to a town. Thus both the glamour of modern urban utilities and the new employment opportunities would exert a strong pull, drawing population to the urban centres. But clearly only a certain category of the population can hope to compete successfully for employment within the new urban milieu. This comprises those with some literate ability in terms of being able either to read or write or do both. There are, of course, others who, though not possessing this qualification, would feel confident because of their youth, of finding some way of surviving in the city as unskilled labour of various kinds. Thus we shall expect changes (a) in the socia characteristics of Nigerian towns measurable in terms of educational attainments and (b) in the demographic conditions measurable in termsl of a greater proportion of young adult males and females in the urban centres.

In Nigeria, educational opportunities came with European missionaries who first arrived on the scene about 1838.[23] Their area of initial activity was around Lagos from where they extended their influence to cover all of Western Nigeria and most of the East. The political agreement between the British administration and the Northern Nigerian Emirs at the time of the subjugation of the latter was to the effect, among other things, that Christian missionaries would be discouraged from proselytizing in the North. The result of this policy was to keep the level of education and literacy (except in Arabic) very low in that part of the country. The 1952 Census distinguished three categories of educational attainments. These were:

(*a*) At least a Standard II education (4 years of schooling).
(*b*) Ability to read and write in Roman script.
(*c*) Literacy in Arabic.

Returns for all three categories are available for Northern Nigerian towns but not for the other two regions. In Table 14, however, only the first category has been considered since it is this that is more likely to determine types of employment realizable. In general the statistical evidence bears out the historical pattern of the spread of education among the three regions with the West having the highest proportion and the North the least proportion of its population with at least Standard II pass.

TABLE 14   NIGERIAN TOWNS: LITERATES AS PERCENTAGE OF TOTAL POPULATION (1952 CENSUS)

$$National = 6 \cdot 1 \%$$

REGIONS	NORTH	EAST	WEST
REGIONAL AVERAGE	1·5	11·6	16·9
Towns with pop.			
Over 80,000	6·6	—	12·6
40–80,000	4·4	26·6	7·9
20–40,000	7·6	5·6	9·8
10–20,000	1·4	5·8	6·4
5–10,000	1·8	6·4	6·4

The position in the towns shows certain interesting features. In Northern Nigeria the educated elements, as one would expect, show a tendency to gravitate to the towns. The result is that for all classes of towns except the low-medium (10,000–20,000) size, the average percentage of literate element is very much higher than the regional average. Although generally towns with over 20,000 people have a higher percentage of literates than those below, size does not appear to be an important factor here. Again the size-class of towns from 40,000 to 80,000 people which includes a number of traditional Hausa cities like Sokoto, Zaria and Katsina has a much lower average percentage than the next lower class—a fact which no doubt has some interesting relation with their emphasis on craft occupations which we have already noticed.

Eastern Nigeria again shows its typical pattern in which the larger towns have a very high percentage of literates and the classes below have a much lower average percentage varying inversely with size but generally below the regional average.

The position in Western Nigeria is certainly curious. Although all classes of towns have a percentage higher than the national average, even the largest towns have a percentage lower than the regional aver-

Plate 9   Ilesha town (air photograph)
Plate 10 The inside of a Yoruba compound

Plate 11   Palace and palace ground of a small Yoruba town (Shagamu)
Plate 12   Brazilian architecture in Lagos

age. This is a situation which indicates a thriving rural economy which attracts a larger proportion of literates than do employment opportunities even in the largest centres. In general there seems to be some direct relation with size, although towns in the range 20,000 to 40,000 seem to attract a disproportionately larger percentage of literates. Inspection of the data shows that this size-class contains a number of provincial and divisional headquarters such as Akure, Ondo, Sapele, Owo, Shagamu, Ijebu-Ode and Ado-Ekiti where some of the oldest missionary schools in the region are to be found.

The religious characteristics of Nigerian towns also offer some insight into the pattern of life in different parts of the country. The 1952 Census recognized three broad religious divisions—Moslems, Christians and Animists. Table 15 shows the pattern of distribution among regions and size-classes of towns. It shows, for instance, that for the country as a whole, Moslems comprise 35 per cent, Christians 30 per cent and Animists another 35 per cent. The Northern Region, however, is predominantly Moslem; the Eastern Region has hardly any sizeable population of Moslems. The position is clearly reversed with respect to the Christians, the East being largely Christian and the North hardly so. The Western Region has about the same proportion of its population in both religious groups. With regard to the Animists, the Eastern Region tops with almost half of its population being so categorized. The other two regions also have a substantial percentage of Animists. They form nearly one-quarter of the Northern and one-third of the Western Regional population.

While reflecting the regional preponderance of Moslems in Northern Nigerian towns, Table 15 shows some interesting deviations especially among towns in the size-class 20,000-40,000 as well as the very smallest towns. The relatively low Moslem, high Christian and Animist populations of towns in the former class are due to the inclusion in this class of two major towns of the Middle Belt—Jos and Offa. Small towns in the Middle Belt are also important for raising the average in the size-class 5,000-10,000 towns. Thus, as far as the percentage of Christians are concerned, the Middle Belt towns of Kabba (70 per cent), Kafanchan (63·8 per cent), Bukuru (58·5 per cent) and Idah (26·8 per cent) have helped to raise the value of the average.

In Eastern Nigeria the large towns are predominantly Christian while almost all other classes of towns are predominantly Animist. Of equal interest is the fact that below the class of the very large towns, the in-

TABLE 15 (A)   NIGERIAN TOWNS—MOSLEMS AS PERCENTAGE OF TOTAL POPULATION

National = 35·3%

REGIONS	NORTH	EAST	WEST
REGIONAL AVERAGE	73·0	0·4	32·8
Towns with pop.			
Over 80,000	94·0	—	55·5
40-80,000	90·8	4·9	37·4
20-40,000	74·8	0·2	38·0
10-20,000	95·3	0·4	31·7
5-10,000	86·1	0·7	24·2

TABLE 15 (B)   NIGERIAN TOWNS—CHRISTIANS AS PERCENTAGE OF TOTAL POPULATION

National = 29·8

REGIONS	NORTH	EAST	WEST
REGIONAL AVERAGE	2·7	50·0	36·9
Towns with pop.			
Over 80,000	5·9	—	33·7
40-80,000	7·6	87·0	27·9
20-40,000	19·1	21·6	45·2
10-20,000	2·8	25·4	37·0
5-10,000	5·7	32·0	48·8

TABLE 15 (C)   NIGERIAN TOWNS: ANIMISTS AS PERCENTAGE OF TOTAL POPULATION

National = 34·7

REGIONS	NORTH	EAST	WEST
REGIONAL AVERAGE	24·3	49·6	30·3
Towns with pop.			
Over 80,000	0·1	—	10·8
40-80,000	1·5	8·1	36·1
20-40,000	7·7	78·2	16·9
10-20,000	1·8	74·1	31·3
5-10,000	6·8	67·3	27·0

verse relation between size and specific variables is preserved. Thus the percentage of Christians and Moslems decreases with increasing size while that of Animists, whose preponderance in a town may be taken to indicate a lower level of economic development, increases with increasing size.

The situation in Western Nigeria shows no clear pattern. The percentage of Moslems tends roughly to decrease as town size decreases. Christians tend also roughly to be more important in smaller than in larger towns. With Animists, both the class of largest towns and the class 20,000 to 40,000 show relatively low percentages. Especially with the latter class, it is important to point out that this is the same class in which we found a relatively high proportion of literates and which includes many of the provincial and divisional headquarters.

As far as the demographic characteristics of Nigerian towns are concerned, the available data allows us to examine only restricted aspects of the situation. The absence of vital statistics and the fact that there has been only one real census in the country's history make it impossible to discuss question of growth rates among urban centres. Equally difficult is the estimation of differential birth and death rates between urban centres and the rest of the country, and the contribution to the size of urban population by both natural increase and rural-urban migration. What is available is a breakdown into sex and age classes. Five age classes are recognized for each sex. These are 0-2 years, 2-6 years, 7-14 years, 15-19 years, 50 years and above. For our purpose these have been grouped into three, namely, children (which include all age classes from 0 to 14), adults (those from 15 to 49), and aged (those over 50 years). As interesting indices of the demographic structure of cities, two of the possible age-sex ratios have been chosen. These are:

(a) males as a percentage of the total population;
(b) adult males and females as a percentage of the total male and female population.

Table 16 indicates the situation as between regions and among different sizes of towns. With the exception of towns between 10,000 to 40,000 in Eastern Nigeria and the very small towns of Western Nigeria, Table 16 (a) shows that most towns have a higher proportion of males than is the position for the country as a whole. As between the regions, it is seen that the West, which is the most urbanized, has a higher proportion of males than the North and the East. However, Northern towns of nearly all classes tend to be slightly more dominated by males than by females, while in the West, except for the very largest towns and those in the range 10,000 to 20,000, the reverse is the case. In Eastern Nigeria the large towns are clearly male-dominated, while for

TABLE 16 (A)   NIGERIAN TOWNS—MALES AS PERCENTAGE OF TOTAL
POPULATION

National $= 48\cdot9\%$

REGIONS	NORTH	EAST	WEST
REGIONAL AVERAGE	48·9	48·3	49·5
Towns with pop.			
Over 80,000	50·64	—	50·28
40–80,000	50·06	62·8	49·70
20–40,000	51·88	46·8	49·41
10–20,000	49·20	47·7	50·26
5–10,000	50·50	50·9	47·95

TABLE 16 (B)   NIGERIAN TOWNS—ADULT MALES AND FEMALES AS PER-
CENTAGE OF TOTAL MALE AND FEMALE POPULATION

National: Adult Male $= 46\cdot6\%$; Adult Female $= 46\cdot1\%$

REGIONS	NORTH		EAST		WEST	
	Male	*Female*	*Male*	*Female*	*Male*	*Female*
REGIONAL AVERAGE	46·1	50·2	46·8	44·1	47·6	46·6
Towns with pop.						
Over 80,000	53·6	54·9	—	—	37·4	39·1
40–80,000	51·3	54·9	60·7	50·8	46·6	48·0
20–40,000	51·7	51·8	48·7	53·6	44·8	47·6
10–20,000	49·7	54·4	48·8	53·2	42·9	46·1
5–10,000	47·5	52·5	49·4	54·4	43·5	46·2

the other classes of towns below them there is found the usual pattern
whereby the choice variable (i.e. the degree of male dominance) varies
inversely with the size of the towns.

The adult component of the urban population presents another
feature of interest. Northern Nigerian towns consist clearly more of
adults of the middle age-range than of either children or the aged.
Western Nigerian towns are again the reverse with children and the
aged being more important than younger adult males and females. In
Eastern Nigeria the figures show that, except for the larger towns, adult
males are fewer than children and the aged, but not so with adult
females. For all regions and for all size-classes, however, adult females
tend to be proportionately more numerous than adult males. The only
exceptions are the large towns of Eastern Nigeria, which are dominated
by adult males.

Conclusion

The 1952 Census thus allows us some glimpse of the increasing differentiation that was becoming apparent among Nigerian towns. With regard to the various urban characteristics, there are indications of differences due to regional location or to size. These indications, however, were of a very weak kind and do not enable us to make any definitive statements about the effect of size or region on the various characteristics considered. Moreover, we have not examined the nature of the interrelationships which might give us further insight into the process of urbanization in Nigeria. In the next chapter we shall deal with these matters. In particular we shall attempt to provide the theoretical framework which will help us to understand the full impact of the colonial régime on the pattern and chacteristics of urbanization in Nigeria.

References

1. P. A. Talbot, *The Peoples of Southern Nigeria*, Vol. 1, London, 1926, p. 104.
2. K. O. Dike, *Trade and Politics in the Niger Delta, 1830-85*, Oxford, 1956, p. 24.
3. H. M. Waddell, *Twenty-nine Years in the West Indies and Central Africa*, London, 1863, p. 314.
4. MacGregor Laird and R. A. K. Oldfield, *Narrative of an Expedition into the interior of Africa, 1832-34*, London, 1937, Vol. 1, p. 392.
5. Ibid., p. 165.
6. Allan McPhee, *The Economic Revolution in British West Africa*, London, 1926, p. 4.
7. See K. O. Dike, op. cit., pp. 81-96 and S. Biobaku, *The Egba and their Neighbours, 1842-72*, Oxford, 1957, pp. 64-95.
8. L. P. Mair, *Native Policies in Africa*, London, 1936, p. 12.
9. See M. G. Smith, *The Economy of Hansa Communities of Zaria*, Colonial Research Studies, No. 16, London, 1955.
10. L. P. Mair, op. cit., p. 120.
11. *The Nigerian Handbook*, Lagos, 1919, p. 98.
12. *The Nigerian Handbook*, London, 1936, p. 212.
13. *The Nigerian Handbook*, Lagos, 1917, p. 79.
14. *The Nigerian Handbook*, Lagos, 1924, p. 176.
15. H. Barth, *Travels and Discoveries in North and Central Africa 1848-1855*, London, Centenary Edition, 1965, Vol. 1, p. 299.
16. Otunba Payne, *Table of Principal Events in Yoruba History*, Lagos, 1893, p. 8.

17. Archdeacon H. Johnson, Letter to Henry Venn, 8 February 1877, CMS Archives, CA2/055.
18. Otunba Payne, op. cit., p. 10.
19. Report of Select Committee on Africa, London, 1965, No. 7065, p. 279.
20. Letter by Merchants and Residents of Lagos to Governor Freeman, December 1862, CO 147/4, Vol. 2.
21. Archdeacon H. Johnson, Letter to Henry Venn, 8 February 1877, *Church Missionary Society Archives*, CA2/055.
22. Nigeria, Department of Statistics, *Population Census of the Eastern Region of Nigeria, 1953*, Lagos, 1956, p. 20.
23. See J. F. A. Ajayi, *Christian Missions in Nigeria, 1841-91*, London, 1965, pp. 133-41.

6 Analysis of the Pattern of Nigerian Urbanization

The description of the characteristics of Nigerian towns gave some insight into the variety of urban conditions in the country but did not explain the cause and pattern of this variety. Although we observed that for some variables there was a tendency to vary with size, we also noticed that, for others, size was of hardly any significance. Moreover, in some cases regional contrasts were so much more vivid that they obscured the effect of size variation. Yet there is no doubt that, by 1952, in spite of the persistence of strong regional contrasts, the British had largely succeeded in welding Nigeria together into a single economic entity.

Given this fact, any understanding of urbanization in Nigeria must regard the towns and cities as forming a spatial system whose individual units interacted amongst themselves and reacted with the rural areas to promote the economic development of the country. In this chapter, therefore, we shall try, with the aid of conceptual and analytical tools, to explain the pattern of urbanization in 1952. The date 1952 is, of course, fixed by the data available, but the pattern revealed is important both because even today much of it has not changed materially and for the reason that, even where there have been changes, the position in 1952 serves as a useful bench-mark against which to measure these changes.

Conceptual basis of analysis: the 'central place' theory

According to Smailes, towns grow in particular places to discharge necessary functions.[1] Of these functions, the most important are those of trading and manufacturing. Other functions performed by towns are social, cultural and administrative. In Nigeria, until after 1952, manufacturing was relatively unimportant. Especially in the era of British domination, trade was the dominating function of Nigerian towns.

The most articulated theoretical formulation concerning cities as a spatial system of trading centres is that by the German geographer, Walter Christaller.[2] His ideas, commonly referred to as the Central Place Theory, have been further elaborated upon by another German, an economist, by the name August Lösch.[3] According to this theory, a system of cities results from an economy that is largely devoted to trading and similar tertiary activities. This is because such an economy requires that certain goods and services which cannot be provided everywhere should be made available at central places for the benefit of the population within defined tributary areas. Such a requirement leads to the generation of a system of cities, first, because the prices of these central goods and services vary with the distance from the point of supply and, secondly, because these central goods and services differ in terms of

    (i) the minimum amount of purchasing power necessary to support a single supplier;
    (ii) the frequency of the demand for the goods and services and
    (iii) the amount that can be purchased on each visit by a consumer.

These ideas underline the two concepts of the threshold level and the range of a central good.[4] The threshold level of a central good can be defined as the minimum sales level (measured by the population, income or purchasing power) required in a central place to make it worth providing that good. For instance, the threshold level for a confectionery shop is smaller than that for a motor showroom. The range of a good, on the other hand, can be defined as the radial distance which delineates the market area of a central place for the good. It has both a lower and an upper limit. The lower limit incorporates the threshold purchasing power for the supply of the good; the upper limit represents the point beyond which the central place is no longer able to sell the good. Each central good has different limits to its range both because of the differing internal economic characteristics of the supplying firms which determine the threshold level (in the case of the lower limit) and because of competition between central places supplying the good (in the case of the upper limit).

On the basis of both the threshold level and the range, central goods and services can be arrayed in an ordered fashion. Low order goods will be those with small threshold levels and relatively short range. They are characterized by their relatively low price, frequent demands for them and the relatively small size of supplying units. As a result they tend to be found in most central places. Examples of such goods and services are drugs, foodstuffs, hairdressing, shoe-repairs, and so on. High order goods are those with high threshold levels and relatively long range. They are characterized by their high prices, the infrequent demand for

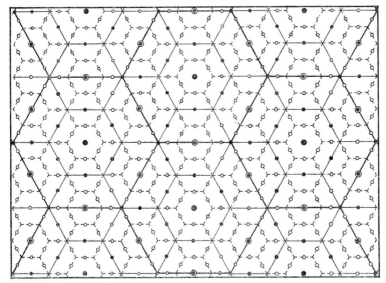

Figure 12   Theoretical market area of towns (after Christaller)

them and the large size of the supplying unit. As a result they tend to be found in fewer centres, each of which serves a number of other smaller centres.

The idea of an ordered system among goods and services leads naturally to the conception of an ordered system among the urban centres which provide them. Christaller postulates that among cities there exists a hierarchy such that lower order centres distribute lower order goods and services and their trade areas 'nest' within the trade areas of higher order centres (Fig. 12). The latter, while distributing similar goods and services as all the centres below them, also provide other goods and services of a higher order and with longer range. Articulation within such a system of cities is provided by a hierarchy of routeways, with high-order traffic routeways leading to the major centres and low-order traffic routeways leading to the smaller centres.

Within any given area of the world, the conditions that every place must have access to an urban centre and that the aggregate cost of transportation should be minimum, lead theoretically not to a circular but to a hexagonal shape for the trade areas of the cities, given a uniform distribution of population or purchasing power. Fundamentally, the Central Place Theory conceived the mode of transportation which gives rise both to the hierarchical system of urban centres and the hexagonal pattern of their trade areas as a given, uniform and invariant factor as long as a market economy exists. Movement, in fact, could be on foot, on animals, or on animal-drawn wheeled carriages as in medieval Europe or much of Africa until the twentieth century. It could also be by railways and automobiles, as in twentieth century Europe and the United States. Differences in the mode of movement would be reflected not in the pattern of distribution of the centres, but in the range of the goods and services, in the spacing apart of the centres, perhaps in the physical characteristics of the centres (since such different transport media may reflect more fundamental differences in technological capability) and in the nature of the goods and services being marketed.

Vining has provided the most comprehensive criticism of the Central Place Theory as conceived of by Christaller.[5] Although he accepts the existence of different sizes of cities with different ranges for the goods and services they provide, he doubts whether these are organized in any formal hierarchical system. According to him, 'the structure as it would be observed would seem to be characterized by continuity and not by a discreteness that is suggested by the idea of some definite number of types of places'. He also doubted whether the range of a central place (i.e. its trade area) could properly be shown to take any definite geometrical shape and went on to demonstrate convincingly that the notion of a 'range' of goods and services was valid only for activities which yield such goods and services not shipped by rail.

Vining's most important contribution, however, appears to be in his discussion of the stability or otherwise of a system of cities. For this, he introduced the concept of statistical equilibrium. To quote him:

'The typical form of the distribution that is thought by many to be stable will be stable only if the passages of individuals are mutually compensatory when this particular form is established. This is a limiting form, representing an equilibrium situation. . . . Through a continuing process of births, deaths, movements into and movements out of designated small partitionings of a large area, a particular form of density configuration is established. The passages of individuals from sub-area to sub-area do not alter this form. But if the form of the distribution were arbitrarily altered—for example, *suppose that by the actions of some all-powerful authority individuals and equipments were moved about in such a way that all central places were made the same size* —then these passages of individuals would tend to change this arbitrarily established distribution. And if the original distribution does in fact conform with the idea of a state of statistical equilibrium, then the

arbitrarily established equal distribution of individuals among designated sub-areas would be changed, through a process of undirected
individual passages from sub-area to sub-areas, back to the original
distribution. This would not mean a re-establishment of the old cities
but rather a development in time of a system of central places having
the same general features of form.'[6]

Although suggesting that interference with the system of cities by an
'all-powerful authority' such as a colonial government would lead
eventually to a re-adjustment, Vining, like Christaller and Lösch, did
not pursue further these questions of the dynamics of the system. In
their bibliographical survey of this field, Berry and Pred noted that
'little evidence has been provided about the ways in which central place
systems are changing'.[7] They claimed that the available fragmentary
evidence, such as it was, showed that such change 'is characterized by
the progressive upward shifting of central functions to higher order
centres, with the resulting accelerated growth of these higher order
centres'.

Of the dynamic elements leading to this shifting of central functions,
perhaps the most crucial is transport. This determines the varying
ranges of goods, the extent of market areas and the variety of establishments that can agglomerate profitably in a centre. Moreover, it determines the efficient distance apart of central places. Nevertheless, changes
in transportation media and their effectiveness will lead to a general
shift of functions to higher order centres only where such changes are
'organic' (in the sense of having grown from within rather than being
imposed from outside the system of cities) or are pervasive throughout
the system at about the same time; where, for instance, as in the USA,
the change may be due to a progressive 'automobility' of families,
irrespective of where they are. On the other hand, in places such as an
underdeveloped country, where changing transportation technology is
selective in its incidence and restricted in its area of concentration, it is
easy to see that the shifting of central functions would not be everywhere to the higher order centres, nor would the resulting accelerated
growth be a feature only of higher order centres.

In short, the theoretical questions raised by this study are these:
what happens when on a system of cities developed under one set of
market and transport conditions a new, faster, more effective, more
capacious transport system is imposed? What happens when this is done
in a rather selective manner as to the area served? What happens

when the new spatial economic integration which is achieved by this new transport system focuses the flow of commodities within the system on a few selected points, with a view to facilitating the export of these commodities out of the country? What is the nature of the adjustments that can be assumed to be taking place within the system in consequence of this new development? What effects would these adjustments have on the efficiency of the system and the growth of the economy?

The importance of the pattern of transport development

The chapters tracing the history of urbanism in Northern Nigeria as well as in Yorubaland emphasized the importance of trading activities in these areas well before the advent of the European. As we have seen, this was a trade involving long-distance movements, the exchange of diverse products and the use of some currency as media and units of exchange. For these trading activities, transport was restricted to human porterage or to animals. This system of transport had a serious limiting effect on the amount of trade goods that could be carried over great distances on one trip. The result is to give rise to a marketing organization based on a certain periodicity of activities. We have already indicated the relationship which existed between types of goods and the periodicity of their vending. Thus certain goods such as foodstuffs were available at the market every day; others only at intervals of four days; others at intervals of eight days and still others at intervals of sixteen days, and so on. The order of importance among urban centres has also been shown to be related to how many of such types of market function within the city. The implication of this situation in the northern and western parts of the country was that by the time of the British advent the system of cities had evolved some order of importance among themselves. Such an order was based on the favourable location for international or interregional trade or on levels of political pre-eminence or on both. The various kingdoms in the country had their metropolitan centres, and their subsidiary towns were organized in a descending order of importance.

For our purpose, it is immaterial whether the organization of the towns took on a hierarchical form with discrete grades of towns or whether it assumed the form of a continuous size distribution among the cities. The important point is that the variation in their size and importance should be related to their importance in the trading economy. Similarly, the question of whether the trade area of each town was hexagonal and 'nesting' in the trade areas of a higher order twon is not of great significance. Once we relax the assumption of an even distribution of population and of purchasing power, these situations take on more complex forms and their hexagonality is not easily demonstrable in the real life situation.

It was into these systems of cities generated both by traditional trading activities everywhere in the country and by the pre-industrial level of technology that the British introduced a more sophisticated trading organization and a more advanced transport technology. At the time of their advent, the British could be said to have two choices before them. One was to improve the system of internal exchange in the hope that the increasing returns from this would lead to greater trading activities with Europe; the other was to concentrate on what they could profitably exploit and export from the country in the hope that this would have some incidental beneficial effect on internal exchange.

To have taken the first choice would have meant that the British colonial venture was not to serve the interest of the British people but that of the Nigerians primarily. It would also imply that any development and innovations brought by them would be undertaken or accepted within the traditional order of importance among the cities. For example, if the railway were to be introduced, it would be first to link existing important centres, and only after would it serve less important centres. The exception would be the few smaller centres fortunate enough to lie on the direct link between two important centres. If such a situation had obtained in Nigeria, it is easy to see that development would be in the manner hypothesized by Berry and Pred, namely, that there would be a progressive upward shifting of central functions to higher order centres with the accelerated growth of these higher order centres.

However, the British did not come to Nigeria to uphold or enhance the traditional system. In their concern to exploit the resources of the country in a way most remunerative to their imperial interest, they acted as 'the all-powerful authority' of Vining, moving individuals and equipment about in such a way as would appear to a 'Nigerian' at the time as entirely arbitrary. From this point of view, one can see the seventy or eighty years of British administrative control of the country between 1885 and 1960 as imposing a new but 'arbitrary' spatial integration on Nigeria.

The most important basis for this new integration had been provided by the Berlin Conference of 1884. At that Conference the doctrine of 'effective occupation' had been enunciated as a touchstone of the right of any of the European powers to enjoy a semi-monopolistic privilege in exploiting the resources of any given area of the continent. One of the most decisive ways of indicating such effective occupation was by constructing railway lines in the territory. Thus, while the French were busy with their various ambitious railway projects from the coast inland to the Niger, the British also conceived of a number of rail-lines within the area now known as Nigeria.

The major consideration for any of these lines was quite naturally its economic profitability to the British investors. A line was considered viable if it opened up areas which could grow or produce such crops as the British industrialists would buy, areas which had valuable mineral deposits, or areas, especially coastal sites, with good accessibility to Europe for the export of these commodities. Various exploration teams surveyed proposed routeways to decide on their viability. The result of the report of one of these teams, for instance, necessitated by-passing Oyo city, then the metropolis of Yorubaland, in order to keep closely within the forest belt with its high potential for the export of palm produce. Nonetheless, it is true that as much as it was consistent with their economic interest, the British tried to link major centres by rail-line.

The main railway lines in Nigeria were constructed between 1895 and 1930 (Fig. 13). The western line began from Lagos in 1895 and had reached Ibadan by 1900. It bypassed Ijebu-Ode and Shagamu, and connected Abeokuta to both Lagos and Ibadan. The line was pushed forward to Ilorin in 1908, bypassing such other important centres in Yorubaland as Oyo, Ife, Ilesha and Ogbomosho. Progress beyond Ilorin was again hindered for a while because of political rivalry between Northern and Southern Nigeria, but in 1909 the railway reached Jebba. It continued to Minna, reaching there in 1912 about the same time as another line from Baro through Minna to Kano was being opened.

This event meant that, by 1912, a new integration had been imposed on a strip of area some 700 miles long from Lagos on the coast to Kano in the extreme north. One immediate result of this was that it paved the way for the amalgamation of Northern and Southern Nigeria in 1914. In the next two decades the rest of the present railway network was completed. In 1913 an eastern line based on Port Harcourt was begun. It reached the coalfields at Enugu in 1916, Makurdi on the Benue River

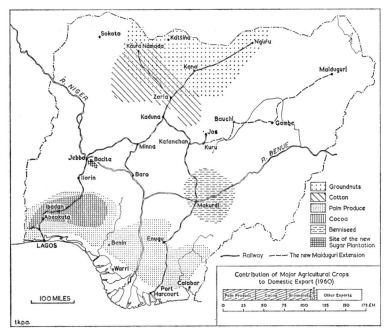

Figure 13   Export crop-producing areas

in 1923 and joined up with the Lagos-Kano line at Kaduna in 1926, a
branch from it reaching Jos in 1927. In the latter year the Lagos-Kano
line was extended to Nguru and two years later another branch from
Zaria on the main line reached Kaura Namoda.

The effect of this new spatial integration on production and trade was
spectacular. Groundnut export from the Kano region, for instance,
showed an increase within two years of almost 1,000 per cent—from
less than 2,000 tons in 1911, before the arrival of the railway, to about
20,000 tons in 1913, a year after the railway reached Kano. Indeed,
according to Harrison Church, in the twenty-five years before the
Second World War, the railway caused the exports of groundnuts to
increase 200 times, of cocoa 30 times, of tin 12 times and the internal
trade in fish to develop a hundredfold.[8] One reason for this, as Hodder
shows in his study of tin-mining on the Jos Plateau, was the remarkable
shortening of travel time. According to him, before the railway reached
the Jos Plateau, the journey from the tin mines to the coast took thirty-
five days and cost £29 10s. a ton. With a connection to the coast at Port

Harcourt in 1927, not only was the journey reduced to less than thirty-five hours, but the cost came down to £8 per ton, while exports rose from 10,926 tons in 1927 to 13,069 in 1928.[9]

River transport, although of great antiquity in Nigeria, has not been an effective means of spatial integration in the country. While it provides the cheapest haulage costs and the longest average length of haul in the country, it accounts in most years for less than 15 per cent of all goods moved.[10] There are in Nigeria approximately 4,000 miles of waterways navigable by river craft. Because of the absence of river conservancy, the flow of water in these waterways is hardly controlled and the effective navigation season is restricted to between six and eight weeks a year except for canoes. Moreover, most of the waterways pass through areas of relatively sparse population either in the Middle Belt of the country or the swampy lagoon and delta area. In consequence there are only about two dozen river-towns, most of these being small towns in the Niger delta (Fig. 10) where scarcity of dry land rather than trade had encouraged the concentration of people on the few dry spots. Onitsha, Lokoja, Makurdi and Yola are the most important river-towns while centres like Sapele, Warri, Burutu and Calabar combine seaport functions with their riverside location. What the effects of improvement in the navigation of the River Niger with the completion of the Kainji Dam will be for urban development is too early to say. Possibly it could lead to the growth of Yelwa as a major centre for trade in the north-western corner of the country.

Compared to river transport, roads are of very recent date in Nigeria and their impact on urban development has only started to be felt in the last two decades. Although the first roads for motor traffic were built in about 1900, it was not until 1919 that road construction can be said to have begun in earnest. A report of an enquiry of 1907 instituted by Lord Elgin, the then Secretary of State for the Colonies, into the state of the roads and road traffic throughout the Dependent Empire revealed that there was a total of fifty-four miles of road suitable for wheeled traffic in the whole of Southern Nigeria.[11] One major reason which limited the expansion of the roads at this time was that road vehicles were largely of the heavy type which tore up the lightly-made roads. The damaged surface of the roads in turn shortened the lives of the motor vehicles. This fact made motor transport so costly that it was seriously argued that motor vehicles would never displace head carriage in areas away from the railway. The problem remained unsolved until the light Ford vehicles were invented in the USA and imported into Nigeria. In 1920, 325 vehicles were imported into Lagos. The number rose to 1,027 in the next year, and though it fell to 80 in 1922, the number rose to 310 in 1923.[12]

For some time the progress and development of a road network were subordinated to the needs of the railway. In 1927, however, a trunk-road policy was formulated, giving the roads an independent existence from the railway. The policy set out to organize the roads into three grades, namely, Trunk A, Trunk B and minor roads. Trunk A roads were to be constructed and maintained in the form of a rigid framework on which the rest of the road system would be built up. The basic components of this structure were to be two roads running from the ports of Lagos and Port Harcourt to the northern boundary; and four east-west roads, two south and two north of the Niger-Benue Rivers. The system was designed to link the Federal and Regional capitals, connect these with other large towns and the ports and afford communication between Nigeria and neighbouring territories. Trunk B roads were to be constructed by the regional governments to connect provincial or divisional headquarters and other large towns with the Trunk A system, with one another, with the ports or with stations on the rail line. Minor roads were to be built to serve as feeders to the trunk road system and were to be maintained by local or native authorities.

One measure of the general ineffectiveness of road transport until very recently is the fact that even today parts of the two north-south roads have not been completely built. Of the four east-west roads, only the two in the south have been completed. In 1953, at the beginning of the demise of the colonial administration, the position was even worse. Large stretches of the two north-south roads were unsurfaced and there was only one east-west road in the south. The other east-west road in the north was poorly surfaced and only seasonally usable over large sections. At that date there were in Nigeria only 28,000 miles of roads of which 17 per cent were Trunk A, 20 per cent were Trunk B and 63 per cent were minor. Of these roads, only 1,900 miles or less than 7 per cent had bituminous surfacing and half of these were in Western Nigeria. Also in 1953 the number of commercial and private vehicles licensed was only 22,900, of which the commercial represented just under one half. Even in 1960, when this number rose to over 53,000, it gave a ratio of one vehicle per 660 persons which is one of the lowest in Africa.[13]

Table 17 shows the effect of this state of affairs in the share of road transport in the movement of traffic in Nigeria.[14] It underlines the vast superiority of the railway over the road and therefore the greater trade involvement of towns on the rail line vis-à-vis those which were served only by the road system. The table, however, also gives indication of the dynamic nature of the situation and the growing importance of road transport. Today, road transport is perhaps the fastest growing means of movement in the country. Its advantages derive from the speed and regularity of the service which it offers, its flexibility regarding the size of load carried, the ease and speed of transhipment, door-to-door delivery which minimizes handling costs, risk of damage, pilferage and the need for packaging. More recently its competitive ability has been further enchanced by improvements in vehicle design, better and more widespread servicing facilities, numerous fuel stations and the construction of better roads.

TABLE 17   ESTIMATED DISTRIBUTION OF TRAFFIC IN NIGERIA

	(million ton-miles)					
	1938-39	%	1948-49	%	1952-53	%
RAIL	315	66	658	63	827	61
ROAD	100	21	300	29	400	30
RIVERS	60	13	85	8	120	9
AIR	—	—	—	—	0·2	—
TOTAL	475	100	1,043	100	1,347	100

To sum up, the new economy that resulted from the British colonial administration was based increasingly on a fast and more efficient transport system as well as on novel economic institutions, machines and equipment. As such it developed its own critical nodes, notably at the ports, at a number of centres on the rail line and on major roads leading to rail lines. Some centres also developed as river ports in consequence of the more effective use of the lower reaches of the Niger and the Benue. Although on a widely different scale and with greater intensity and pervasiveness than in the pre-colonial period, trade remained the life blood of the urban centres whether called into being by the new economy or locationally favoured by its transport system. However, trade was largely oriented to export, channelled exclusively to the two major ports of Lagos and Port Harcourt instead of being made to circulate internally and keep alive the important trade functions of many of the old and existing urban centres. Industries played hardly any part in the colonial economy, for Nigeria, like other colonial territories past and present, was seen as a market for the manufactures of the 'mother country' rather than a place for setting up competing industries.

The implications of this new spatial integration on the urban system which the British met in Nigeria and to which they added only in a very limited way are fundamental for an understanding not only of the complex process of urbanization in Nigeria today, but also of the relation of this process to the need and capabilities for rapid economic development in the country. For cities exist as points of economic articulation, and the reason for their existence can only be understood in terms of the economic system they grew up to serve. Conceptually, it could be argued that for each economic system there is a system of cities which are major nodes for the transport routes and for the movement of people, goods and ideas. And as the economy that gave these nodes their existence changes, so also does the relative importance of the nodes.

The effect of regional economic differentiation

The explanation of the pattern of urbanization in Nigeria within the framework of the Central Place Theory poses a number of questions which we shall now investigate. It has already been suggested in Chapter 2 that the true urban centres are those where people are employed largely in non-agricultural activities. It has also been hypothesized that there is a strong tendency for this proportion of the population to increase with the size of the city. If the Central Place Theory holds, we may expect a strong correlation to exist between size of cities and the proportion of people employed in non-agricultural activities. On the other hand if, as suggested, the order of importance among the cities has been seriously disturbed by the activities of the colonial administration, then such an order, even if it exists, would have been seriously weakened.

Moreover, the Central Place Theory generally assumes the existence of a homogenous area of uniform population and purchasing power. In Nigeria such homogeneity does not exist. One important effect of the development of modern transport has been to encourage significant regional specialization in agricultural production which today underlies major variations in regional incomes in the country. These regional variations in income and purchasing power would clearly affect the types of goods and services which towns can provide and probably the

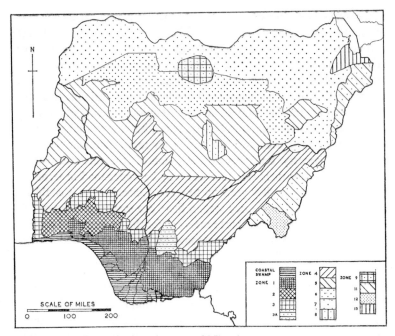

Figure 14   The agricultural zones of Nigeria

number of those required to provide them. Fig. 14 shows the agricultural zones of Nigeria based on the 1951 Sample Census of Agriculture
(see Appendix 2 for a description of each zone). Although fourteen
zones are recognized, the last two (12 and 13) are too small in area to be
relevant for our purpose. The remaining twelve zones have been
grouped into eight broad regions as a result of merging zones 5, 6, 8
(the Middle Belt) and zones 7, 9, 11 (the Sudan Belt).

A two-criteria analysis of variance was performed on the average
proportion of the male population in the four main classes of non-
agricultural activities and the result is shown in Table 18. The analysis
was on the basis of eight agricultural regions and four size-classes of
towns (5,000-10,000; 10,000-20,000; 20,000-40,000; and over 40,000).
Averages of the percentage of males in particular occupational groups
among each class of towns were used because the number of towns in
each of the 8 × 4 cells was uneven. Analysis of variance as a statistical
decision method requires that the number of entries in each cell be the
same.

Table 18 gives an unequivocal statement that variation in the character of agricultural regions has an important influence on the proportion of non-agricultural population in a city. It also shows that the occupational groups most sensitive to this variation are the administrative and professional as well as the 'other occupations'. The influence of town size, however, while significant, is shown to be not unequivocally so except again in the case of the administrative-professional class. This analysis thus bears out some of the features of the urban scene that were beginning to be apparent from the description of urban characteristics in the preceding chapter. It emphasizes that regional economic characteristics affect the proportion of non-agricultural workers in Nigerian towns, so that the wealthier the region, the greater is this proportion.

TABLE 18 ANALYSIS OF VARIANCE OF THE INFLUENCE OF TOWN-SIZE AND AGRI-CULTURAL REGION ON THE DISTRIBUTION OF THE URBAN NON-AGRICUL-TURAL POPULATION (1952 CENSUS)

Occupational groups Sources of variation		Crafts	Trading and Clerical	Administr. and Profession	Other Occupations	Degrees of freedom
BETWEEN	Var. est.	18·74	50·97	26·74	140·74	7
REGIONS	Var. ratio	4·56**	4·29**	5·56***	7·25***	
BETWEEN	Var. est.	17·93	53·42	32·53	85·92	3
SIZE CLASSES	Var. ratio	4·36*	4·50*	6·76**	4·43*	
RESIDUAL	Var. est.	4·11	11·88	4·81	19·40	21
TOTAL	Var. est.	40·78	116·27	64·08	246·06	31

*** Significant at 0·1%† ** at 1·0% * at 5·0%
† An 0·1% level means that the relationship is most certainly significant;
  1·0% level is also highly significant, while 5% level is only probably significant.

The dimensions of urbanization in Nigeria

Although the analysis of variance has revealed the importance for Nigerian towns of location within particular agricultural regions, there are important dimensions of the urbanization process which have not been investigated. Intuitively it is possible to conceive of four such dimensions, all of which are related to the readjustment of traditional urbanization in Nigeria to both the new integration of transport and the novel economic and political conditions. The first and perhaps the most obvious is the economic dimension. The effect of locational change among economic centres should show at once in aggregate, if not in per capita, income of the individual towns and cities. It should also be reflected in major shifts in their demand for goods and services, in the sales volume of their businesses as well as in prices. These shifts would be in consequence of the selective migration of the main income-earning group, namely, the young men and women between the ages of fifteen and forty-nine, from the bypassed and 'stranded' cities to centres with a decisive locational advantage for the new economy.

Secondly, there is the demographic dimension which should serve as a useful index of the adjustment going on. The favourably located centres would tend to show an increase in the number of young people, most of whom would be unmarried, as well as a relatively small number of children and the aged. The 'stranded' centres would tend to be the obverse of this, with relatively more children and an aged population.

Thirdly, the effect of this demographic situation would be very telling on the social and physical conditions in the towns. The growing centres would tend to attract the more educated and will expose them to the challenge of meeting people of other ethnic and racial origins. The hustle and bustle of the new centres, with their congested housing, their overloaded sanitation systems, as well as the excitement these centres provide for finding new jobs, forming new relationships and joining new associations would contrast sharply with the rather somnolent social life, the mass of unoccupied and underoccupied dwellings, and the poorly maintained sanitation system of the stranded centres.

Fourthly, the contrasts in the economic and demographic circumstances of the cities are bound to have immense repercussions on their administrative efficiency. Cities which have lost most of their young and active population through massive emigration would have problems in raising enough revenue from rates and taxes to maintain their basic services. They are also likely to find these losses cumulative since it is these same young and enterprising people who, if they had stayed, could have been impelled to find ways and means of improving the economic conditions of the cities.

These four dimensions as at present described are no more than broad generalizations or hypotheses to be tested before their validity is established. Lack of suitable data, however, constitutes a major problem in this respect. Nonetheless, a judicious use of the mass of information contained in the 1952 Census of Nigeria provides a fairly adequate picture of the situation which remains true for large parts of the country even today. Thus, as far as the economic dimension is con-

TABLE 19   LIST OF 32 VARIABLES RECORDED FOR EACH TOWN IN THE 1952
CENSUS

1. TOTAL POPULATION	18. MALE: TRADING AND CRAFT
2. TOTAL MALE	19. MALE: ADMINISTRATIVE AND
3. TOTAL FEMALE	PROFESSIONAL
4. HAUSA/FULANI	20. MALE: OTHER OCCUPATIONS
5. IBO	21. MALE: OTHER MALES
6. YORUBA	22. FEMALE: LESS THAN 2 YEARS
7. OTHER NORTHERN TRIBES	23. FEMALE: 2-6 YEARS
8. OTHER SOUTHERN TRIBES	24. FEMALE: 7-14 YEARS
9. NON-NIGERIANS	25. FEMALE: 15-49 YEARS
10. STD. II PASS AND OVER	26. FEMALE: 50 YEARS AND OVER
11. ABLE TO READ AND WRITE	27. FEMALE: AGRICULTURE AND
12. MALE: LESS THAN 2 YEARS	FISHING
13. MALE: 2-6 YEARS	28. FEMALE: TRADING AND CRAFT
14. MALE: 7-14 YEARS	29. FEMALE: OTHER FEMALES
15. MALE: 15-49 YEARS	30. MOSLEMS
16. MALE: 50 YEARS AND OVER	31. CHRISTIANS
17. MALE: AGRICULTURE AND FISHING	32. ANIMISTS

cerned, the Census has information on the proportion of the population
of cities in the various non-agricultural occupations such as trading,
craft, administration and the professions. For the demographic dimension there is information on age and sex distribution. Information on
the proportion of the urban population attaining an educational qualification of at least Standard Two pass, professing Christian, Moslem or
Animist religious belief and belonging to various ethnic groups gives
some impression of social conditions in the cities. There is no data on
administrative efficiency of the cities although inferences on this can be
made logically from the results of the test for the other three dimensions.

The 1952 Census provides data on 32 variables for each town covering demographic, occupational, ethnic, educational and religious
characteristics. These thirty-two variables are listed in Table 19. One
increasingly important multivariate technique of analysis which can be
used to test the validity of our hypotheses and gain further insight into
the process of urbanization in Nigeria is factor analysis. According to
Cooley and Johnes, the rationale of modern factor analysis is to determine the minimum number of independent dimensions which account
for most of the variances in a set of variables.[15] This technique is based
on the assumption that variables (such as age, sex, occupational and
educational characteristics) relating to a class of objects or phenomena
(such as cities) must correlate significantly one with another. This

intercorrelation among the variables, it is further assumed, reflects the existence of common factors or traits among the objects. Factor analysis attempts to identify these traits or common factors or dimensions and uses them as a new set of reference variables to descrbe thei objects. Usually these common factors are much fewer in number than the original variables from which they have been extracted. Thus, to illustrate, four variables relating to the proportion of children, sex ratio, level of education and percentage of Animists in the population of a number of cities could intercorrelate in such a manner as to reflect a common trait of economic backwardness among these cities. On the basis of this new reference factor or trait, the individual object (or cities) can then be given scores which can be high or low, negative or positive depending on how strongly or otherwise they reflect this trait or its opposite.

A basic requirement of factor analysis is thus the matrix of intercorrelations. For Nigerian cities, each of the thirty-two variables has been correlated with all the others and the result is shown in Appendix 3. Details of the analysis of this matrix need not concern us here. Suffice it to say that the purpose of the analysis is to bring out:

(a) the common factors or traits which are present in all the variables. These factors represent that portion of total variance which correlate with certain of the variables and on which, therefore, they are said to load.

(b) the unique or specific factor which is that portion or the total variance which does not correlate with any other variable.

The analysis reveals the existence of twenty-three common factors with the sum of their independent common variance or communality being 28·752 (see Appendixes 4 and 5). Of this sum, seven common factors accounted for 24·240 or 84·3 per cent of the total variance. For all practical purposes, therefore, it can be assumed that these seven common factors represent the most important dimensions of the process of urbanization in Nigeria.

Table 20 shows the relative importances of each of these seven factors after the initial results have been rotated to ensure that each factor is independent of the others. The table reveals that the first factor alone accounts for 5·23 or 21·5 per cent of the total common variance for the seven factors whilst the seventh factor accounts for only 1·28 or 5·3 per

Variable No. Name	Factor number 1	2	3	4	5	6	7	Communality 7 Factors
Sum squares over variables	5·230	5·102	4·877	3·229	2·978	1·545	1·281	
1. TOTPOP	-0·392	-0·085	-0·140	0·063	-0·074	0·036	-0·180	0·224
2. TOTM	-0·353	-0·030	0·115	0·042	-0·887	0·012	0·065	0·931
3. TOTF	0·354	0·032	-0·108	-0·037	0·887	-0·019	-0·064	0·931
4. HA/FU	-0·084	0·921	0·100	0·123	-0·006	0·068	-0·157	0·910
5. IBO	0·131	-0·310	0·187	-0·749	-0·116	-0·184	-0·136	0·775
6. YORUBA	-0·035	-0·591	-0·244	0·572	0·105	0·189	-0·123	0·799
7. ONORTH	-0·204	0·518	0·183	0·101	-0·022	-0·208	0·306	0·491
8. OSOUTH	-0·178	-0·255	-0·037	-0·129	-0·123	-0·055	0·609	0·504
9. NONNIG	-0·535	0·124	0·245	-0·065	-0·394	-0·006	0·111	0·534
10. STDII	-0·645	-0·600	-0·038	-0·181	0·150	0·033	0·111	0·846
11. RANDW	-0·520	0·326	0·071	0·028	0·026	-0·040	-0·071	0·390
12. MLESS2	0·372	-0·099	-0·786	0·262	0·047	0·033	-0·101	0·848
13. M2-6	0·254	0·026	-0·716	-0·135	0·439	0·065	0·262	0·862
14. M7-I4	0·025	-0·289	-0·530	-0·416	0·294	-0·029	-0·321	0·729
15. MI5-49	-0·238	0·044	0·806	-0·227	-0·404	0·008	0·114	0·936
16. M50+	0·010	0·243	-0·033	0·780	0·318	-0·043	-0·164	0·798
17. MAG/FH	0·872	0·098	-0·053	0·117	0·186	0·012	-0·199	0·860
18. MTD/CT	-0·736	0·107	0·137	0·163	-0·104	0·314	0·020	0·708
19. ADMIN	-0·792	0·061	0·213	-0·019	0·183	-0·018	0·071	0·715
20. OOCCUP	-0·717	0·021	0·337	0·058	-0·299	0·041	0·181	0·756
21. OMALES	0·056	-0·209	-0·488	-0·287	0·400	-0·328	0·113	0·648
22. FLESS2	0·269	-0·207	-0·767	0·274	-0·241	0·076	-0·051	0·845
23. F2-6	-0·038	-0·213	-0·717	-0·292	-0·062	0·099	0·347	0·781
24. F7-14	-0·097	0·573	-0·500	-0·233	-0·114	-0·051	-0·334	0·769
25. FI5-49	-0·062	0·249	0·855	-0·324	-0·049	0·024	0·119	0·919
26. F50+	0·044	0·331	-0·000	0·701	0·464	-0·083	-0·153	0·848
27. FAG/FH	0·610	-0·605	-0·043	-0·091	0·049	-0·014	-0·087	0·757
28. FTD/CT	-0·330	0·059	-0·043	0·131	0·033	-0·846	-0·008	0·849
29. OFEMLS	-0·420	0·533	0·061	0·089	0·005	-0·635	-0·116	0·889
30. MOSLEM	-0·097	0·815	0·046	0·411	0·041	0·114	-0·202	0·900
31. XTIANS	0·292	-0·754	-0·219	-0·031	-0·002	0·093	0·169	0·740
32. ANIMIS	0·456	-0·535	0·063	-0·442	0·089	-0·189	0·112	0·749

cent. In other words, the first factor is over four times as significant as the seventh.

The question of interpreting each of these factors or giving it a name is one of logical inference from inspecting the variables with which it strongly correlates (or is loaded) either positively or negatively. In subsequent discussion of each factor, these variables are extracted along with their correlation. It can easily be shown that factors one and six describe aspects of the economic conditions of Nigerian cities; factors two, four and seven aspects of the social conditions; and factors three and five aspects of the demographic conditions.

Furthermore, for the 293 Nigerian cities for which data were available, we now have new scores on each of the seven factors. For each factor, these scores have been plotted on a map to make it easy to appreciate the spatial pattern of urban development in the country. To interpret each of these maps successfully, one must bear in mind the significance of the high or low values and the positive or negative signs of the variables correlating strongly with the factor.

Factor One

This factor loaded heavily on the variables listed below. Both the positive and negative loadings are listed since this helps to emphasize certain inverse relationships among the variables.

Negative		Positive	
19. ADMIN/PROFESSIONAL	−0·792	17. MALE: AGRIC/FISHING	0·872
18. MALE: TRADING/CRAFT	−0·736	27. FEMALE: AGRIC/FISHING	0·610
20. MALE: OTHER OCCUP.	−0·717		
10. STD. II PASS AND OVER	−0·645		
9. NON-NIGERIANS	−0·535		
11. ABLE TO READ AND WRITE	−0·520		

It is obvious that with high negative loadings on male occupational groupings such as administration, the professions, trading, crafts and other occupations and the high positive loadings on male and female occupations in agriculture and fishing, this is the factor of *urban economic function*. A city which scores a high negative value will be one where the non-agricultural functions are more important than the agricultural. These are the really urban functions and their greater importance in a city can be taken as a sign of growth. The list also shows a close relation of the urban economic functions with high educational

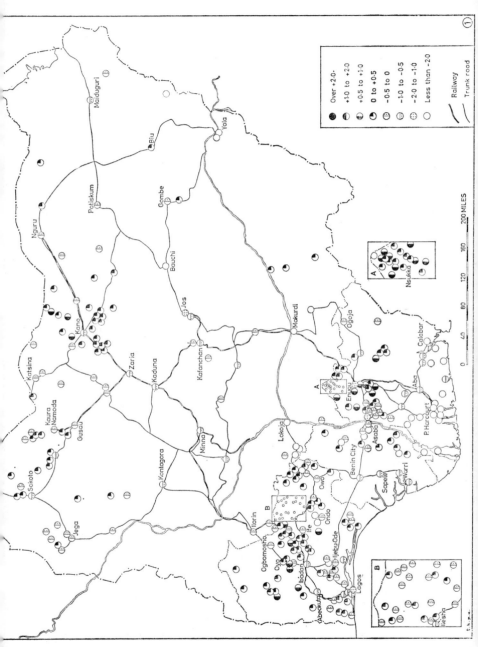

Figure 15   Nigerian towns: spatial distribution of scores on Factor One

attainment (Standard II pass and over) and ability to read and write. Moreover, it emphasizes that where urban economic functions are so important, there you will expect to find a concentration of Non-Nigerians.

In the earlier part of this chapter, we have stressed that by 1952 the location of transportation routes, especially the railway and the ports, was crucial for the economic development of Nigeria cities. We pointed out that cities favourably located on these routes were those which were growing, while those away from them were declining. If this were true, we would expect to see cities which were growing scoring high minus values, and those declining scoring high positive values.

Fig. 15 shows the distribution of the scores by each city in Nigeria and to a large extent justifies our expectations. Important modern cities like Lagos, Enugu and Jos on the rail lines had the highest negative scores between $-2 \cdot 0$ and $-1 \cdot 0$. Other major centres on the rail line, on the coast and on the trunk roads had scores between $-1 \cdot 0$ and $-0 \cdot 5$. By contrast and irrespective of their size many centres not so favourably located returned positive scores indicating a high dependence on agriculture and fishing. Generally, however, the highest positive scores were returned by small towns in northern Onitsha Province (around Nsukka), in Oyo Province and in Kano Province. (See Appendix 6 for the individual scores of towns.)

Factor Two

Negative		Positive	
31. CHRISTIANS	$-0 \cdot 754$	4. HAUSA/FULANI	$0 \cdot 921$
27. FEMALE: AGRIC/		30. MOSLEMS	$0 \cdot 815$
FISHING	$-0 \cdot 605$	29. OTHER FEMALES	$0 \cdot 533$
10. STD. II PASS AND OVER	$-0 \cdot 600$	7. OTHER NORTHERN TRIBES	$0 \cdot 518$
6. YORUBA	$-0 \cdot 591$	11. ABLE TO READ AND WRITE	$0 \cdot 326$
24. FEMALE: 7-14 YEARS	$-0 \cdot 573$		
32. ANIMISTS	$-0 \cdot 535$		
5. IBO	$-0 \cdot 310$		

As a matter of logical inference, this factor can be identified as one contrasting Southern versus Northern urbanism (*Regional Factor*). It helps to define more clearly some aspects of the social conditions in Nigerian cities. The factor, for instance, emphasizes the tendency for southern towns to have a higher proportion of literates (Std. II and over) due no doubt to the importance of the adherence to Christianity in the population. Interestingly enough, these southern towns also show

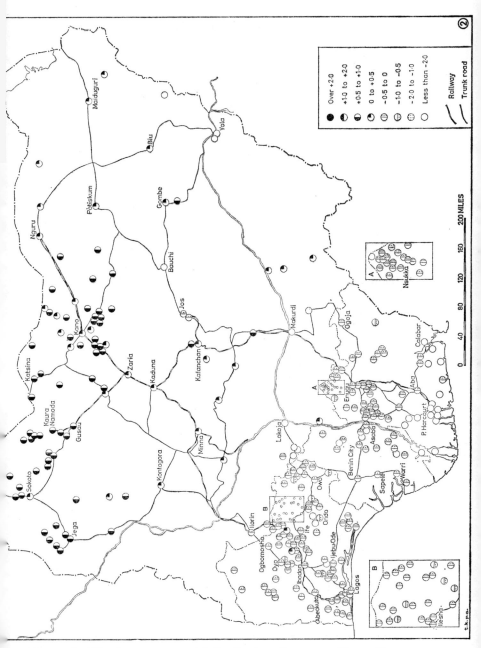

Figure 16   Nigerian towns: spatial distribution of scores on Factor Two

a stronger residuum of Animist population than do northern towns. Moreover, there is a higher proportion of young females in southern towns and a greater tendency for females to be involved in primary activities while living in the towns.

The northern towns, by contrast, are shown to be largely Moslem; and with this religion goes the ability to read and write largely in Arabic. The relatively high score of the variable 'other females' also underlines the situation among Moslems of keeping a large number of females in 'purdah' and often out of employment.

Fig. 16 strongly confirms the interpretation of this factor. The fact that the scores of most cities are highly clustered (in the south between −0·5 and 0; in the north between 0·5 and 1·0) also points to the attributive nature of this factor. The two Yoruba towns which return positive scores on this factor are Oshogbo and Iwo, both of which, for their size group, have the highest proportion of Moslems in the Region. The similarity of the scores of the northern Yoruba towns of Offa and Ilorin with those of the south emphasizes their cultural similarity with the south.

Factor Three

Negative		Positive	
12. MALE: LESS THAN 2 YEARS	−0·786	15. MALE: 15-49 YEARS	0·806
22. FEMALE: LESS THAN 2 YEARS	−0·767	25. FEMALES: 15-49 YEARS	0·855
23. FEMALE: 2-6 YEARS	−0·717		
13. MALE: 2-6 YEARS	−0·716		
14. MALE: 7-14 YEARS	−0·530		
24. FEMALE: 7-14 YEARS	−0·500		
21. MALE: OTHER MALES	−0·488		

Clearly, this is the *demographic factor* in which the importance of children is put against that of adults in the population. If we accept the hypothesis on the demographic dimension of urbanization in Nigeria, we would expect that most cities on the main transport routes whose economy have been shown to be growing would return high positive scores to emphasize the predominance of adults in their population. We would expect cities which are not so favourably located to return high negative scores indicating the mass emigration of adults and the importance of children in the population. Moreover, in cities on a major transport route but with a large survival of traditional urbanism—

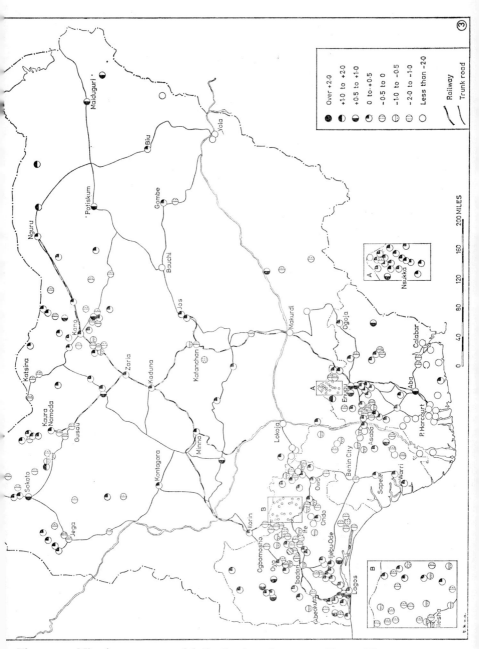

Figure 17   Nigerian towns: spatial distribution of scores on Factor Three

for instance, Ibadan, Abeokuta, Kano and Zaria—we may expect low negative scores because of the tendency towards 'de-urbanization' in the older half of the cities which may cancel out positive gains from the immigration of young adults into the cities.

Fig. 17 describes the pattern of scores-distribution on this factor. It shows that by and large our thesis concerning the demographic structure of towns on major transport routes is valid. Even places like Ibadan, Abeokuta and Benin City returned negative scores as was expected. Traditional northern cities like Kano and Zaria, however, returned positive scores indicating that some of the effects of their traditional base is being obliterated or obscured as a result of massive immigration in recent times.

The figure, however, poses questions especially in Eastern Nigeria (e.g. around Nsukka) but also in Northern and Western Nigeria with regard to places where we would expect negative but we find positive scores. Perhaps the migration of adults away from stranded areas is more complex than it seems at first sight, but no other reason for this phenomenon is apparent.

Factor Four

Negative		Positive	
5. IBO	− 0·749	16. MALE: 50 YEARS AND OVER	
32. ANIMISTS	− 0·442		0·780
14. MALE: 7–14 YEARS	− 0·416	26. FEMALE: 50 YEARS AND OVER	
25. FEMALE: 15–49 YEARS	− 0·324		0·701
		6. YORUBA	0·572
		30. MOSLEM	0·411

This factor may be called the *Ibo Factor*. It extracts those variables which were attributes of Eastern Nigerian towns in 1952 and contrasts them with the rest of the country but especially with Yoruba towns. Ibo towns, for instance, are shown to have proportionally slightly more Animists, more male children and more adult females than other towns. Compared with Ibo towns, the others have a more aged population. Fig. 18 in general confirms the pattern but leaves a residue, especially in Northern Nigeria, which is not easy to interpret. The towns with negative score here, for example Minna, Kafanchan and Jos, stand out because of having more than the typical northern proportion of Animists. It is difficult to see these northern towns having negative scores because of Ibo migration, although the pattern of age distribution with special

Plate 13   Ibadan, 1851 (Impression by Mrs D. Hinderer)
Plate 14   The city of Ibadan, looking east

Plate 15   The ridge across Ibadan in the background with the immigrant
            half of the city in the foreground
Plate 16   Gbagi Commercial Centre

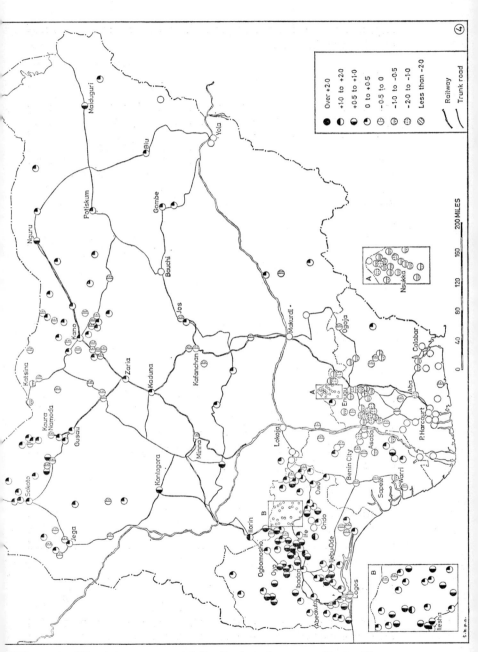

Figure 18   Nigerian towns: spatial distribution of scores on Factor Four

respect to male children 7-14 years old and female 15-49 years may contribute to the score.

Factor Five

Negative		Positive	
2. TOTAL MALE	−0·887	3. TOTAL FEMALE	0·887
15. MALE: 15-49 YEARS	−0·404	26. FEMALE: 50 YEARS AND OVER	
9. NON-NIGERIANS	−0·394		0·464
		13. MALE: 2-6 YEARS	0·439
		21. OTHER MALES	0·4C0
		16. MALE: 50 YEARS AND OVER	0·318

This factor has been called the *Male Dominance Factor*. It further underscores the pattern traced by Factor Three, although emphasis here is on the sex rather than the age-sex composition of the population. This factor is seen to have substantial negative loadings on adult males and non-Nigerians, the latter being known to have a very unbalanced sex ratio. The positive loadings of this factor reveals some interesting relations between the young and aged male population and the female population. On the basis of our hypothesis of urban re-adjustment we can expect most of the favourably located centres to have negative scores while the remote centres have positive scores. Fig. 19 shows the pattern. Towns like Aba, Enugu, Ibadan, Jos, Lagos, Kaduna and Minna return high negative scores as expected. The position in the traditional cities of the far north, however, confounds this interpretation. Kano, Katsina, Maiduguri, Sokoto and Zaria all return high positive scores, possibly indicating a strong female superiority in number. The other variables on which this factor is positively loaded give some indication that the excess females in the population of these Northern cities are probably the old ones (50 years and over) whose presence is correlated with that of old men (50 years and over) and male children (2-6 years).

One other anomaly is revealed by the towns around Nsukka which return negative scores where they are expected to return positive. The reason for this is not clear although it tallies with the pattern revealed by Factor Three.

Factor Six

Negative		Positive	
29. OTHER FEMALES	−0·635	28. FEMALE: TRADING/CRAFT	0·846
21. OTHER MALES	−0·328	18. MALE: TRADING/CRAFT	0·314

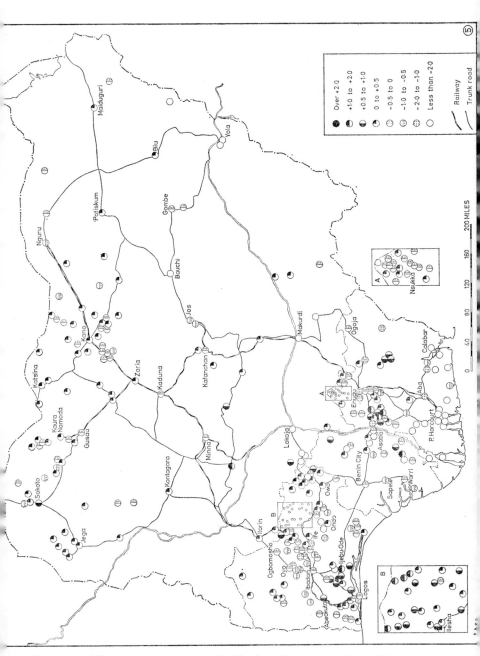

Figure 19   Nigerian towns: spatial distribution of scores on Factor Five

This is a very interesting factor which, for want of a better term, can be described as the *Female Urban Employment Factor*. The factor contrasts a situation in which a substantial proportion of the women are involved in urban employment—basically trading and craft—with one in which most of them are not employed or are unemployable because of age. The factor shows that these situations are partly related to similar ones among the male population. In interpreting this factor, it is necessary to bear in mind that the issue of women's participation in trade and related urban activities is largely culturally determined. Thus among the Yoruba, as we have seen in Chapter 4, this is a time-honoured tradition. In the Northern Region the effect of Islamic teaching about the keeping of women in purdah would tend to militate against this, although it need not prevent them from engaging actively in craft production. In the Eastern Region, most trading and craft-work is in the hands of the men, the women being either confined to household duties or they help with agricultural work.

On the face of it, therefore, positive scores would be expected on this factor by towns in Western Nigeria and negative scores elsewhere in the country. Fig. 20 depicts the position and to a large extent it supports this hypothesis. Most towns in Western Nigeria return positive as against negative scores in other parts of the country. The most spectacular anomaly, however, is revealed by towns in the densely settled zone around Kano. Some of these towns like Wudil, Wurno and Gammo returned over 50 per cent of their female population engaged in trading or craft. It is possible to interpret this phenomenon around Kano in terms of the great tradition of trading and craft activities in these areas as well as the high competition for survival in what is the most coveted area of Northern Nigeria. It may be that because of the small size of holdings here, the women are forced to supplement family income by trading and craft production.

Factor Seven

Negative		Positive	
24. FEMALE: 7-14 YEARS	−0·334	8. OTHER SOUTHERN TRIBES	0·609
14. MALE: 7-14 YEARS	−0·321	23. FEMALE: 2-6 YEARS	0·347
		7. OTHER NORTHERN TRIBES	0·309

This factor may be described as the *Minority Factor* since the variable on which it loaded the most was 'Other Tribes' both northern and southern. We would therefore expect positive scores on this factor

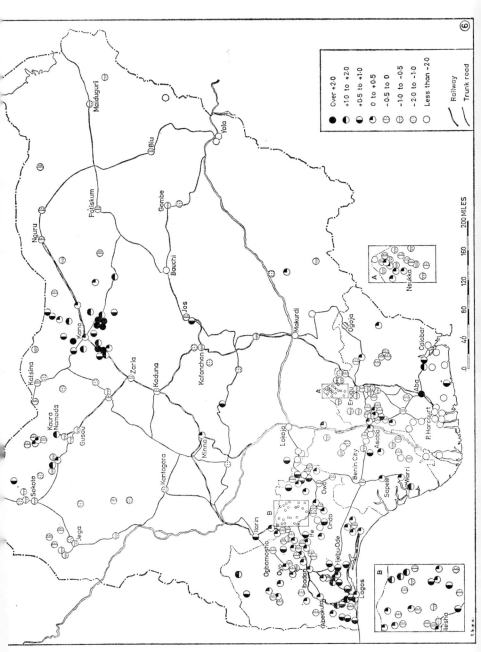

Figure 20   Nigerian towns: spatial distribution of scores on Factor Six

in areas such as the Mid-Western Region, non-Ibo areas of Eastern Nigeria, the Middle Belt Region and Bornu Province of Northern Nigeria. It is rather difficult to interpret the female children variable that went with this factor or the basis for the contrast, though weak, with the adolescent male and female. One possible explanation is that the age class 7-14 is that of school-children. Because of a relative poverty of educational institutions in these minority areas, there is a tendency for their towns to lose children of this age class to towns elsewhere for purposes of education. This is a plausible inference although it should not be overstressed.

Fig. 21 by and large bears out this interpretation. The position is particularly clear in the Mid-West. Except for Asaba and Abbi, every other town returned a positive score on this factor. In Western Nigeria many towns close to the Mid-Western boundary also returned positive scores, no doubt reflecting the tendency of non-Yoruba groups to migrate from the Mid-West. In the North and East the position is largely as expected, most scores being negative.

The factor analysis of the characteristics of Nigerian towns in 1952 underlines the complexity of the urbanization process in Nigeria up to then and attempts to unravel the major strands in an intricate situation. Four of these strands bear re-emphasis. First, the analysis shows that a considerable re-adjustment is going on among Nigerian towns which is particularly reflected in their demographic structure. The general pattern of adjustment is by way of migration of the adult males and females to the thriving centres, especially along the rail-line but also on the coast, the major rivers and some of the main roads. In these centres there is a general predominance of the age-group 15-49 and a relative unimportance of children under the age of 15 and elderly people over the age of 49. This position is reversed in towns, especially the large, traditional centres which have been by-passed by the major arteries of colonial trade connections.

Secondly, this simple picture is modified by sharp cultural differences within the country. Of special importance are differences between the northern and southern parts of the country deriving from religion and the prevalence of literacy, especially of the type based on the Arabic language. This literacy factor dating from the medieval proselytization of Islam may underline the more essentially urban character of northern as opposed to southern Nigerian towns. Even within the south, a striking cultural contrast between Ibo and Yoruba areas does appear

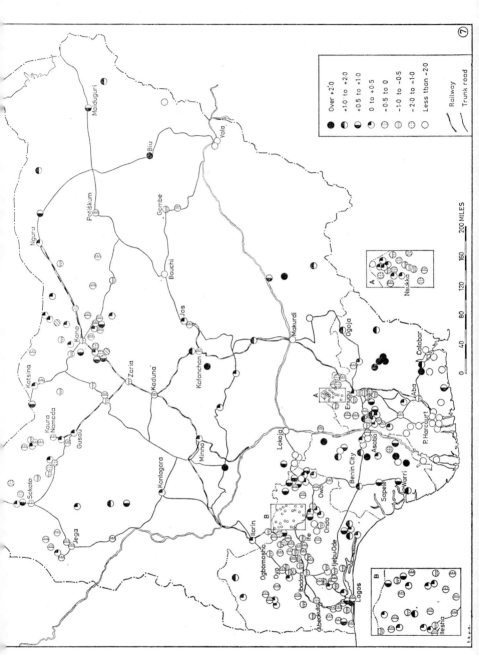

Figure 21 Nigerian towns: spatial distribution of scores on Factor Seven

to affect the character of their cities. This contrast is especially under-lined by the importance of Animists in Ibo towns and Moslems in Yoruba towns. That the importance of Animists may be related to the essentially first-generation, rural-urban migrant nature of Eastern Nigerian towns is indicated by the close relation of this factor with the relatively younger population. The traditionally established position of Yoruba towns, on the other hand, is shown by the importance of the aged population in them.

Thirdly, as a special form of cultural factor there is the role of women in urban economic activities. Here the Yoruba towns stand out clearly as reflecting the prevailing norm of female economic independence. In the north, where the Islamic religion and the institution of purdah restrict most women from participating openly in economic life, the position around Kano stands out as anomalous. It has been suggested that the development here in spite of religion may be related to the long tradition of acute economic competition and the general evolved status of Hausa women in this area.

Fourthly, there is the comment on the minority groups and the non-Nigerians. The former predominate in the few towns in their part of the country but seem to lose their children of school-going age to towns in other areas probably for the purpose of education. The non-Nigerian migrants are shown to be predominantly adult male and to include relatively fewer females, both children and adult.

These various strands in the urbanization process determine the quality of life in different Nigerian towns. They affect the form of social organization and societal activities. They influence the nature of politi-cal relations in the town. However, in turn they are seriously affected by the vigour of economic activities in the country as a whole and the relative economic importance of the individual towns within the system. Our examination so far has concentrated on the adjustment going on within the system of towns due to changes in the general economic and social conditions of the country. At the level of the individual town, however, this examination has been only superficial. There are ques-tions relating, for instance, to the implications of these changes to the internal structure of the individual city, to the organization and loca-tion of various institutions within the city, to the local pattern of population distribution and movement and to the segregational ten-dencies operating among residences and workplaces in the city. These are questions of equally vital importance for an understanding of urbanization in Nigeria and the second part of this book is devoted entirely to providing answers to them.

References

1. A. E. Smailes, *The Geography of Towns*, London, 1953, p. 44.
2. Walter Christaller, *Die zentralen Orte in Suddeutschland*, Jena, 1933.
3. August Lösch, *The Economics of Location* (trans. by W. H. Woglom), New Haven, 1954.
4. See B. J. L. Berry and W. L. Garrison, 'Recent developments of Central Place Theory', *Papers and Proceedings of the Regional Science Association*, Vol. 4, 1958, pp. 107-120.
5. Rutledge Vining, 'A Description of Certain Spatial Aspects of an Economic System', *Economic Development and Cultural Change*, Vol. 3, No. 2, January 1955, pp. 147-95.
6. Ibid., pp. 187, 189.
7. B. J. L. Berry and A. Pred, *Central Place Studies*, Regional Science Research Institute, Bibliography Series No. 1, Philadelphia, 1961.
8. R. J. Harrison-Church, 'The evolution of railways in French and British West Africa', *Congrès International de Géographie*, Lisbon, 1949, Tome 4, p. 113.
9. B. W. Hodder, 'Tin Mining on the Jos Plateau', *Economic Geography*, Vol. 35, No. 2, April 1959, p. 110.
10. In 1954-55 the charges per ton-mile and average haul of various media were given as follows (Source: *UAC Statistical and Economic Review*, No. 14, September 1954):

	Average haul (in miles)	Average charge per ton-mile in pence
Road feeder services (Nigerian railway)	42	7·25
Nigerian railway	473	2·73
Niger river fleet	530	2·34

11. Papers relating to Mechanical Transport in the Colonies, Col. 4589, 1909, pp. 22-4.
12. Allan McPhee, *The Economic Revolution in British West Africa*, London, 1926, pp. 115-16.
13. *UAC Statistical and Economic Review*, No. 25, March 1961, pp. 1-44.
14. International Bank for Reconstruction and Development, *Report on the Economic Development of Nigeria*, Baltimore, 1955, p. 59.
15. K. W. Cooley and P. R. Johnes, *Multivariate Procedures for the Behavioral Sciences*, New York, 1952, p. 151.

Part Two   Types of Urban Development

7 Theory of Urban Growth and Development

The preceding chapters have considered the process of urbanization as it operates over the whole country. We have tried to show that, within the broad theory of urbanization, economic conditions dating from the medieval period have given rise to systems of cities within Nigeria. The modern period with its greater technological sophistication has, however, imposed a new order of importance on these cities. The result is a situation that is not easily explained, although it has been possible through the use of both conceptual and analytical tools to gain some valuable insight into the nature of the processes at work.

It is equally interesting to interpret the forces which have shaped the internal form of Nigerian cities. Obviously the structure of a city is the result of growth over a long period. Most theories attempting to explain the internal structure of cities therefore seek largely to understand the pattern of their growth. The situation presented by cities in under-developed countries has not given rise to any formal theory of city growth and structure. In the advanced industrialized countries, however, certain theories have been suggested to explain the nature of city growth. Three of these theories have become relatively well-known, especially among scholars of urbanism in the United States of America. Each throws some light on the pattern of urban growth but it can be seriously criticized on the grounds of its assumptions. The three theories will be discussed in brief and evaluated in so far as they help us to understand the internal structure of Nigerian cities.

Theories of urban growth

The concentric zone theory of urban growth derives from Professor Burgess and dates from 1923. According to him, cities (American cities, in particular) differentiate into five major zones as they grow (Fig. 22, top left).[1] These are:

Zone 1: The central business district.
Zone 2: The zone of transition comprising areas of residential deterioration due to the increasing encroachment of business and industry from Zone 1.

Zone 3: Zone of independent workingmen's homes largely comprising residences of second generation immigrants into the city.

Zone 4: Zone of better residences—the neighbourhood of the middle class, the small business men, professional people, clerks and salesmen.

Zone 5: The commuters' zone—a ring of encircling small cities, towns and hamlets which serve as dormitory suburbs for the wealthier city dwellers.

Burgess's theory has been criticized on various grounds.[2] There have been criticisms of the zonal concept itself. Implicit in this concept is the fact that growth takes place along the broad margin of successive zones, whereas the more observable tendency is for growth to concentrate along radial lines, that is, the routeways, which cut across the zones. Another criticism relates to the assumption of zonal homogeneity. More important have been criticisms of the generality of the theory. Here it must be noted that, while Burgess himself believed that the zonal pattern found expression in all American cities, others who have had to defend the validity of some of his hypotheses have generally narrowed the coverage to growing 'commercial-industrial' cities of the USA.

Of the major critics of the zonal concept of Burgess, only Homer Hoyt provided an alternative theory. He introduced two new elements into the theoretical conception. These are (a) the effects of land-pricing or rent, and (b) the influence of the major transport routes on the pattern of urban growth.[3] According to him, as a city grows, population and businesses are attracted to it. In their desire for the choicest location, these compete for land, especially in the centre of the city. Central location is considered extremely valuable because, among other reasons, it represents the point of minimum aggregate travel to and from every other point within the city. As a result of the intense competition, land values at the centre rise sharply and only businesses can afford to occupy this location. Thus is created the Central Business District.

The rise in land values or rent gradually spreads from the centre outward. However, instead of this rise taking place along a broad circular front as Burgess suggests, Hoyt postulates that it is particularly concentrated along the main transport routes which, as it were, represent lines of least resistance. From empirical work done in a number of

American cities, Hoyt further suggests that growth along any particular transport route would consist of similar types of land use.[4] The result is the emergence of a star-shaped pattern of city growth in which different types of land use radiate from the Central Business District along particular sectors towards the periphery of the city (Fig. 22, top right). Thus a high-rent residential area in the eastern quadrant of a city would tend to migrate outward, keeping always in the eastern quadrant. A low-quality housing area, if located in the southern quadrant, would tend to extend outward to the very margin of the city in that sector.

   Whatever the relevance of Hoyt's theory to the American situation, three reasons make it unrealistic in the Nigerian situation. The first is the assumption of a *laissez-faire* economic system in which people and businesses compete for land and the highest bidder wins. The evidence in traditional Nigerian cities, such as it is (as well as in pre-industrial cities of Europe and Asia), suggests the deliberate allocation of a particular area of the city to certain uses. Thus the palace, the castle, or the cathedral may occupy an extensive area in the centre of the city for reasons other than economic. Similarly, parts of a city may become well-known for particular crafts or kinds of trade for reasons which defy economic rationalization. Secondly, until the rise of joint-stock enterprises and the factory system, businesses were never on such a scale as to require to be segregated or to need land so much as to give the latter a scarcity value. There is thus no serious competition for land, and the money value attached to it by way of urban land-rent provides a rather weak index of its value. Moreover, the technology of modern transport which, as it improves, tends to generate functional differentiation and specialization of areas, is even today still far from pervasive in many Nigerian cities. The situation in many of these centres remains in this respect very reminiscent of the pre-industrial conditions in medieval Europe. Thirdly, as pointed out above, where modern transport is poorly developed, people are satisfied with less regulated and poorer means of communication. In such a situation, the traditional *élite* are found close to the centre of the city in locations which help to minimize the effort of getting about the city.

   Another criticism of Burgess's theory seeks to show that in many cities growth takes place not around a single nucleus but around several separate nuclei.[5] These nuclei may have existed from the very origin of the city, or develop as the growth of the city stimulates migration and specialization (Fig. 22, bottom left). Their separate existence results

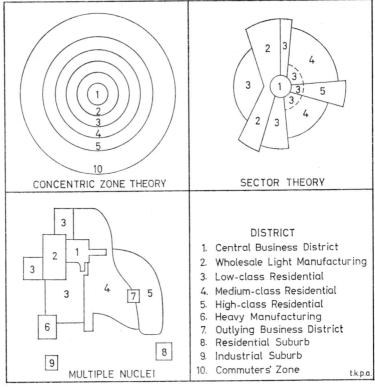

CONCENTRIC ZONE THEORY

SECTOR THEORY

MULTIPLE NUCLEI

DISTRICT
1. Central Business District
2. Wholesale Light Manufacturing
3. Low-class Residential
4. Medium-class Residential
5. High-class Residential
6. Heavy Manufacturing
7. Outlying Business District
8. Residential Suburb
9. Industrial Suburb
10. Commuters' Zone

t.k.p.a.

Figure 22   Three generalizations of the internal structure of cities

either from their need for specialized facilities or because of the detrimental effect on one another of the set of activities carried out in each centre. The number of nuclei varies greatly from city to city, although the general tendency is that the larger the city, the more numerous and specialized are the nuclei. Once the nuclei have formed, the other types of land-use already identified then develop around them. London exemplifies this type of conformation. Here, 'the City' and Westminster originated as separate nuclei, the former as the centre of finance and commerce, the latter as the centre of political life

It should be obvious that the so-called multiple-nuclei theory is not so much a theory as a warning not to assume the existence of a single urban nucleus as suggested by the two preceding theories. In a sense, this is an attempt to destroy the idealized construct of those theories by calling attention to the greater complexity of growth. The theories of Burgess and Hoyt assume that urban growth involves no more than an expansion of each land-use region *ad infinitum*. They fail to appreciate that urban growth is the result of autonomous and often external influences whose effect on a city in many cases is the creation of a new centre of activities. Even in the USA this type of situation is commonly visible. A city such as Chicago, which started as a commercial-transportation centre, grew rapidly as it began to attract industries to itself. The new industries did not seek location within or even around the former commercial centre. Rather they created a new centre for themselves miles away from the 'Loop' or Central Business District.

It may be, of course, that here we are dealing with different types of growth. The growth envisaged by Burgess and Hoyt may be likened to the 'natural growth process' of human population involving the slow, almost imperceptible change in the character and extent of the function-areas of a city. On the other hand, the growth assumed in the multiple nuclei theory is relatively more dramatic, sometimes divergent but infinitely more impressive in terms of its effect on the city's size and structure.

In succeeding chapters it will be seen how the idea of multiple nuclei is fundamental in understanding the nature of Nigerian cities. The nature of the divergent forces which have brought about the situation will be further explored and their more subtle effects on the total character of the city discussed. Neither the Burgess nor the Hoyt theory is totally irrelevant and the partial understanding which they provide will also be indicated.

Theories of city retail structure

All the theories of urban growth and structure which have been considered so far have been concerned primarily with the evolution of the residential regions within a city. True they each recognize the existence and crucial importance of the Central Business District, but in all cases they virtually assume that outside this area there are no other substantial business concentrations in a city. Though less known, there have been just as many attempts to explain the retail structure of cities as there have been to explain the total urban structure. These attempts fall into two main groups. The first and earlier attempts belong essentially to the pre-Second World War period; the second group is largely post-

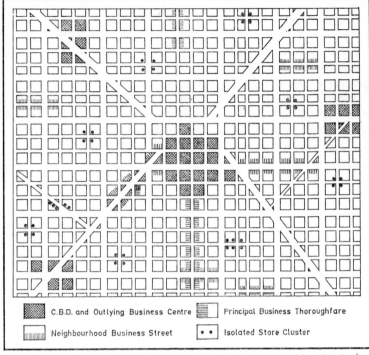

C.B.D. and Outlying Business Centre ▓   Principal Business Thoroughfare

Neighbourhood Business Street   • •   Isolated Store Cluster

(After : Proudfoot)

Figure 23   Theoretical construct of city retail structure

war. Like the other essays in theoretical explanation of the urban phenomenon, all the attempts stem from the USA.

The best known of the pre-Second World War studies is that by Michael Proudfoot in 1937. From detailed studies of Chicago, Philadelphia, Cleveland, Atalanta and Des Moines, and reconnaissance studies of four others, Proudfoot concluded that businesses in cities tend to have five types of conformation (Fig. 23). These, he listed as follows[6]:

(a) *The Central Business District* where is concentrated a multiplicity of functions, including retailing, finance, wholesale and administration as well as light industries;

(b) *The Outlying Business Centres*—miniature types of Central Business District found at the focal points of intra-city transportation;

(c) *The Principal Business Thoroughfares* which combine the functions of a traffic artery and a business street although it has little depth beyond the street frontage;

(d) *The Neighbourhood Business Streets* which form the real centres of neighbourhood economic life throughout the city with groceries, meat, fruit and vegetable, drug and other convenience goods predominating; and

(e) *The Isolated Store Cluster* comprising two or more complementary convenience-goods stores and representing the final and individually the least significant type of city retail structure.

The five types identified by Proudfoot can be grouped broadly into two classes: (a) a cluster or nucleated class comprising the Central Business District, the Outlying Business Centre and the Isolated Store Cluster, and (b) a string-street or arterial class comprising the Principal Business Thoroughfare and the Neighbourhood Business Street. Postwar studies, especially those of Garrison and Berry,[7] tried to provide theoretical support for these two forms of business groupings in cities. They ask the questions as to what factors generate a business structure comprising basic nucleated types of various orders in addition to string-street types of business centres.

Of the important operating factors, three groups are identified. A first group comprises population distribution, income levels and available purchasing power within the urban area. Differences in the incidence of purchasing power are shown to be the cause of differences between functions located in nucleated and string-street centres. A second group of factors includes the pattern of transport and traffic facilities within cities, as well as the directional flow of traffic. This group of factors can be included under the general definition of accessibility. The third group relates to the characteristics of business establishments, the minimum size of market necessary to support them as well as the location and characteristics of potential competitors.

Essential to an understanding of how these factors underlie the size and distribution of retail centres in cities are two notions with which we are already familiar, namely, the range of a good and the threshold sales level.[8] The theoretical framework provided for understanding the retail structure of cities is, in fact, an extension of the Central Place Theory of Walter Christaller already outlined in Chapter 6. Deriving from this, it can be shown that any large city with great purchasing power will give rise to a hierarchical structuring of business centres from the single, most complex centre (the Central Business District) through increasing numbers at intermediate levels to the large number of centres at the lowest level. Higher level centres perform the functions characteristic of lower level centres, plus some additional functions which they perform for the service areas of the set of lower level centres falling within their sphere of trading influence. The most complex centre performs specialized functions for the entire urban area.

One weakness of the explanation provided by this extension of the central place theory is that it does not cover the case of string-street types of development. It has been suggested that it is because this type of retail structure serves different demands from those of nucleated centres.[9] These are demands not for immediate consumer goods purchased from the home, but presumably demands associated with people moving along major urban transportation routes. Spatial distribution of demands in this case is not approximated by the population or housing map, as in the case of nucleated centres, but by the traffic-flow map. Moreover, shopping seems to be done not by people walking to several stores in a centre, but is of a single-purpose character from a car parked near the store. Hence businesses need not nucleate in centres to minimize the costs of shopping; they can string along major traffic arteries and still be located centrally to the maximum profit areas at their command.

Many of the theoretical arguments for the string-type shopping areas are clearly presumptions. They reveal that these are developments within urban areas which have so far escaped the catch-net of central place theory. They also bear evidence to the fact that we are still groping for a definitive theory to account for the pattern of retail distribution in cities. Yet a much more fundamental question is the extent to which all these help towards the understanding of the emerging commercial landscape in Nigerian cities.

In this respect there are three points worth mentioning. The first is the emphasis on purchasing power of the population. Although in the theoretical explanation this is a variable dependent on population density, it is also strongly related to *per capita* income. For many types of business, there is a strict condition of entry determined by the level of per capita, disposable income of the urban population. Where this is low, as in many parts of Nigeria, few businesses will be found, and there will be hardly any strong tendency towards a hierarchical structuring in their location. As income rises, however, more and more businesses will be attracted, and only then can a pattern approximating to that described above emerge.

In the second place, even if income rises enough to begin to encourage this type of retail structure to emerge, there is a problem related to the conformation of certain retail functions in different cultural settings. For instance, retail types like groceries, butchery and a number of others have no formal existence in Nigerian cities, their functions being performed in market places. This gives markets an important place in the retail structure of Nigerian cities which they do not have in the American city. But there are indications that to a large extent this fact may also be explained by the income variable. In other words, it may be that as Nigeria develops, and the *per capita* income of its peoples increases, the capital stock of the average market woman will be such that a small market stall will cease to be adequate for her retailing needs. Or perhaps the average buyer will have so much money to spend over a greater variety of goods that he begins to prefer shopping at a supermarket than rambling around the market as it is at present constituted. In either case, a substantial rise in the income of the people may initiate a major decline in the importance of markets in Nigerian cities.

Thirdly, the types of retail and commercial activities considered in the theories have developed their own form of technology. There are the specialized functional units such as the various types of goods stores, showrooms, luncheon places, hotels, finance houses, banks, brokers' offices, law offices, insurance houses, garages and petrol stations. All of these are space-consuming, and access to them either for goods delivery or personal service involves the use of various types of vehicle—railway freight trucks, lorries, motor cars, motor cycles, bicycles or a long walk. Communication with business houses involves the use of the post office, the telephone, the teleprinter and, more recently, television. These are the symbols of modern commercial activities. The competing need of the various businesses for choice sites and for the most accessible location forces some order into their arrangement in space if they are to function efficiently. Moreover, irrespective of whether the businesses are found in the USA, in Europe or in Africa, a condition for their efficient functioning is the orderly arrangement of their location.

Nonetheless, it would be taking an extreme view to expect the retail structure of every city to be simply a replica of that of another. Differences there must surely be, especially in the internal arrangement of their units. The chance effect of historical origin, the vagaries of land tenure, the local variation of relief and drainage and innumerable other factors may affect the detail. However, a pattern begins to appear, the product of the operation of economic and technological rules which, once released from their original culture area, are no longer culture-bound. And whether in Europe or America, in Asia or in Africa, they tend to impose a certain pattern and order on the internal arrangement of land-uses within cities.

The remaining chapters of this book are an attempt to examine the extent to which these theories help to explain the structure of Nigerian cities. Since many of the cities have had a longer history than most American cities that provided the empirical data for the theories, we should expect some interesting deviations. These deviations, however, would be no more than we might expect to find if we were to test the theories against European cities with strong medieval roots. But although in Europe modern technological development represents a direct growth from these roots, in Nigeria it is an alien importation of many bewildering dimensions. Thus, while its impact has been and continues to be gradually absorbed in cities in the advanced countries of Europe and America, its effect on Nigerian cities has been more dramatic and often less easy to assimilate. In short, while modern technology has served to transform medieval European cities into modern European cities, its effect in Nigeria so far has been to create twin-cities—one traditional and one modern.

The interaction between these two provides the really exciting basis for understanding the emerging urban forms and functions in Nigeria. The larger the traditional urban mass, the clearer and more comprehensible is the nature of the interaction. These considerations, in particular, have conditioned the choice of Ibadan and Lagos for our present study. The former represents the highest achievement of pre-European, pre-industrial urbanism in Nigeria; the latter is the leviathan of our modern industry-oriented urbanism. The former depicts many of the characteristics of similarly old cities in the country, such as Ife, Oyo, Iwo, Sokoto, Kano and Zaria; the latter provides glimpses of situations yet to be experienced by many of the modern urban developments such as Kaduna, Jos, Port Harcourt, Aba and Enugu. Between them they provide a conspectus of the problems of growth and development in present-day Nigerian cities.

References

1. For the detailed characterization of these zones, see E. W. Burgess, 'The Growth of the City: An Introduction to a Research Project', *Publications of the American Sociological Society*, No. 18, 1924, pp. 85-97; reprinted in R. E. Park, E. W. Burgess and R. D. McKenzie, *The City*, Chicago, 1925, pp. 47-62.

2. Much in this section is derived from Leo F. Schnore, 'On the Spatial Structure of Cities in the Two Americas', in Philip Hauser and Leo F. Schore (Eds), *The Study of Urbanization*, New York, 1965, pp. 349-56. See also J. A. Quinn, 'The Burgess Zonal Hypothesis and its critics', *American Sociological Review*, Vol. 5, 1940, pp. 210-18; M. A. Alihan, *Social Ecology: A Critical Analysis*, New York, 1938, pp. 224-5; M. R. Davie, 'The Pattern of Urban Growth' in G. P. Murdock (Ed.) *Studies in the Science of Society*, New Haven, 1937, pp. 133-61.

3. Homer Hoyt, *One Hundred Years of Land Values in Chicago*, Chicago, 1933.

4. Homer Hoyt, *The Structure and Growth of Residential Neighbourhoods in American Cities*, Washington, D.C., Federal Housing Administration, 1939.

5. Chauncy D. Harris and E. L. Ullman, 'The Nature of Cities', *The Annals of the American Academy of Political and Social Science*, Vol. 242, November 1945, pp. 7-17.

6. For detailed characterization of each type, see Michael J. Proudfoot, 'City Retail Structure', *Economic Geography*, Vol. 13, No. 4, October 1937, pp. 425-8.

7. See W. L. Garrison, B. J. L. Berry, D. F. Marble, J. D. Nystuen and R. L. Morrill, *Studies of Highway Development and Geographic Change*, Seattle, 1959, pp. 39-66; and B. J. L. Berry, *Commercial Structure and Commercial Blight*, Department of Geography, University of Chicago, Research Paper No. 85, Chicago, 1963.

8. See p. 138.

9. W. L. Garrison *et al.*, op. cit., p. 58.

8 Ibadan, a Traditional Metropolis

As far as Nigerian cities are concerned, Ibadan is a city of relatively recent origin. Its claims to city status carry none of the customary sanctions of a crowned head, a palace or a hereditary line of chiefs. Yet, in a very real sense, it is the pinnacle of pre-European urbanism in Nigeria, the largest purely African city and the emporium for the commerce of an extensive region. The reason for its existence confirms the logic of the urbanization process as indicated in Chapter 2. It grew because an effective power-class was able to guarantee internal peace and security to its specialists, both agricultural and non-agricultural.

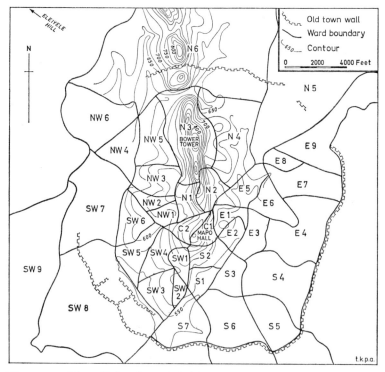

Figure 24   The relief and ward divisions of Ibadan, 1952

Like Rome, it grew to an unequalled size because it could subject extensive areas to its domination and control.

There is something about the site of Ibadan which seems to predispose it to serve as a point of concentration for human groups. Three times the site has served for the foundation of cities, the present city being the third. The site is dominated by a range of lateritized quartzitic hills trending generally in a northwest-southeast direction (Fig. 24). The highest of these hills (Eleiyele Hill) rises over 100 feet above the surrounding country and gives a very wide view over the plains. The defensive advantage of such a situation must have attracted the first settlers to this area. Moreover, Ibadan is located close to the boundary between forest and grassland. Its annual average rainfall of 48 inches (taken over 47 years) makes it drier than many places (Ilorin, Bida and Kaduna) farther north within the savanna grassland region. Its name, in fact, is said to be a corruption of 'Eba-Odan', which translates as 'near the grassland'. Its ease of access to grassland country ensures nearness to land more easily cleared and cultivated than the forests. On the other hand, its situation just within the forest belt ensures protection and refuge from aggressive neighbours. Furthermore, given the development of commercial exchanges, a settlement so located should provide an important meeting place for the exchange o the products of the grassland and the forest.

According to Akinyele, the local historian of Ibadan, the first group of people to inhabit this area was comprised of 'fugitives from justice, wild and wicked men expelled from adjacent towns, rebels and robbers'.[1] This motley collection of people did not found a town. That was left to a member of the colonizing group from Ife who, in the general exodus from that hearth of the Yoruba people, came in this direction. His name was Lagelu. Within a short time, Akinyele continues, the town of Ibadan began to derive great advantages from its frontier location. It became a market for, on the one hand, the Ijebus and Egbas whose territories lie partly or wholly in the forest belt and, on the other, the Oyos who mostly inhabit the grassland region. This first Ibadan was near the Awotan Market, to the north-west of the present city not far from the waterworks.

Whatever the importance of Ibadan at this time, it was not such as to prevent summary judgment being delivered against it by its much stronger neighbours. Oral tradition has it that because of failure to maintain certain strict propriety in connection with the Egungun cult,

Ibadan was placed under a siege and completely destroyed.[2] One of the few survivors was Lagelu and his children, together with whom he took refuge on one of the nearby hills. This hill is known today as Oke Ibadan (the hill of Ibadan) and there is annual ritual and festivity on the site both to commemorate these events and to worship at the shrine of Lagelu who was buried there.[3]

However, Lagelu survived the turmoil, and when peace returned he came down to found a second Ibadan. The site of this second town was a few miles farther south at what is now Oja Iba—the central market of the city. With time, this town became included in the Gbagura province of Egba territory. It was never a very big town and its area was probably less than 3 square miles in extent. According to Johnson, the second Ibadan consisted of the central market and about half a mile of houses around. Part of the town wall was still visible as late as 1913 when the grammar school of the city was established.[4]

This second foundation survived until the early nineteenth century. By then Yorubaland was enveloped in an unprecedented internecine struggle in which many towns and cities were completely destroyed. The Egba who inhabited Ibadan and an extensive region all around had unwittingly supported the armies of the Ife, Ijebu and Oyo peoples in their attempt to destroy the capital of the neighbouring kingdom of Owu. With Owu destroyed, the allied armies turned on the Egbas and systematically destroyed every one of their settlements. The only exception was Ibadan which, nonetheless, the inhabitants deserted.[5] Seeing this, the armies quartered their forces within it. What began as a war camp about 1829, however, grew so rapidly that it was no longer reasonable to think of breaking it up. In this way the present Ibadan was founded.

The growth of Ibadan up to 1850

From its very beginning, Ibadan was marked by the heterogeneity of its population. This comprised the armies of Ife, Ijebu and Oyo and some of the friendly Egbas. The Ife and the Oyo settled around the present Oja Iba and Mapo Hall while the Ijebu settled at Isale-Ijebu towards the south. A few of the Egba inhabitants who returned with the allied armies took up residence to the west in a quarter now known as Yiosa.

This lack of homogeneity created considerable problems for the city in its initial phase. In particular, it gave rise to a constant struggle for ascendancy among the three principal communities. In the event the Oyo element came to predominate and Ibadan became a largely Oyo town. This, however, did not necessarily make it easy for Ibadan to adopt the customs and traditions of Oyo. The fact was that, as a primarily military settlement, the city attracted a large motley of people, especially of the daring, the adventurous and numerous others anxious to escape the stifling traditionalism of other Yoruba cities. According to Awe, 'as the settlement grew, these came not only from among the Oyo-Yoruba, but from all parts of the Yoruba country; indeed a survey of the various compounds in Ibadan indicates that every Yoruba town had a son in Ibadan. . . . Ambitious young men eager to get on, crafts-men looking for better opportunities for their trade, and rich men bored with life in their own towns came there; also from overseas came later on in the century a handful of Sierra Leone and Brazilian immigrants, descendants of those formerly carried into trans-Atlantic slavery, and now finding their way back to the Yoruba country.'[6]

With such a population, new ways of doing things and novel forms of organization prevailed. This was particularly evident in the form of government that the city evolved. With no historical traditions, ascriptive claims based on heredity gave place to competition; the conferment of titles and recognition was based purely on a man's wealth. By 1851 the result was that government in Ibadan was divided into two spheres, the military and the civil, and there were four main lines of chiefs.[7] Two of these belonged to the military. The more important was headed by the Balogun or General of the Army; the other by the Seriki, leader of the younger men with less military experience. The two other lines of chiefs were composed of civilians. One was the line of the *Bale*, or civil head of the town whose subordinate chiefs were designated by their order of sitting to his right and left at meetings; the other was the line of the Iyalode or the head of the town's womenfolk. She too had subordinates designated in a manner similar to that of the Bale.

Ibadan thus had no hereditary crowned head and no formal palace as in other Yoruba towns. Without an Oba or a palace, there could be no Oba's market—a common feature of Yoruba towns. Instead, what we have is the market of the Ibashorun, a title of the Balogun which recognized his important military position within the Oyo Empire as a whole.[8]

By 1851 Ibadan had grown remarkably. In that year arrived the first

European to the city, the Rev. David Hinderer of the Church Missionary Society. Hinderer has left a very detailed description (Plate 13) of the city at this date which is worth quoting *in extenso* because of the light it throws on the later development of the city. According to him:

'Ibadan is a large Yoruba town, almost as large as Abeokuta, but a good number of Egbas reside there as well. The predominant part of the inhabitants are heathen, though the large number of Mohammedans also are by no means without influence, especially as their warlike disposition seems to suit the chiefs as well.

'The most populous part of the town is situated on part of a range of hills running northwest-southeasterly whilst the more widely built and more cleanly parts of it occupy extensive portions of the plains below the hills on every side.

'The town is surrounded with mud walls all around to the extent of about fifteen miles.

'To define the population of such a place with any degree of certainty is almost more than one could venture to undertake. We seemed to agree pretty well in our calculation about Abeokuta which we thought to contain about 60,000 inhabitants. But Captain Beecroft, Her Majesty's Consul-General of the Bight on his visit here at the beginning of this year made sure of 100,000 and to this day contends for that number. Ibadan, I should say, contains pretty well the same number of inhabitants as Abeokuta, with the exception of those farmers of the latter place who constantly live in farm villages.

'Though Ibadan is professedly a town of warriors, or as they frequently style it "a war encampment", yet there is a good deal of industry to be seen in and about the town. There are the weavers, the tailors, the tanners, leather dressers and saddlers, the iron smelter and the blacksmith, a kind of country sawyer and carpenter, and last but not least, the potters, the palm-oil and nut-oil and the soap manufacturers of the female sex to be seen in all parts of the town, some of them very busily engaged in their respective occupations.

'There are a great many markets all over the town for vending the productions of their farms, such as yams, beans, corn, cotton and food prepared as well as other necessaries of life, *but there is one large market especially for home and foreign manufactures, with all kinds of European articles which have yet been imported*. These are brought here principally through the Egba and Ijebu country from Lagos and Badagry; whilst on the other hand, traders from the interior bring their ivory, some superior home manufactured articles, especially clothes, a large quantity of rock salt used as medicine, especially for horses and, at seasons, loads of very fine large onions grown at Ilorin and, above all, their hundreds of slaves.

'The slave market is not public but, as in Abeokuta, it is held in large private houses. . . .'[9]

The problem of feeding such a large agglomeration of warriors, craftsmen and traders must have been immense. In the nineteenth century a solution was found in the institution of slavery. According to Johnson, slaves, when they had not been chosen to serve as soldiers or as wives if they were females, were usually sent to the farms, each to be employed in his or her line of work.[10] The chiefs had large farms and farm houses containing from a hundred to over a thousand souls. The men were engaged in clearing the bush, cultivating the soil, cutting palm nuts and doing other male work; the women in making palm oil, nut oil, soap, weaving mats, rearing poultry and the smaller cattle, cultivating kitchen vegetables of all kinds for the weekly markets, spinning cotton and shelling palm nuts. All were engaged as 'hands in time of harvest'. The result was that food was actually cheaper in Ibadan, though a military capital, than in many other cities.

Hinderer confirmed this dependence of the urban economy of Ibadan on slaves and slavery. He noted that 'the chiefs and headwarriors have all extensive farms, some of them have hundreds of slaves, and a few, I was told, even some thousands of them for whom they build fortified hamlets and small villages. (I found afterwards cause to disbelieve the statement of the "thousands" as to Ibadan at present. Oluyole, the late Basorun, used to have so many; and Ali, the late General of Ilorin is said to have had a village of 26,000 slaves of his own, all working in irons.)'[11]

By the beginning of the second half of the nineteenth century, Ibadan was already a large city. It had grown out of the disastrous upheavals of the Yoruba country in the early nineteenth century and had attracted diverse sorts to itself. Its size made it a market of no mean importance, and craftsmen of various descriptions found an effective demand for the products of their skills. Moreover, as Hinderer pointed out, even at that date the city had thrown up its system of shopping places, the various grades of markets, the premier among which served almost as a central business district where the largest variety of goods was to be found.

The growth of Ibadan, 1851-1900

However, the economy of Ibadan depended heavily on slaves. If the city had to grow, then the ranks of the slaves had to be constantly replenished and augmented. In the second half of the nineteenth century, therefore, the growth of Ibadan depended on the size of the area of Yorubaland which it could dominate. By the time the British arrived in

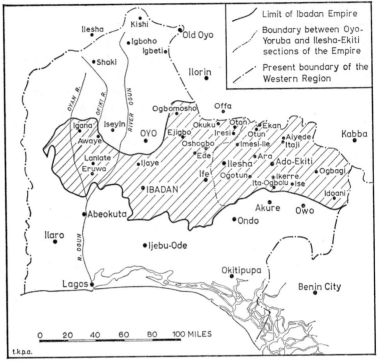

Figure 25   The Ibadan Empire, 1861-93

1893, this empire covered some 20,000 square miles and extended over much of northern and eastern Yorubaland (Fig. 25).

The movement to expand the sphere of influence of Ibadan is said to have begun with Ibikunle, the Balogun of Ibadan from 1851 to 1862. To the east, this meant expansion into the Ekiti country where many of the small towns were easily subjugated. To the west, most of the Ibarapa and south-western Oyo towns came under Ibadan. In each of the conquered towns, the Ibadan placed a resident consul or Ajele, who acted much in the manner of the later British officers. He oversaw the day-to-day administration of the town, ensured that it remained loyal and paid its annual tribute, and that in times of war it sent a troop of soldiers to augment the fighting force of Ibadan. In return, Ibadan provided some form of security and protection, especially against the external threat from the Fulani.

The responsibility for security, however, did not stop Ibadan from pillaging and raiding on occasions even the towns which had accepted its overlordship. Apart from the fact that this was the easiest way for the various military lords in Ibadan to amass riches and wealth, it was also the most convenient means of keeping up the supply of slaves. On such occasions the slaves poured into the city in large numbers. Sometimes, as in 1874, the congestion from the influx encouraged the spread of an epidemic. In that year Johnson reported that 'this epidemic was increased by the dead bodies of Ado captives who died by the hundreds and whom their cruel masters have left unburied'.[12]

Ibadan's political pre-eminence throughout the second half of the nineteenth century made it the emporium for trade in the region. Of the major trade-routes from the coast during the period, two converged on Ibadan. These comprised the routes through the Ijebu country and through Abeokuta. North of Ibadan these routes provided important links with diverse parts of the country even as far north as Kano.[13] The intensive commercial activities meant that the population of Ibadan was also growing rapidly during this period. By 1858 the position was such that it was necessary to build a new town wall which came to be known as Odi Ibikunle (Ibikunle's Wall) after the Balogun who suggested, planned and superintended the carrying out of the work.[14] In 1890 Millson described the city as counting 'over 200,000 souls, while within the walls at least 120,000 people are gathered. Its sea of brown roofs covers an area of nearly 16 square miles and the ditches and walls of hardened clay which surround it are more than 18 miles in circumference.'[15]

The thatched roofs, however, were a constant danger for, apart from outbreaks of smallpox, that of fire was the greatest hazard of living in Ibadan in the nineteenth century. In the month of January 1857 alone, no fewer than four major conflagrations were reported.[16] One of the first innovations made by Europeans coming into Ibadan therefore was a roofing material that was more fire-resistant than the ordinary thatch. In 1854 the European missionaries in Ibadan put up the first iron roofs in the city.[17] In the next half century, but especially after 1900, iron roofs replaced thatch all over the city. Although they resolved the problem of fire, they did not significantly alter the impression of 'a sea of brown roofs' since the iron sheets quickly turned rusty brown on exposure to the elements.

In 1893 the British succeeded in negotiating military disengagement between the Ibadan and the Fulani based at Ilorin. In this way they succeeded in creating conditions of peace and security so necessary if Ibadan was to derive further advantages from its favourable location for trade. In that year too they posted a Resident in Ibadan. The arrival of the British Resident marked the end of the era of Ibadan's political dominance and the beginning of the era of its emergence as a modern regional commercial centre. At first the Resident concentrated on administrative reforms. A Council of Chiefs was set up consisting of the Bale and the Balogun as well as eight to twelve other minor chiefs. Rules were made for keeping the town clean, providing a prison, holding open courts and generally putting the administration of justice on a better footing than before.[18] Then in 1901 the railway from Lagos reached Ibadan and ushered in a new era of growth based on the favourable location of the city for trade over a very extensive region.

The growth of Ibadan, 1901-52

The railway was the instrument of a new order in Nigeria in which the overseeing of security throughout the length and breadth of the country gradually came to devolve on a central administration in Lagos. It also represented a new system of commercial articulation in which the produce of the land was garnered for export to the outside world through the port of Lagos. The agents of this new articulation were the European merchants. As the railway wound its way into the interior, they followed closely in its wake. Their arrival gave rise to still further novel departures from traditional usages.

In Ibadan the British Resident requested the Council to agree to the demarcation and survey of a special part of the city for the European traders. After initial opposition by the Council, various European firms were in 1903 granted leasehold to land for varying terms of up to fifty years in consideration of an annual rental of between £5 and £8 per acre.[19] The operation of pegging out the boundaries of these plots was such a novelty that it came to be used as the name of the district. Thus the new European Business District in Ibadan was called *Gbagi* which, in the vernacular, meant 'to peg'.

In the immediate years following the arrival of the European traders, a major concern was the search for a profitable commodity of trade in order to raise the purchasing power of the populace for buying imported goods from Europe. Rubber was first decided upon, and until the output from the Malayan plantations in 1913 broke the boom, the region around Ibadan, like similar areas of tropical forest, was the scene of

Plate 17   University of Ibadan Teaching Hospital
Plate 18   Houses on Bodija Estate, Ibadan

Plate 19   A small African store in Ibadan

active rubber collection from wild trees. Cotton cultivation for export
was also encouraged. In 1903 new seeds and cotton ginning machines
were introduced and the Ibadan Council was persuaded to grant a lease
of about four square miles of land to the British Cotton Growers'
Association for fifty years. Nevertheless, in spite of the activities of the
Association, and of the system of cash loans to farmers by the Bank of
British West Africa, cotton production never became important in the
Ibadan region.

It was not until after 1910 with the extensive cultivation of cocoa in
the region, especially east of Ibadan, that there grew up considerable
purchasing power in the rural areas sufficient to support numerous
commercial activities in Ibadan. By 1918 many European firms, already
established in Lagos, had opened branches in Ibadan. Their list included the African and Eastern Trade Corporation, Miller Brothers,
G. B. Ollivant and Co., Patterson and Zochonis Ltd, G. Gottschalk and
Co., W. B. MacIver and Co., the Société Commerciale et Industrielle
de L'Afrique Occidentale, John Holt and Co. (Liverpool) Ltd, Lagos
Stores Ltd, John Walkden and Co., the Anglo-Colonial Trading Corporation, Dyer and Wintle Ltd and H. B. Russell and Co. Ltd.[20] Their
activities covered both the import of manufactured articles and the
export of local agricultural produce, notably cocoa, palm oil, palm
kernel, rubber, hides and skins. By contrast, Lebanese traders who had
also arrived in Ibadan soon after 1901 specialized almost exclusively in
the sales of imported cotton textiles and numerous cheap fancy goods.

This rise in the commercial importance of Ibadan attracted a number
of people into the city. It encouraged further diversification in the
character of its population based, this time, not so much on ethnic origin
as on education and level of income. Soon complaints began to be heard
of some of the effects of this increasing intermixture. Elgee reported in
1914 that 'the railway now began to show itself not entirely an unmixed
blessing, for with its advent came many partially educated clerks and
such like from Lagos who often misled their illiterate brethren by bad
advice'.[21] Over the years, as the railway linked diverse parts of the
country together and as the road linkages were extended and improved,
more and more people speaking different languages and with varying
educational qualifications migrated into Ibadan. There came from the
east the Ibos, the Ibibios, the Efiks and the Ijaws; from the mid-west
the Edos, the Ishan and the Urhobos, and from the north the Hausas,
the Nupes and the Igbirras. In 1946 Ibadan was made the headquarters

of the Western Provinces and began to attract still more of the clerical and executive types as well as more Europeans.

Meanwhile, various social and sanitary programmes were initiated which helped to improve the environmental conditions, reduced mortality and stimulated a rise in the total population. As early as 1900, attempts were made to drain the swamps in the town, notably that at Oranyan. In June 1901 the first dispensary was built in the town. In 1903 a beginning was made with smallpox vaccination which was made compulsory in 1905. The number of successful vaccinations rose from 46 in 1904 to 13,000 in 1907. In 1906 the first primary school (the Bale's school) was opened in the city. This was followed in 1913 by the opening of the grammar school by the Church Missionary Society. For peace and orderly government, a civil police force of 20 was inaugurated in 1903 with its number increasing to 85 by 1907.

The progress made by Ibadan over the period was being faithfully reflected in the various censuses of the country. Unlike in Lagos, however, there was no formal counting of heads until 1952. Most of the figures before 1952 were based on estimates and guesswork. The only exception was for those immigrants into the city—Europeans, non-Nigerians and Nigerians—who were recorded as living in the Ibadan Township. The Nigerians in the group were usually those who had come up to Ibadan as employees of the railway or the commercial firms. In 1921 the total population of the township was given as 2,233 (compared to Lagos, 99,690), and, as a result, Ibadan was classified as a second-class township.

The smallness of the Ibadan township population compared with that of Lagos underlines the fact that, in this era of legitimate commerce, Ibadan was bound to find its position inferior to that of Lagos and that with time it would have to yield pride of place to this rising metropolis. The figure of 2,233, however, does not represent the total number of immigrants into Ibadan at this time. Many Yorubas, especially from neighbouring groups like Ijebu, Ijesha, Oyo and Egba, who came into Ibadan at this time resided in the city proper and were not counted as part of the township population. In Lagos, by contrast, because the population had grown largely by immigration, every individual was counted as living in the township.

The breakdown of the 1921 figures (Table 21) on the basis of race or nationality and education provides an interesting insight into the character of the two centres at this time. It showed the concentration of

TABLE 21 IMMIGRANT TOWNSHIP POPULATION IN IBADAN AND LAGOS
COMPARED (1921 CENSUS)

(a) Nationality

	Ibadan	Lagos
EUROPEAN	58	1,210
NON-EUROPEAN	20	77
Non-Africans	78	1,287
NON-NIGERIANS	145	7,264
NAT. OF N. PROV.	649	9,760
NAT. OF S. PROV.	1,361	81,379
Africans	2,155	98,403
TOTAL	2,233	99,690

(b) Education

	Ibadan	Lagos
EDUCATED	310	11,547
PARTIALLY EDUCATED	253	16,902
ILLITERATE	1,670	71,241
TOTAL	2,233	99,690

major commercial activities in Lagos (cf. figures for Europeans and
educated people) and the comparative weakness of Ibadan considering
its overall size and the fact of its being on the rail-line. The 1931 Census
did not provide us with a similar breakdown for levels of education.
What it provided was an equally interesting breakdown on the basis of
sex and nationality (Table 22) for the total urban area. It showed that
in Ibadan, as in many other traditional cities in the country, there was a
preponderance of females over males. By contrast, in Lagos as in other
newer centres males were found in the majority.

The phenomenon of a relatively large female population in the older
traditional Nigerian cities, it has been stressed, represents an adjustment

TABLE 22 SEX AND NATIONALITY CHARACTERISTICS OF IBADAN AND
LAGOS POPULATION COMPARED (1931 CENSUS)

	Ibadan	Lagos	*Other Africans*	Ibadan	Lagos
MALE	167,497	70,227	MALE	—	4,506
FEMALE	219,636	55,881	FEMALE	—	2,605
TOTAL	387,133	126,108	TOTAL	—	7,111
Nigerians			*Non-Africans*		
MALE	167,321	64,519	MALE	176	1,202
FEMALE	219,586	53,035	FEMALE	50	241
TOTAL	386,907	117,554	TOTAL	226	1,443

Sources: H. B. Cox, Census of the Southern Provinces, Vol. 3 of the
Census of Nigeria, 1931, *London,* 1932, *p.* 24;
and N. J. Brooke, Census of the Northern Provinces, Vol. 2 of the
Census of Nigeria, 1931, *London,* 1933, *pp.* 59-62.

to the new economic conditions in which the role of these cities has been drastically altered. No longer can their inhabitants thrive on their craft and skill, for these have been rendered useless by the penetration of cheaply manufactured substitutes from Europe. No longer can they easily manipulate the trade of their cities, for now there are better organized and financed European business houses. No longer can they depend for their income on booty from annual raids on their weaker neighbours. In the circumstances, the erstwhile proud soldiers or sons of military chiefs, the former blacksmiths, the woodworkers or the ex-traders in slaves, must all learn the new ways. If they cannot, they must return to farming, the most elemental of human occupations. For farming, while it may not make them rich or guarantee them social position, at least ensures them against starvation and death. And may be, if the land yields some of the crops in great demand for export, they may still be able to save enough to give the next generation a start. So they accept the inevitable and depart into the rural areas to farm during weekdays and return to the cities over the weekend. Sometimes they prefer to move out completely to any one of the newly developing centres, especially Lagos. But in all cases, they continue to regard their erstwhile cities as their real home. Here they come back to build houses when it becomes financially feasible to do so. Here they may even leave their wives and children while they go away for periods on end.

In Ibadan this unusual picture of urban-rural migration is clearly exemplified. Mitchell reports that 'farmers in the *abas* or *abules* within the so-called Ibadan "urban area" spend on the average four nights of every week on their farms and three in Ibadan'.[22] He noted that modern transport had probably aided the movement, especially since the Second World War when petrol had been plentiful and prices of cocoa high. In the Ibadan Division alone four thousand villages, classified as 'other villages' in the 1952 Census, and with a population each of under a hundred, were 'discovered' during the census-taking. Most of them did not exist before the war or were then only small collections of huts. The trend which Mitchell noticed was also confirmed by Morgan who emphasized that many of the farmers no longer returned to Ibadan each week except for the two major festivals of Oke 'Badan in March and the Egungun in June.[23]

The criss-cross pattern of movements into and out of Ibadan no doubt emphasizes the complexity of the problems of development in the city. It certainly underscores the difficulty of using figures given for the city at the different censuses to tell a story of uninterrupted and rapid growth. The question to which no answer is available is, of course, what population does the census figure depict—permanent residents, those who regard Ibadan as their home, those residing within the continuous built-up area, or these plus people in surrounding villages?

By 1952 the census returned a figure of 459,196 for the city. This represented an annual rate of growth of only 0·8 per cent (compound interest) over the 21-year period from 1931. The comparable rates from 1911 to 1952 are shown in the accompanying table (Table 23) based on the various estimates of the total population provided. Does this slow rate of growth indicate the increasing tempo of de-urbanization, especially from the Second World War period as suggested by Mitchell or only the greater accuracy of the 1952 count?

TABLE 23   RATE OF GROWTH OF THE POPULATION OF IBADAN

	Total population	% Rate of growth
1911 ESTIMATE	175,000	—
1921 ESTIMATE	238,075	3·1
1931 ESTIMATE	387,133	5·0
1952 CENSUS	459,196	0·8

What all this means then is that although Ibadan as an important commercial centre was attracting an increasing number of immigrants, the effect on the total population was lost as a result of the opposite outward movement of people in the older half of the city. The breakdown of the 1952 figures demonstrates this fact amply. Compared with the 2,233 people in the township in 1921, the total number of non-Yoruba immigrants in 1952 had risen to 24,364, giving an annual growth rate of 8 per cent per annum (compound interest) over the period. This increase was just sufficient to tilt the balance as between the sexes so that Ibadan in 1952 had an excess of 14,912 males and came to show a pattern of sex distribution typical of the growing new centres. The percentage distribution was 51·6 per cent male and 48·4 per cent female. Of the 24,364 non-Yoruba immigrants, about 16,000 came from the Eastern and Mid-Western regions and 8,000 from the North. Some 400 people were classified as non-Nigerians.

The growth of Ibadan after 1952

The year 1952 has special significance for the growth of Ibadan because in that year the city became the capital of a semi-autonomous

Western Region. Since 1946 it had in fact served as headquarters of the Western Provinces. Within the colonial set-up, this earlier development was not of dramatic significance. The whole administrative organization, for instance, was contained within a single, long building called the Secretariat. The change in 1952 involved substantial transfer of political power from the British Colonial Office to the nationals of the country and began the process of ministerial appointments and cabinet rule. In terms of the administrative set-up this meant rapid expansion of staff and building in Ibadan. Where before a single block was adequate to house all the officials and clerks, now some dozen or more blocks had to be built to house the various ministries.

More than ever before, Ibadan became the focal point of political and economic activities for a region some 42,000 square miles in area. Its importance was further enhanced by the presence since 1948 of what was, until recently, the only University College, and also the most modern and best equipped teaching hospital (The University College Teaching Hospital) in the whole country (Plate 17). The increasing concentration of so many people (senior civil servants, university teachers, professionals, technicians, etc.) earning income well above the average for the region, substantially increased purchasing power in the city. By 1961, for instance, of total tax assessment units in the region earning over £300 per annum, some 53 per cent were concentrated in Ibadan alone.[24] This compares with the figure of 17 per cent for units earning less than £300 per annum.

This remarkable concentration of purchasing power in the city stimulated rapid growth in commerce and in employment opportunities. Numerous new firms were established and many of the older ones expanded. No figure exists for the number of new stores opened or of increases in the total volume of trade within the city. One fairly satisfactory index of the rapid growth of commercial activities in the city during the period is provided by the consumption of electricity by commercial and industrial enterprises (Table 24). The table shows over a tenfold increase in consumption in the short spell of nine years. In particular, the column showing increases as the percentage of consumption of the previous year clearly depicts the remarkable increase in the period 1959 to 1961 just around the independence of the country.

Although commercial activities were increasing in tempo, Ibadan did not succeed in attracting many industries. The Industrial Directory provided by the Federal Ministry of Commerce and Industry shows

TABLE 24   UNITS OF ELECTRICITY CONSUMED BY COMMERCIAL AND
INDUSTRIAL BUILDINGS IN IBADAN, 1955-64

Year	No. of units consumed (in millions)	% Change over 1955	% Increase over previous year
1955-56	1·625	100	—
1956-57	2·944	181	181
1957-58	3·165	194	108
1958-59	3·765	231	119
1959-60	6·429	396	171
1960-61	11·258	694	175
1961-62	13·388	824	119
1962-63	15·157	931	113
1963-64	17·656	1,086	116

Sources: Western Nigeria Statistical Bulletin, December 1960, p. 109;
1963, p. 12.

that in 1963 Ibadan had only 47 industrial establishments employing
over 10 people. Of these, only 9 employed more than 100 people. The
breakdown of the industries by size of employment is shown in Table
25. The only really big industry in the city is the Nigerian Tobacco
Industry with an annual turnover of £4 million and a region-wide
market. Most of the other industries of fairly large size are soft drinks,
furniture-making and tyre-retreading establishments.[25] By contrast
there are over 2,000 small-scale industries in the city employing fewer
than 10 people and usually no more than 5.[26] Most of these comprise
single-owner tailoring establishments, barbers' shops, photographic
studios, dry-cleaning, shoe-repairing and printing establishments as
well as cornmills, bakeries, beer parlours and petrol stations.

TABLE 25   NUMBER OF LARGE-SCALE INDUSTRIES IN IBADAN BY SIZE OF
EMPLOYMENT, 1963

No. of people employed	No. of establishments	% of total establishments
10-24	10	21·3
25-49	20	42·6
50-99	8	17·0
100-199	6	12·8
200-499	2	4·2
500-999	1	2·1
TOTAL	47	100

Source: Industrial Directory, Federal Ministry of Commerce and
Industry, Lagos, 1964.

Such a poor industrial base underlines the relatively slow rate of growth of the city compared with Lagos. The 1963 Census gave a figure of 625,000 for Ibadan, or a 2·8 per cent increase per annum since 1952. While this represents a considerable improvement on the earlier rate and indicates substantial immigration into the city during the period, it hardly compares with the 9 per cent per annum growth rate for Lagos during the period. The latter figure is, moreover, an understatement of the position in Lagos since it relates to increases within the municipality alone rather than to the spectacular concentration within the Greater Lagos area.

Conclusion

Today, and in spite of recent development, Ibadan remains a city with a dual personality. Its pre-European foundation constitutes a significant proportion of the city. Although this has been outstripped by the newer development in terms of area, it still commands attention because of its almost unbelievable density of buildings, their spectacular deterioration and virtual absence of adequate sanitation. Moreover, its inhabitants live their lives apart from the modern immigrants. The differences in their wealth, education, acquired skills, social customs and attitudes emphasize the social distance between the two sections of the city. Yet, given the democratic nature of elections into the city council, the numerical superiority of the traditional urbanites has helped to concentrate power in their hands. This advantage has been used to stem the tide of change, to resist the movement for slum clearance, and to prevent the participation of many enlightened and imaginative individuals in the administration of the city.

The weakness of its administrative machinery constitutes a major problem for the development of the city. Up to now, it has had the effect of preserving sharply contrasting residential neighbourhoods and non-residential districts in the two halves of the city. In the next chapter, therefore, an analysis of the internal structure of the city is offered and an attempt made to indicate broadly the forces which have operated to give rise to this structure. In this way, it is hoped the problems of the older and newer parts of the city will be highlighted. This should provide a useful basis for comparison with the completely different kind of urban development in Lagos.

References

1. I. B. Akinyele, *The Outlines of Ibadan History*, Lagos, 1946.
2. The Egungun cult is the cult of the ancestors. It is represented by masquerades, whom women are not allowed to know. The alleged crime of the Ibadans at this time was that an iconoclastic member of their community chose to break this rule in the open market-place by disrobing one of the masquerades.
3. Oke Ibadan is one of the two hills to the north-west of the artificial lake at Eleiyele that forms the reservoir for the water supply to Ibadan.
4. Bishop A. B. Akinyele recorded this fact in the record of the founding of the school. See also S. Johnson, *The History of the Yorubas*, London, 1921, p. 244.
5. C. H. Elgee, *The Evolution of Ibadan*, Lagos, 1914, p. 2. S. Johnson, op. cit., p. 224.
6. Bolanle Awe, 'Ibadan, its early beginnings', in P. C. Lloyd, A. L. Mabogunje and B. Awe (Eds), *The City of Ibadan*, London, 1967, p. 14.
7. Ibid.
8. Oja 'ba in Ibadan is a shortened form of Oja Iba and not of Oja Oba as in other Yoruba towns. Iba, in turn, is a shortened form of Ibashorun, a title taken by Oluyole, one of the most distinguished military leaders of the early Oyo-Yoruba immigrants.
9. D. Hinderer, *Journals*, September 1851, CMS Archives, CA3/049.
10. S. Johnson, op. cit., p. 325.
11. D. Hinderer, op. cit.
12. S. Johnson, *Journals*, CMS, CA2/058, June 1874.
13. D. Hinderer, *Journals*, CMS, CA2/049, September 1851.
14. J. Johnson, *The History of the Yorubas*, London, 1921, p. 327.
15. Alvan Millson, 'The Yoruba Country, West Africa', *Proceedings of the Royal Geographical Society*, Vol. 13, No. 10, October 1891, p. 583.
16. J. Barber, *Journals*, CMS, CA2/021, January-March 1857.
17. J. T. Kefer, *Journals*, CMS, CA2/059, January-June 1854.
18. C. H. Elgee, op. cit., p. 7.
19. Ibid., p. 13.
20. See Allister Macmillan, *The Red Book of West Africa*, London, 1920, pp. 63-118.
21. C. H. Elgee, op. cit., p. 11.
22. N. C. Mitchell, 'Some Comments on the Growth and Character of Ibadan's Population', *Research Notes, Department of Geography, University College, Ibadan*, No. 4, December, 1953, pp. 9-10. *Aba* or *abule* means a hamlet.
23. W. B. Morgan, 'The change from shifting to fixed settlements in Southern Nigeria', *Research Notes, Department of Geography, University College, Ibadan*, No. 7, April 1955, pp. 14-25.

24. See *Western Nigeria Statistical Bulletin*, June-December 1963.
25. See R. A. Akinola, 'The Industrial Structure of Ibadan', *Nigerian Geographical Journal*, Vol. 7, No. 2, December 1964, pp. 115-30.
26. Ibadan Town Planning Authority, *Industrial Survey*, 1963, unpublished returns.

9 The Internal Structure of Ibadan

The various theories of urban growth and development which were considered in Chapter 7 were all consistent in putting the chief business district in the fundamentally central position in a city. Both the concentric zone and the sector theories of urban growth idealized this Central Business District as a single, continuous area from where influences are transmitted radially to the periphery of the city. In place of this, the idea of twin central districts is one of the fundamental modifications to the theories that are called for in any attempt to understand the internal structure of traditional Nigerian cities. For, as has already been emphasized, these cities today represent an amalgam of two different urban processes, each of which still has its centre of intense activity and both of which continue to flourish side by side. In places like Kano and Zaria in Northern Nigeria, these two centres and their surrounding residential tracts are kept virtually distinct and separate by a wide tract of green land. The traditional city, confined within its ancient town-wall, continues to be referred to as *birni* (or 'the city'); and the new city growing rapidly to one side of it is designated *sabon gari* (or 'the new town').

In Ibadan, although part of the new development is distinguished as *sabo* (a corruption of the Hausa *sabon gari*), there is no visible demarcation between the old city and the new town. Both merge along a hazy zone of varying width where the roofing material of corrugated iron sheets is only partly rusty. The centre of the old city remains the Iba Market, and that of the new city is Gbagi, the 'pegged-out' commercial area. Both centres are so strikingly different in appearance, though not in basic functions, that it is necessary to attempt their detailed characterization.

Iba Market—the traditional urban nucleus

Iba Market is the oldest market in the city, situated on the ridge of hills in the centre of the old city (Plate 14). The map showing the stages in the growth of Ibadan (Fig. 26) emphasizes the centrality of its position. Like all Yoruba markets, it is held in the open, with a few stalls

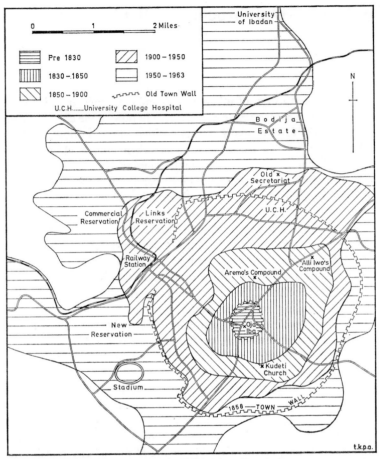

Figure 26   Stages in the growth of Ibadan, 1830-1963

to provide shade and shelter for those traders who care to sell their wares throughout the day. The market area used to be about 10 acres of hardened lateritic soil. About forty years ago the market was cut across by two roads, one running north to south and passing by Mapo Hall, the other running west to east from the Gbagi area. This invasion of the market area by roads has encouraged considerable encroachment by residential buildings. The effect today is that while the area of the market has been reduced to less than three acres, marketing activities spill out along all the roads that enter the market. Over a decade ago the position had become sufficiently serious for all roads to the market except the north-south road to be closed to vehicular traffic.

Like other urban markets in Yorubaland, the Iba Market is held throughout the day but especially from late evening to late at night. As the centre of traditional urbanism, Iba Market serves not only an economic but also a social and political function. As a social centre, it is a point of meeting for such occasions as the outing ceremony of youth societies, the burial obsequies of an aged parent or grandparent, or the festivities pertaining to individual families or sections of the city. Politically, here is where much news of local events is disseminated and, in particular, where the ceremony of installing the titular head of the city is held. A plaque in the market marks the exact site at which this ceremony is performed.

As a centre for commercial transactions, we have already seen the importance of Iba Market for long-distance trade even by the mid-nineteenth century. Hinderer's description of the market on occasions when caravans from the coast met those from the interior has been quoted *in extenso* in the preceding chapter to convey a vivid picture of the market in those days. Today the caravans have been replaced by fleets of lorries which convey to Iba Market goods and articles from an extensive hinterland. Except for the expensive hardwares of foreign manufacture, virtually any article can be purchased at Iba Market. Its distinctive character within the city is its specialization in craft articles of local manufacture. It is also noted for the relatively cheap price at which food commodities and small livestock—especially poultry, sheep and goats—can be got. As a marketing institution, it is popular because most articles can be purchased here in their smallest quantity.

Because of its variety of functions, Iba Market is a focal point for pedestrian and vehicular traffic in the city. This is particularly true in the early evenings when taxi-cabs converge here, bringing numerous passengers to the market. Lorries also carry goods (e.g. kolanuts) away from the market or bring in traders from other towns. However, since the volume of trade carried on by any single trader in any one day is not usually large, there is little need for large freight trucks and side-street off-loading facilities. Nonetheless, where the volume of trade is great or the articles being sold demand it, shops have replaced open-air vending of goods. Such small shops line the streets leading away from the market and their restocking does involve occasional visits of large freight trucks.

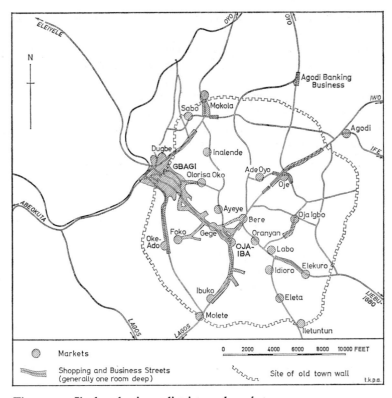

Figure 27   Ibadan: business districts and markets

Although the Iba Market occupies a premier position in the traditional commercial activities of the city, there are, within Ibadan, a
number of other markets serving neighbourhood as well as specialized
marketing functions (Fig. 27). Because of the diversity of the goods
more frequently sold and the periodicity of marketing activities, it is
not easy today to identify a hierarchy among the markets below the Iba
Market. Generally most markets operate every day during the daytime.
The intensity of marketing activities seems to be related either to the
income density in the neighbourhood or to the specialized character of
the market. Thus Dugbe Market, located roughly in the middle of the
immigrant half of the city close by the Gbagi Business District, is easily
the most important day market in the city. The commodities vended
range from imported groceries, chinawares and haberdashery to locally

produced vegetables and fruits. In this respect it is replicated farther north in the Mokola Market which is also a day-time daily market, in the immigrant half of the city. Gege and Ayeye Markets, a little to the west of Iba Market on the other hand, specialize in locally produced foodstuffs while Oje in the north-east is unique as an eight-day market serving alternately for the selling of traditional woven cloth and home-made soap. There are a number of other day-time markets specializing in the sale of foodstuffs but in areas where income density is inadequate to support daily trading activities. Such markets function on a periodic basis at four-day intervals. They are noted for their location on the edge of the older part of the city and include Ibuko, Eleta, Elekuro and Oja Igbo. At these markets the city establishes a direct relation with its rural districts. Every four days there is an influx into the city of people offering the produce of their farms directly for sale to the city women.

In spite of modern developments, these traditional forms of trading activities remain very strong within the city. A large part of their strength and resilience derives from the dominant position of women in their operation. Although only few of the women trade on a scale which can be described as large, for the majority the attraction of the market is that it allows small-scale, petty trading at negligible overhead costs and, by the same token, for little profit. Given the Yoruba society, the strong emphasis on the financial independence of women, and the generally low level of income, it is difficult to foresee a time when the market in its essential aspects will disappear from the urban scene. Within Ibadan and for as long as this situation subsists, Iba Market will continue to play its major role as the most important trading area for the older and relatively poorer half of the city.

Gbagi Business District

Gbagi is the modern central business district of the city. It is 'central' only in the sense of being the most important concentration of business activities in the city. In geographic terms, however, it is well displaced from the city centre towards the western margin (Plate 16).

The origin of the centre dates from 1903, two years after the city had been connected to Lagos by a rail-line. The dependence on the rail-line is clearly reflected in the close proximity of the centre to the railway station. As already pointed out, this area was divided into leasehold plots early in the century and allocated by the Ibadan Council on an annual rental basis of between £5 and £8. Elgee noted that in 1906 'in

210 URBANIZATION IN NIGERIA

the case of land leased to settlers, it was ordered that broad streets be pegged out and not allowed to be built on, with a view to construction when funds permitted'.

It has already been indicated that all this 'pegging out' activity served to give the area its local name. More than this, however, it represented a rationale of space organization different in type and scale from that of Iba Market. Every European firm had its plot, just as every trader had his small position in the market. But whereas the position in the market carried no investment, the commercial plot received large-scale investment in the form of shop-buildings, offices, banks and stores. Once these structures had been put up, it was not easy to relocate them. They were space-consuming and fairly permanent. A situation like that at Iba Market where roads were cut through the market easily would here have posed real difficulties.

The Gbagi Business District covers an area of nearly 350 acres. It is served by four major roads which run almost parallel in their western half but converge to form a single street at their eastern end (Fig. 28). To the west they are all linked by another street running almost north-south. Unlike the Iba Market, the need of vehicles for parking space and an unrestricted flow dominates the layout and building design in this new business area. Furthermore, the great demand for land gives scarcity value to plots within the district and encourages competition for choice sites. Initially this competition was not reflected in the rent paid for the land. The system of long leases and the compulsory acquisitions of land by government obscured the situation for a time. Although the chief rent-deciding factor was nearness to the railway station, the land immediately adjacent to the station itself was acquired by government at hardly any rent and is still not completely built over today. Beyond it, however, begins the commercial area proper where the effect of competition is already starting to lead to significant areal differentiation within the district.

As must be obvious, the ability to compete for a choice site is dependent on rent-paying capacity. The latter in turn is greatly affected by the scale of operation. In Ibadan the scale of operation is closely related to the racial complexion of Nigerian trade. Bauer observed in 1949 that about 85 per cent of the import trade of Nigeria was handled by European firms, about 10 per cent by Levantine and Indian firms, and about 5 per cent by African firms.[1] Even with national independence, it is still true to say that as much as 80 per cent of the country's import trade is in

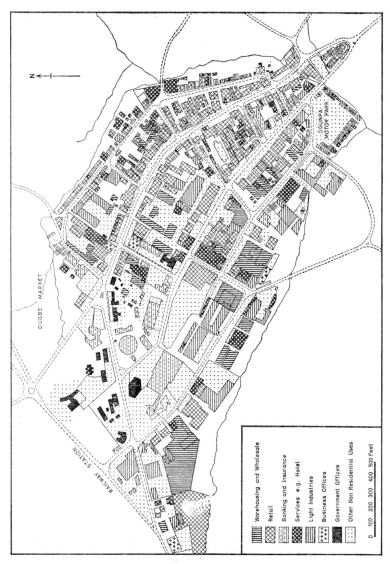

Figure 28   Gbagi Business District

the hands of European firms. These firms are distinguished by the large-scale nature of their operations which ensures their highly competitive position. The result is that their location in Ibadan is closest to the railway station after the government acquisition.

In the last ten years the scarcity value of land in Gbagi is more clearly reflected in the number of multi-storey buildings being constructed. The major departmental stores, notably the Kingsway and A. G. Leventis, occupying many square feet of area, now rise to three or four floors. The Co-operative building, the Finance Corporation building and Cocoa House each rises over ten floors and contains numerous offices. Most other businesses have been increasing their total floor space by building higher and bigger.

On the eastern side away from the railway station the European firms are succeeded by the Levantine and Indian firms. These usually occupy two-storey buildings of which the bottom storey is used as a shop and the upper storey as a residence. Most of these buildings occupy relatively restricted space, giving no more than thirty to forty feet of frontage on the street. The shops are very specialized, dealing largely in textiles, articles of clothing and some jewelry. They extend as far as the Ogunpa Stream which marks the eastern edge of the Gbagi Business District proper. Beyond, it is succeeded by a long line of small one-storey African shops.

To the south and north the margins of the Gbagi Business District are marked by a line of motor sales and repair garages, notably those of J. Allen (Ford cars mainly), the United Trading Company (Opel cars), the S.C.O.A. (Peugeot) and A. G. Leventis (Mercedes) on the south and that of C.F.A.O. (Morris) on the north. The need of these semi-industrial businesses for relatively cheaper land on which to build their largely one-storey structures probably explains their preference for peripheral location.

The theory of the retail structure of towns leads us to expect that, given a certain income density, there would be generated other lower-order retail concentrations within the city at some distance away from the Gbagi Central Business District.[2] In the descending hierarchical order postulated by Proudfoot, the next type of retail conformation we should expect is that of an outlying business centre—a miniature central business district at focal points of intra-city transportation and featuring such retail units as clothing, furniture and shoe stores, motor showrooms and an admixture of convenience-goods stores. Although no

such conformation has fully emerged in Ibadan, it is possible to specu-
late on where they may be expected to develop. Already there is an
interesting concentration developing at Mokola in the north-west and
Molete in the south-west, both areas being almost equidistant from the
Gbagi area. Both areas have motor-showrooms and furniture stores at
present as well as an admixture of convenience-goods stores. No other
part of the city shows any such retail elements. In fact, in the larger
eastern portion of the city where the level of income is generally low,
only the lowest-order retail concentrations of neighbourhood business
street type is found. Usually, as if to emphasize their neighbourhood
importance, such business streets terminate in the local markets.

In terms of the amount of business transacted, Ibadan can be said to
have a principal business thoroughfare. This comprises the road leading
from the Gbagi Business District eastward as far as Bere, a distance of
over a mile. Both sides of the thoroughfare are lined by a continuous
succession of small African stores (Plate 19) occupying single-storey
buildings and usually only one room deep. As a principal business thoroughfare, the stretch of road shows a succession of trade. The first half-
mile from the Gbagi Business District specializes in imported hardware
and enamel, leather and plastic goods, small electrical wares and a wide
range of convenience goods. The section just beyond the Agbeni
Methodist Church concentrates on local foodstuffs. The final section,
east of the junction of Ayeye Street, specializes in cheap school text-
books.

The interaction of the twin centres

To understand the internal structure of Ibadan it is necessary to
appreciate the nature of the interaction of these two major centres of
economic activity in the city—Iba Market and Gbagi. Up to now,
Ibadan has no important area of industrial concentration so that no
other nucleus needs to be considered at this stage. Clearly, the Gbagi
Business District is the major centre of gravity of economic activity in
Ibadan. As a result, it tends to dominate the Iba Market and to influence locational decisions everywhere in the city. For most people
there is invariably a need to go to Gbagi either to work or to shop and
there is therefore a great advantage in living not too far away from the
district. Theoretically, such a situation would tend to encourage a high
concentration of residences around this centre. Since, however, in
urban life there are other values and satisfactions that people are

anxious to maximize, e.g. spacious dwellings, quiet, privacy, open grounds, etc., not everyone reacts equally to this pull of the centre. But indifference to the pull depends on two conditions, namely, high income and a convenient means of daily transportation to the centre.

In Ibadan, while these conditions are met in the ever-expanding, peripheral areas on the western part of the city where the wealthier people live, the eastern periphery contains largely low income people who can hardly afford the cost of motorized transport to the Gbagi Business Centre. The immediate effect of this is to put a definite limit to continued eastward expansion of the city and to encourage a process of residential concentration within the area already built-up before 1900. Indeed, it is notable that in spite of the remarkable increase in its population since the nineteenth century, the traditional city, checked to the west by the new developments after 1901, has not even today expanded on the eastern side beyond the 1851 wall. Rather in an attempt not to be too far away from the Gbagi Business District, new residences have tended to fill in every available space within the traditional city, and to create conditions of hazardous congestion. This effect of the Gbagi Business District becomes clearer when we consider the details of the residential districts of Ibadan. Nevertheless, since the social and economic characteristics of the population also underlie the contrasts in the residential districts, we shall begin by turning attention to these.

The spatial pattern of socio-economic characteristics

(a) The age and sex distribution

Table 26 shows the age and sex distribution of the Ibadan population in 1952. It contrasts this with the national and regional situation so as to emphasize the pattern of deviation in Ibadan. The most important fact that emerges is that adult males and females form a lower proportion, while children, especially those under 2 years of age, form a higher proportion of the total population of the city than is the case for either the region or the country as a whole. This situation is the reverse of what might be expected in a growing modern centre and becomes understandable only when we investigate the detailed distribution within Ibadan itself.

In 1952, the city of Ibadan was divided into 39 wards varying in area from about 30 acres to over a square mile of densely built-up area. These wards lie astride a ridge of hills trending generally north-west to

TABLE 26   IBADAN: AGE AND SEX DISTRIBUTION

	IBADAN		WEST REGION		NIGERIA	
	Male	Female	Male	Female	Male	Female
Sex distribution	51·6	48·4	49·5	50·5	48·9	51·1
0-2 YEARS	15·8	16·6	11·4	12·1	11·1	12·8
3-6 YEARS	18·6	18·6	18·1	17·1	18·0	16·9
7-14 YEARS	20·9	19·8	18·0	16·1	17·0	15·4
15-49 YEARS	36·6	36·8	45·3	46·6	46·6	46·4
50 + YEARS	8·1	8·2	7·2	8·1	7·3	8·5
	100·0	100·0	100·0	100·0	100·0	100·0

south-east (see Fig. 24). This ridge represents, in general, not only a physical watershed but also a major socio-economic divide in the city (Plate 15). To the east of it lives the indigenous population; to the west the immigrants. The indigenous population, however, spills over the ridge and especially in the southern half predominates in wards along the western slope as far as the Ogunpa Stream. By contrast, the immigrants spill over eastward on the north to check further expansion of the indigenous Ibadan in this direction. In short, we find that the two central wards, all of the nine east wards and all the seven south wards are occupied by indigenous Ibadan. The indigenous population also predominates in at least four of the six north wards, in five of the nine south-west wards and in three of the six north-west wards. The nine wards in which immigrants predominate are, however, individually some of the largest in the city and have been growing very rapidly in the last decade.

Fig. 29 shows the variation in the relative importance of adult males in the population of the various wards. It reveals a higher concentration in the north-west immigrant section while in the rest of the city, especially in the areas of indigenous population, it shows a relative predominance of children. This is clearly in keeping with the thesis of de-urbanization outlined in Chapter 5 which stresses that in those traditional centres where the economic base had been undermined by modern development, the adults have tended to emigrate. In the case of Ibadan, the only other major urban centre that could offer better employment opportunities is Lagos. Since, however, it is unlikely that emigrants to Lagos would leave their children behind (considering the better social facilities in Lagos), we conclude that most of the movements out of the city are to rural areas for less than permanent residence. The situation in Ward SW8, which records one of the lowest proportions

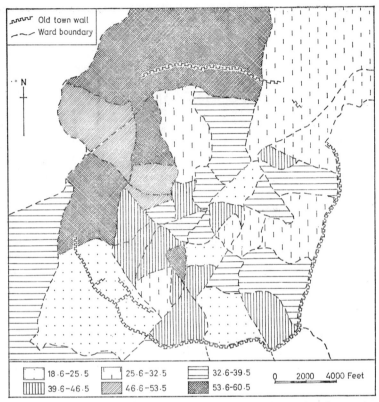

Figure 29   Ibadan: adult males as a percentage of the total male population (1952 Census)

of adult males, is related to the concentration in this area of most of the grammar schools in the city with their boarding houses.

(b) Ethnic distribution

Ibadan is, of course, a Yoruba city and the centre of the most prosperous cocoa-producing area of the region. As such, it has attracted a large number of Yoruba who are not 'indigenes' in the sense of the early nineteenth century immigrants who now think of themselves as 'Ibadan' and distinct from other subgroups of the Yorubas. The immigrant Yoruba groups comprise Ijebus, Egbas, Ijeshas, Oyos and, more recently, Ekitis and Ondos. Unfortunately the 1952 Census provides no breakdown of the Yoruba on the basis of provincial derivation so

that it tends to understate the extent to which the population of Ibadan
is made up of immigrants and is heterogeneous in composition.

Table 27 describes the ethnic composition in Ibadan and compares it
with both the regional and national situation. It shows, for instance,
that in 1952 only about 5 per cent of the total population of the city was
not Yoruba compared with nearly 30 per cent for the region and 83 per
cent for the whole country.

TABLE 27   IBADAN: ETHNIC COMPOSITION, 1952

	IBADAN	WEST REGION	NATIONAL
YORUBA	94·7	70·8	17·0
HAUSA/FULANI	1·2	0·8	28·2
IBO	1·6	5·9	18·0
OTHER NORTHERN TRIBES	0·5	0·3	11·3
OTHER SOUTHERN TRIBES	1·9	22·0	25·4
NON-NIGERIANS	0·1	0·2	0·1
	100·0	100·0	100·0

On the face of it, these figures tend to belie the high degree of ethnic
heetrogeneity which one associates with a city the size of Ibadan. Four
points, however, need be made with respect to these figures. In the
first place, as has been mentioned above, the high figure for Yoruba in
Ibadan obscures the very significant immigration of non-Ibadan Yoruba
into the city. Secondly, the relatively higher regional figure for non-
Yoruba reflects the fact that before the creation of the Mid-West Region
the Western Region contained a significant non-Yoruba population,
notably Ibo and Edo. It is this that raises the regional percentage of
Ibo and other southern tribes in the regional distribution and under-
mines the impression of heterogeneity in the Ibadan population. Thirdly
the position with regard to the Hausa Fulani and other northern tribes
is perhaps more typical of the relation of Ibadan to the region as a whole.
The proportion of these groups to the total population in Ibadan is
about half as much again as in the region. The implication of this is
that, as one would expect, Ibadan attracts proportionally more northern
migrants than does the region as a whole. Lastly, there is the group of
non-Nigerian immigrants for whom Ibadan's attractive power appears
to be less than that of the region and about the same as for the whole
country. Here the picture is grossly distorted because of the inclusion
of Lagos in the Western Region. In 1952, Lagos in fact accounted for
22 per cent of all non-Nigerians in the country and 74 per cent of all

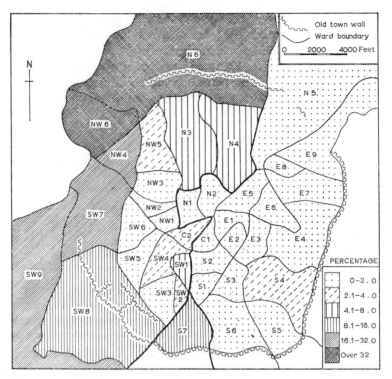

Figure 30   Ibadan: percentage of non-Yorubas in wards

those in the Western Region. When the figures for Lagos are excluded, the regional percentage comes down to 0·05 compared with 0·1 for Ibadan—a result consistent with the greater relative pull Ibadan exerts on even this class of immigrant.

Fig. 30 shows the spatial pattern of ethnic segregation in the city. Basically it shows that the eastern half of the city is predominantly Yoruba while the western half has a significant proportion of non-Yoruba. Attention is drawn to the interval of the shading which is made geometric in order to emphasize the relatively small degree of heterogeneity. Furthermore, the thick line running north-north-east to south-south-west is crucial. Although on both sides of it are wards with a relatively low percentage of non-Yoruba, the line, based on observation, virtually separates wards where the predominant Yoruba population is Ibadan-born (i.e. those east of the line) and wards where most of these are non-Ibadan immigrants (i.e. those west of the line). What is equally interesting is that a comparison of Fig. 30 with Fig. 24 shows that this line runs for most of its course along the crest of the ridge. To this extent, it is easy to appreciate the importance of this feature not only as a physical divide but also as a demographic and socio-economic divide in the city.

(c) Education and religious characteristics

Table 28 shows the educational and religious characteristics of the population of Ibadan. It emphasizes that, compared with the region and the nation, the city has a higher proportion of its population with at least Standard Two pass but it has a lower proportion able to read and write than the region. The reason for this second situation is not clear but is probably related to the preponderance of Moslems in the Ibadan population. In other words, following the history of literacy development in the country which has been due largely to Christian missionary efforts one can expect a negative correlation between the proportion of the population which is Moslem and the proportion able to read and write.

TABLE 28   IBADAN: EDUCATIONAL AND RELIGIOUS CHARACTERISTICS, 1952

	IBADAN	WEST REGION	NATIONAL
STD. II AND OVER	14·2	7·5	3·7
ABLE TO READ AND WRITE	8·9	9·4	2·4
ILLITERATES	76·9	83·1	93·9
MOSLEMS	59·9	32·8	35·3
CHRISTIANS	32·2	36·9	29·8
ANIMIST	7·9	30·3	34·7

The spatial pattern of variation of these variables, however, does not strongly support this supposition. Fig. 31, which shows the distribution of the percentage of Moslems (a) and the percentage of literates (b) does not indicate a sufficient correlation. It is true that Ward SW7 with the lowest percentage of Moslems also has the highest percentage of literates and that a number of wards with a very high Moslem population (SW1, SW2, and S7) have some of the lowest percentages of literates but the position is far from consistent and some areas with a relatively high proportion of Moslems also show a relatively high percentage of literates.

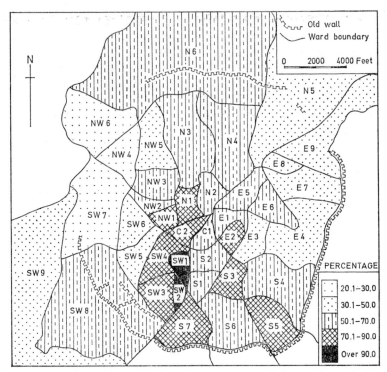

Figure 31 (*a*)   Ibadan: Moslems as percentage of the total population (1952 Census)

(*d*) *Economic characteristics*

Ibadan's role as a major trading and craft centre is clearly brought out in Table 29. The table shows that although a substantial proportion of both the male and female population is involved in agricultural activities, this is very much less than either the regional or the national average. By contrast, the proportion of the non-agricultural male population is three times as much as the regional and four times as much as the national proportion. The importance of women in the trading activities of the city is also well brought out by the table.

Fig. 32 shows the spatial distribution of the various occupations. It shows, for instance, that the agricultural males tend to be important in a belt running north-east to south-west in the eastern half of the city. Areas towards the eastern periphery tend to be less agricultural—a fact no doubt indicative of some progress in suburban development. To the

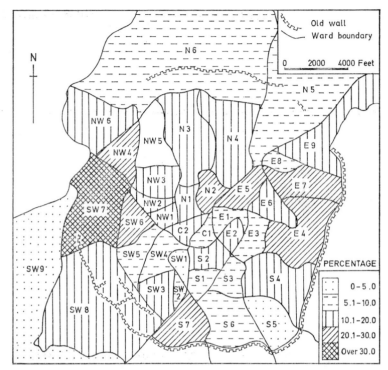

Figure 31 (b)   Ibadan: Literates as percentage of the total population (1952 Census)

west, the predominance of immigrants with no claims to local agricultural land is reflected in the low percentage of males in agriculture.

The map for craft shows a concentration in the centre of the city with two wards—N1 around Bere Square and SW6 near Ogunpa dominat-

TABLE 29   OCCUPATIONAL STRUCTURE OF IBADAN, 1952

	IBADAN		WESTERN REGION		NATIONAL	
	Male	*Female*	*Male*	*Female*	*Male*	*Female*
AGRICULTURE/FISHING	21·6	20·7	36·9	37·0	42·7	32·1
TRADING, ETC.	12·0	29·1	5·3	14·1	3·4	11·2
CRAFT	13·4	—	4·1	—	3·3	—
A DMIISTRATIVE/						
PROFESSIONAL	5·3	—	2·2	—	1·5	—
OTHER OCCUPATIONS	9·6	—	5·0	—	3·7	—
OTHERS	38·1	50·2	46·5	48·9	45·4	56·7

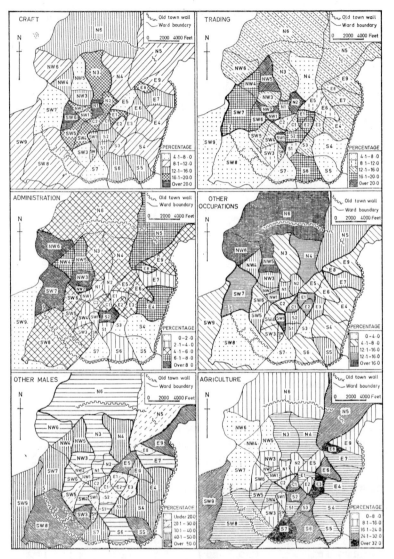

Figure 32   Ibadan: percentage of male population in different occupations (1952 Census)

ing. The wards with largely immigrant population do not show a strong orientation to craft. Compared with the map of ethnic derivations, it is clear that trading and administrative occupations are the essential economic functions of immigrants in Ibadan. The two other maps— 'other occupied males' and 'other males' are more difficult to interpret. In the case of the former, it appears that there are two broad groups of activities included. One group is probably oriented to the needs of immigrants and hence is found in wards on the western periphery of the city; the other is probably tied to traditional needs and hence is found in the centre of the city. The map representing the distribution of the residual male population excites certain interesting comments. Low residual male population characterizes a belt running across the city with a generally north-west-southeast alignment. It excludes much of the immigrant wards where it can be assumed that children will tend to be unoccupied and in school. It also leaves out most of the eastern wards where the map of literacy shows some fairly high percentages.

To conclude this section of the socio-economic characteristics of Ibadan, two facts should now be evident. The first is that there is by and large a basic contrast in the socio-economic characteristics of the indigenous and immigrant population of Ibadan. The former tends to be more homogeneous, largely Moslem, less literate, more agricultural and with a relatively higher proportion of children among its population. The immigrants are heterogeneous, largely Christian, more literate, occupied largely in trade and administration and with a relatively higher proportion of adult males and females. As against this is the second fact that the spatial pattern of distribution for these variables shows no clear-cut tendencies. Hardly any two maps show a high degree of correspondence and it has been difficult to establish, purely on the basis of the maps, which variables show any strong tendency to vary with each other.

In the circumstance, a statistical examination of variables which intuitively can be expected to correlate with each other was undertaken. Table 30 shows the result of investigating a possible relationship between the social and economic characteristics of the population. Two aspects of the table demand attention: the direction of the relationship between the variables, whether positive or negative; and the level of significance of the relationship. From the table it is clear that an educational level of attainment of at least Standard II is correlated positively with craft activities, administration and the professions and negatively with trading and other occupations. The relationship, however, is significant only in the case of administration and professional activities. The same pattern is clear in the case of the relationship between all those able to read and write in Roman script and the various occupational groupings. Non-Yorubas are shown to feature positively in all non-agricultural activities but the relationship is only clearly significant with respect to administrative and professional and particularly with regard to other occupations. In fact, the correlation in the latter case is sufficiently high that clearly it can be said that more than half the explanations ($r^2 = 0.52$) for the pattern of distribution of those engaged in 'other occupations' is provided by the distribution of the non-Yorubas. Lastly, the presence of a large Moslem population is shown to lead to a somewhat lower proportion of people with education of at least Standard II level—the inverse correlation co-efficient, however, being significant only at the 5 per cent level.

TABLE 30   CORRELATION BETWEEN SELECTED SOCIAL AND ECONOMIC VARIABLES

	7 Std. II pass and above	8 Total literate	9 Non- Yorubas	10 Moslems
1. NON-AGRIC. FEMALES		−0·04	+0·18	+0·18
2. NON-AGRIC. MALES		0·02	+0·64***	−0·10
3. MALES—TRADING	−0·12	−0·12	+0·28	
4. —CRAFT	+0·18	+0·24	+0·32	
5. ADM/PROF.	+0·40**	+0·43**	+0·47**	
6. MALES—OTHER OCCUPATIONS	−0·28	−0·29	+0·72***	
7. STD. II PASS AND ABOVE			+0·27	−0·33*

*** Significant at 0·1% level
**   „   „ 1·0% level
*   „   „ 5·0% level

The nature of the residential districts

The social and economic characteristics provide an important background to understanding the types of residential districts in the city. Fig. 33 is an attempt to divide the city into seven broad residential regions. Basically, however, these regions fall into three broad types:

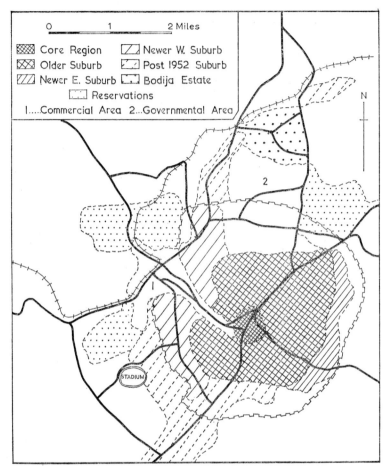

Figure 33   Ibadan: residential regions

(a) Older, low quality residential districts comprising the core region and the older suburbs;

(b) Newer, low to medium quality residential districts comprising the newer eastern and western suburbs as well as the post-1952 suburbs;

(c) High quality residential districts comprising the Bodija Housing Estate and the Reservations.

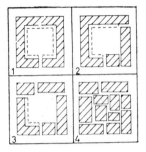

Figure 34 The traditional compound: stages in the process of 'growth by fission'

(a) *The older residential districts*

These districts are found in the central areas of the city. They are occupied largely by the indigenous Ibadan population and the early non-Ibadan Yoruba immigrants. Their physical character can be understood only in terms of changes leading to the disintegration of traditional compounds as a result of a process which the writer has described elsewhere as 'growth by fission'.[3] Fundamentally, growth by fission is due to the breakdown in the control-mechanism within the extended family system. This control-mechanism resided, as it were, in the powers of the head of an extended family over the family land at a time when every member of the family depended in one way or the other on agricultural land for his source of income. With modern developments, many members of a family can now turn to non-agricultural employment, and even those in agriculture can look forward to highly profitable returns from cocoa cultivation. As a result, the powers of the head of the extended family have been greatly weakened and the cohesiveness of the family considerably impaired. Add to this the disruptive influence of both Islam and Christianity in their preference for the nuclear family (polygamous or monogamous) and some of the factors contributing to the disintegration of the compound and the individualization of housing units become clear.

The result is that the traditional compound has been broken up into a number of separate housing units (Fig. 34). Evidence of the physical assault on the compounds is literally obvious in the rough edges of some of the new housing units. This development must be seen in

Plate 20 Lagos Marina in the 1880s
Plate 21 The port of Lagos today

Plate 22   Lagos Island with Carter Bridge in the background
Plate 23   An old 'colonial-type' house

conjunction with the pull of the Gbagi Commercial Centre which tended to check any expansion eastward. The result has been that this break-up of the traditional compound in the eastern half of the city has gone hand in hand with the concentration of new buildings on every available space within and around the compound. Today a large part of this area is characterized by the closely-packed and jumbled nature of numerous houses, many of which are only one storey high.

Fig. 35 shows the population and accommodation densities in the city. Within the limits of the older, low quality residential districts, it shows two areas with the highest density of population in the city. Their figures ranged from 600 to 1,000 persons per acre. Both areas are contiguous to the two commercial centres—Gbagi and Oja Iba—in the city. The high density near Oja Iba is, in fact, coincident with the core region. Here, however, high population density has not given rise to high accommodation densities. This situation results from the advanced stage of the individualization of housing which has been shown to be characteristic of this area. This has meant the presence of many small, one-storey houses with average dimensions of about 25 ft. × 40 ft. and an average of four rooms. A room for the purpose of the map is any enclosed space which is inhabited irrespective of its size and it is not infrequent that the size of rooms in this part of the city is no more than 8 ft. × 10 ft.

The high density area close to Gbagi comprises Agbeni, Amunigun and Agbokojo districts of the city. These are the areas occupied by the early twentieth-century immigrants into the city. The quality of houses is only a shade better than those around Oja Iba, the basic distinction being that most of them are plastered with cement and have not resulted from the physical break-up of pre-existing compounds. A good number of houses, while conforming to the rectangular layout of compounds, were built from the start as individual units. The immigrant character of the area is shown in the high accommodation densities of the area. The figure of 4·6 persons per habitable room is the highest in the city. Part of the reason for congestion here is the relatively high rent paid for rooms in the neighbourhood, since this is where young, uneducated, immigrants just arriving in the city and without much of an income tend to concentrate. Elsewhere in the area of the older suburb, population densities remain relatively high, varying generally between 200 and 400 persons per acre. Accommodation densities tend to vary between 2·5 to 4·0 persons per habitable room.

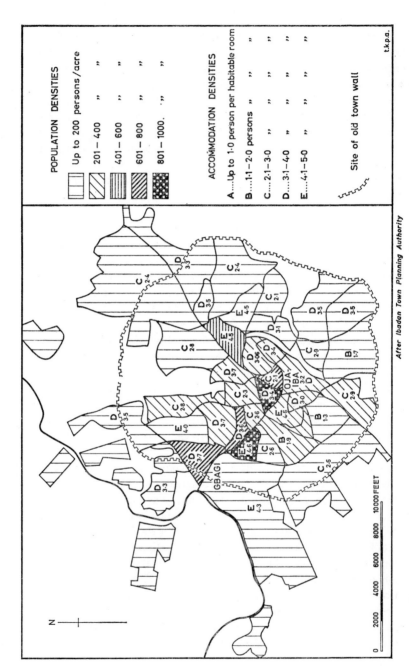

Figure 35   Ibadan: resident population and accommodation densities

(b) The newer residential districts

The area of low to medium quality residential districts stands out on Fig. 35 as having generally lower population densities usually below 200 persons per acre. The only exception is Ward NW4 (Ekotedo) where densities are in the range 600 to 800. In spite of the relatively low population densities, however, accommodation densities are not much lower than in the older suburb. The explanation of this fact takes different form in different parts of the area and underlines the basic division of residential districts here into three regions—the newer eastern suburb, the newer western suburb and the post-1952 suburb.

The newer eastern suburb represents an extension of the older suburb occupied by the indigenous Ibadan. Most of its residents are younger members of families for whom there is no longer any land within the old family compound. Often their new houses, mainly bungalows of four to six rooms, are built in the modern fashion to contain an immediate family group. The majority of these people are farmers who can afford to build only with mud, but those who are wealthy farmers or prosperous traders and contractors build their new houses more solidly with bricks and cement plaster and sometimes with more than one storey. The more attractive appearance of these houses has paid dividends in the form of rent from letting out rooms to some of the service population, notably teachers, who work in numerous schools newly established on this eastern edge of the city. The location of these schools on the outskirts of the built-up area in 1955, when free primary education was introduced by the Regional Government, is one useful indicator of the congested conditions within the older suburb.

The newer western suburb in many ways sharply contrasts with the newer eastern suburb. Most of its population is immigrant and, unlike the older immigrant suburb, comprises a sizeable proportion of non-Yoruba elements, notably Ibo, Hausa, Edo, Nupe, Urhobo and Ibibio. These non-Yoruba elements settle largely in the north-western part of the city and their concentration here is partly responsible for the high population density of the Ekotedo area. In the early phase of immigration into the area, the City Council divided land here into building plots. It put these out on leasehold for ninety-nine years, first to indigenous speculators in land. Some of the far-sighted ones built houses on their plots and let them to the incoming migrants. Many others, particularly in the south-west, sold their rights privately. In the southwest, most of the buyers of leasehold rights were the business-minded

Ijebu traders, a neighbouring Yoruba subgroup whose capital city is some forty miles south of Ibadan. Because of their greater wealth, the houses they built were superior in design (mainly Brazilian-type), construction and taste to most of those in the north-west or anywhere else in the city at the time. This south-western suburb, deriving other advantages from its nearness to the commercial centre and to numerous secondary educational institutions, attracted a higher class of residents, among them professional people such as doctors, lawyers and teachers as well as a large number of white-collar workers in business and the Civil Service. The latter group came to be numerically dominant after 1939, when Ibadan was made the headquarters of the Western Provinces and increased even more after 1952 when the city became the capital of an almost autonomous region.

Because in the 1930s and 1940s most of the new immigrants to the south-west suburb were young men, often just leaving school, the houses were built as tenement houses. They consisted of a double row of rooms opening on a common passage that led at one end out to the street and at the other to a backyard with a common kitchen, bathroom and latrine. The idea was to build the house so that a number of young bachelors could each rent a room. If one married, he could rent two or three rooms in a row. The average bungalow had six to ten rooms; the average two-storeyed building twelve to twenty rooms. There are a few instances of three or four-storeyed buildings with thirty to forty rooms on a plot 50 ft. × 100 ft.

Except for laying out plots, the city council undertook no improvement in the suburbs. In the north-west the streets were marked but not actually constructed. As a result, encroachments by greedy house-owners has tended to obliterate them and today only a few provide easy access to houses by vehicular transport. In the south-west, by contrast, through the exertions of the residents, the streets are laid out, though not always kept in good repair because of the incessant erosion by the heavy rains.

The post-1952 suburb arose out of the need to provide accommodation for a somewhat different class of Nigerians coming into Ibadan after 1952. The aftermath of the political autonomy of the region has been a sharp increase in the demand for better qualified officers in the Civil Service. Commerce also felt a need to keep up with the times by encouraging the Nigerianization of many of their posts. The professional and entrepreneurial class was also greatly augmented, especially as a result of the ever expanding opportunities that were being created for the exercise of individual talent and ability. Apart from these groups, there was the new class of politicians both at the regional and local levels.

These various groups demanded more spacious accommodation, better equipped with modern sanitary and household amenities. At first, most of the houses were built in the new Brazilian style but were let out on the 'open apartment' system. In this system, an individual rents one of the two rows of three or four rooms on the floor of a house. Along with this go a separate kitchen, storeroom and toilet facilities. Since all the rooms open on a corridor shared with the family opposite, the apartment is not really self-contained, hence the term 'open apartment'. Later, more variety of layout and design were noticeable in the construction of houses in this suburb—all calculated to give privacy and ensure a greater degree of comfort and convenience to the occupier.

The largest area of post-1952 development is in the south-west of the city beyond the nineteenth century city wall. Similar development, although on a much smaller scale, has taken place in the north-west and north-east of the city as well as in pockets of formerly unbuilt areas within the older and newer suburbs. Because of their background, most of the residents are monogamous; because of their age, with few children; and because of their immigrant origin, with few dependants. Yet, owing to the configuration of ward boundaries such that the areas in post-1952 development are included along with older areas of high accommodation densities, their extent is only slightly apparent on Fig. 35.

(c) *High quality residential districts*

High quality residential districts comprise the five 'Reservations' to the north, north-west and south-west of the city as well as the Bodija Estate. These areas are distinguished by their very low population and accommodation densities which do not stand out clearly in Fig. 35 because of the tendency already noted for wards on the city borders to be very large and highly variable in character. In these residential districts, houses are set in the midst of extensive lawns, often hedged round with shrubs and flowering plants such as *bougainvillaea*, *allamanda* and *hibiscus*. The average density is two to four houses per acre with not infrequent instances of houses with more than an acre of garden.

The Reservations developed initially as a means of providing accommodation for a special type of immigrants into Ibadan, namely, the Europeans. The first Europeans to arrive were the missionaries in 1851 who were lodged in the south-eastern part of the city in what was then a newly growing suburb. In 1893, with the expansion of British influence into the hinterland of Lagos, a British Resident was posted to Ibadan. He established the Residency on Agodi Hill just outside the city wall to the north. This later grew to become one of the five large residential districts specially reserved for Europeans. However, the first real reservation came with the railway, which reached Ibadan in 1901. This was the Jericho Reservation, west of the city wall and centering on the Jericho Hospital. By 1931 the Europeans in the city numbered about 150, and most were engaged on the railway, in local administration, in the medical services and in trade.

When in 1939 Ibadan became the headquarters of the Western Provinces, a large secretariat was built not far from the former Residency. Many more Europeans moved into Ibadan and swelled the population in the Agodi and Jericho Reservations. Since then, Ibadan has continued to atttact Europeans, either as civil servants or as managers of the many commercial and industrial enterprises. By 1952 their number had reached more than two thousand, and three new Reservations had to be established—the Commercial, the Links and the New Reservations.

Up to 1952 the Reservations were occupied almost exclusively by Europeans. Since that date there has been an influx of Nigerians of similar status due to the political changes in that year. This has led to a remarkable expansion of the area of the Reservations. Today, although part of the Reservation land has passed from public to private ownership, the high-class character of dwellings in the area continues to be preserved.

As an alternative method of providing high-class residential facilities, the Regional Government in 1959 established a Housing Corporation which provided the first planned housing estate in the city. The Bodija Housing Estate, as it is called, is north of the city and covers an area of nearly 400 acres (Plate 18). When completed it is to have about 1,200 houses of varying sizes with facilities for shopping, religious and educational needs as well as a playing-field. By 1965 most of the houses had been built. Those built by private arrangement are on plots ranging from $\frac{1}{4}$ acre to one acre and are of varying architectural design and construction but approved by the Town Planning Authority. All classes of houses are provided with modern facilities and conveniences including a garden. The idea is to have a 'balanced community' of various income groups on the estate. Nonetheless, in spite of what is evidently a mistaken philosophy of neighbourhood development, the Bodija Estate has failed to attract most members of the low-income classes largely because of the relatively high deposit required and the high monthly mortgage repayment. The result is that the size of housing has not been a major indicator of differences in income and most of its inhabitants belong to the class of white-collar civil servants and professionals.

North of the Bodija Estate are the campuses of the University of Ibadan and the local branch of the University of Ife. Both together are about five square miles in area and provide accommodation for most of their senior staff as well as the students. With the exception of the quarters for the junior staff, which tend to be congested, the residences on the campuses have the same character, population and accommodation densities as the Reservations.

Conclusion

As a city with great potential for future growth, Ibadan presents two major problems in terms of its internal structure. These are the problems of its slum areas and of easy circulation within the city. The former affects the comfort, aesthetic pleasure and convenience of living in the city, the latter the efficiency with which the city performs its functions as a business and a future industrial centre.

Fig. 36 shows the housing conditions within the city. It emphasizes that something like 50 per cent of the city area is occupied by slum dwellings. These are dwellings usually built of mud, having no identifiable sanitation facilities and generally in conditions of physical deterioration. The area of bad slums in which over 70 per cent of the buildings have a deteriorated structure covers much of the core region and the older suburbs. To this is added part of the newer suburbs both in the east and the north-west where jerry-building has been very common and the structures are deteriorating rapidly. The areal extent of the slums, however, does not adequately emphasize the serious nature of the problem; for the slum areas have not only the highest housing densities but also the highest population densities in the city. It is therefore more realistic to talk of some 70-80 per cent of the population of the city living in virtual slum conditions. Moreover, a large propor-

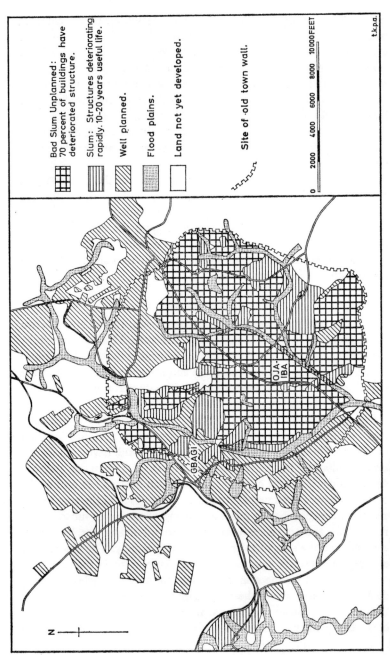

Figure 36   Ibadan: housing conditions

tion of the slum-dwellers are indigenous Ibadan. This fact tends to complicate any rational discussion of the need for slum clearance since it appears that its implication is that those who consider themselves 'owners of the city' (or as they popularly assert 'sons of the soil') would be disturbed in their occupation of land in their city.

It is difficult to see a quick solution to the problem. In the first place, there is the situation created by the existence of twin centres in the city. The more active and expansive business centre (Gbagi) is located on the edge of the slum area. Unlike what one might expect in typical European city, the expansion of this centre does not provide a means of gradually eliminating the slum and transforming the city centre at costs which would be borne largely by private business enterprises. Instead, the extension of the business centre goes on at the expense of relatively good buildings of about the same age as the business centre itself. The old slum remains untouched, a sprawling blot of substandard housing in the city, requiring vast sums of public money and imaginative planning to clear and redevelop.

Unlike in many developed countries, the slum areas are, however, not coincident with areas of moral and social deviance, criminality and deliquency. As a result, their impact on public conscience has been rather weak. In fact, life in the slum area is particularly integrated, satisfying to the full the warmth of intimate human relations. As a result, discontent with the slum conditions comes from those living outside rather than inhabitants of the slum area itself.

Furthermore, the city authority continues to treat this older half of the city occupied by the indigenous population as a special area. It is an area to which all the by-laws and regulations of the Town Planning Ordinance do not extend. Houses are sited anywhere at will and oriented in any direction. A house-owner may suddenly find the front-age of his house blocked by a new construction going up. Worse still, he may discover that all the household effluent and slop water now flow past his frontage, and he can do hardly anything about it. There are no regulations as to density of housing, design and quality of even a minimum level of convenience in the houses. All of this makes the slum really squalid and unhealthy.

The problem of efficient circulation within the city is, in a sense, closely related to that of the slum. With the virtual lack of planning con-trol in the most populous half of the city, the density of motorable roads through this section is extremely low. There are large parts of the city where the nearest motorable road is at least a quarter of a mile away. Moreover, most of the roads, tend to be narrow, usually no more than twenty-two to thirty feet wide, and are usually winding. The result is that traffic is densest on the three relatively straight roads which run the length and breadth of the city. Two of these—the Oyo Road—Ijebu-By-Pass and the Ogunmola—Oja-Iba Road—run north to south across the city and are linked by the third—an east-west road— from the Railway Station to Bere Square.

One other aspect of circulation arises from the wide separation of some of the important work-places (the various government ministries and the universities) and most of the medium to high-class residential districts from where the employees come. The former are largely to the north of the city, the latter to the south. The daily morning northward flow and afternoon southward flow of the traffic so generated has a flood-like effect and tends to bank up traffic making for the major north-south routes from other directions. Although traffic congestion has not reached a dimension such as to have a seriously adverse effect on efficiency, the conditions do occasionally become intolerable.

Already attempts are being made to improve the routeway density by pushing new roads through densely built-up areas. So far, most of these have served simply to improve access to residential properties. More important are the plans to build a ring road to divert through-traffic away from the two main north-south roads. At present, only the south-west section of the ring road has been built. However, because of the failure to complete the ring road, the south-west stretch itself, instead of serving as a high-speed transit routeway, is being treated as an access road and new houses are springing up on both sides of it.

Ease of circulation is bound to become a major constraint on the efficiency of economic operation within the city. Even assuming the relatively slow rate of growth of 2·8 per cent per annum (compound interest) between 1952 and 1963, the population of Ibadan will pass the one million mark by 1970. By then the need to have a master-plan both for redevelopment at the centre and for expansion at the periphery will have become acute. So far, administrative ditherings about the powers of the Town Planning Authority have virtually paralysed the latter as an effective agency for overseeing the growth and development of the city.

References

1. P. T. Bauer, *West African Trade*, London, 1954, p. 65.
2. See pp. 179-82.
3. See A. L. Mabogunje, 'The Growth of Residential Districts in Ibadan', *Geographical Review*, Vol. 52, No. 1, January 1962, pp. 56-77.

10 Lagos, the Rise of a Modern Metropolis

In many ways Lagos is the most spectacular of that class of Nigerian cities which owe their growth and development largely to European influence. Here the chance concentration of traffic imposed by the construction of the railways in 1895 and the later improvement of port facilities in 1914 gave Lagos maximum significance in the predominantly export-trade orientation of the Nigerian economy. Except for Port Harcourt, no other city in the country is favoured by being the joint termini of major land and sea routes. Nonetheless, for many towns and cities whose location remains of relevance to the modern economy, Lagos represents a type both in its rapid rate of growth and in the nature of the problems which are involved in such growth. However, the sheer magnitude of Lagos puts it in a class by itself and compounds many of its problems. For, when the era of industrial development began, the port location and the political pre-eminence gave Lagos a peculiar advantage and transformed it into the major focus of the urbanization process in the whole country.

The weakness of the traditional foundation

Unlike many other new towns such as Kaduna, Minna, Jos, Enugu, Aba and Port Harcourt, Lagos is not exactly a European creation. Before the advent of the European there had been a small town on the site. Because the settlement was so small it was easy to obliterate much of it. This fact provides the major contrast to the situation in Ibadan. In its origin, the most important single reason for the settlement on Lagos Island was defence. The exact date of the settlement is unknown, but the evidence seems to suggest early in the seventeenth century.[1] The first settlers were Awori, members of a subgroup of the Yoruba, whose land extends for nearly 40 miles inland from the coast. At first this community built their small town on the mainland at Ebute Metta not far from Lagos Island. However, the insecurity of this mainland location, due probably to the hostile activities of the neighbouring tribes of Ijebu and Egbado, decided them to break up their town and remove first to the island of Iddo and later to Lagos Island.

Iddo Island covers an area of only about one square mile. Although it was ideal from the point of view of defence, it could hardly supply much of the agricultural needs of the people. The danger of attack from the interior, however, hindered the inhabitants from making extensive farms on the mainland. Hence, notwithstanding that the soil was very sandy and much less fertile, Lagos Island came to be preferred for farming. It was this use of the island which led to its receiving the name *Oko*, meaning 'a farm', later corrupted to Eko. George, however, believes that the name is Bini in origin and is derived from another settlement in Benin peopled by captives of war.[2] The name 'Lagos' was given to the island by the Portuguese, probably about the middle of the eighteenth century.[3]

Up to the end of the eighteenth century, the settlement of Lagos led a very placid existence. Adams estimated its population at no more than 5,000 when he visited it about 1800. However, he excluded from this estimate the 'two or three populous villages on the north side of Cradoo lake (the lagoon) over which the caboceer (or Oba) of Lagos had jurisdiction'.[4] Even then it was probably a much smaller town than Ardrah (Porto Novo), whose population he estimated as between 7,000 and 10,000. During the next fifty years the population of Lagos more than doubled owing largely to the immigration of three different classes of people, namely slaves and slavers, the 'Brazilians', and the 'Sierra Leone immigrants'.

Although Lagos had been involved in the slave-trade since the eighteenth century, it was not until after 1821 that it became an important slaving port on the West African coast.[5] Three events had conjoined to give Lagos this late pre-eminence. The first was the French Revolution after 1790. The new French Government ordered French traders to relinquish the trade and also declared war on other European nations who continued to carry on the trade.[6] In November 1794, and again in August 1797, French squadrons successfully swept the whole of the West coast of Africa capturing ships of all nationalities as they went along.[7] It was in these circumstances that first the English traders, and later those of other nationalities turned their attention to Lagos, whose situation offered greater protection against molestation by roving ships of the French squadron. Thus, of ninety-two ships which cleared from Liverpool for the whole of Africa in 1797, none went to Ardrah (Porto Novo) whereas four went to Lagos.[8]

The two other events served simply to confirm this advantage of Lagos. The first was the act passed against the slave-trade by the British

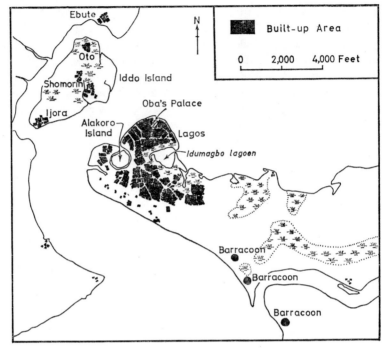

Figure 37   Lagos in 1850

Parliament in 1807. From then on, the British Royal Squadron more or less took over from where the French Navy left off and Lagos continued to provide the most effective hide-out for the slavers. The other event was the Yoruba wars taking place immediately north of Lagos. These wars against the Owu and the Egba people for the first time made Yoruba people offer their kinsmen in large numbers for sale to the European slave-dealers. Until then the Yoruba were the traders, and their slaves consisted largely of Hausa brought from farther inland.[9] With the source-area now centred on Yorubaland itself, from about 1831 Lagos became assured of a hinterland and its population grew as both the slaves, mostly Egba, and the slavers poured into it.

Of these slaves, many were exported to Brazil and came to be known as 'Brazilians'. In Brazil many of them, having succeeded by industry, frugality or good conduct in purchasing their freedom and that of their wives and children, later returned to Lagos. By 1851 they numbered some 130 families.[10] Other slaves were, however, more fortunate in being rescued in mid-Atlantic by British ships of the Royal Naval Squadron, and resettled in Freetown, Sierra Leone. Here they learnt to read and write and to engage in various crafts as well as in trading.[11] A group of them under a certain John Ferguson, having amassed some wealth, purchased a vessel, hired a white man to navigate her and began commercial trading down the West African coast.[12] In 1838, on one of these trips, they sighted Lagos and recognized it as the port from where they had been exported. In the next three years (1839-41), more than 250 of these Sierra Leone immigrants returned to Lagos.

Thus by 1850, the year before Britain's active connections with Lagos began, the population of Lagos had grown well beyond the 5,000 of 1800. But it is doubtful whether, even so, it was more than 20,000. However, compared with Ibadan, Lagos was a very small town occupying a small part of a small island (Fig. 37). Being small, its effect on later development was limited, and a large proportion of its population could easily be absorbed into modern urban activities. This weakness of the traditional foundation turned out to be one of the major advantages of Lagos as a Yoruba town. When its period of rapid growth came, Lagos was even more fortunate in having at the helm of affairs people who were anxious to see it grow into a modern city.

Lagos as a colonial outlier, 1851-1900

The first fifty years of British influence in Lagos were not years of rapid growth, but of consolidation. Lagos in 1851 was still the most important slave port on the West African coast. The trade in slaves was vigorously encouraged and actively participated in by Kosoko, the Oba, who had the support of most of the interior chiefs. Kosoko, however, had come to the throne by forcibly deposing Akitoye, his less energetic uncle. In exile at Badagry, the latter had declared himself favourably disposed to the termination of slave-trading in Lagos. The British Government therefore decided to intervene militarily in the politics of Lagos and to restore Akitoye to the throne. The result was the bombardment of Lagos in December 1851.

The first effect of the bombardment was a substantial decrease in the population of Lagos. According to an eye-witness account, nearly half of the town was destroyed especially as a result of a widespread conflagration that followed the explosion of a large gnupowder magazine on the western part of the island.[13] Moreover, with the certainty of defeat, a large proportion of the population deserted the town. Kosoko himself made away with about 2,000 followers in 50 or 60 large canoes.[14] Many slaves seized the opportunity to abscond back to their homes in the interior. In fact, for months after the British intervention, it was necessary to appeal to people to return to the island. Jones mentions that, by February 1852, upward of 5,000 of the inhabitants had returned to the town.

The news of the bombardment of Lagos and of the installation of Akitoye as the Oba of Lagos, however, had the effect of attracting to Lagos new groups of people. The first was that of European merchants. In 1852, five of them arrived, namely, Sandeman, Scala (an Italian), Grotte (a German), Diedrichsen (agents for Messrs. W. Oswald of Hamburg), and Johanssen. Two more arrived in 1853, namely Banner and McCoskry. Within a decade there were several others, notably Southam Wike, Chillingworth, Regis Aine (a French firm) and Madam Pittiluga, a spinster of Austrian descent.[15] Bowen mentions that by 1855, there were also several American firms engaged in trade in Lagos.[16] Most of these merchants, it will be noticed, were not British, and it was some time before the British element came to predominate. This was facilitated in 1889 by the departure of the French firms, who used to be the leading merchants in Lagos, as a result of the introduction of a system of trade by the use of specie to replace the old practice of trade by barter.[17] Throughout the nineteenth century, however, the number of Europeans in Lagos was never very great. In 1866 it was only 42; by the end of the century it had risen to about 250.

A second group of immigrants into Lagos in 1852 was that of missionaries. Soon after the news of the defeat of Kosoko reached Badagri, Gollmer, a missionary of the Church Missionary Society, decided to shift the centre of his activity from the latter place to Lagos. He was joined later by Wesleyan missionaries, and in 1862 by a Roman Catholic Father, by name Borghero, from Whydah. In number the missionaries were not a very important group, but in their wake came a fresh group of Sierra Leone immigrants who had settled in Badagri and Abeokuta. A number of Egba Christian refugees also joined them in 1867 as a result of the outbreak of hostilities in Abeokuta against European missionaries and their converts. With them came other refugees from the city of Ijaiye which was destroyed by Ibadan in 1865.

The number of Brazilian immigrants in Lagos was also considerably augmented after 1851. Like the Sierra Leone immigrants, they too were socially more accomplished than the indigenous inhabitants, although less educated than the former. A large proportion was Roman Catholic. A good number were artisans and their influence has survived in the popular architectural design of houses which, though less common now in Lagos, is still widespread throughout southern Nigeria. In 1862, when the first Catholic missionary arrived in Lagos, he estimated the number of 'Brazilians' at 3,000.[18] Nine years later, in 1871, they were joined by more of their kind from St Helena and Brazil. By 1873 the acting Administrator of Lagos commented that 'next to the natives of the place and the interior, the Brazilian Emancipados are the most numerous. They are constantly arriving by every opportunity at Lagos, I presume in consequence of the late Emancipation Law in Brazil; their number is estimated by some from 4,000 to 6,000.'[19]

One immediate effect of the arrival of so many non-natives was to emphasize the serious limitations of Consular Authority in Lagos. It could, for instance, ensure no effective protection to property, and from the European merchants' point of view it had no mode of enforcing the payment of debts due to them. To a great extent it was to rectify this position that the move was made in 1861 to have Lagos ceded formally to Britain as a colony.

With the cession came orderly government and a regular administration of justice. In 1862 a constabulary was set up consisting of some 100 Hausa freed slaves. Their number was increased first to 250 in 1865, and again to 500 in 1892. They served not only to police the town, but also as a fighting force when the need arose. To help them in the early days after the cession and until 1870, two companies of the West Indian Regiment were kept at Ebute Metta on the mainland. A Police Court was established in 1862 at Olowogbowo, but was removed to Tinubu in 1869 where it became the Supreme Court of the Lagos Colony in 1888. Apart from the Constabulary and the Court, a prison was started in Lagos in 1875, an enclosure with mud walls and two to three mud houses. This was rebuilt in 1888 and again more recently.

Lagos soon became known in the interior as a free colony, and many slaves, having escaped from their masters, made for it. McCoskry indicated that most of those coming into Lagos before 1865 were from Whydah, Abeokuta, Ibadan and Ijebu.[20] A large proportion of them, on arriving in Lagos, enlisted in the Hausa Force, while many others were simply declared liberated or apprenticed to artisans. By 1889 Moloney asserted that the population of Lagos was 'augmented to no inconsiderable extent by the number of escaped slaves who succeed from time to time in reaching the colony, and in thus securing their natural liberty'.[21] With the capitulation of Ijebu-Ode in 1892, many more slaves arrived in Lagos, several of whom, according to Carter, were Hausa who were absorbed in the Police Force.[22]

These increases in the population of Lagos were from 1866 faithfully recorded in censuses. The first census in that year gave a figure of 25,083 for the town. A second census was conducted in 1871 and after that date at decennial intervals. Table 31 gives some idea of the pattern of growth. Although it can hardly be doubted that these censuses were at best only rough indications of the position, the 1·1 per cent annual rate of growth which they give for the 30-year period cannot be regarded as excessive. Some idea of the inaccuracies to which the censuses are subject can, however, be realized, for instance, in the supposed decline in the population between 1881 and 1891. The census officer for 1891 suggested that the figure for 1881 had been faked owing 'to the fact that the enumerators in 1881 were paid by the head, according to the number of people each of them recorded'.[23] In spite of this, throughout the period, the population gradually increased with the expansion of the trade of Lagos and the consolidation of its position as the most important port for legitimate commerce on the West African coast.

TABLE 31 GROWTH OF LAGOS IN THE NINETEENTH CENTURY: POPULATION

	Total	% Increase or decrease
1871	28,518	—
1881	37,452	+23·9
1891	32,508	−15·2
1901	39,387	+17·5

The growth of legitimate commerce

The commerce on which the very life of Lagos depended was threatened in the early years of the colonial régime by the political instability in the interior. In 1865 and again in 1872 the Egba had closed the trade routes to Lagos in retaliation for certain actions of the Lagos government. It thus became clear that to ensure the progress of trade in Lagos, stable political conditions had to be extended over its economic hinterland. In consequence, the first political addition to Lagos was made in 1863 and consisted of Badagri, Palma and Lekki. In the same year Ado and Oke-Odan to the west of Lagos were added and, between 1883 and 1895, Appa, the Jekri country as far as Mollume, Ogbo Mahin,

Itebu and Aiyesan, Igbessa, Ilaro and Kotono were included in the Lagos territory.[24] A western boundary for this territory was agreed on with the French in 1889 and an eastern boundary with the Niger Coast Protectorate in 1898.

All this territory, however, was coastal and extended inland for only a few miles. Beyond were the more organized Yoruba kingdoms. The nearest to Lagos were the Egba and the Ijebu kingdoms. These two kingdoms controlled the trade routes to Lagos from the interior. The Lagos government entered into treaty agreement with the former in 1893 to guarantee the free flow of trade. A similar move was rebuffed by the Ijebu a year before, and as a result their chief town, Ijebu-Ode, was attacked and subjugated. The defeat of the Ijebu kingdom was followed by attempts to set up a system of British Residents at key towns in Yorubaland to ensure a free road policy throughout this vast hinterland of Lagos. As mentioned in a previous chapter, one was located in Ibadan in 1893. Others were placed at Oyo, Ogbomosho and Odo Otin and their authority was backed up by armed garrisons. By 1900 this policy, according to Burns, 'had resulted in an immediate increase in the prosperity of the people, and this was reflected in a marked degree in Lagos, which as the capital and port of the Colony, rapidly gained in importance'.[25]

By itself the extension of the Pax Britannica over such an extensive area would not have resulted in the growth of Lagos unless the area involved was productive and means were available for transporting its produce to Lagos. Over the whole of the Yoruba country the average annual rainfall is over 40 inches, and with temperatures always above 64·4°F, the oil-palm thrives in abundance even without cultivation. From about 1810 its fruits became important as raw material for the industrial revolution in Britain owing to changes in social customs and industrial technology. Although as early as 1800 Adams had mentioned that palm oil could be obtained abundantly and cheaply in Lagos, it was kept out almost completely from the commerce of Lagos because of the greater prosperity from the slave-trade.[26] In fact, until 1851, the slaving interests in Lagos and Abeokuta had succeeded in closing the Ogun River to trade in palm oil which had, in consequence, been diverted to Badagri. After that date, the Ogun River and a number of north-south land routes became important routeways for the palm oil trade. Apart from these, Lagos also derived much of its trade from the ancient east-west route along the lagoon. McCoskry, in fact, believes that up to 1865 a great proportion of the palm oil brought to Lagos came from the banks of the lagoon from towns such as Ikorodu, Epe and Ejinrin.[27] The last-named port was said to supply as much as 60,000 to 70,000 gallons of palm oil per week to Lagos in 1853.[28]

The convergence of so many routes on Lagos led to a remarkable growth of its trade. Between 1862 and 1900 the value of its exports rose from £62,000 to over £885,000. In the same period, imports rose from £78,000 to over £830,000. The growth of trade, however, was not continuous and a period of high prosperity was followed by one of depression.[29] However, throughout the period it was so remunerative that the colony was self-supporting and self-protecting. For the first few years after the establishment of Consular Authority, there was a parliamentary grant of £2,000 a year which dropped in 1863 to £1,000, and then ceased. From thenceforth revenue rose from £16,000 to nearly £210,000 by the end of the century. So constant was the surplus of revenue over expenditure that, in 1896, before it was necessary to raise money by loan for the large capital expenditure on bridges and the railway, there was a credit balance of over £50,000 invested in Britain.[30]

Various other institutions to aid the further growth of trade were established during the period. A mail steamer service between Lagos and Britain began to operate in 1853. A bank was opened in 1891 by Mr G. W. Neville soon after the government had inaugurated its own Treasury Savings Bank. This bank later became the Bank of British West Africa. An oil mill was established along what is now Oil Mill Street in 1865. Telephone communication was introduced in 1892. Then in 1897 came the foundation of the Lagos Chamber of Commerce for the purpose of promoting the commerce and the public interest of the town.

One major handicap to trade and increased prosperity remained in the sand-bar at the entrance to the Lagos Lagoon. In the first decade after 1851, most ships unloaded their cargo and passengers outside the bar which were then conveyed by surf-boats to the Lagos beach. The operation was, however, very tricky and required extremely skilful manoeuvres which only members of the Fanti tribe of Ghana had mastered.[31] After 1861, ships began to venture across the bar. Burton mentions that there were three passages over the bar—the canoe, the boat and the ship passage.[32] Usually only two of the passages were usable—the ship or western, and the canoe or eastern passage. Neither of these passages was safe. Hutchinson mentions that 'even men-of-war of large tonnage and steamers of 200 horsepower, which one would think ought to have sufficient weight to keep them steady, took in water through their bull's eye'.[33] Graver casualties were common. The average deaths, not including Europeans, were 14 per annum, and in 1858 there were 45 casualties. Escapes were very rare because of the presence of numerous sharks which often swam close alongside a boat waiting for the victims of wrecking.

A temporary solution was found in the use of a special type of iron steamer to serve as bar tenders. These steamers, weighing each 120 tons and drawing only 6 ft of water with a horsepower variously estimated as 80 and 160, succeeding in plying for mail and cargo across the bar.[34] This solution, however, was costly in terms both of human lives and expense. A report on the situation was submitted by Messrs Coode, Son & Matthews in 1896 which showed that the average annual cost of trans-shipment over the bar was in the region of £25,000.[35] To this must be added direct expenditure by government such as the appointment of a Harbour Master in 1861, numerous surveys of the bar, the setting up of buoys to mark the deep-water channel and the provision of tide tables to help the bar tenders.

What with the costly expenditure and the high mortality occasioned by the dangerous bar passage, it is no wonder that, as Burton remarked, no one visited Lagos for the first time without proposing a solution.[36] By the end of the century three proposals were receiving serious consideration. Of these, only that put forward by Messrs Coode and Partners in 1892 sought to solve the problem permanently, and it was ultimately adopted. It consisted of building into deep water two stone moles from the shoreline on both sides of the entrance to stabilize the direction of the channel. A third mole—the west training wall—was to be included to guide the flow of water and so effect the scouring of the entrance channel (Fig. 38). The proposal envisaged little recurrent dredging after the initial one giving the entrance a depth of 25 ft. Its earlier estimated cost of £830,000 was later brought down to £797,000 in 1898.

Nonetheless, building such moles required large quantities of stone. The nearest outcrop of hard, stony rocks to Lagos is some 60 miles inland near Abeokuta, and until this could be reached nothing could be done about improving the entry to the port of Lagos. The Lagos Government had begun to construct a railway in 1895, and this reached Abeokuta in 1898. The event marked a turning point in the history of

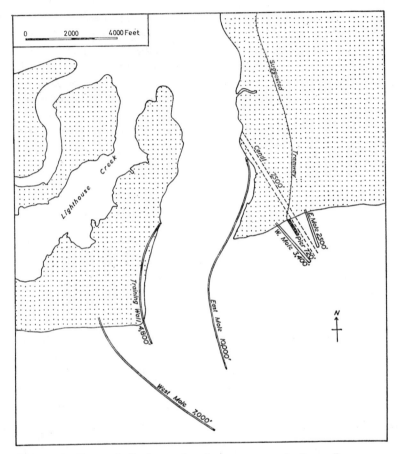

Figure 38   Proposals for improving the entrance to the Lagos Lagoon

Lagos. Within two decades the harbour entrance was improved. The trade of Lagos soared as imports and exports flowed in and out more easily. More and more people flocked into Lagos, and the town experienced a phenomenal growth in population as well as in area. However, in 1900 this rosy future was still no more than a dream.

The development of port functions

One of the most important factors which helped the development of the port of Lagos was the series of constitutional changes which gradually raised the town after 1900 to the status of the capital of the Colony and Protectorate of Nigeria. At the beginning of the century, Lagos was no more than an isolated colony of Britain. Its Governor, however, exercised some form of political supervision over the affairs of Yorubaland, which was made a Protectorate of Lagos. The first of the series of constitutional changes began in 1906 when Lagos and its protectorate of Yorubaland were amalgamated with the Protectorate of Southern Nigeria, which then comprised what was formerly the Niger Coast Protectorate. The new political unit was designated the Colony and Protectorate of Southern Nigeria and Lagos was made the seat of government. Eight years later, in 1914, the process reached an inevitable conclusion when the unit was amalgamated with the Northern Protecorates to form the single country—Nigeria—with Lagos retained as the capital city. The immediate effect of this enhanced position of Lagos was to bring to a close the controversy about whether Lagos should be the main port terminal for the new rail-line into the interior. Once this was resolved and the railway was extended to Kano and Kaura Namoda, Lagos found itself with an extensive hinterland, penetrating more than 700 miles into the interior of the country and including part of the French Niger Territory.

With the first amalgamation of 1906, the revenue of Lagos rose from over £$\frac{1}{2}$ million in 1905 to over 1 million, and it was felt that the time was ripe for implementing the mole proposal of Messrs Coode and Partners.[37] In May 1907 the steam dredger *Egerton* arrived and the minimum bar draught was increased to 10$\frac{1}{2}$ feet by the end of the year. Stones for the first of the moles (the eastern) were brought by train from Abeokuta to Iddo and transferred by barges to the Signal Station Wharf where its landward root was located. The construction of the mole went on from 1908 to 1913 when it was completed to a length of 7,315 ft. The western mole was begun in 1912 and the west training wall in 1915. Nonetheless, it was not until 1917, when the western mole was extended enough to exercise an influence, that the depth of water was sufficient to enable ships to enter the harbour the whole year round. Before then, a maximum depth of 19 ft had been achieved in 1914, and the first ocean-going vessel had crossed the bar into the harbour, but in 1915 the depth of water had decreased to 17 ft. Throughout 1917, a constant official draught of 19$\frac{1}{2}$ ft. was maintained. This rose to 25 ft. in 1928 and to 27 ft in 1936, below which figure it has never fallen.

Concurrent with the gradual improvement of the bar draught was the development of berthing facilities. In 1907, at the commencement of the harbour works, the port of Lagos consisted of two wharves—the Customs and Iddo Wharves—apart from a number of privately-owned small jetties and piers, projecting in front of 'factories' along the Marina. The Customs Wharf had grown from the Customs Pier of the 1860s along which steamers carrying dutiable cargo had berthed. In 1907, it was only 300 ft long. Iddo Wharf, on the other hand, was built at the beginning of the Lagos Railway Schemes in 1895 and measured 100 ft. In 1904 it was extended to 450 ft. Besides these two wharves, there was at Apapa in 1907 the Government Vessels Department's floating dock. It was constructed the previous year and had a lifting capacity of only 400 tons.

With the commencement of the harbour works, the Consulting Engineers were asked to make proposals for immediate wharf developments.[38] They recommended the extension of Customs Wharf by 344 ft and the provision alongside of a depth of 22 ft of water by dredging. The extension was completed in 1913. Local businesses soon found the provision grossly inadequate and suggested the construction at Wilmot Point or Apapa of either a wharf or a pier system of ship accommodation instead of the quay (marginal) type proposed by the Consulting Engineers. The proximity of the Customs Wharf to the commercial centre, however, was a major point in favour of its further extension in preference to new constructions at Wilmot Point or Apapa.

Apapa was finally chosen, but what turned the scale in its favour was the need for a port terminus for the railway. The annual maintenance cost of the Iddo Wharf was increasing owing to heavy corrosion of its steel girders. Its extension was inadvisable owing to the possibility of danger to shipping from its nearness to Carter Bridge. By 1920 it became impractical to continue to use it for external traffic and the Railway decided to give it up. Apapa, being on the mainland and necessitating no great expense in bridge construction (a wharf at Wilmot Point would have necessitated providing a wide bridge over Five Cowrie Creek) became the obvious choice. Construction of a quay 1,500 ft long and a wharf with four-storey transit sheds was completed in 1926, and this served Lagos until 1950.[39]

Two other special commodity wharves were constructed about the same time. In 1919 a Coal Wharf was built at Ijora on Iddo Island, westward of the former Iddo wharf, to receive coal from Enugu for electricity generation and the railways in the western zone. Later, in 1933, a

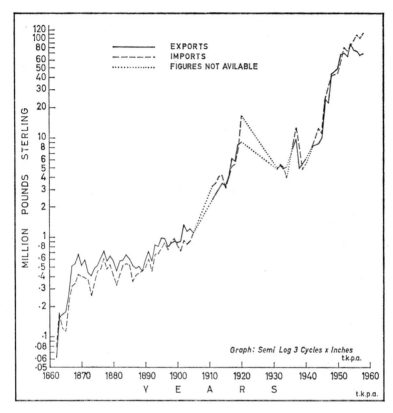

Figure 39   Growth of trade in Lagos, 1862-1958

Petroleum Jetty was constructed at Apapa, north of the general cargo wharf, to reduce the risk of fire.

The effect of the improvement to the port of Lagos combined with the extension of the railways and the development of roads after 1920 was phenomenal for the growth of trade in Lagos. Although trade had been rising steadily after the pacification of the immediate hinterland of Lagos in 1893, it soared upward after 1917. Fig. 39 shows the trend in the value of Lagos exports and imports during the period and dramatically underlines the remarkable growth that took place. Exports from Lagos not only increased in value and volume, but also became highly diversified. Apart from palm oil and kernels, after 1912 Lagos exported groundnuts, cocoa, cotton, tin, hides and skins. This diversification ensured a steady flow of economic activity in the port. Earlier in the century, when palm produce formed most of Lagos exports, there was regularly a peak in the October-March period and a trough in the April-September period. With a greater variety of produce and improved storage facilities, this simple seasonal pattern was evened out.

The greater efficiency of the Lagos port in handling the increased trade was reflected in the changing character and capacity of the shipping it handled. While in 1894 some 441 ships were handled with a tonnage of about 383,000, in 1946, when the country was just recovering from the effect of the Second World War, the tonnage rose to over 1·5 million although the number of ships was only 402. Moreover, the switch-over of effort from war-time to peace-time production after 1945 further increased the all-year-round efficiency of operation. Indeed, so great was the volume of traffic that by 1953 berthing capacity in the port was proving highly inadequate. To cope with the new situation, it was necessary to considerably extend and improve the facilities. This involved the reclamation of about 100 acres of lagoon on the Marina shoals (Plate 21) and the construction of 2,650 ft of quay plus transit sheds. Additions and adjustments to the original plan brought the completion cost of the project to £3¼ million. The extension was formally opened in 1956, but was only fully completed in 1958.[40]

The result was again a remarkable increase in shipping and tonnage handled, both of which are clearly indicated in the following table.

TABLE 32   GROWTH OF SHIPPING AND TONNAGE IN LAGOS

	1938	1946	1954	1958	1962
NO. OF SHIPS ENTERED	695	402	1,331	1,989	2,233
NET REGISTERED TONNAGE ('000's)	1,960	1,529	3,079	4,433	5,569

Within Nigeria, Lagos maintained its lead as the premier port although its relative importance vis-à-vis the other ports remained hardly changed. In 1958 it accounted for 56 per cent of the total number of ships entered in Nigeria, and 64 per cent of their net registered tonnage. In fact, if Dakar's trade in bunker oil was excluded, Lagos by 1954 had become the most important West African port both by value of trade and by tonnage handled.

The move to industrialization

Although this growth of port traffic itself implied increased employment opportunities, its effect in widening the scope of commercial activities in Lagos was perhaps more important.[41] In this respect, it is necessary to distinguish between the export and the import traffic. The export trade of the country is largely in primary agricultural produce which is bought by the various Regional Marketing Boards acting through numerous licensed buying agents. By the time these products reach Lagos, they are on their way out of the country. As a result, they contribute very little directly to the vigour of commercial life in Lagos.

It is the imported manufactured goods which provide the grist of the local trade of Lagos. Since most of the headquarters of business houses are here, the first and subsequent stages in breaking the bulk of goods imported take place in Lagos. This calls into being numerous retailers participating at different levels of the distributive process. As the volume of trade increases, so the number of such retailers multiplies. Up to 1949, both the volume and the value of imported goods had remained well below those of export, but from 1950 the position began to change owing to further relaxation of the post-war import control as a result of the improvement in the gold and dollar reserves of the Sterling Area. By 1955 the value of imports had risen so high that for the first time since 1922 the balance of trade turned against Nigeria. There was in that year an adverse balance of some £4 million which increased to nearly £18 million in 1956, to £25 million in 1957 and by 1960 it was nearing £60 million.

Most of the commodities that showed marked increases in their importation were consumer goods, notably cotton piece goods, private cars, petroleum, fish, corrugated iron sheets and cement. Although a sizeable proportion of these goods was destined for the interior, there is no doubt that Lagos itself constituted their most important market. This is so not only because a higher percentage of the population of Lagos was involved in the money-exchange economy, but more because Lagos represents the greatest single concentration of purchasing power in the country. A comparison of Tables 33A and 33B showing employment and earnings for a single month (September 1956) for Lagos and the three regions of Nigeria emphasizes this point.[42] Expressed as a percentage of the total adult male population of each area, the wage and salaried section constituted 84 per cent in Lagos, 4·5 per cent in the Western Region, 3·4 per cent in the Eastern Region and only

TABLE 33   EMPLOYMENT AND EARNINGS BY REGIONS, SEPTEMBER 1956

A. Number employed

	Lagos	Western Region	Eastern Region	Northern Region
FEDERAL GOVERNMENT	15,379	4,116	2,633	3,065
REGIONAL GOVERNMENT	—	22,117	13,153	25,585
LOCAL GOVT. COUNCILS	3,220	22,787	15,951	43,773
PUBLIC CORPORATIONS	24,720	12,886	22,610	15,912
COMMERCIAL & OTHERS	54,237	27,203	23,299	63,325
TOTAL	97,556	89,109	77,646	151,660

B. Cash earnings (£)

	Lagos	Western Region	Eastern Region	Northern Region
FEDERAL GOVERNMENT	319,997	69,372	43,219	53,634
REGIONAL GOVERNMENT	—	297,131	179,604	320,255
LOCAL GOVT. COUNCILS	29,154	177,580	96,044	248,848
PUBLIC CORPORATIONS	441,706	142,740	240,934	195,412
COMMERCIAL & OTHERS	635,347	213,289	220,387	438,466
TOTAL	1,426,204	900,112	780,188	1,256,615

2·9 per cent in the Northern Region. The average annual earnings for each salaried person came to £187 in Lagos, £131 in Western Nigeria, £120 in Eastern Nigeria and £100 in Northern Nigeria.

These figures, however, while showing the superiority of Lagos over any other urban centre in Nigeria, still represent a poor index of the actual position, for what is clear about Lagos is the great inequality of income. This is due to the fact that, like all big and rapidly growing cities, Lagos tends at the one end to attract the rural poor (persons lacking both assets and urban skills), while at the other to give immense opportunity to many others to express personal talents and manipulate private property for spectacular monetary gains. As a result, its population contains a more than proportionate number of individuals with some of the highest incomes in the country. It is this fact that underlines the commercial dominance of Lagos. And since most of the imported articles that are so much in demand are manufactured consumer goods for which there is usually a high income elasticity, one would expect a city like Lagos to generate a very high sales volume for these articles.

The adverse balance of trade that followed after 1955 in the wake of the increasing importation of so much consumer goods posed a serious threat to the economic growth of the country. One way of improving the position, therefore, has been to encourage local industrialization initially on the basis of import substitution. Granted the importance of the existing market in Lagos, it is obvious that it offered an inconsiderable attraction to industrialists. Moreover, there is the fact that as a port city it also offers the uncommon advantage of single transhipment costs for imported factory machines, equipment and raw materials. To these two factors must be added the fact that infrastructural facilities (electricity, water supply, health, medical and educational institutions) are the best developed and, in some cases, the cheapest in the country, public transport facilities are fairly adequate, skilled and unskilled labour is abundant, and accessibility, both national and international, is easy.

Preparatory schemes for industrial development in Lagos began soon after the Second World War, but they did not start to show results until after 1951. Before that date there were in Lagos no more than fifteen major industrial establishments, of which at least five were public utilities. These included the Ijora electricity power plant, the Nigerian railway workship, the Public Works Department sawmills and mechanical workshops, the Government Printing Works and the marine Dockyard, wharves and port installations. Of private industrial establishments, the most important were a soap factory employing about 500 people, a brewery, cold storage installations, a metal containers manufacturing workshop, and three large newspaper printing presses. The remaining industrial enterprises of which Lagos could boast at the time were numerous small workshops and corn mills, each employing less than 20 people.

A Department of Commerce and Industries was set up in 1948 charged with the duty, among many others, of 'developing secondary industries on the widest possible scale by methods that will ensure the maximum possible participation by Nigerians themselves in economic industrial enterprises'.[43] At about the same time a scheme to reclaim an extensive area of some 1,000 acres at Apapa was begun. Of these, some 230 acres were to be laid out as an industrial estate, especially for large-scale foreign-owned industrial enterprises. Another industrial estate, this time for small to medium scale Nigerian enterprises, was established at Yaba and provided good workshop accommodation at reasonable rentals. Unplanned industrial areas developed at Iganmu, east of Apapa, and also at Mushin just outside the municipal boundary. In 1958 the Western Nigerian Government also established a 300-acre industrial estate at Ikeja close to Mushin.

By 1959 an Industrial Survey carried out by the Industrial Section of the Federal Ministry of Commerce and Industry (from November 1957 to August 1959) showed that there were by then in Lagos about 2,400 industrial units employing about 40,000 individuals. This figure grossly understates the position since the Survey was limited to Ikoyi, Lagos Island, Ijora, Iddo Island, Ebute Metta and Apapa. Yaba was not surveyed, nor were the areas such as Mushin and Ikeja which were outside the municipality, but they contained some of the more important industries in the Lagos area. An analysis of labour strength for the units surveyed is shown in the Table 34. It emphasizes the predominance of small-scale units in the industrial character of Lagos. Although not as detailed as the table for Ibadan concerning industries employing more than 10 persons, it underlines the contrast between the two cities. For while Ibadan had only 47 of such units in 1964, even in 1959 and in spite of the incompleteness of the data, Lagos already boasted of nearly 300 relatively large industrial enterprises.

TABLE 34   INDUSTRIAL LABOUR STRENGTH ANALYSIS, LAGOS, 1959

No. of employees	No. of Industries	%
Under 4	1,672	69
4-9	457	19
10-19	104	5
20 and over	186	7
TOTAL	2,419	100

The growth of population, 1901-50

All these developments in commerce, port functions and industrialization gave rise to a phenomenal increase in the population of Lagos. The period after 1950 when Lagos was entering the era of industrialization was, however, so different in its rate of population growth that it needs to be considered separately. Indeed, while the annual rate of growth was only 3·4 per cent between 1901 and 1950, it jumped to 18·6 per cent per annum between 1951 and 1963.

Table 35 shows the growth of the population and the area of Lagos for the period 1901 to 1950. All the censuses, like previous ones, were based on a house-to-house enumeration and, like them, because of the circumstances of Lagos, they must be taken as only more or less accurate. The trend they depict is, however, clear. The population of Lagos was increasing at a rate faster than anything that had gone before. The rate

TABLE 35   GROWTH OF LAGOS IN THE TWENTIETH CENTURY

Year of Census	Area covered by Census (sq. mls.)	Total population	Annual rate of increase
1891	1·55	32,508	
1901	(Not available)	41,847*	2·5
1911	18·00	73,766	5·7
1921	20·17	99,690	3·1
1931	25·59	126,108	2·3
1950	27·22	230,256	3·3

* The census for the first time included the population of Iddo Island and Ebute Metta (2,460).

was most rapid in the period 1901 to 1910; it was retarded during the next decade by a combination of disastrous circumstances. These included the 1914-18 War, the influenza epidemic which broke out soon after the war, and the post-war slump in trade. This trend continued after 1925 owing to more deaths from bubonic plague as well as to the general world economic depression. The latter resulted in the fall in prices of Nigerian exports and a general decline in the activity of the port of Lagos, which is reflected in the lower rate of population growth between 1921-31. The Second World War stimulated a new upward trend which by 1950 had had the effect of raising the population to almost twice the size of the 1931 population.

The rapid growth of population in Lagos was accounted for partly by natural increase and partly by a fresh wave of immigration from all over Nigeria and West Africa. In the first decade of the century, the excess of births over deaths was negligible. It rose phenomenally after 1911, partly because of large-scale immigration into Lagos of younger people of child-bearing age, and partly as a result of improved sanitary conditions which brought down the death rate. The honour of inaugurating this new development goes to Sir William MacGregor, who became the Governor of Lagos in 1899. During his five years of office the island saw more advances in health and sanitary reforms than it had known since the coming of the Europeans.

The major reforms, many of which were completed after Mac-Gregor's departure, were connected with water supply, sewage disposal and anti-mosquito precautions. Apart from the £13,000 spent on sinking new wells and repairing old ones after 1900, a large water-works, described as the biggest of its kind in West Africa, was completed in 1915 at Iju, on the Ogun River, 17 miles from Lagos. This was capable of supplying 2·5 million gallons daily, sufficient for a population of 115,000 so that its expansion was uncalled for until recently. The effect of the introduction of piped water (Plate 28) into Lagos was almost dramatic. Not only did it considerably reduce the incidence of dysentery but, according to Dr Turner, it led to the almost total elimination of the guinea worm disease.[44]

A system of sewage disposal was organized in the European section of the town and centred on the dejection jetty near the junction of the Old Customs House Street and the Marina. Complaints by residents of this neighbourhood, however, soon prompted the government to construct a new dejection jetty on Victoria Island to which sewage was brought from all over the town by a Sanitary Tramway between 1907 and 1933. Later, disintegrator installations were substituted and the collection of the sewage was farmed out to contractors. This system has continued to function with varying degrees of efficiency since then.

Of the various improvements, perhaps none had a greater effect on the health of the population than the anti-mosquito operations. Once Sir Ronald Ross had discovered in 1897 that the malaria parasites were carried by the *anopheles* mosquitoes, no efforts were spared to destroy their breeding places. Governor MacGregor initiated the operation by directing that all water-tanks in government quarters were to be rendered mosquito-proof and all government premises subjected to periodical inspection to ensure that no stagnant water was allowed to accumulate. He also ordered every official's house to be equipped with a mosquito-proof room and its tenants were advised to use mosquito-nets and wear mosquito-boots.

With the African population, a vigorous campaign of education in the prevention of malaria and other diseases was launched. Under the instigation of MacGregor, a Lagos Ladies' League was formed in 1901. Its main object was 'the administration of quinine to children and the combating of infant mortality'.[45] In 1902 the Massey Street Dispensary was opened, and in 1908 a Municipal Board of Health was established. It was this Board which in succeeding decades carried out a most comprehensive programme to rid Lagos of mosquitoes. The programme included house-to-house inspections by sanitary and anti-mosquito inspectors; the catching of adult mosquitoes in dwelling places; the use of gas oil and mixture of Paris green as larvicides; the filling of crab holes; the disposal of water-containing receptacles; the construction and maintenance of earth drains; and the stocking of wells with fish. In certain parts of the town, re-afforestation, particularly with casuarina and eucalyptus, was pursued vigorously as an anti-mosquito measure. By 1942 over 80,000 young seedlings had been transplanted. The most effective single measure against mosquitoes, however, was the reclamation of swamps. Despite the activities of previous administrations before 1900, swamps still covered a large extent of Lagos (Fig. 40). One of these, the Kokomaiko, had proved extremely intractable, but under MacGregor it was so thoroughly drained that by 1905 houses were already going up on it. Much of the material used in reclaiming this particular swamp was obtained by cutting a canal 25 ft wide, through the island from north to south. This canal, which was most appropriately named after MacGregor, forms the trunk of several smaller canals draining the whole swamp between the town and Ikoyi. In 1903, swamps around Elegbata, Alakoro and Idumagbo were reclaimed by granting plots of swampland to individuals on condition that they were reclaimed. From the 1920s onward, the Lagos Town Council, which superseded the Municipal Board of Health, reclaimed the north-east Ikoyi swamps, the swamps at Okepa, Mekunwen, Oke Suna, Elesin, Igbo Road, Obalende and others at Ijora, Ebute Metta and the Railway Reservation. The Lagos Executive Development Board, created in 1929, undertook the reclamation of the Idumagbo and Isalegangan lagoons in pursuance of its town-planning schemes, drained the swamps east of its new Yaba Layout in 1933 and at Apapa in 1946. In all, nearly 1,000 acres of swamp land were reclaimed between 1900 and 1946.

The improved health conditions in Lagos were clearly reflected in the falling death rate. At the close of the nineteenth century, the average death rate was over 40 per 1,000, but between 1911 and 1917, it fell to less than 30. It exceeded 30 again between 1918 and 1924 during the influenza epidemic, but since 1928 it has been below 20. This falling death rate, however, must also be seen against the background of the increasingly youthful character of the population of Lagos. In fact the proportion of persons below thirty years of age rose in Lagos from about 62 per cent in 1921 and 1931 to over 67 per cent in 1950. In the latter census, for instance, the number of persons in each of the age groups 20-24 and 25-29 was larger than the youngest age group (under 5 years of age). These facts point to the importance of immigrants in the population of Lagos. By 1950, in spite of the fact that growth by

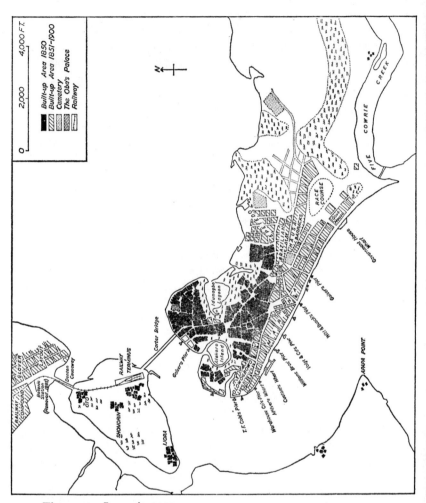

Figure 40   Lagos in 1900

natural increase rose more than ever before, its relative contribution to the total fell from 41 per cent in 1931 to about 37 per cent.

The most important factor stimulating immigration into Lagos during the period 1901-50 was the increasingly widening gap in employment opportunities between Lagos and the rest of the country. This gap became more pronounced with the Second World War when, owing to shortage of supplies, many employers in the country had to dismiss most of their staff. So great was the influx into Lagos of unemployed people at this time that, in order to ensure that many of those normally resident in Lagos had a chance of securing employment, the registration of workers in Lagos—both currently employed and unemployed—was closed to people from the provinces by a series of Orders, Nos. 202, 234, 271 of 1944, and Nos. 6 and 7 of 1945.[46] Even then, more people continued to flock into Lagos, but after 1945 their number was swelled by a fresh stream of immigrants, namely, ex-servicemen. The general demobilization of troops serving overseas had begun in October 1945. In the same year an Ordinance (the Employment of Ex-servicemen Ordinance, No. 48 of 1945) was passed. This made it incumbent on all employers of not less than ten Africans to register and then to employ ex-servicemen, until 10 per cent of their normal establishment consisted of ex-servicemen. By 1948 a record of the number of ex-servicemen absorbed by such employers shows the position as follows:

TABLE 36   EMPLOYMENT OF EX-SERVICEMEN BY REGIONS, 1948*

	Ex-servicemen employed	Civilians employed	TOTAL
NORTHERN REGION	9,474	71,444	80,918
EASTERN REGION	7,883	54,112	61,995
WESTERN REGION	4,074	46,987	51,061
LAGOS	6,001	47,102	53,103
TOTAL	27,432	219,645	247,077

*Information in respect of Nigeria for the year 1948, Lagos, 1950, p. 15.

What is most striking from the figures is that, compared with the regions, each of which had population of over five million, Lagos, with its population of only about 200,000, was easily the most important employment centre in the country. The 1950 Census further elaborated the position. It showed that of 202,000 persons in Lagos aged 5 years and above, some 119,000 (i.e. 59 per cent) were gainfully occupied.

There was employment for both males and females, even though at a ratio of 2 to 1. The Census Officer, however, commented that this proportion of gainfully occupied males and females, high compared with most countries, was due, on the one hand, to the employment in various undertakings of large numbers of young persons under 15 years of age and, on the other, to the fact that many housewives combine with their duties as home-makers some gainful occupation, usually trading. Thus three out of every four women gainfully occupied were employed in trading, while 70 per cent of the males were employed in four occupations, namely craftsmen and production process workers (30 per cent), clerical and related workers (14 per cent), labourers (14 per cent) and domestic and personal service workers (12 per cent).

Demographic characteristics of the population

An important aspect of the large number of immigrants into Lagos during this period is the diversity of ethnic groups represented. Before 1931 no figures are given of Yoruba immigrants, although it is known that they were considerable. Table 37, however, shows that in 1931 and 1950 they were the most important single group of immigrants. Within the Yoruba area the source region of most of these immigrants comprised the Colony, Abeokuta, Ijebu, Ondo, Oyo and Ilorin Provinces. Both the 1931 and the 1950 Censuses gave the contribution of each of the provinces and helped to underline certain minor trends in the migration into Lagos from the Yoruba area. Table 38 shows that in 1931 Abeokuta and Oyo Provinces accounted for more than half the Yoruba immigrants. By 1950, although their absolute contribution had increased, their relative importance had declined. The most spectacular increase between 1931 and 1950 was from Ijebu Province, its relative

TABLE 37   PROPORTION OF IMMIGRANTS IN LAGOS, 1911–50

	Total population	(a) Yoruba immigrants	(b) Non-Yoruba immigrants	(c)	(d)	(e)
1911	73,766	—	14,478	—	20%	—
1921	99,690	—	23,045	—	32%	—
1931	126,108	45,811	28,468	36%	23%	59%
1950	230,256	85,042	61,057	37%	26%	63%

(c) Yoruba immigrants as percentage of total population.
(d) Non-Yoruba immigrants as percentage of total population.
(e) Total of immigrants as percentage of total population.

TABLE 38   PROVINCIAL DERIVATION OF YORUBA IMMIGRANTS

Provinces	Total number		Percentage	
	1931	*1950*	*1931*	*1950*
COLONY	3,604	8,610	8	10
ABEOKUTA	11,765	20,242	26	24
IJEBU	6,968	19,566	13	23
ONDO	2,408	6,277	5	7
OYO	13,350	17,786	29	21
ILORIN	7,716	12,561	19	15
TOTAL	45,811	85,042	100	100

importance rising from 13 per cent in 1931 to 23 per cent in 1950. The number of Ijebu in Lagos in 1950 becomes even more significant when seen against the background of their province of origin. It represents almost 6 per cent of the total population of the province (348,024 in 1952) compared with the 0·7 to 3 per cent for most of the other Yoruba provinces. In other words, for Ijebu people, more than for any other Yoruba group, Lagos by 1950 represented a vital centre to which to emigrate.

Nonetheless, although the total number of Yoruba immigrants had risen by about 85 per cent between 1931 and 1950, the rise in the case of the non-Yoruba had been of the order of 115 per cent. Non-Yoruba immigrants are divided into three classes, namely, natives of Nigeria, Africans (i.e. those from other African countries), and non-Africans (i.e. Europeans and Asians mainly). Among the natives of Nigeria, the most important ethnic groups represented in Lagos were the Ibo, the Ijaw, the Edo and the Hausa. Their contribution to the population from 1911 to 1950 is shown in Table 39. The most striking fact from the table is the phenomenal rise of the number of Ibo, from less than 300

TABLE 39   NON-YORUBA NATIVE IMMIGRANTS, 1911-50

	Total number				Percentage of total native immigrants			
	1911	*1921*	*1931*	*1950*	*1911*	*1921*	*1931*	*1950*
IBO	264	1,609	5,147	25,577	5	16	26	47
IJAW	264	1,097	1,327	3,500	5	11	7	6
EDO	291	1,463	3,324	6,800	5	15	16	13
HAUSA	3,533	3,951	3,593	3,725	65	50	18	7
OTHERS	1,125	1,764	6,777	14,483	20	8	33	27
TOTAL	5,477	9,884	20,168	54,085	100	100	100	100

in 1911 to nearly 26,000 by 1950. Nearly half of the Ibo came from the single province of Owerri, while less than 15 per cent came from Ogoja and Rivers Provinces. The number from Owerri Province, unlike the case of Ijebu Province, represented only about 0·6 per cent of the total provincial population (2,077,891 in 1952) so that emigration to Lagos from that province can hardly be said to be phenomenal. Moreover, it is noteworthy that the major influx of Ibo into Lagos began just before 1931, about the time when the eastern line of the railway was completed from Port Harcourt, through the Ibo country, to join the western line at Kaduna. Both the Ijaw and Edo maintained their relative position during the period, although they both increased greatly in absolute terms. The position of the Hausa immigrants is most curious. Throughout the period they showed relatively little change in their total number although their relative importance declined.

Of non-Nigerians, four countries on the west coast provided the bulk of the African immigrants (Table 40). They were Ghana-Togoland, Sierra Leone, Liberia and Dahomey. At no period was their contribution ever more than 10 per cent of the total population. By 1950 both their absolute contribution and their relative importance showed a marked decline. Among the Europeans, the major groups represented were British, French and German. Most of them were involved in administration either in government or in commerce. Very few were technicians as Lagos was then far from being an industrial city. The preponderance of British nationals is understandable since Nigeria was

TABLE 40   NON-NIGERIAN IMMIGRANTS INTO LAGOS, 1911-50

	1911	1921	1931	1950
Africans				
GHANA-TOGOLAND	634	1,192	1,140	1,736
SIERRA LEONE	940	1,373	1,187	631
LIBERIA	2,680	1,707	1,273	—
DAHOMEY	1,493	1,857	2,567	3,873
OTHERS	609	1,135	944	283
TOTAL	6,356	7,264	7,111	6,523
Europeans and Asians				
BRITISH	484	992	1,053	2,044
FRENCH	21	26	37	178
GERMANS	73	3	34	—
SYRIANS & LEBANESE	36	53	134	288
TOTAL	614	1,074	1,258	2,510

by 1950 still a colony of Britain with the upper cadres of its Civil Service manned almost exclusively by British people. Most of the French and Germans were engaged in commerce and repair services for vehicles. The rise and decline in the number of Germans reflected the changing relation between Britain and Germany before and during the war years. Among the Asians the most important were the Syrians and Lebanese. Their immigration into Lagos dates from 1902. Although their number continued to increase during the period, even in 1950 it remained small compared with their great importance in the commercial life of Lagos.

There is no greater index of the highly immigrant origin of most of the population of Lagos than the age and sex composition. Throughout the period Lagos remained a predominantly male and very youthful city. But while the sex ratio has been moving since 1921 towards an equalization, the age composition has been showing an increasing proportion in the under 30 years of age group. Table 41 gives the detail of the position from 1891 to 1950. What is perhaps more revealing is the position in the different ethnic groups that make up the total population. This is shown graphically in Fig. 41.

Among the Yoruba who formed the majority of the population, the sex ratio expressed as the number of males per 100 females, was 119 (1921), 110 (1931), and 104 (1950). In no age class was it ever greater than 130. The only exception occurred in 1921 when in the 15-30 years class it rose to 140. Throughout the period, therefore, the Yoruba as a group, both migrant and Lagos-born, were the nearest to being a balanced community in Lagos.

Among the other Nigerian immigrants, the position was strikingly different. The Ibo, for instance, had a ratio of 322 in 1921 which was still as high as 186 in 1950. However, the greatest absolute imbalance among them had shifted by 1950 from the age group 15-30 years to the 30-51 years. This is a reflection that, among the younger Ibo immigrants both sexes were almost equally represented. Over the same period, 1921-50, Edo immigrants were nearest to achieving equalization. The position among them shifted from 530 (1921) to 134 (1950). As with the Ibos, however, the greatest disproportion was in the older age classes. The Hausa immigrants showed here again rather peculiar characteristics. In the first place, the sex ratio among them remained almost constant at about 130. Secondly, it was the older immigrants, particularly those between 30 and 50 years of age, that were most important among

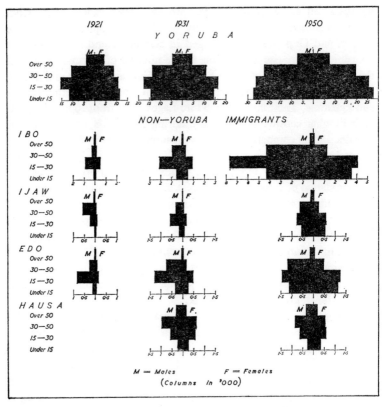

Figure 41   Lagos: age-sex distribution of native immigrants, 1921-50

TABLE 41   AGE AND SEX CHARACTERISTICS OF POPULATION, 1891-1950

	Males	Females	Males per 100 Females	% of total population under 30
1891	13,520	14,998	90	—
1901	21,176	20,671	102	—
1911	39,865	33,901	118	—
1921	57,337	42,353	135	62·2
1931	70,227	55,881	126	62·1
1950	124,858	105,398	119	67·3

them. This is probably an indication that most Hausa had come down to trade and not to seek for paid employment, trading being an occupation that would require older rather than younger immigrants. It appeared also that a large proportion of them were not permanent residents, but were constantly on the move between Lagos and Northern Nigeria. This fact would explain the very low proportion of Hausa under the age of 15 in Lagos.

Among the non-Nigerians, the Africans showed no remarkable disproportion between the sexes, the exception being among immigrants from Dahomey. With the latter, the males were always more numerous than the females except in the age class under 15 years. The Sierra Leoneans showed the best balance, never higher than 120. In fact, in 1950, Sierra Leoneans in Lagos between the ages of 15 and 30 years showed more females than males. Europeans and Asians showed a very large imbalance between the sexes up to 1931, but the gap has narrowed considerably since then. Among the British, the ratio fell from 552 (1931) to 172 (1950); among the French from 800 (1931) to 162 (1950); and among Syrians and Lebanese from 212 (1931) to 159 (1950). More European and Asian women have thus come into Lagos during the 19 years between the two censuses. Another notable change has been the increase in the number of European and Asian children in Lagos since 1931. Before that date neither the British nor the French thought Lagos safe enough for the health of their children. Since then, conditions have changed and numerous facilities have been created for rearing and educating non-African children in Lagos.

The metropolitan explosion: the post-1951 period

The rapid industrial development which took place in Lagos after 1950 resulted not only in an unprecedented rate of growth (Fig. 42) but also in the spectacular spatial expansion of the continuous built-up area beyond the legal confines of the municipality. Within the municipal boundary itself the population rose from 230,256 in 1950 to over 650,000 in 1963. This gave an enormous rate of annual growth of over 9 per cent per annum (compound interest). This remarkable growth in the population of Lagos was the combined result of an increased rate both of natural increase (see Table 42) and of immigration. The former was due to a sharp decline in death rate especially among infants as well as to an increase in birth rate. All of these reflected the tremendous improvement in social amenities in the period after 1950 best typified

TABLE 42   VITAL STATISTICS: LAGOS 1945-59

Per 1,000 of population	1945	1957	1958	1959
CRUDE BIRTH RATE	44·8	49·1	50·4	55·8
CRUDE DEATH RATE	23·3	14·2	12·7	13·6
INFANT MORTALITY RATE*	128·0	80·2	79·9	77·0
RATE OF NATURAL INCREASE	21·5	34·9	37·7	42·2

* deaths under one year of age per 1,000 live births

Source: Annual Reports of the Federal Medical Services, 1957, 1958, 1959, Lagos, Government Printer, 1960, 1961, 1962.

in the provision of medical facilities. Up to 1950 Lagos had only two general hospitals, a maternity hospital, four dispensaries, an orthopaedic hospital, a mental hospital, a tuberculosis sanatorium, an infectious diseases hospital, a dental centre and a school clinic. It also provided a Domiciliary Midwifery Service. In the succeeding seven years, it had added to these another general hospital on the mainland, a new maternity hospital and, most important, a fully-fledged teaching hospital of the University of Lagos. Compared with the rest of the country, Lagos, by 1958, had the best health facilities. Its ratio of population per hospital bed was 262 compared to 1,959 for the Western Region (including the Mid-West Region), 1,210 for the Eastern Region and 4,000 for the Northern Region. Similarly its ratio of population per doctor was 2,000 compared to 21,000 for the Western Region, 52,000 for the Eastern Region, and 99,000 for the Northern Region.

Growth by natural increase, however, probably accounted for no more than a third of the growth of population in Lagos since 1951. The rest was made up by renewed immigration at a rate unequalled in the history of the city. There are no figures to document the details of this spectacular influx but the broad pattern is clear. More Yoruba, particularly from Ijebu and Abeokuta Provinces, which are the nearest, moved into Lagos. Of the non-Yoruba, the Ibo remained the most important group. From field investigations carried out in 1961, it appeared that the trend towards a numerical equalization of the sexes among the Ibo was temporarily reversed and many more young Ibo men were to be found than Ibo women. An increase in the number of Hausa was particularly striking, and was accompanied by a significant change in the age and sex structure in favour of younger men of 25 to 40 years of age. These new immigrants had come to Lagos as members of the

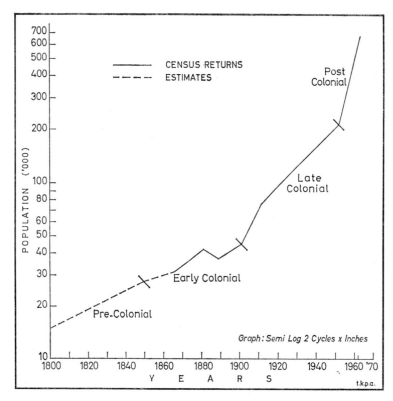

Figure 42   Growth of population in Lagos, 1800-1962

enlarged Federal Civil Service so that their social and economic status was much higher than was the case among the Hausa population of Lagos before 1950.

Of non-Nigerians, the position among the Africans and Asians is obscure. It is less so in the case of Europeans (including Americans) because of the new conditions governing their entry into the country. A larger proportion of those coming into Lagos after 1950 is made up of technicians, engineers, commercial salesmen and businessmen, for each of whom an entry permit had to be obtained from the Federal Government through the Ministry of Commerce and Industry. The Annual Report of the Ministry indicates the number of those granted such permits as 218 in 1956, 272 in 1957 and 598 in 1958. Figures since then are not available, but there is no doubt that the trend continued.

It was reckoned that by 1957 the total European population had risen to about 7,000 compared with less than 3,000 in 1950.

This remarkable growth of population within Lagos gives no indication of the fact that a large proportion, especially of the unskilled labour force on which Lagos depends, now lives outside of the municipality in what were formerly distinct and separate communities. Compared to Lagos itself, these communities (Table 43) have undergone within 11 years (1952-63) a staggering rate of growth. Their combined population had increased from about 60,000 in 1952 to nearly half a million in 1963. Added to the figure for Lagos, this brings the total population of the continuous built-up area to well over a million. In short, by 1963 Lagos had burst through the confines of its municipal boundaries, and, like rapidly industrializing cities everywhere in the world, was engulfing neighbouring small communities in a dramatic 'metropolitan explosion'.

TABLE 43   GROWTH OF POPULATION OF COMMUNITIES AROUND LAGOS 1952-63

Community	1952	1963	Annual rate (%) of growth
MUSHIN	32,079		
BARIGA	175		
SOMOLU	} 5,309	} 312,063	21·3
BAJULAIYE			
BASHUA, ETC.			
OSHODI-SHOGUNLE	4,274	23,391	16·7
IKEJA	6,705	36,923	16·8
AJEROMI	12,951	52,245	13·5
TOTAL	61,493	424,622	19·3

Such an 'explosion' always creates innumerable problems. A most important one relates to the usual time-lag of administrative adjustments to the new situation. In particular, district councils formerly concerned with overseeing the needs of predominantly rural communities become suddenly faced with the entirely different problems of a restless urban group. The need of this group for such basic amenities as good roads, water supply, sanitation, shopping areas and recreational grounds invokes hardly any responses from the council. Within a short time the tolerable rural conditions are changed to the menacing squalor of an urban slum. A sharp line of contrast is now drawn as between conditions in the municipality and those in its immediate surroundings; for instance, between Apapa and Yaba on the one hand, and Ajegunle and Somolu on the other.

A United Nations Team which reported in 1964 made the obvious point that what was now needed was the creation of either an administrative or a planning region of Greater Lagos.[47] As was to be expected, there has been a considerable dragging of feet on the issue which involves both the Federal and the Western Regional Governments. Irrespective of their decision, there is no doubt that Lagos, in terms of the municipality, no longer has an independent existence. The succeeding analysis of the structure of the city is therefore concerned not just with the municipality but with the whole of the continuous built-up area stretching north to Ikeja and including on the south-west both Ajegunle and Ajeromi.

References

1. Durate Pacheco Pereira, the Portuguese geographer, in his *Esmeral-do de Situ Orbis*, published in 1505 (Trans. Ed. G. H. T. Kimble, Hakluyt Society Series II, Vol. 79, London 1937, p. 124) described the Lagos Lagoon and, although he indicated the existence of the large city of Geebu (Ijebu-Ode) further inland, made no mention of any settlement on the island in the Lagoon. Similarly, Petrus Plaucius in his map of 1594, *L'Afrique Occidentale*, Anvers, 1594 (*Monumenta Cartographica Africae et Aegypti*, Tome V, Fasc. 1 (Ed. Youssouf Kamal), 1951, p. 1541) showed the lagoon and the island but gave no name to the latter. The first reference to the island as Ichoo (or Eko, the name by which the settlement is locally known) is in a map of 1659 entitled *L'Afrique au nord de l'équateur* by the Dutch cartographer L. Blaeu (see Youssouf Kamal (Ed.), op. cit., p. 1551). M. D'Avezac in his *Notice sur le pays et le peuple des Yebous en Afrique*, Paris, 1841, p. 4, also mentions that, during the seventeenth century, the name Ichoo began to appear on maps of lesser known Dutch cartographers. D. O. Dapper's *Description de L'Afrique*, Amsterdam, 1686, p. 307, also showed Ichoo on a map and called the settlement in the neighbourhood Curamo, adding besides that 'the Dutch come here to buy cotton cloths which they carry to the Gold Coast'.
2. J. O. George, *Historical Notes on the Yoruba Country and its tribes*, Lagos, 1884, p. 24.
3. There is some controversy about whether the name is a corrupted version of *Laguo* in Rio de Laguo—the name by which the lagoon was known to the Portuguese—or whether the island was given the name after the town of Lagos in Portugal. See C. P. Lucas,

Historical Geography of the British Colonies, Vol. 3, Oxford, 1894, p. 221.

4. Captain John Adams, *Sketches taken during ten voyages to Africa between the years 1786 and 1800*, London, 1923, p. 27.

5. Otunba Payne, *Table of Principal Events in Yoruba History*, 1893, p. 1, ascribes the earliest beginning of the trade in slaves in Lagos to Akinsemoyin, who became the Oba of Lagos in 1704.

6. Captain John Adams, op. cit., p. 78.

7. L. Abson to A. Dalzel, 14-22 December 1794, Treasury Papers, Public Record Office, London (T70/1570) and 27 August 1797 (T70/1574); Citoyen Denian to Pierre Bonon, 20 August 1797, Archives Nationales (AN.C6/27); P. Bonon to le Ministre de la Marine et des Colonies, 10 Vendémiaire, Au. 10. (AN.C6/27).

8. Liverpool Ships to Africa, 1797, Treasury Papers, Public Record Office, London (T70/1575).

9. See Captain John Adams, op. cit., p. 80.

10. B. Campbell, letter dated 28 December 1853. See William N. M. Geary, *Nigeria under British Rule*, London, 1947, p. 29.

11. For the conditions of life of these freed slaves in Sierra Leone, see Christopher Fyfe, 'Four Sierra Leone Recaptives', *Journal of African History*, Vol. 2, No. 1, London, 1961, pp. 77-85.

12. T. B. Freeman, *Missionary Notices*, Vol. 9, December 1841.

13. Consul Beecroft, Letter to Viscount Palmerston, 3 January 1852, *Papers relative to the Reduction of Lagos*, No. 69, London, 1852.

14. Captain Jones, Letter to Commodore Bruce, 29 December 1851, *Papers relative to the Reduction of Lagos*, No. 70, Inclosure 2, London, 1852.

15. P. A. Talbot, *The Peoples of Southern Nigeria*, Vol. 1, London, 1926, p. 104.

16. T. J. Bowen, *Adventures and Missionary Labours in several countries in the Interior of Africa from 1849-1856*, Charleston, 1857.

17. P. A. Talbot, op. cit., p. 124.

18. M. J. Bane, *Catholic Pioneers in West Africa*, Dublin, 1956, p. 146.

19. See R. R. Kuczynski, *Demographic Survey of the British Colonial Empire*, Vol. 1, London, 1948, p. 673.

20. Report of the Select Committee on Africa, London, 1865, p. 71.

21. See R. R. Kuczynski, op. cit., p. 674.

22. Governor Carter, *Letter to Lord Knutsford, June 24th 1892*, C.O. 806/357, Incl. No. 133.

23. H. N. G. Thompson, *Census of Lagos, 1931*, Vol. IV of the Census of Nigeria, London, 1932, p. 1.

24. A. C. Burns, *History of Nigeria*, London, 1929, p. 128.

25. A. C. Burns, ibid., p. 207.

26. Captain John Adams, op. cit., p. 107.

27. *Report of the Select Committee on Africa*, London, 1865, p. 73.

28. Thomas J. Hutchinson, *Impressions of Western Africa*, London, 1858, p. 77.

29. B. W. Hodder, 'The Growth of trade at Lagos, Nigeria', *Tijdschrift voor Economische en Sociale Geografie*, 50ste Jaargang, No. 10, October 1959, pp. 197-202.
30. Sir William N. M. Geary, op. cit., p. 41.
31. W. B. Baikie, *Narrative of an Exploring Voyage*, London, 1856, pp. 21-22.
32. R. F. Burton, *Wanderings in West Africa*, London, 1863, p. 207.
33. T. J. Hutchinson, op. cit., p. 73.
34. R. F. Burton, *Wanderings in West Africa*, London, 1863, p. 209.
35. Messrs Coode, Son and Matthews, *Report on the Lagos Harbour*, March 1896, para. 36.
36. R. F. Burton, op. cit., p. 208.
37. Sir W. N. M. Geary, op. cit., p. 146.
38. *Correspondence on Lagos Harbour*, 1904-10.
39. See *History of Lagos Harbour*, Ministry of Transport, Lagos, Departmental Notes, 1956.
40. Messrs Coode and Co., *Apapa Wharf Extension Completion Report*, London, 1958.
41. Total daily employment of dock labour rose from an average of 234 in 1938 to nearly 6,500 in 1959. (See *Annual Report of the Port Dept.* 1938, p. 9, and 5th *Annual Report of Nigerian Ports Authority*, 1960, p. 119.)
42. *Annual Report of the Department of Labour* for the year 1956-7, Lagos, 1959.
43. *Annual Report of the Department of Commerce and Industries*, 1949-50, Lagos.
44. *Census of Nigeria*, Vol. 1, London, 1932, p. 127.
45. *Colonial Report*, Lagos, 1900-1, p. 10.
46. *Annual Report on the Department of Labour, 1945*, Lagos, 1946, p. 12.
47. United Nations Report, *Metropolitan Lagos*, Prepared for the Government of Nigeria by Otto Koenigsberger, Charles Abrams, Susumu Kobe, Maurice Shapiro and Michael Wheeler. Appointed under the United Nations Programme of Technical Assistance, 1964.

Although less traditional than Ibadan, Lagos exhibits an internal structure which in part can also be explained in terms of the twin-centre concept. Much of the differences between the two cities is due to the island situation of the initial settlement, the smallness of the traditional town and the fact that the major development of Lagos took place in the era of modern commercial expansion and industrial growth.

The island of Lagos has an extreme east-west length of about $3\frac{1}{4}$ miles and an extreme north-south breadth of about $1\frac{1}{4}$ miles. Its total area is thus about four square miles. It is a low-lying island consisting largely of sand and originally covered by swamps and a coarse type of grass interspersed with clusters of large trees. The highest part of the island is in the extreme north-west (Fig. 43) and is just over 20 feet. This low eminence extends south-eastwards at a slightly lower elevation to form an east-west backbone to the island. Until the present century, much of the island was taken up by lagoons and swamps. The largest of the lagoons was the Idumagbo Lagoon on the north, an expanse of shallow water covering some 40 acres. A short distance to the east was the Isalegangan Lagoon, a narrow, elongated body of water about 12 acres in area. On the west were the Elegbata and Alakoro Creeks, the latter forming a natural moat around Alakoro Island. The largest areas of swamps were to be found to the east of the island and consisted of the North and South Ikoyi Swamps and the Okesuna Swamp.

The numerous lagoons and swamps separated the settlement into blocks. Sometimes they served the very useful purpose of localizing the ravages of the ever recurrent fires which were commonplace before the era of corrugated iron sheets. Most of the time, however, they constituted a threat to the health of the people. The lagoons were used as dumping grounds for all refuse and, apart from being an eyesore during low water, they polluted drinking water. The swamps bred mosquitoes whose bites, although at first not associated with malaria, were extremely offensive. The task of reclaiming the swamps and adding some 1,000 acres of new land to the area of Lagos Island began in earnest only with the arrival of Governor MacGregor in 1899. Today Lagos

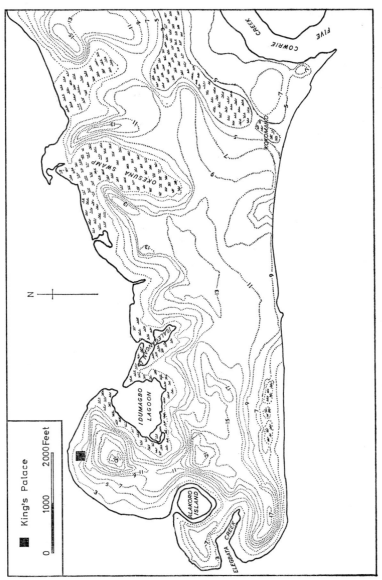

Figure 43   The physical characteristics of Lagos

Island has been relieved of virtually all its swamps although on the mainland there still exist extensive swamp areas which are in the process of being reclaimed.

The traditional centre and spatial organization

Considering the physical character of the island before recent times, it is easy to appreciate why the oldest and densest concentration of housing was on the highest ground to the north-west of the island and extending down to the shore (Plate 22). Morgan states that in 1853 the town occupied no more than a third of the total area of the island.[1] As in other Yoruba towns, the palace of the Oba stood in the centre of this town, within an extensive palace ground covering over 8 acres (see Fig. 37). This palace is believed to have been sited on what was formerly a pepper (*iganran*) farm, hence its name 'Iga Idunganran' or the Pepper Palace. Oral tradition asserts that this first palace was replaced early in the eighteenth century by a new one built by the Portuguese, probably in appreciation of the trading monopoly granted them by Oba Akinsemoyin. In 1863 this palace was described as 'a red-tiled and partially whitewashed barn backed by trees of the noblest stature'.[2] Today the tiles have disappeared but the iron columns remain as do parts of the original walls.

Not far from the palace was the Obun Eko Market with a shoreline extension in the Ebute Ero Market. The Obun Eko Market is the real central market in Lagos but because of its more advantageous location for trade along the lagoon, the Ebute Ero (the Haven of the Visitors) has grown to become more important. This is a daily market specializing in both foodstuffs and craft products and attended not only by the townspeople but also by Ijebu and Awori along the lagoon. Partly because of the smallness of the island area and the greater intensity of economic life in Lagos, neither the Obun Eko nor the Ebute Ero Market exercises anything like the influence of Iba Market in Ibadan on contemporary conditions in Lagos. Indeed, such has been the pace of development in Lagos that Ebute Ero Market has had to be moved from its original site close to the Palace to a location farther north. In 1960, on the eve of the country's independence, it had to be destroyed as its physical condition had deteriorated to such an extent that it was an eyesore. The market has now been rebuilt close to another market— Egerton Square Market—together with which it continues to play an important part in the distributive trade of Lagos. It is not clear whether, like Iba Market in Ibadan, Obun Eko served also as an evening market. However, it continues to serve as a four-day periodic market apart from its other function as a daily market and performs a highly specialized function as a kolanut market every 16 days.

In 1898, Lagos Island was served by fourteen other markets apart from Obun Eko and Ebute Ero.[3] This large number of markets emphasizes the quarter organization of traditional Lagos, the isolation from each other of portions of the island, and the poor and undeveloped stage of transport. As the quarter system of organization became less important and circulation within the island became both easy and inexpensive, the number of markets has tended to be drastically reduced. By 1940 only three of the earlier sixteen markets—Obun Eko, Ebute Ero and Faji had survived. The rest had disappeared and have been replaced by only six others—Idumagbo, Egerton Square, Lewis Street, Olowu Street, Great Bridge Street and Obalende Markets.

Since the 1940s also, the dominant position of Ebute Ero had been successfully challenged by Idumagbo Market. This is a new market a little way south of Ebute Ero Market, developed on the reclaimed site of the former Idumagbo Lagoon. Because of its relative nearness to the modern Business District on the Marina, this market has become noted for the abundant supply of imported or locally manufactured articles and its section—Jankara—which handles this speciality, sells at what are considered extremely cheap prices. More recently, with the abandoning of Ebute Ero Market, the agricultural produce section of Idumagbo Market has become considerably augmented and has overflowed into the adjoining open space which was formerly Oko Awo Playground.

Table 44 shows the relative importance in 1960 of the eight markets on Lagos Island (minus Ebute Ero) based on the number and types of sellers in the market. The dominant position of Idumagbo on the Island is clearly brought out, and the tendency towards a three-tier hierarchical organization emphasized. The lowest-order markets, namely Faji, Obun Eko, Olowu Street, Great Bridge Street and Obalende, sell lowest-order goods such as foodstuffs and meat but vary in the total number of sellers because of the inclusion of some specialized branch of trade. Thus Obun Eko (V) is an important fresh fish market and so also is Great Bridge Street (VII) while Olowu Street (VI) is noted for its charcoal, firewood, wood and planks, and Faji Market (IV) for both its fish section and sundry services (pepper grinders, stockfish cutters, etc.). The next order of markets comprises both Egerton

TABLE 44 TYPES AND NUMBERS OF SELLERS IN LAGOS MARKETS*

	I	II	III	IV	V	VI	VII	VIII	IX	X	XI	XII
1. FOODSTUFFS	424	208	222	12	48	56	2	10	386	128	12	263
2. VEGETABLES AND FRUIT	124	121	164	86	29	12	12	17	178	127	30	175
3. CONDIMENTS	336	176	193	38	30	38	41	10	342	72	26	247
4. VEGETABLE OIL	54	40	32	16	16	24	6	8	128	18	4	74
5. MEAT	80	44	58	40	—	—	—	14	74	46	30	64
6. DRIED MEAT	—	—	—	—	—	—	—	—	74	—	—	—
7. FISH (FRESH)	56	104	50	25	96	—	64	9	80	14	18	46
8. DRIED FISH	68	26	48	14	—	—	6	2	84	22	—	42
9. STOCKFISH	61	65	32	24	—	—	—	4	56	12	—	35
10. POULTRY	97	30	42	—	—	—	—	—	187	15	—	63
11. SHEEP AND GOATS	—	—	—	—	—	—	—	—	80	—	—	—
12. KOLANUTS	84	31	49	—	—	—	6	—	—	12	10	—
13. NATIVE MEDICINE	—	6	—	—	17	34	—	3	68	—	—	58
14. FIREWOOD	64	—	—	—	—	27	—	—	—	—	—	24
15. CHARCOAL	40	—	—	—	—	14	—	—	—	—	—	—
16. WOOD AND PLANKS	30	—	6	—	—	—	—	—	—	—	—	—
17. MATTRESSES	107	—	3	—	—	—	—	—	—	—	—	—
18. MATS	56	20	5	—	—	—	—	—	—	—	—	—
19. POTTERY	84	—	49	—	—	—	—	—	42	—	—	25
20. NATIVE CLOTH	262	76	31	—	—	—	—	—	—	—	—	—
21. IMPORTED TEXTILES	310	120	36	—	—	—	—	8	114	39	—	72
22. CHINA AND ENAMELWARE	341	172	32	—	—	—	—	—	156	29	—	86
23. TINNED FOOD, ETC.	142	40	8	10	—	—	—	—	169	37	—	69
24. SUNDRY GOODS	84	35	42	12	—	—	—	3	138	12	16	49
25. PEPPER GRINDERS	12	12	36	21	—	—	—	1	94	3	—	78
26. STOCKFISH CUTTERS	65	42	—	6	—	—	—	—	12	—	—	—
27. FOOD STALL	—	—	—	—	—	—	16	1	52	30	—	9
28. SEWING MISTRESSES	—	—	—	—	—	—	—	—	5	—	—	36
TOTAL	2989	1368	1138	304	236	205	153	90	2519	616	146	1515

* *Source:* Field Survey in 1960. *Markets represented are:*

I	*Idumagbo*	II	*Egerton Square*	III	*Lewis Street*
IV	*Faji Market*	V	*Obun Eko*	VI	*Olowu Street*
VII	*Great Bridge Street*	VIII	*Obalende*	IX	*Oyingbo*
X	*Ijero*	XI	*Sabo (Yaba)*	XII	*Mushin (Daily)*

Square (II) and Lewis Street (III) both of which sell everything in the lowest-order market as well as imported articles. They also provide services such as pepper grinding, stockfish cutting and food provision. Idumagbo's premier position appears to be based on the sale of more expensive goods like native cloth, mattresses, wood and planks, and mats. On the mainland there appear to be two other systems of markets. One, based on Oyingbo (IX), has as subsidiary centres the markets at Ijero, Yaba, Ojuelegba and Apapa; the other based on Mushin (XII) has Odi-Olowo and Somolu markets as subsidiaries.

Superimposed on this system of daily markets is the phenomenon of periodic markets. Traditionally, periodic markets serve the function of replenishing the stocks of grocers in a situation in which there is no refrigeratory equipment. As Hodder had noticed elsewhere, such periodic markets tend to operate as 'rings', often of four markets, each market operating once in four days. Until recently there were six periodic markets in the Lagos area, namely Ebute Ero, Obun Eko, Oyingbo, Mushin, Iganmu and Apapa. These markets were organized as two rings with Oyingbo and Mushin being in both rings. Since the 1950s, however, the ring system has broken down both on Lagos Island and in Apapa with the result that major periodic activities are now concentrated only on Oyingbo and Mushin Markets. These activities are excluded from the consideration of their size in Table 44.

Finally there is the Iddo Wholesale Food Market which is related in a very special way to the railway terminus at Iddo. Most of the commodities sold here have been involved in long hauls by railway from the northern parts of the country. They include rice, beans, onions, maize, dried fish, eggs and groundnut oil. All have a common characteristic, except for onions and eggs, of being non-perishable. The market itself was reconstructed in 1959 and now consists of 117 new stalls. Stall spaces are larger than in the daily markets and are provided with large doors which can be kept under lock and key.

The reason for describing the marketing system in Lagos in such detail is to stress its very traditional origin. As in Ibadan, the markets represent focal points of community organization. Moreover, as in Ibadan, the most important part of the market was located close by the palace of the Oba, together with which it formed the centre of the traditional town. Even today important ceremonial functions connected with the installation of the Oba of Lagos are carried out at the Enu-Owa end of the Obun Eko Market. However, unlike in Ibadan, the orientation of traffic routes has tended to by-pass the older part of Lagos and condemned it to a condition of steady degradation and neglect.

The Marina and other modern business centres

While the traditional centre of Old Lagos is to the north of the island, the southern shores began to be occupied after 1851 by incoming European merchants. As the nineteenth century progressed, this area developed as a new but important centre of trade. In 1861 McCoskry, one of the merchants, during a period when he acted as Governor, began the construction of a broad road, 60 ft wide, along the waterfront which became known as the Marina.[4] Soon after, another street, also 40 ft wide, was begun about one hundred yards behind the Marina and was named Broad Street. These two streets form today the main arteries of the modern Central Business District of Lagos, an area more commonly referred to as the 'Marina'.

In the nineteenth century the trading establishments of the European merchants were known as 'factories'. These were buildings storied in their front part and containing the shop below and the residence above. Inside the walls on three sides, these buildings faced inward.[5] They were occupied by blacksmiths, coopers and carpenters, by stores for produce, and by the cook. In the open space formed by the courtyard, beneath the shade of large trees, the Africans who had come great distances in their canoes lay about and talked, went to sleep, or haggled about trade. Each factory had opposite it on the lagoon side a pier (Plate 23) where the water was deep enough to berth vessels of those days alongside. Between the wharves there was plenty of space for the canoes coming from long distances to the north, east and west to discharge produce and to receive, on the spot, goods in return.

During the twentieth century much of this has changed. All the 'factories' have disappeared and have been replaced by more modern multi-storey buildings. The numerous piers in front of them were also dismantled with the construction of a modern port at Apapa in 1926 and greater governmental supervision of import and export for fiscal purposes. Today, such has been the development in Lagos that its nucleations of commercial businesses do give rise to a pattern approximating to that generalized by Proudfoot (see Chapter 7).

The most important of these nucleations is the *Central Business District* which, as we have seen, developed around the twin arteries of

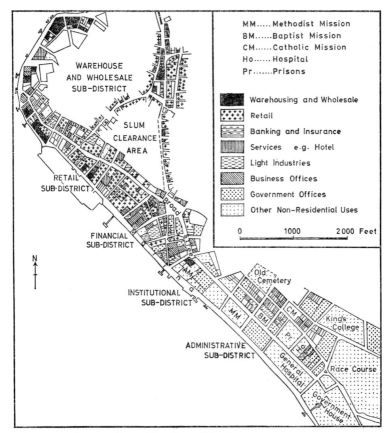

Figure 44   Lagos: Central Business District

the Marina and Broad Street. In this district is concentrated a multiplicity of functions including wholesaling, retailing, financing, cultural
activities and administration. Fig. 44 shows that each of these functions
tends to be dominant in parts of the Central Business District, giving
rise to five main sub-districts. First there is the warehouse and wholesale sub-district for which produce stores and warehouses are the most
distinctive land-use (Table 45). Second there is the retail sub-district
which is, of course, the heart of the CBD. Most of the houses here are
three- or four-storied, although many new ones are going to much
greater heights. The most characteristic form of land-use in this sub-
district is the department store. This is defined by the British Census

of Distribution as 'a large shop with annual sales exceeding £100,000, and with sales greater than £5,000 in each of several commodity groups one of which is clothing. Shops classified under this heading usually sell women's clothing, household textiles and soft furnishings, furniture and domestic hardware, and they may sell men's wear, food and other items'.[6] In Lagos, no figures of annual sales are available but the other criteria have been used to identify department stores. The oldest and most important of the department stores is the Kingsway Store. Opened in 1948, it has a total floor area, on three floors, of 100,000 square feet. Other notable department stores include the Union Trading Company, A. G. Leventis, the G. B. Ollivant and the K. Chellaram Stores.

TABLE 45   SUMMARY OF LAND-USE INTENSITY

(expressed as the number of floors of buildings occupied by each function)

	Wholesale	Retail	Finance	Administration
PRODUCE STORES	14	—	—	—
WAREHOUSES	25	—	—	—
WHOLESALE DEPARTMENTS	4	4	—	—
STORE ROOMS	2	31	8	—
MOTOR SERVICING	7	3	3	3
PRINTING	4	2	4	3
BUSINESS (GOVERN-MENTAL) OFFICES	45	98	78	186
SHIPPING LINES	3	8	2	—
TRAVEL AGENCIES	1	3	1	—
DEPARTMENTAL STORES	2	20	1	—
HARDWARE AND BUILDING MATERIALS	—	22	2	1
TECHNICAL AND MOTOR SHOWROOMS	—	17	11	—
ELECTRICAL AND RADIO SHOPS	—	14	—	—
CHEMIST AND DRUGGIST	—	7	2	—
SHOES	—	5	2	—
HABERDASHERY	—	5	—	—
SUPERMARKETS	—	1	—	—
HOTELS	2	10	—	8
BANKS	5	14	37	3
INSURANCE	4	4	9	—

Source: Field Survey in 1960.

The finance sub-district is found to the east of the retail sub-district. At its centre is the Central Bank of Nigeria, a seven-storied building dating only from 1959 (Plate 24). Scattered around the Central Bank are various British, American and Nigerian banks and insurance houses, many of which have been reconstructed into multi-storied buildings in the last few years. Farther east are found various religious and educational institutions including the Anglican Cathedral of Lagos, the First Baptist Church, the Methodist Boys' High School, St Mary's Convent School and the Anglican Girls' School. The location of these various institutions along the Marina and Broad Street dates from the 1850s but they represent the least intensive use of land in the CBD. Many of the buildings have in recent years been converted to headquarters or administrative offices of the various religious denominations. Lastly there is the administrative sub-district to the extreme east comprising both the municipal and the federal government offices. Because of the rapid constitutional development since 1951, this sub-district has experienced the most phenomenal changes. From being contained in a single large Secretariat building, government business overflowed into many adjoining houses, some of which had to be rebuilt as multi-storied structures to provide space for the numerous new ministries. Further expansion came with national independence in 1960 when the need of numerous foreign embassies, consulates and commissions for office accommodation led to a spurt of new buildings of the most modern design. Many of these buildings rise to unprecedented heights and a few are veritable sky-scrapers rising to over 25 floors.

The Central Business District in Lagos is clearly much more highly developed and more specialized than that of Ibadan. In fact it draws to itself a large day-time population not only from all parts of Lagos but also from Abeokuta and Ibadan which are some sixty and ninety miles away respectively. Many middle-class families in these towns make a monthly or quarterly trip to Lagos for some of their shopping. The superiority of the Central Business District in Lagos to that in Ibadan is, no doubt, due to a greater concentration of income in the former. This same factor underlines the fact that, unlike Ibadan, Lagos shows a clearer evidence of the development of other modern retail conformations besides the Central Business District in other parts of the city.

Thus in at least four locations (Fig. 45) there is an indication of the development of *outlying business centres*. These locations are at (1) Sabo in Yaba, (2) Oyingbo in Ebute Metta, (3) Idumota inter-section of

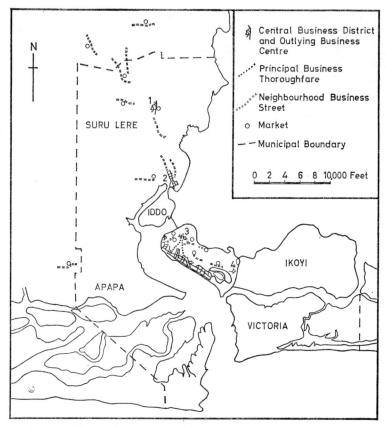

Figure 45   The retail structure of Lagos

Victoria and Balogun-Ereko Streets, both of which are business thoroughfares, and (4) Araromi at the eastern end of Lagos Island. At each of these centres, the two major elements in the nucleation are a departmental or large provision store and a bank. The Sabo nucleation shows two banks, two large provision stores, and numerous closely-spaced small African shops. In the Oyingbo nucleation there are two department stores (Bhojson and Marks & Spencer), one supermarket (Leventis), a bank, a hotel, motor showrooms, hardware and building material stores and a concentration of small African convenience goods shops. Some of the functions represented in the Idumagbo Centre include a department store, a radio and television showroom, a jewellery store, three banks and two insurance offices. The Araromi nucleation is still rather rudimentary and shows as yet only a large provision store and a bank. Nonetheless, at each of these centres there is evidence of a growing intensity of land use indicated by the increasing development of multi-storied buildings, the ground floors of which are designed to serve as shops.

Equally obvious in the case of Lagos is the existence of *principal business thoroughfares*. There are two of such thoroughfares in Lagos. One is Victoria Street; the other is Balogun-Ereko Street. As with similar streets elsewhere they combine the two functions of a business street and a traffic artery. As business streets, they differ from the CBD in having little depth much beyond the street frontage and consist largely of single or two-storied buildings of rather restricted floor space, varying between 200 and 400 square feet. Their strongest attraction derives from their specialized sales character as can be seen from Table 46. Their specialization in the sale of textiles and haberdashery is, apart from anything else, the spatial expression of local trade organization whereby the large European firms handle most of the importation of textiles into the country but sell wholesale, often direct from the warehouse, to Syrians and African businessmen. This secondary group of sellers, unable to compete for land in the CBD, find the traffic arteries to and from the latter an invaluable location for their purpose.

Lagos also shows clear evidence of the two lower orders of business conformations, namely the neighbourhood business street and the isolated store cluster. What is so interesting is the way in which the

TABLE 46   TYPES OF SHOP ALONG THE PRINCIPAL BUSINESS THOROUGH-
FARES

(Figures are based on a field survey carried out in 1961)

| | NUMBER | | | % | | |
	Balogun	Ereko	Victoria	Balogun	Ereko	Victoria
TEXTILES AND HABERDASHERY	47	35	47	71	85	56
MIXED RETAIL	1	—	12	1·5	—	14
BUSINESS OFFICE	11	2	14	17	5	17
FURNITURE STORE	1	1	1	1·5	2·5	1
SHOE STORES	—	—	2	—	—	2
OTHERS	6	3	8	9	7·5	10
TOTAL	66	41	84	100	100	100

former tends to occur as a complementary adjunct to local markets which have been and remain the real centre of neighbourhood economic life. Indeed, most of the *neighbourhood business streets* take their source, as it were, from the markets and extend away from them generally along major mass transportation routes. Some of the more notable ones include Lewis Street deriving from Lewis Street Market; Tokunbo and Massey-Agarawu Streets which are related to Faji Market; Egerton and John Streets which are related to Egerton Street Market; Denton and Oyingbo Street which are related to Oyingbo Market; and the Agege Motor Road which is related to Mushin Market. That the retail conformation along these streets is related to their nearness to markets is further emphasized by the importance of women shop-owners, most of whom concentrate on such convenience goods as food and drinks and tend to avoid those that require some special knowledge or expertise such as drugs, electrical goods, tools, and spare parts for vehicles. An analysis of the type of shop commonly found along them confirms that over 60 per cent are either selling convenience goods on a scale too large for stalls in a market or are performing services the equipment for which requires to be properly housed and protected.

Port development and industrial concentrations

Until recently the traditional centre and the modern Central Business District provided the major nuclei around which the city of Lagos developed. From 1926 onwards, and especially since 1950, a new nucleus was established at Apapa with the construction of the port. However, as long as Apapa served only as a port, its focal importance was not very great. Since 1950, when the land in its immediate vicinity was developed as an industrial estate, it has begun to exert a strong influence on the pattern of land development in Lagos.

The Apapa Industrial Estate is easily the most important industrial concentration in Lagos. Its 230 acres of reclaimed and developed land provided ample space for numerous large industrial plants. The most important industries represented include food and drinks, transport—particularly motor assembly and repairs—building and construction engineering, and metal industries. Table 47 shows that of some 43,000 industrial workers in Lagos in 1959, over one-third were employed in Apapa alone. If Iganmu were included, the proportion would come to nearly half. The table also shows the relative importance of Apapa with respect to specific categories of industries. If Iganmu were included,

TABLE 47 · LOCATION OF THE INDUSTRIAL LABOUR FORCE, 1959 (PERCENTAGE DISTRIBUTION)

Types of Industry / Location	Food and Drinks	Textiles and Clothing	Wood and Leather	Building and Construction	Printing	Metal	Engineering	Transport	TOTAL
APAPA	50·9	1·4	13·3	49·3	—	31·2	21·3	47·1	35·6
IGANMU	23·4	—	16·8	10·4	9·0	1·2	—	1·5	7·2
LAGOS ISLAND	13·7	63·1	14·3	6·5	58·8	34·7	30·8	18·0	21·4
IDDO-IJORA	—	2·0	17·5	3·9	—	7·4	39·1	8·8	9·7
EBUTE METTA WEST	0·3	5·8	3·6	10·1	13·5	4·1	5·0	16·6	9·3
EBUTE METTA EAST	4·6	24·7	29·2	18·3	6·2	8·9	3·8	6·2	13·6
YABA ESTATE	1·9	0·4	0·9	0·8	10·6	—	—	0·5	1·0
MUSHIN	5·2	2·6	4·4	0·7	1·9	12·5	—	1·3	2·2
Percentage Total	100·0	100·0	100·0	100·0	100·0	100·0	100·0	100·0	100·0
TOTAL LABOUR	2,796	3,659	3,922	13,829	1,732	2,121	4,621	10,247	42,927

Source: Based on a survey carried out by the Federal Ministry of Commerce and Industry.

for instance, Apapa would account for nearly 75 per cent of the industrial labour force in foods and drinks, 60 per cent in building and construction and 50 per cent in transport. In general, however, the use of the labour force as an index of industrial concentration understates the importance of Apapa for in contrast to the numerous, small-scale industrial units found in most other parts of the municipality, Apapa has mainly large, heavily capitalized, modern industrial plants. These include, for instance, the brewery at Iganmu employing 650 individuals, the soap factory occupying an area of nine acres and employing 700 workers; the four building contracting firms of Taylor Woodrow (Nigeria) Ltd, G. Cappa Ltd, Borini Prono & Co. Ltd and the Coast Construction (Nigeria) Ltd which, between them, account for nearly 18 per cent of the total industrial labour; the five motor assembly plants, the largest of which cost over half a million pounds; and there is, of course, the port and dockyard of the Nigerian Ports Authority providing shipbuilding and repair facilities.

The industrial concentration at Apapa has grown so rapidly that it has linked up with the development at Iganmu. The pressure for more land for industrial development in this nucleus has led the Lagos Executive Development Board to seek to raise a loan from the Commonwealth Development Finance Corporation to reclaim and develop 376 acres of low-lying swamp at Ijora which is contiguous to Iganmu. As a matter of urgency and to meet a limited number of priority demands, the Board has already developed approximately 50 acres of this site even before the loan agreement has been settled.

Within the municipality another major industrial nucleus is represented by the workshops of the Nigerian Railway Corporation in Ebute Metta West. This concentration of industrial activities is, in fact, the oldest in Lagos, dating from 1895 when the construction of the railway was begun. Occupying part of the 1,100-acre land of the Railway Compound, the Industrial Section of the Nigerian Railway Corporation at Ebute Metta employs over 2,000 workers representing more than half the total industrial labour force in that part of the city. Close by the Railway Compound have developed in recent years some relatively large civil engineering establishments, notably E. J. Delany & Co. Ltd employing some 1,400 people and Dys Trocca Valsesra & Co. Ltd employing over 800. There are also major motor repair establishments, notably Leventis Motors, Mandilas and Karaberis, and Arab Brothers.

Since 1958 two other industrial nuclei have developed, this time outside the municipality of Lagos: one is at Mushin; the other at Ikeja. Although Mushin in 1959 showed a relatively low proportion of the industrial labour force (2·2 per cent), the concentration here has been growing rapidly and includes a number of medium-size factories manufacturing, among other things, furniture, food products and interior-sprung mattresses. It also includes a bicycle assembly plant and a large printing press. The concentration is largely unplanned and simply spreads out on both sides of the Lagos-Agege Road. The other nucleus at Ikeja has, by contrast, grown as a planned industrial estate like Apapa. The estate is some 300 acres in area and is adequately supplied with all facilities to aid industrial operation. Most of the factories are medium to large size occupying plots varying from 2 to 10 acres. Many employ labour varying from 200 to 500. Some of the most important factories are Guinness Nigeria Ltd (beer and stout production); Asbestos Cement Products Ltd, the Steel and Wire Factory, Tower Aluminium Ltd, Imperial Chemical Industries Ltd and British Paints Ltd.

Internal circulation

The four industrial concentrations at Apapa, Ebute Metta, Mushin and Ikeja as well as the Central Business District (Marina) and the traditional centre around Obun Eko on Lagos Island constitute the six major nuclei which today exercise a considerable influence on the internal structure of and circulation within Lagos. The role of the industrial nuclei are quite recent and emphasize the growing dissimilarity between Lagos and Ibadan. However, until they developed, Lagos was, like the latter town, essentially a twin-centre urban area. As early as 1899 it was suggested that a tramway should link both centres to the new Railway Terminus at Iddo, and so with the growing development at Ebute Metta.[7] The tramway was completed in 1902 and conveyed both passengers and freight between the two places. Its route ran from the Marina, northward through Balogun Square, Ereko, Idunmota and to Iddo. There were two trams for regular working and the service was at 45-minute intervals, later shortened to 30 minutes. The number of trams was increased to four in 1910 and the average fare for a mile was roughly a penny.

However, by 1913 it had become necessary to close down the passenger and goods-carrying activities of the tramway. Two reasons were mainly responsible for this. The first was the rather tight-fisted policy of the government with regard to providing the necessary outlay for new rolling stock and thus helping to make operation economic. The second was the unfortunate but fundamental error of adopting the 2 ft 6 in. track gauge as against the 3 ft 6 in. gauge. According to Miller, 'had the 3 ft 6 in. gauge been adopted, faster running could have taken place and through working of wagons from Lagos wharves to the main line railway would, no doubt, have considerably increased the revenue. Moreover, the trams could have run over the railway lines to Ebute Metta and there branched out into the streets again.'[8] Thus Lagos missed the opportunity of having a suburban high-speed tram service which would have helped to move large masses of people more quickly and efficiently than motor-buses can do in the narrow, ill-laid out streets and save the city some of its present problems of traffic congestion.

By then, however, road transport was becoming a major feature of urban activities in Lagos. In 1907 the city was reported as having ten miles of road suitable for wheeled traffic as well as two motor-cars, bicycles, horses and rickshaws.[9] In the next three decades the number of registered motor vehicles rose to 7,507, that of bicycles to 7,603, while rickshaws and go-carts stood at 28. Indeed, by 1946, the amount of vehicular traffic in Lagos had risen to such great intensity that some form of control had to be devised (Plate 29). A one-way system of traffic was introduced along many of the major roads, notably Victoria, Balogun, Bamgbose and Igbosere, and greater attention was paid to instituting traffic notices and signs at numerous dangerous approaches.

While private motor vehicles allowed the higher income classes to extend to the farthermost edge of the municipality in Ikoyi, Yaba and Apapa, it was the provision of cheap, mass transit media that facilitated the rapid expansion of Lagos. A cheap bus service was begun in 1915 when a Lagos family had two or three buses running within Lagos Island. Really effective services, however, began only in 1929 and since then they have improved both in their scope and efficiency. These services were provided by numerous private entrepreneurs, the most important of whom was the Greek family of J. N. Zarpas. Theirs was easily the most efficient, the most reliable and the best organized bus transport service and ran from Obalende on Ikoyi Island to Idi-Oro and Apapa on the mainland. In 1958 the business was bought by the Municipal Authority for a sum of about half-a-million pounds to form the basis of a municipal public transport service.

Plate 24   The Central Business District of Lagos

Plate 25   A lane in Old Lagos
Plate 26   A street scene in Somolu

The period of the take-over coincided with the period of the metropolitan explosion of Lagos. The bus service, therefore, although owned by the Lagos City Council, extended its operation beyond the city limits into the new low-rent residential suburbs sprawling away on the northern margin of the city. The average charge per mile on any route is roughly 2d. and the highest charge for a single trip, notably from Obalende to Apapa, a distance of nearly eight miles, is only 11d. On the whole it is estimated that nearly 100,000 passengers are moved daily by bus from one point to another within the metropolitan districts.

With the metropolitan explosion, the railway has become increasingly involved in intra-city transportation, especially during the morning and late afternoon rush hours. It moves workers mainly from the Apapa industrial and port district to the residential areas, especially those north of Ebute Metta. No figures are available for the total number of passengers involved in this daily movement, but a consideration of Table 48 gives some idea of the magnitude and extent of the traffic. The table shows that, after Oshodi, traffic diminishes so sharply that it emphasizes the limit of the metropolitan area, at least as in 1960. The large number of passengers at Apapa Local, Iganmu, Yaba and Mushin and the very low average value of tickets per passenger emphasizes that traffic from these stations, particularly from Iganmu, is short-distance and within the metropolitan area. In fact from field observation it is known that most of the factory hands and dock labour at Apapa and Iganmu come from Mushin and the low-grade residential districts to the north and east of Yaba for which the Yaba station is the converging point.

The distribution of the socio-economic characteristics of the population

An understanding of the location of the major nuclei in Lagos facilitates an appreciation of the pattern of distribution of various socio-economic groups and the character of residential districts within the city. However, like other cities in the world which have 'exploded' beyond their administrative limits, metropolitan Lagos has the problem of not being regarded as an entity for statistical purposes. The result is that while data exist for the municipality, there is nothing comparable for the rest of the metropolitan area. Even the data for the municipality are not completely satisfactory. In the first place they refer to the 1952 Census and depict a situation which, although it may not have changed substantially, is clearly in the past. Secondly the data exist

TABLE 48   RAILWAY PASSENGER TRAFFIC, 1960

	Number	Receipts (£)	Average value of tickets (£)
LAGOS TOWN OFFICE	1,622	8,915	5·5
LAGOS TERMINUS	116,379	93,787	0·8
APAPA LOCAL	217,001	4,150	0·02
IGANMU SIDING	97,561	779	0·008
EBUTE METTA	81,359	5,110	0·06
EBUTE METTA JUNCTION	108,398	5,113	0·05
YABA	172,620	3,933	0·02
MUSHIN	313,599	10,087	0·03
OSHODI	93,859	1,659	0·02
SHOGUNLE HALT	16,634	435	0·03
IKEJA	14,173	350	0·02
AGEGE	168,324	13,888	0·08

Source: Annual Report, The Nigerian Railway Corporation 1960, Lagos, 1961.

only for wards, which are rather large units for our purpose. The smallest of these wards, for instance, contains over 15,000 people while the largest contains over 66,000. All the same, as long as these reservations are borne in mind, the essential socio-economic characteristics of different parts of Lagos can be depicted.

Table 49 shows the percentage of the population belonging to different sex and ethnic groups. It emphasizes that, except in Ward G (Ikoyi Island), Yoruba are the dominant ethnic group in Lagos. In Wards A and B, which comprise much of old Lagos, they form over 90 per cent of the population while in Ward F (Ebute Metta) they are

TABLE 49   ETHNIC AND SEX DISTRIBUTION IN LAGOS, 1952 (% DISTRIBUTION)

		ETHNIC ORIGIN						SEX	
Wards	Total Pop.	Yoruba	Ibo	Hausa Fulani	Other Northern Tribes	Other Southern Tribes	Non-Nigerians	Males	Female
A	37,450	91·70	2·14	0·69	0·21	0·89	1·59	50·48	49·52
B	40,034	92·33	1·36	1·60	1·68	1·16	0·51	50·53	49·47
C	74,472	75·41	7·99	0·73	0·20	4·00	4·00	53·37	46·63
D	21,761	53·27	26·18	11·07	0·18	7·36	3·91	56·09	43·91
E	37,682	52·40	27·70	3·66	0·53	6·10	4·16	56·56	43·44
F	38,534	82·73	6·69	1·00	0·37	3·44	2·29	52·84	47·16
G	17,474	30·27	33·61	3·92	0·66	9·78	10·00	60·20	39·80
TOTAL	267,407	73·29	11·92	1·55	0·60	8·27	3·30	53·58	46·42

Source: 1952 Census of Nigeria, Lagos, 1953.
Wards with a percentage greater than those for the municipality as a whole are in italic.

over 80 per cent. The wards where their proportion is least—Ward D (Apapa), Ward E (Yaba) and Ward G (Ikoyi)—are whose where immigrant groups, especially those of Ibo origin, account for over 25 per cent of the population. The Hausas are important in Apapa (Ward D) and non-Nigerians in Ikoyi (Ward G). In other words, as we move farther north, east and west away from central Lagos, the percentage of non-Yorubas increases. A sample survey of ethnic distribution in Mushin and Somolu showed Yorubas as comprising 64 per cent and 40 per cent respectively and Ibos 24 per cent and 37 per cent respectively in these areas, a situation still confirming the tendency noted above.

One interesting feature of the distribution is presented by the comparison of ethnic and sex distribution. It is seen that, although everywhere in Lagos males tend to be more numerous than female, the imbalance is greatest in those wards where non-Yoruba elements predominate. In other words, the imbalance noted in Chapter 10 among immigrants into Lagos is now seen against the background of the wards where most of them tend to concentrate. The high imbalance of Ward G (Ikoyi) is no doubt due to the presence of young, unmarried, male English administrative officers and their not-infrequently young unmarried male (Ibo) domestic servants.

The imbalance in the sex distribution is made more age-specific in Table 50. This table strongly underlines the immigrant character of this extra male population. For it shows that, while for most other age classes there is in all wards an excess of female to male, the reverse is

TABLE 50   LAGOS: AGE-SEX DISTRIBUTION BY WARDS (1952 CENSUS)

Wards	MALES				FEMALES			
	Total Males	0-14	15-49	50+	Total Females	0-14	15-49	50+
A	18,904	*36·7*	57·7	*5·6*	18,546	37·5	*56·8*	5·7
B	20,229	*36·8*	57·6	*5·6*	19,805	37·6	57·0	5·4
C	39,748	37·6	57·4	*5·0*	34,724	38·9	55·3	*5·8*
D	12,206	33·5	63·5	3·0	9,555	*40·5*	*56·8*	2·7
E	21,313	33·1	*63·0*	3·9	16,369	*41·5*	54·7	3·8
F	20,361	*36·2*	59·9	3·9	18,173	*39·7*	56·3	4·0
G	10,519	27·9	*69·2*	2·9	6,955	*40·3*	57·0	2·7
LAGOS	143,280	35·5	60·0	4·5	124,127	38·9	56·3	4·8

Source: 1952 Census of Nigeria, Lagos, 1953
Wards with proportions greater than those for the municipality as a whole are in italic.

true for the age class 15-49. This implies that most of the immigrants are young and male, and the three wards of Apapa, Yaba and Ikoyi are still the major centres of concentration. Furthermore, the table emphasizes the relative unimportance of children and the aged in those wards where immigrants tend to concentrate.

Other characteristics of a social nature relate to the educational status and religious profession of the population. Table 51 depicts the picture in 1952 and reveals still more interesting features of the population. In the first place it shows that by and large the older wards on Lagos Island have a relatively lower proportion of their population who are educated. In general there seems to exist a tendency for low educational achievement to go hand in hand with the profession of Islam. The immigrant wards, by contrast, show a higher proportion of Christians and a correspondingly higher proportion of educated people. The pattern of distribution of the educated people among the wards allows some further insight into the characteristics of the immigrants into Lagos. It appears that, by and large, most of the educated people, that is, those who would aspire to the white-collar professions tend to concentrate on Yaba (Ward E) in particular and to a lesser extent on Ebute Metta (Ward F). Ward G (Ikoyi), which shows the highest proportion of young adult males and Ibo, however, shows a relatively low proportion of educated people and a relatively high proportion of Animists. Considering the greater tendency of Ibos to be Animists, it

TABLE 51   LAGOS: EDUCATIONAL AND RELIGIOUS DISTRIBUTION BY WARDS (% DISTRIBUTION)

		EDUCATION		RELIGION		
Wards	Total Pop.	Std. II and over	Able to read and write	Moslems	Christians	Animist
A	37,450	20·34	*12·32*	*61·92*	37·10	0·31
B	40,034	16·39	8·88	*67·06*	30·84	2·11
C	74,472	*28·95*	*18·69*	45·62	52·56	1·82
D	21,761	*28·53*	4·51	24·37	*71·30*	*4·33*
E	37,682	*36·65*	*13·20*	21·97	*76·64*	1·39
F	38,534	*30·71*	9·00	34·23	*63·31*	1·83
G	17,474	25·19	6·80	23·05	*67·65*	9·29
LAGOS	267,407	26·92	12·23	42·14	54·49	3·37

Source: 1952 Census of Nigeria, Lagos, 1953.
Wards with proportions greater than those for the municipality as a whole are in italic.

seems fair to assume that Ibo immigrants to Ward G have low educational qualifications and are Animist in their religion.

One would expect these social traits to have economic correlates especially in terms of the occupational distribution of the population. Table 52 shows the occupational distribution of both males and females by wards. Unlike in Ibadan, where agriculture accounted for over 20 per cent of the male and female population, Lagos has less than 3 per cent of its male and female population so classified. In fact the proportion in most wards is considerably less than this. The exception is Ikoyi Island where, in 1952, there were areas still occupied by fishermen and small farmers. The position has changed since then, most of Ikoyi Island having now been drained and built-up.

The fact that the 1952 Census came before the era of industrial growth in Lagos is reflected in the relatively low proportion of the population in craft and related occupations. Indeed this is a proportion much lower than that of Ibadan (13·4 per cent). One indication that much of the craft occupations recorded are small-scale, requiring only a little education, is revealed by the higher proportion in the older immigrant wards of Obalende (Ward C) and Ebute Metta (Ward F). Trading, however, is clearly one of the major activities of the older, non-immigrant wards on Lagos Island (Wards A and B). The fact that this is an activity which traditionally requires relatively little training is also brought out by the relatively low proportion of educated people in the population of these wards. This relation is still further emphasized by the higher participation of women in trade in these latter wards

E 52   LAGOS: OCCUPATIONAL DISTRIBUTION BY WARDS, 1953

ds	Agri & fishing	Craft	Trade	Admin	Other occupations	Other males	Agri & fishing	Trade & clerical	Other females
	0·93	7·21	18·59	5·05	25·26	41·96	1·01	34·72	63·94
	2·27	8·27	18·49	9·00	21·02	39·24	5·42	33·10	61·48
	1·62	9·70	15·88	8·50	20·10	40·08	1·46	30·50	66·91
	1·39	8·06	10·49	14·82	24·68	40·55	1·17	20·02	78·81
	2·57	6·02	10·04	18·50	22·74	40·08	1·01	12·73	86·27
	2·10	9·42	15·51	10·99	19·78	41·29	1·76	27·34	70·64
	11·41	2·86	7·23	15·33	31·50	31·46	5·55	8·17	86·28
S	2·53	7·94	14·59	11·01	22·49	2·22	2·22	26·68	70·70

ce: 1952 Census of Nigeria, Lagos, 1953.
ds with proportions greater than those for the municipality as a whole are in italic.

where educated individuals are disproportionately fewer. Trading, however, is more of a cultural trait among Yoruba women and thus tends to be less important in those wards where non-Yoruba immigrants are important.

The importance of Lagos as the capital city of the country and the headquarters of most organizations, business or otherwise, is emphasized by the relatively high proportion of the population occupied in administrative or professional employments. Yaba (Ward E), which has the highest percentage of educated people, also shows the highest percentage in administration and the professions. It is followed by Ikoyi (Ward G) and Apapa (Ward D). The older wards on Lagos Island are distinguished by their very low proportion in this category.

Of activities classified under the heading 'Other occupations', there is no doubt that domestic service constitutes an important item. This is particularly so in Ward G (Ikoyi), which records the highest proportion in this category. Ikoyi is largely a dormitory ward where craft and trading are relatively unimportant but where live the 'senior service' men and their 'houseboys'. This situation would also explain the relatively high proportion in Ward D (Apapa) and to a lesser extent in Ward E (Yaba). By contrast the high proportion in this category recorded in Ward A (Old Lagos) is more likely due to numerous petty traditional employments not easily classifiable.

One final point of interest in Table 52 relates to the categories 'Other males' and 'Other females'. Compared with Ibadan, Lagos shows much higher proportions in these categories. The suggestion that this may represent a higher proportion of unemployed people in Lagos is not likely to explain this situation adequately. A more realistic inference, based on the fact that the percentage increases in the immigrant wards which have higher literacy figures, would be that most of the unemployed persons are children of immigrants as well as others who have come to Lagos to take advantage of the greater availability of educational facilities.

For Mushin and Somolu, where the 1952 figures have no relevance to the present situation, the sample survey of 1960 indicated that 59 per cent and 72 per cent respectively of the occupied males were classed as engaged in craft and trading. The preponderance of these two occupational groups which have been shown to be those requiring the least training is a useful pointer to the social and educational background of most of the immigrant population of these districts.

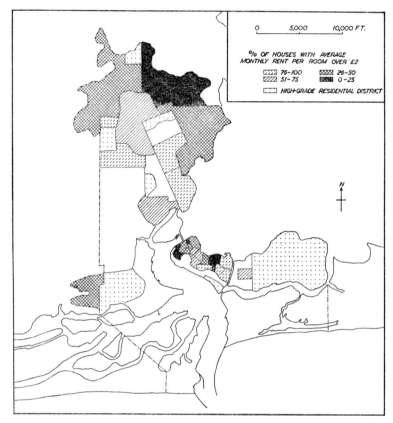

Figure 46   Average monthly rentals in Lagos

The residential districts of Greater Lagos

One useful index which summarizes these various characteristics of the population in so far as they determine the residential structure of Lagos is rent paid for accommodation. It has been suggested that, in an economic system characterized by private ownership of buildings and by competitive selling and renting of dwellings without governmental restrictions such as rent controls or price ceilings, all the various factors that make a house or apartment desirable to potential owners or occupants become integrated into a single measure of desirability—its market value—either in the form of sale value or rental value.[10] Under such conditions as exist in Lagos, it can therefore be assumed that rents paid per room afford the best available measure of the desirability of residential districts. Ability to pay, in turn, is determined by those socio-economic variables, especially education and occupation, which we have already considered.

A rent-distribution map (Fig. 46) of Greater Lagos was produced from the result of a sample survey of 605 houses carried out in August 1960. This survey enquired, among other things, into the nature of household amenities, the availability of internal water supply, the type of kitchen arrangement (whether shared or self-contained), the type of toilet facilities (whether bucket- or water-system), electricity supply as well as rent paid per room per month. A correlation of these various factors and rent gave the following coefficients. These emphasize that all four variables vary directly as rent. The highest coefficient is that of rent and internal water supply. On this result, the existence in a house of an internal water supply is shown to explain nearly 70 per cent of the variation in rent paid. The provision of modern toilet facilities and of electricity, while not explaining very much of the variation, is shown to vary significantly with rent. There is, of course, no doubt that considerations other than household amenities do enter into the determination of rent. Low rents, for instance, may sometimes represent special concessions to either relations or tenants of long residence or tenants occupying comparatively small rooms in a house of much larger rooms. On the other hand, high rents may reflect nearness to main centres of business as well as general accessibility.

TABLE 53   CORRELATION COEFFICIENT FOR RENT AND OTHER VARIABLES

Variables	Correlation Coefficient
RENT AND WATER SUPPLY	$+0.83$***
RENT AND KITCHEN ARRANGEMENT	$+0.30$
RENT AND TOILET FACILITIES	$+0.47$**
RENT AND ELECTRICITY SUPPLY	$+0.51$**

*** Significant at 0.1%
**   „   „ 1.0%
*   „   „ 5.0%

In classifying residential districts, however, it is important, as in Ibadan, to include the special case of government and privately-owned reservations where senior officials in the civil service, commerce and industry reside. Although rents are paid here, they are calculated on the basis of a certain percentage of the monthly salary of the occupier and, in general, they tend to be much lower than the rent for comparable accommodation elsewhere in the city. Yet there is no doubt that residences in these reservations belong to the very highest grade of those found in the metropolitan area within Lagos. For this reason, the reservations are graded as high while other districts have been graded medium or low. Using a rent of £2 per room per month as an index of fair quality, districts where more than 50 per cent of the houses are let at a monthly rent of £2 or more per room have been graded as medium; those with only 50 per cent or less have been graded as low. The medium grade is further sub-divided into two—medium (100-76 per cent) and lower medium (75-51 per cent).

Although this division is purely arbitrary, it shows a regional distribution that is not without significance. The medium grade includes most of the newly developed districts on Lagos Island and the planned districts on the mainland while the low grade is made up of the older districts on Lagos Island and those others on the mainland which, though new, lack essential household equipment and facilities, and are poorly maintained. Districts in the lower medium grade show some of the characteristics of both groups. They are planned and well laid out but have failed generally to preserve the same standard of upkeep as those of the medium grade. On the whole, although other criteria enter into the regional character of residential districts in Lagos, the rent factor more than any other is important in giving a fairly clear indication of their groupings.

The following residential districts are identified and they have been grouped under their grades with the rent index, i.e. percentage of houses with monthly rental of £2 or more, shown in brackets.

A. HIGH GRADE RESIDENTIAL DISTRICTS

1. East Marina and Victoria Island
2. Ikoyi
3. Apapa
4. The 'Railway Compound'
5. North Yaba
6. Itire Estate
7. Palm Grove Estate
8. Maryland
9. Ikeja Reservation and Housing Estate

B. MEDIUM GRADE RESIDENTIAL DISTRICTS

10. Surulere Estate (100)
11. Yaba—Ebute Metta East (85/93)
12. North-Eastern Lagos—Lafiaji (100)
    Brazilian Quarter (86)
    Oke Suna (78)
    Araromi (77)

C. LOWER MEDIUM GRADE RESIDENTIAL DISTRICTS
13. Western Mainland—Ebute Metta West (75)
                        Ojuelegba   (63)
14. Central Lagos   —Isalegangan   (65)
                        Oko-Awo   (56)
15. Obalende   (57)

D. LOW GRADE RESIDENTIAL DISTRICTS
16. Old Lagos—
      Faji   (56)   Ereko-Agarawu   (37)
      Idunshagbe   (50)   Olowogbowo   (25)
      Idunmota-Alakoro   (50)   Offin-Itolo   (21)
      Idumagbo   (46)   Ebute Ero   (21)
17. North Central Lagos—Okepopo   (41)
                        Epetedo   (21)
18. Mushin   (35)
19. Yaba East   (28)
20. Somolu   (9)
21. Ajegunle-Ajeromi (23)

(a) High grade residential districts

The nine districts in this grade have the common characteristics of being well planned layouts. Most of them are of very recent date and, apart from one or two exceptions, have been specially developed by government or government-sponsored agencies. The density of housing is generally much lower than the average for Lagos and most houses stand in the midst of well-kept lawns surrounded by neatly trimmed hedges. Except for blocks of flats, the houses are generally single-family houses. Tenements are completely unknown. Here are to be found the most important members of the community in all spheres of activity in Lagos.

The oldest of the high grade residential districts is that of East Marina. Dating from the 1850s when the British Consul established the Consulate here, this district today accommodates the political leaders of the Federation. Here is the Governor's Lodge, the Prime Minister's Lodge and the lodges of a few other high-ranking Ministers of State. The remaining members of this political *élite* as well as most of the top civil servants are to be found in the Ikoyi Reservation. Like the reservations in Ibadan, Ikoyi was developed in the late 1920s to provide extra space for the increasing number of European civil servants coming to Lagos. Up to 1952 it retained this exclusive character. With the political development of the country since then, it has become not only considerably mixed in its population but has also vastly expanded its area. The programme of expansion had involved extensive land reclamation of the swampy parts of Ikoyi Island on the north-east, south-east and south-west.

Most of the other high grade residential districts have developed in response to the need to provide satisfactory accommodation for the top classes in commerce and industry. Apart from the 'Railway Compound', which dates from the closing years of the nineteenth century, most of the other high grade districts date only from the 1950s. A veritable indication of the differences in age among the various districts in this grade is the style of housing. In the older districts, housing tends to be largely of the 'colonial' type (Plate 23), replicating as much as possible the typical English country-house even including the fireplace. They are usually two-storeys high and painted white, with wide balconies, tiled roofs and a generous use of timber in their interior panelling. Houses in the newer districts are more light and airy in their style and show a variety of delightful and elegant modern tropical designs.

(b) Medium grade residential districts

The three districts included here share the common characteristics of having been planned and laid out during this century, the Surulere Estate being the most recent. All of them show a very high percentage of houses with more than the minimum of household amenities. The majority of landlords are of the professional classes and tenants in 'white-collar' employments show a predilection for these districts. Density of housing is generally about 12 to 16 per acre. There are very few houses with gardens and fewer still with garages except on the newly developed Surulere Estate (Plate 27).

The oldest of these regions is north-eastern Lagos where the Brazilian Quarter stands out as a distinctive social area. Although some impressive Brazilian-style storied buildings are still to be found in this area, the majority of houses are modest, small-size bungalows which, along Bamgbose and Igbosere roads, show an almost continuous wallage with hardly any interruption between the houses. Since 1918 this district has been extended eastward to the reclaimed areas of Lafiaji, Oke Suna and Araromi. Together they constitute an area highly desired by 'white-collar' workers in government and commerce who seek to be close to their place of work on the Marina.

Yaba and Ebute Metta are another area much desired by 'white-collar' workers. Ebute Metta, however, being much older than Yaba, has tended also to attract people on a slightly lower socio-economic scale with the result that its houses are not as well preserved as those of the latter. The development of the two districts spans a period of nearly seventy years from the Glover layout of 1867 to the new 'garden city' layout of the 1930s. The layout is on the gridiron pattern with housing blocks varying in shape from squarish in Ebute Metta to rectangular in Yaba. A new development which today also houses mainly 'white-collar' workers and people in the middle-income range is the Surulere Estate. Originally designed principally to resettle the large number of families displaced in the 1956 slum clearance of Central Lagos and to provide relatively cheap housing for the lower income group, this Estate has with time come to change its character. The displaced people, finding the trifling rent of 25s per month which they have to pay for their subsidized accommodation still too much for their purse, have in many instances let out their houses and moved to cheaper residences in Somolu and Mushin. Apart from such accommodation in Surulere, the Lagos Executive Development Board provided houses for sale at moderate prices to members of the middle income group in this area. Private development in Itire nearby houses people of the same socio-economic class.

(c) Lower medium grade residential districts

This grade comprises those districts which, though planned, started as slum areas. Partly for this reason, even atⅰer their new layout, they have not completely excluded the kind of occupiers who tend to make the district return to slum conditions. A good example is provided by Isalegangan and Oko Awo districts as well as adjacent parts of Idumagbo and Idunshagbe, all of which were involved in the earlier slum clearance of the 1930s. These districts constitute an oasis of planned layout in a wilderness of confused housing. The main north-south through road is Idumagbo Avenue, a wide street of which the traffic flow has, however, been considerably reduced by the crowd of petty traders lining it on both sides with their movable 'counters'. Indeed it is the preponderance of petty traders in the population of these districts that has, in spite of the relatively good provision of household amenities, led to a generally lower standard of neighbourhood upkeep.

Obalende also shares these characteristics but it is further distinguished by the large number of Ghanaians and Togolese in its population. It has not been possible to discover how this local concentration of Ghanaians and Togolese came about. A map of 1911 shows the area as planned for a Hausa Settlement adjacent to the Barracks of the Hausa Constabulary, which is now the Nigeria Police Force. But the Hausa population in Lagos was never, until recently, very large, and it is possible the non-Nigerians were encouraged to purchase land not taken up by the Hausa, a situation not unlike that at Mokola in Ibadan.

The western mainland districts lie to the west of the rail-line and are separated by the 'Railway Compound' into Ebute Metta West in the south and Ojuelegba in the north. These districts began to develop in a most unsatisfactory manner at about the same time as Yaba and Ebute Metta to the east were being laid out and planned. Although they were declared town-planning areas about 1930, their major development came after the Second World War and consisted primarily of speculative building of large, storied houses with numerous rooms for hire to immigrants coming into Lagos at this time. Because of their newness, most houses have amenities above the average for Lagos, but new houses in remote situations in Ojuelegba are still without light or adequate toilet arrangements.

(d) Low grade residential districts

This grade of district has the characteristic of never having been planned. It includes the oldest districts on Lagos Island with their narrow, confused lanes and generally poor housing conditions and the newly developed low-class residential districts outside the municipality. In the case of the latter, the poor conditions have been due to the speed and excessively speculative nature of their development, the absence of an effective planning authority and the general difficulty of extending the framework of basic amenities across the municipal boundary.

Old Lagos comprises all the districts in the western one-third of the island which were, in the early growth of Lagos, established on the available dry spots. The nucleus of the region is in the extreme northwest in Idumagbo where is to be found the Oba's Palace as well as those of his chiefs. The region has been affected by most of the changes in Lagos and, as is only to be expected, it has suffered the greatest deterioration. Since the growth of Lagos has been largely by immigration, the old town found itself hemmed in by the development of new districts occupied by stranger population. Family ties, moreover, made it difficult for many of the indigenous Lagos inhabitants to move out of the old town. The result was that as their population grew, particularly with the improved medical facilities of the present century, dwelling accommodation became more scarce. Former compounds were broken up into unit houses and any space left unoccupied was enclosed by insubstantial structures such as bamboo, wood or corrugated iron sheets.

The districts remain predominantly Yoruba, most of whom are engaged in trading or crafts. Housing conditions are indescribably squalid. Access to many houses is by narrow foot-paths (Plate 25) which also serve as drains for household water. Household equipment and facilities are most inadequate, and even where they exist they are very unsatisfactory. It is no wonder that rents here are some of the lowest in Lagos except where the advantage of location such as at Olowogbowo, Faji and Idunmota increases them. Although the general insanitary conditions here gave rise to the outbreak of cholera in 1929 and led to slum clearance, first in the 1930s and again in 1956, the worst areas of squalid and unwholesome dwellings still remain untouched.

East of Old Lagos are the districts of Epetedo and Okepopo grouped together as North Central Lagos. Epetedo was settled about 1862 with the return of Kosoko and his retinue from Epe, hence the name Epetedo. The district was specifically granted to Oshodi Tappa, a Lieutenant of Kosoko, who divided it up into blocks among his own men. Each block was built up as a single, large rectangular compound (still referred to as a 'court') with numerous dwelling places and enclosing a large open space. Today the continuity of the compound has been disrupted, though the rectangular pattern is preserved. In its place have developed individual houses of varying sizes, shapes and storeys. Inasa Court, for instance, has 23 houses, Oshodi Court 20 houses, Oloko Court 18 houses and Fagbohun Court 10 houses. Inasa Court also contains an Islamic School and a corn mill. In both Epetedo and Okepopo the houses are rather old and accommodate largely related individuals. Yoruba are numerically the most important group although the Bini form a significant minority. Ibo and Ijaw are also to be found. Housing conditions are poor and population densities are quite staggering. Inasa Court, for instance, with an area of about one acre, has an estimated population of almost 600 people. Most of these are artisans and traders, although the younger generations, being educated, turn to 'white-collar' employment.

Far off to the north but still within the municipality, the need to provide cheap accommodation for the low-income population serving educational and other institutions around Yaba gave rise to the development of an unplanned, low grade suburb at Yaba East. It was based on existing small hamlets at Ijesha, Oja, Onitiri, Onike and Iwaya in an area which was in the 1930s considered unsuitable for development because of its liability to seasonal flooding. There are as yet no well developed street connections between the hamlets, and the quality of housing varies enormously from the cheap, mud bungalows of the 1940s to the stone-and-mortar storeyed buildings put up in recent times. The nearness to Yaba has helped to ensure the provision of some household equipment and facilities although many houses in 1960 were still without an internal water supply (71 per cent) and without electricity (29 per cent). Initially, the class of people attracted were cooks, gardeners, stewards and artisans who could hardly afford the high rents in Yaba itself. This class still forms a sizeable proportion of the population and occupies houses where the rents are low (occupants of 50 per cent of houses surveyed pay rents of £1 10s a room or less, and 72 per cent less than £2). Ibos are strongly represented in this group. In the area as a whole they account for more than one-third of the population. Higher income groups have been attracted to parts of the area, particularly to Onike, either as owner-occupiers or tenants of the better designed houses.

Outside the municipal boundary, Mushin offers to the low income workers cheap tenements and to the higher income groups cheap land. The result has been the development of a suburb of very mixed character. The most striking feature is a layout of streets which has been incidental to the sale of regular plots of land and which the local authority has done little to improve. The main axis for this development is the Agege Motor Road. Along this road three or four-storied tenement buildings containing from 24 to 40 rooms are common. Elsewhere in the area, however, poorer houses, mainly mud-built cement-plastered bungalows, are to be found. Artisans and young clerks of Yoruba (64 per cent) or Ibo (24 per cent) extraction who are attracted by the low rents and are prepared to tolerate the low housing conditions predominate. Less than 30 per cent of houses are let for over £2 but then less than 35 per cent have piped water and less than 70 per cent have electricity. In 40 per cent of the houses, water is procured from wells and in 43 per cent pit latrines are in use.

Somolu is the most recent of the suburbs with almost 94 per cent of its houses built since 1950. It is perhaps an indication of its newness that it wears all the appearance of an immature, semi-rural suburb. Indeed, tenants are known to have stayed on here because of the ease of getting land for part-time farming. Somolu consists of a number of hamlets—Somolu, Bashua, Bajulaiye, and Bariga—which have now been engulfed by Lagos. As with Mushin, there is the outline of a layout but the local authority has paid little attention to the streets or to their proper alignment. Conditions are on the whole worse than in the former place, for Somolu is less mixed as a suburb. The standard of house construction is much lower and mud houses show their faces unashamedly (Plate 26). There are very few storied buildings, and most bungalows contain 8 to 10 rooms. Housing conditions are indescribably poor and less than 10 per cent of the houses have piped water. Electricity is available in less than 30 per cent of the houses and toilet facilities in over 80 per cent of the houses are either pit latrines or are non-existent.

It is no wonder that, as one landlord complained, tenants hardly ever stay for more than six months. Most of them are usually new arrivals, with non-Yoruba, particularly Ibo, predominating. Many are labourers, artisans and petty traders who were initially attracted both by the greater ease of finding accommodation and by the very low rents. Less than 10 per cent of the houses charge more than £2 per room and 67 per cent charge less than £1 10s. As they become more settled, the new arrivals look for accommodation in better suburbs and tend to move either to Mushin or Ojuelegba or Ebute Metta West.

In the extreme south-west close to Apapa but outside the municipality, there have developed since the 1950s low grade residences to house dock-workers and factory-hands. This suburb, known as Ajegunle-Ajeromi, developed on the crest of two parallel east-west sand ridges which are separated by a marshy depression. The streets are not developed and like Somolu and Mushin are most inconvenient for vehicular traffic. As far as housing conditions go, this district has a status midway between Mushin and Somolu. The houses are on the whole fairly substantial as at Mushin, with many being two-storied and having 16 to 20 rooms. But as in Somolu the standard of household equipment and facilities is very low. Turnover of tenants is, however, also low due largely to the fact that there is no better suburb within a convenient distance of the Apapa Industrial Estate. As in Somolu, the non-Yoruba groups are well represented, with Ibo predominating. The

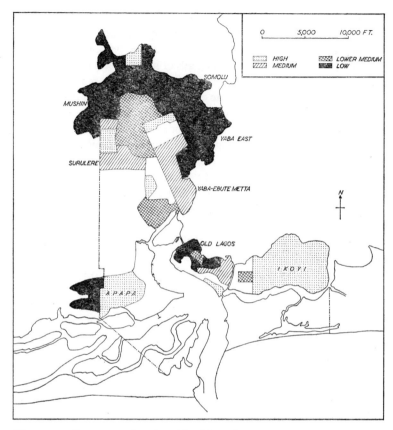

Figure 47   Lagos: grades of residential regions

region, however, attracts very few people in the higher income group.

Fig. 47 shows the spatial relations of these various grades of residential regions. It indicates that, but for the development in Mushin, Somolu and Ajegunle-Ajeromi, housing conditions tend to improve, in general, away from Old Lagos. In the present situation of Lagos, it is both this ancient core and the peripheral areas of the metropolitan district that feel most the impact of recent developments. In the case of the core area, the impact has resulted from the expansion of the Central Business District; with the periphereal areas, it is due to the almost 'explosive' character of metropolitan growth.

The process whereby the business area of a city expands horizontally to adjoining streets and district is, of course, not peculiar to Lagos. The form of invasion of one type of land use by another is, moreover, a healthy sign of development which can hardly be prevented. However, in Lagos, both because of certain details of its population structure and because the process has been artificially induced by municipal slum clearance, its social and economic consequences have been tremendous.

Peter Marris of the Institute of Community Studies in Britain was invited by the Lagos Executive Development Board to report on the social consequences of the Lagos Slum Clearance Scheme. His Report, submitted in 1959, contains a number of observations which are particularly relevant in considering the effects of this form of inevitable functional invasion in a developing African city.[11] In the first place, because the commercial centre is not contiguous with the core area of the city, its expansion has not, as elsewhere in the world, helped in the clearing of the oldest and most insanitary slum areas in the city. The area cleared contained houses which were built about the same time as some of those in the commercial area. Though old, many of these could still have been used to advantage for some decades to come. In the circumstances of Lagos, where population is increasing much faster than new building, the slum clearance of such an area not only stimulates the rapid rise of rents in the areas around but also accentuates the already appalling slum conditions in the core area.

Secondly, there is the problem of the special character of the population involved in the present (and likely to be involved in future) schemes of slum clearance to make room for the expansive commercial centre. It has already been shown that more than 85 per cent of the population of this part of Lagos are Yoruba and that most of them are descendants of the oldest indigenous inhabitants of the city with all that this implies in an African setting. Moreover, this population forms a stable and closely knit community with, according to Marris, about two-thirds having one or more of their brothers or sisters and their parents living no more than 10 to 15 minutes walk away. Slum clearance, therefore, meant a great disruption of social life with all its attendant distress and misery.

What made the misery worse was the economic consequences of the displacement. The nearness of this part of Lagos to the commercial centre has had a tremendous effect on the occupation of the people. Over 80 per cent of both landlords and tenants in this core area have been shown to be traders. Marris found that not only the men but nearly all the women traded profitably from their doorsteps because the centre of Lagos attracts a daily throng of people from outside the neighbourhood. Many of the women, in fact, depend simply on attracting a few shillings from the stream of people who pass along the lanes every day, and find they are out of cigarettes or matches, or need the stimulus of a kolanut to munch. The displacement of such people to the outskirts of the city at Surulere not only damaged their custom but also obliged them to spend more on items such as rent and fares, which had never featured before in their family budget. Detailed sociological considerations of these issues, however, are outside the scope of the present study but the situation underlines certain aspect of the development of the internal structure of a modern city in an African environment.

Unlike the situation in the core area, the effect of the 'metropolitan explosion' on the peripheral areas is only beginning to dawn on the authorities. Metropolitan Lagos at the moment has a population of over a million and is now the largest city in Nigeria. As the capital city of the Republic, it is gradually becoming the culmination of national life, the supereminent market of the country and the destination of an unending stream of the young and ambitious in search of fame and fortune.[12] This situation is bound to make it grow even faster than at present and demands that a master-plan be provided for its development to ensure that some of the worst problems of uncontrolled growth are prevented.

The statutory body charged with the duty of planning control in Lagos is the Lagos Executive Development Board. Up to now, this body has concentrated on the slum clearance of Central Lagos and the development of new housing estates at Surulere, Apapa and Victoria Island. In the meantime, worse slums have developed elsewhere within the metropolitan district but the Board is not concerned with them because they lie outside its legal authority. These slum developments at Somolu, Mushin, Araromi and Ajegunle are in the area of jurisdiction of the Mushin and Ajeromi Local Authorities. The Ikeja Town Planning Authority is the body responsible for planning control over all these authorities. It derives its powers from the Town and Country Planning Law (Western Region No. 6 of 1956) which is based to a large extent on similar legislation in Great Britain. However, because the Planning Authority is poorly endowed and depends to a large extent on the caprices of unenlightened local councils, its influence on development in these areas has been almost negligible.

For many new arrivals by air to the country, it is the peripheral slum areas that provide their first impression of Lagos as they drive from the Airport towards the centre of the city. Moreover, because of the narrow and poorly maintained roads, traffic congestion in these areas largely inhibits movement. Part of the agitation for the extension of the boundary of the Federal Capital to include all these areas has stemmed from frustrations resulting from the unevenness of development on both sides of the municipal boundary. The agitation, however, has a strong overtone of national partisan politics and remains a rather explosive issue. 'Metropolitan explosion', however, is a universal phenomenon which is almost inevitable with economic development. Almost equally universal is the tenacity with which neighbouring local authorities, whose territories are being engulfed by the 'exploding' metropolis, cling to their powers and jurisdiction. Yet in many cases this fact has not prevented the evolution of the same standard of urban housing and amenities on both sides of the legal city. The answer to the problem of metropolitan Lagos, therefore, need not be found in political agitation for boundary extension but in an increasing measure of co-operation in the planned development of the entire metropolitan area.

Already the means for such co-operation exists. Both the Lagos Executive Development Board and the Ikeja Town Planning Authority exchange representatives at each other's meetings. The latter authority has also produced a master-plan to assist orderly development as the 'explosion' extends further into areas as yet unbuilt. Perhaps what is needed is co-operation of a more positive and effective type, something in the form of a Greater Lagos Planning Authority, made up of planning experts insulated from politics, financed initially by both the Federal and the Western Regional Government, and charged specifically with the task of making Greater Lagos a metropolitan capital city of which Nigeria can be truly proud.

References

1. Rev. Williams Morgan, Journal, July–September 1853, *CMS Archives*, London, CA2/071.
2. R. F. Burton, *Abeokuta and the Cameroons Mountains*, London, 1863, p. 18.
3. J. Otunba Payne, *West African Almanack*, Lagos, 1898. The other markets of Lagos in 1898 were Faji, Ereko, Agarawu, Offin, Elegbata, Idunmagbo, Bankole, Balogun, Kosseh, Epetedo, Marina, Victoria, Houssa Town and Ikoyi Road.

4. R. F. Burton, op. cit., pp. 212-213.
5. J. Whitford, *Trading Life in Western and Central Africa*, Liverpool, 1877, p. 90.
6. *UAC Statistical and Economic Review*, No. 12, September 1953, p. 1.
7. Nevil Miller, *Lagos Steam Tramway, 1902-1933*, London, 1958, p. 10.
8. Ibid., p. 26.
9. *Papers relating to Mechanical Transport in the Colonies, 1909*, Col. 4589, pp. 22-4. See also Allan McPhee, *The Economic Revolution in British West Africa*, London, 1926, pp. 115-16.
10. J. Quinn, *Urban Sociology*, New York, 1955.
11. Peter Marris, *Social Change in an African City*, London, 1961.
12. Mark Jefferson, 'The Law of the Primate City', *Geographical Review*, Vol. 29, No. 2, April 1939, pp. 226-32.

12 Conclusion: Problems and Prospect of Urbanization in Nigeria

The preceding chapters have attempted to show the contrasting urban situation represented by Ibadan and Lagos. Both, it has been suggested, represent the highest level of development of particular types of urbanism in Nigeria. For Ibadan it was an urbanism based on pre-industrial technology and oriented largely to the needs of effective administration and trade. Lagos, on the other hand, has grown in an age of modern, industrial technology and is no less important as a centre for efficient administration of a much wider area and for commercial articulation over a very much more extensive territory.

It has been suggested that, irrespective of their contrasting characteristics, both centres are the products of processes different only in degree and not in kind. Functional specialization as a means of increasing human productivity operates in both types of urbanism but at widely different levels of refinement and efficiency. Moreover, as Lampard pointed out, such 'specialization of functions makes inevitably for specialization of areas; it prompts a territorial division of labour between town and country and differentiates town from town. Areal differentiation is, in fact, the spatial corollary of functional specialization and logically serves the same end—economy.'[1] Thus the greater complexity of areal differentiation within Lagos is seen as following from the higher level of functional specialization which that city represents compared with Ibadan. Complex areal differentiation, however, means more complex problems of land-use planning and transport efficiency. These are problems which Lagos has been wrestling with in its various slum clearance projects, estate development, zoning regulations and traffic controls. Most of these problems have hardly become insistent in Ibadan and continue to be treated with casual indifference.

Urbanization in Nigeria thus has to be seen as a development spread out over a wide technological spectrum from pre-industrial to industrial. As national income rises, we can expect an increasingly substantial shift towards modern industrial technology which is bound to have great impact on the character of Nigerian cities. However, as already pointed out, the effectiveness of this impact will be partly conditioned by the extent of the survival of the pre-industrial past. The larger this survival, the less effective the modern impact. This, of course is the short-term view. It is possible that, in the long run, assuming a progressively rising *per capita* income, the position will change for most of the urban centres irrespective of the extent of the survival from the pre-industrial past.

The issue of over-urbanization

This issue of the survival from the past raises the question of whether Nigeria is at present over-urbanized. 'Over-urbanization' is a concept which relates the proportion of a country's population living in urban areas to the level of that country's economic development. Implicit in the concept is the idea of an 'optimum' level of urbanization in respect of a given stage of economic development. Clearly, the concept has significance only in situations in which the goals or objectives of a society are defined unequivocally as the advancement of the economic well-being of the masses of the population. There is no doubt that today such objectives permeate the policies of most countries. However, it is clear that this has not always been the case.

Since 1952 Nigeria has become even more concerned with the economic development of her people and it is from then that the question of whether the country is over-urbanized or not has any relevance. Hoselitz defines the state of 'over-urbanization' in three ways:

(a) when urbanization in a country is running ahead of industrialization and the development of administrative and other service occupations which are characteristically concentrated in cities;
(b) when there is great disproportion between the costs of urban growth and the maintenance of proper facilities for urban dwellers and the earning capacity of the people congregated in cities;
(c) when the migration to the city is due less to the 'pull', i.e. the attractiveness which the city exerts, and more to the 'push' experienced in the rural areas.[2]

Viewed in this way, it is easy to see that Nigeria may be described as 'over-urbanized' from two causes. First, having emerged with numerous urban centres, most of which are not industrial in the modern sense, the country is faced, even from the start, with many people living in urban places for whom no modern urban employment is available. In the second place, the effect of the social amenities provided by the colonial administration has been to lower the death rate everywhere in the country and to force up the survival rate of the people. Thus, especially after 1931, the population of the country has been rising at an annual rate of over 2 per cent. Because of the greater concentration of these amenities in urban centres, their rate of growth has been much higher than the average for the country and has been estimated to be as much as 5 per cent per annum. However, for the rural areas, the impact of this growth of population was staggering. It led to a sharp reduction of the fallow period and a significant decline in soil fertility. The result was a massive exodus of population from rural to urban areas. The influx of migrants into the urban areas has been aggravated in the last ten years by a new wave of unemployed and sometimes unemployable young school leavers from the numerous schools opened in the rural areas since 1955.

Today there is no doubt that Nigeria's level of urbanization is inconsistent with its stage of economic development. In 1952 the Census showed that, of approximately 31 million people, about 6 million or 19 per cent were living in urban centres of 5,000 people and over. For different parts of the country this proportion varied greatly. It was about 49 per cent in Western Nigeria (including what is now the Mid-West), 15 per cent in Eastern Nigeria and 9 per cent in Northern Nigeria. At about this time the stage of economic development measured by the *per capita* income showed that the average Nigerian earned no more

TABLE 54   LEVELS OF URBANIZATION AND ECONOMIC DEVELOPMENT

Country	% of population in urban centres of 5,000 people or more, 1951-53	National income per head (1956) £
TANGANYIKA	4	16
UGANDA	2	20
KENYA	4	26
NIGERIA	19	27
GHANA	17	56
SOUTH AFRICA	36	124
PAKISTAN	13	19
INDIA	17	22
JAMAICA	33	93
UNITED KINGDOM	80	323

Source: U.N. Demographic Yearbook, 1952 *and* 1953 *and the* U.N. Monthly Bulletin of Statistics, 1959

than £27 a year. Comparison with the position in a number of other countries shows (Table 54) that Nigeria is far more urbanized than countries like Kenya or Uganda which have about the same *per capita* income. On the other hand Britain, with her national *per capita* income more than twelve times that of Nigeria, has proportionally only four times as much of its population in urban centres.

Generative and parasitic cities

What all this points to is, of course, that most Nigerian towns are today not functioning effectively in the economy. In return for the investment on social amenities made in them, only a few are making positive productive contributions to the economy. Many others whose contribution is very little or non-existent can be regarded as 'parasitic' in the system. They represent a substantial drag on the rate of economic development in the country.

Two reasons in particular help to make the problem of 'parasitic' towns a serious one. The first is the phenomenon of 'social identification' to which attention has been called in another publication.[3] This relates to the attitude of emigrants from particular urban centres to the social and economic conditions of their home towns. In the colonial period this attitude found expression in the establishment of Improvement Leagues, Progressive Associations and Descendant Unions whose major role was to organize the emigrants to agitate for amenities and progressive administration in their home towns. Since 1950 the emergence of democratic political parties has meant that such emigrants, if they found themselves in positions of power, could do something about this. In consequence, scarce infrastructural investments were diverted to areas where, for some considerable time to come, they cannot generate any significant productive capacity. It is common knowledge that the programme for the installation of various public utilities—electricity, water-supply, medical centres and dispensaries—has not always been guided by the needs of the economy but by the desire to provide amenities for the home towns of the politicians with an eye to winning more votes in the next election.

This is not to say that 'social identification' operates in only a negative manner. Indeed, it has been the basis of significant developmental effort and investment in such vital areas as education. Many a town can boast of a secondary grammar school because of the unstinted effort and the monthly financial contributions of its sons and daughters abroad.

The net result of such effort, apart from spreading enlightenment, has been to raise expectations, to increase the dissatisfaction with the limited opportunity of the home town, and to stimulate further emigration. 'Social identification' thus operates as a contradictory process of diverting scarce capital to areas where it is least effective and, in consequence, making such areas lose more population.

The second reason why 'parasitic urbanism' has serious implications for the economy of the country is the existence of numerous urban communities which cannot support themselves or maintain their facilities and institutions in a tolerable state of efficiency. This situation is thus related to the second condition which Hoselitz defines as indicating a state of 'over-urbanization'. It has been emphasized in Chapter 6 that for many of the towns which are poorly located in terms of the present economy of the country, adjustment has been going on largely by means of their losing the active, income-earning members of their community to those centres which are growing. There is then left a preponderance of children, women and the aged, all of whom earn very little income but incur high costs for the maintenance of proper facilities in the towns. The result is that economic leadership and entrepreneurship which could help to reduce the rate of decline of the towns are lost, administrative efficiency suffers and even social associations and institutions lack the vigour and dynamism which the presence of youthful, enlightened and energetic individuals could have ensured. This is why the infrastructural investment diverted into these centres is so inefficiently utilized and becomes a significant drain on the economy.

Nonetheless, for a developing country, it is on the generative cities that attention must be focused. According to the analysis of Chapter 6, not more than about fifty cities (those with scores of between $-2\cdot0$ and $-0\cdot5$ on Factor One) can be said to be truly generative of growth while another hundred or so (those with scores of between $-0\cdot5$ and $0\cdot0$ on Factor One) are somewhat marginal. Most of these cities have been shown to be mainly trade centres deriving their importance largely from location on the major transport routeways and/or location within relatively rich agricultural regions. Since the 1950s, however, industrial development has added a new dimension to the growth pattern of a number of these cities. This has been particularly so in the case of the major air and sea ports of Lagos, Port Harcourt, Kano and Sapele as well as the regional capitals of Kaduna, Enugu and Ibadan. A few of the trade centres have also succeeded in attracting some industries to themselves. These include places like Aba, Umuahia, Onitsha, Abeokuta and Ilorin.

All these cities, as are only to be expected, have become the major destination of short-distance migration from their immediate rural areas and long-distance migration from other parts of the country. So great has been the influx that one is faced today with the paradoxical situation that it is in the growing centres that unemployment is most pronounced. This failure to create new employment opportunities fast enough to keep pace with the influx of immigrants has had a deleterious effect on the environmental and physical conditions of these cities. With only a fraction of the city population yielding the revenue from which services for so many others have to be provided, it is easy to appreciate why urban equipment and facilities in many of these places are over-used and why the standards and efficiency of urban services are low.

In a very real sense, however, the single most important problem of these growing centres is that of urban management. A city, like any economic organization, requires qualified, enlightened and experienced management to function efficiently and profitably. Three reasons in particular appear to have militated against the emergence of efficient urban management in Nigeria. The first is the failure of governments to recognize the modern role of cities in the economic development of the country. The city is still conceived of as the traditional seat of a natural ruler, whether an Oba or Emir, whose responsibility it is to see to the welfare and development of his subjects. Yet it is common knowledge that few of these natural rulers are enlightened enough to provide the type of leadership which is required. Even in Western Nigeria, where attempts have been made to modernize the traditional city administration, the so-called traditional members are treated as if they were functionally relevant to the role which cities are called upon to play in the present situation of the country.

The continued importance of the traditional rulers in the management of cities has had another effect on the development of these centres. Most traditional rulers have jurisdiction not only over the city but also over a more or less extensive rural district. As such, few cities and towns have an independent existence of their own but are treated as part of a district whose administration is not infrequently dominated by rural members. The city, moreover, has no defined limits and merges imperceptibly with the rural areas. This indeterminacy of the limits of the urban and rural areas and of their spheres of action has often worked against the best interests of the city and left much of its problems un-resolved.

Closely related to this problem is that created by the existence of a group in most cities who regard themselves as 'sons of the soil'. Even in Eastern Nigeria, where urban centres are new creations, villagers on whose land the new cities developed see themselves in this light. As has been pointed out in the previous chapters, these 'sons of the soil' tend on the whole to be poorer, less educated and less enlightened than the immigrants. Yet they wield so great an influence by their ownership of land and, in the case of the older centres, by their numerical majority. In general their attitude to the immigrant communities in the city is a compound of fear and envy of the superior economic position of the latter. The effect has been to discriminate in various ways against the immigrants. Attempts are made as much as possible to exclude them from the city administration. In the North, they are allowed to partici-pate in the administration of only their half of the city and, even then, only under the surveillance of a representative of the traditional authority. In most places they are not allowed to have a freehold title to land and may not expect equal treatment before the customary law. Confronted by such apparent hostility, most immigrants hardly ever see the new city of their adoption as a place in whose overall development they have a stake. For many it is partly this failure to belong locally that rein-forces their sense of social identification with their home town.

While discriminating against the immigrants, the 'sons of the soil' try to protect their own interests as they see them. Their poorer section of the city, which in general tends to deteriorate very quickly under the impact of population growth, is protected as much as possible from any attempt at slum clearance. Regulations and by-laws which tend towards urban renewal are made inoperative in their area of the city. They are exempted from paying the various rates and are encouraged to continue to live their lives oblivious of the rapid changes that have taken place all around them.

A third problem of urban management is the lack of enterprise especially with regard to raising revenue for local development. Much of the revenue of the various councils consists of grants-in-aid from the regional governments. Otherwise, all that the councils receive by way of revenue are the minor fees and licences. Property rating, for instance, is not used as a means of raising revenue in most cities in Nigeria. The exceptions are Lagos, some eight towns in Eastern Nigeria including

Port Harcourt, Enugu, Aba and Umuahia as well as the immigrant sections of the four Northern Nigeria cities of Kaduna, Kano, Zaria and Jos. No town in Western Nigeria undertakes property rating. Furthermore, apart from the somewhat xenophobic attitude to immigrants, no city council in Nigeria has shown that they are aware of the need to create local conditions such as would attract investors from within or outside the country. This responsibility at the moment is regarded as one to be borne only by the regional and federal governments.

The problem of the primate city

These various problems of the generative cities are increased in the case of Lagos by the sheer fact of size. As we have already pointed out, Greater Lagos by 1963 had passed the one million mark and is today the largest city in Black Africa, and the primate city of Nigeria, with Ibadan pushed to second position. Its rapid rate of growth has been due to a favourable conjunction of factors especially the advantages of its port-capital functions for industrial location. It shares these advantages with other port-capital cities on the West African coast like Accra-Tema, Abidjan and Dakar. However, unlike them, Greater Lagos has a much richer hinterland and a more populous country on which to draw. Its rate of growth continues to rise very steeply. Its population having jumped so rapidly from about 250,000 in 1950 to about 1·2 million in 1963, Greater Lagos has been increasing at an annual compound interest rate of 14 per cent. At this rate its population should be close to 5 million in another ten years. Even if, in the ten years after 1963, it increases at only half this rate, the population will be well over 2 million by 1973.

This spectacular rate of growth poses problems relating to the general efficiency of urban functioning and of urban management. The problem of efficiency of urban functioning relates in general to the pattern of land-use development and the volume, density and orientation of traffic within the city. Although the demand for land and housing in Lagos is exceptionally high, there has not developed any real property market. Sales of land, except on the estates of the Lagos Executive Development Board, are conducted almost invariably by private negotiations between individuals and have been the source of innumerable and interminable litigations. Demand for housing remains insatiable owing to a chronic shortage of housing finance. The result is overcrowding and a rapid rate of property deterioration in most parts of Lagos. In the older parts of the city this has led to the creation of indescribably squalid slums. Redevelopment in the 1930s and 1950s has only touched the fringes of the slum. The real problem area is the old core of the city which is relatively far from the modern commercial centre and which gives very little promise of profitable returns from redevelopment. So far, no imaginative proposals have been put forward for the redevelopment of this area but it is clear that the situation cannot be ignored for very long. Whatever happens, it is important to stress that redevelopment in this area must seek to preserve its residential character and as much as possible the social cohesion and stability of its population.

The overall land-use development of the city is meant to be governed by zoning regulations as to the siting, design, quality and use of buildings. Unfortunately these regulations have not been applied with firmness and decisiveness. Outside the municipality the position is even worse. Here, even basic guide lines for urban development such as roads and drains are often non-existent. In much of these areas the private developer constructs his own roads and drains and proceeds to use his land as he thinks fit. The result is a proliferation within metropolitan Lagos of problem areas of localized poor housing, poor environmental sanitation, low accessibility and discordant land-uses.

Furthermore, the present situation in which central business functions are concentrated on the small island of Lagos is leading to an increasingly stultifying traffic problem. This is particularly so because the only connection of the island to the mainland is a single bridge. A second bridge is already under construction and may be ready by 1968. However, if Lagos continues to grow at its present rate and the decentralization of functions from the island does not proceed fast enough, even the second bridge will become inadequate by the time it is completed. As far as the road network itself is concerned, it has been suggested that, except in the areas outside the municipality, there is no shortage of road space. Most traffic problems are therefore due to inefficient administration which allows shopkeepers, builders, street traders and, at night, street sleepers to take possession of the pavements, thereby forcing cyclists and pedestrians to spill over on to the roadway, part of which is being occupied by illegally parked cars.

The problem of inefficient urban management in Lagos, however, is the result of a set of complex factors related partly to the fact that Lagos

is the federal capital of the country and partly to the nature of metropolitan expansion. For administrative purposes, the municipality of
Lagos is managed by the Lagos City Council. Over and above this is a
Federal Ministry of Lagos Affairs which is concerned with the protection and preservation of federal interests in Lagos and with overseeing
the work of both the Lagos City Council and the Lagos Executive
Development Board. Apart from this Ministry, there are seven other
federal ministries which direct policy within Lagos. These are the
Ministries of Education, Health, Labour, Mines and Power, Transport
and Aviation, Works and Surveys as well as Commerce and Industries.
This diffusion of responsibility has led in some cases to the neglect of
vital areas of administrative action such as land-use planning and the
provision of housing. In other cases it has led to conflicts and to a type
of administrative paralysis which makes for further inefficiency.

The nature of the metropolitan expansion has meant that Greater
Lagos now includes parts of a number of administrative divisions outside the municipality. At various times it has been suggested that, for
efficient management, it is necessary to extend the boundaries of Lagos
to cover these new developments. Whatever the merits of this suggestion
there is no doubt that it is an explosive political issue. The region that
is to suffer the loss of area and revenue resulting from such an extension
is not likely to take kindly to the suggestion. Moreover, experience from
other parts of the world shows that such a solution is not only un-
necessary but can also be futile. Since it is difficult to anticipate how far
such an 'exploding metropolis' would extend, it is unlikely that the
extension of boundaries at any one time would provide a lasting solution to the problem.

In consequence, in many cities in similar circumstances what has
been done is not to trouble about the number of administrative divisions
across which the city sprawls but to ensure the existence of a single
planning authority which can oversee the development of the whole
metropolitan area. Thus New York sprawls into 22 counties in three
states, but for planning purposes the whole area is now treated as a
single New York Metropolitan Region. Greater London also includes
the six so-called home counties, under which are numerous subsidiary
local government units such as county boroughs, municipal boroughs,
urban districts and rural districts. For planning purposes, the whole
area used to be under 21 separate planning authorities. In 1965, however, Parliament passed an Act creating the Greater London Council to

replace all of them and to deal with those planning matters that affect the whole conurbation.

The United Nations Team which reported in 1964 suggested that a similar body should be established for Lagos and should be designated the Lagos Metropolitan Development Authority. Its functions should cover, in particular, land and housing, transport, water and waste removal. Its area of jurisdiction should include not only the already developed areas within the metropolitan district but all contiguous areas within $2\frac{1}{2}$ miles from Agege railway station which are adjudged ripe for development and settlement in the near future (Fig. 48). Such a metropolitan district would extend over 115 square miles of territory and should provide a basis for planning the orderly development and growth of this major urbanized area of the country.

Prospect and policy for urbanization in Nigeria

If the policy of the various governments in Nigeria remains that of stimulating economic development through increasing industrialization, then we must expect a marked rise in the proportion of the country's inhabitants who live in urban areas. Even allowing for the contradictory trend of de-urbanization which has been noticed in the currently 'parasitic' cities, there is no doubt that within the next two decades and given a 7 per cent rate of increase of the urban population, something between 25 and 30 per cent of the total Nigerian population can be expected to live in urban centres.

In terms of the expected spatial pattern of distribution of this urban population, certain universal trends need to be borne in mind. The most important is that urbanization based on modern industrial technology tends to be of a selective, highly concentrated type. In other words, the prospect of future urbanization in Nigeria is likely to be the emergence of a few centres of spectacular agglomeration of population comprising the merging together of a number of relatively contiguous cities, towns and villages. It is possible to surmise three axial belts where such developments can be expected within the country. These are the axial belts between Lagos and Ibadan in the west, between Aba and Port Harcourt in the east and between Kano and Kaduna in the north.

Such concentrations of population could aggravate rather than resolve problems of equitable distribution of development throughout the country and this is why, more than at any other time in the history of Nigerias there is a great need for a clearly formulated urbaniza-

Plate 27   Surulere Estate
Plate 28   Water supply in townships

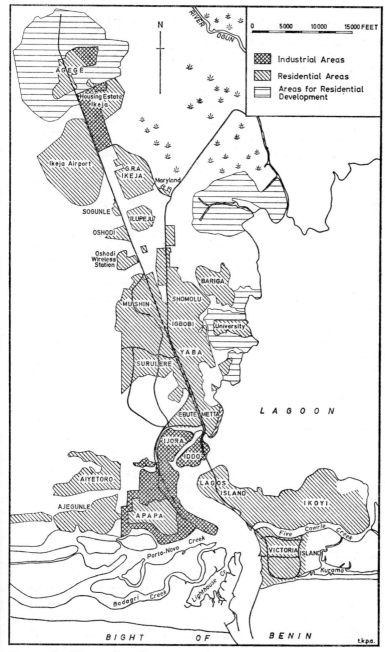

Figure 48   Metropolitan Lagos

tion policy. Such a policy must be based on the realization of the crucial role of urban centres for generating economic development within a given region. Thus a positive urbanization policy must be part of a bigger conception of regional economic planning. There is bound to be disagreement on how such a region should be defined. One idea would be to use the major agricultural regions as currently acknowledged and to encourage industries in such regions to be predominantly those that would have a significant multiplier effect on the regional agricultural economy. In other words, industrial development in the cities within each region should be largely oriented to the processing of raw materials from the region. However, because such economic regions have boundaries which have never been of any administrative significance, another idea is to equate the planning regions with current provincial boundaries. In further support of this view is the belief that provinces, as units of organization, could provide a better basis for stimulating major developmental efforts among local population based on their common historical association and their strong sense of belonging together.

It is obvious that these two ideas are not irreconcilable and a group of provinces can be organized into an economic region. However, in order that the cities may perform efficiently their function as 'growth points' of the economy, it would be necessary to review the nature of their management. As a first step in this direction, it is suggested that the previous colonial system of classifying urban centres should be revived. The class of a town this time should be based on its revenue-raising capacity. This, in turn, should decide the nature of its responsibilities, the scale of its administrative machinery, the range of decisions which it can make and the type and size of infrastructural investments which it can have. Thus a large city with an equally large annual income should be accorded greater autonomy to plan its own economic growth, while smaller towns or large cities with a small revenue-base should be nurtured gradually to enable them to take over an increasing range of activities necessary for their growth and development. Cities should be upgraded as they attain given levels of annual income, this being used along with other yardsticks of administrative efficiency.

Revenue-raising capacity is clearly fundamental to the range of functions cities can perform, and the government should encourage urban centres to seek ways and means of achieving this. Property rating is one such means which has so far not been tried by most urban centres. Another method is for governments to make it possible for cities to borrow from industrial development or other banks a certain proportion of the capital required for particular local projects, provided they can raise the rest locally by their own effort. In Western Nigeria a variant of this method has been invaluable in encouraging towns and cities to provide their own grammar schools. In this case the government offered to provide a grant-in-aid to a town if its people could raise an equivalent amount. It was in this respect that the 'social identification' of émigrés was used to positive advantage, and there is no reason to believe that with proper organization such latent revenue-raising ability cannot be geared to raising capital needed for local industrial development.

One final area of major policy decision is that of data collection. No planning can proceed without the data necessary for knowing even the most elementary facts about the urban areas and the country as a whole. The present study has suffered immensely from its dependence largely on the 1952 Census reports. It has been difficult to describe growth-rate patterns in the country because of an absence of vital statistics. There are no censuses of housing, production and distribution anywhere in the country. Furthermore, most urban centres are not organized internally to facilitate the collection of data about their activities and growth.

In an era of increasing industrialization, these are basic needs which a country can ill afford not to have. For the major thesis of this book is to emphasize that towns and cities are important generating centres for economic growth, and that their efficient management is as crucial to the rate of growth of the country's economy as is the management of any directly productive activity. Efficient management, however, depends on adequate knowledge. This, in turn, depends on the diligent and careful collection of a wide range of relevant data. In the next decade or two, the increasing urbanization of Nigeria will tax to the full the imaginative and organizational resources of the country, especially in resolving the major problems of our cities and towns. The degree of success which attends our efforts in this direction may well determine the chances of the country's take-off to sustained economic growth.

References

1. Eric E. Lampard, 'The history of cities in the economically advanced areas', *Economic Development and Cultural Change*, Vol. 3, No. 2, January 1955, p. 92.
2. Bert F. Hoselitz, 'Urbanization and Economic Development in Asia', *Economic Development and Cultural Change*, Vol. 6, No. 1, October 1957, p. 44.
3. A. L. Mabogunje, 'Urbanization in Nigeria—a Constraint on Economic Development', *Economic Development and Cultural Change*, Vol. 13, No. 4, Part 1, July 1965, pp. 436-8.

Appendix 1

NIGERIAN TOWNS BY POPULATION SIZE (1952 CENSUS)

A. Northern Nigeria

1.	KANO	127,205	38.	MORIKI	10,521
2.	YERWA	56,740	39.	HADEJIA	10,453
3.	ZARIA	53,974	40.	GUMEL	10,406
4.	KATSINA	52,672	41.	AZARE	10,366
5.	SOKOTO	51,986	42.	FUNTUA	9,957
6.	KADUNA	44,540	43.	YARTSAKUWA	9,723
7.	ILORIN	40,994	44.	JIMERA	9,603
8.	GUSAU	40,202	45.	LAFIA	9,519
9.	JOS	38,527	46.	ARGUNGU	9,402
10.	OKENE	32,602	47.	DANBATTA	9,395
11.	KUMO	29,075	48.	KURYA	9,375
12.	NGURU	23,084	49.	MALLUM FASHI	9,330
13.	OFFA	20,668	50.	RINGIN	9,252
14.	BIDA	19,346	51.	MAIKULKI	9,152
15.	KAURA NAMODA	19,146	52.	BIU	9,001
16.	GOMBE	18,483	53.	GWARZO	8,775
17.	MAKURDI	16,713	54.	YOLA	8,573
18.	WURNO	15,880	55.	WAKARI	8,546
19.	GALADI	14,770	56.	BUKURU	8,450
20.	TALATA MAFARA	14,757	57.	GORA	8,220
21.	POTISKUM	14,692	58.	BAMA	8,185
22.	GUMMI	14,608	59.	KIRU	7,816
23.	GANDI	14,273	60.	RIMI	7,735
24.	JANGERU	13,853	61.	ABUJA	7,664
25.	BAUCHI	13,440	62.	KATAMI	7,650
26.	GAYA	12,996	63.	KOKO	7,624
27.	SHINKAFI	12,955	64.	OBEHIRA	7,607
28.	MINNA	12,870	65.	DARKI	7,588
29.	NAFUCE	12,776	66.	GWANDU	7,546
30.	LOKOJA	12,606	67.	YABAKWARI	7,528
31.	BIRNIN KEBBI	12,270	68.	GORA	7,452
32.	GWADA BANA	12,095	69.	IDAH	7,334
33.	MUBI	11,783	70.	KABBA	7,305
34.	GEIDAM	11,032	71.	ALIERO	7,298
35.	JEGA	10,836	72.	DAURA	7,184
36.	ISA	10,800	73.	KAFANCHAN	7,016
37.	GASHUA	10,558	74.	RIMI	6,953

75.	BAKORI	6,898	96.	KONTAGORA	5,665
76.	FADA KWOI	6,763	97.	OKENGWE	5,630
77.	GIYAWA	6,645	98.	WURNO	5,590
78.	DUTSIN MA	6,640	99.	AMBURSA	5,553
79.	GARKO	6,585	100.	INDABO	5,476
80.	RIJAU	6,568	101.	RIKADAWA	5,464
81.	KOFA	6,461	102.	GBOKO	5,360
82.	KEFFI	6,367	103.	GARUNATI	5,350
83.	RUWAN DORUWA	6,326	104.	BARBURA	5,326
84.	GUIMA	6,258	105.	SAYA-SAYA	5,322
85.	BIRNIN KUDU	6,224	106.	KWARRE	5,314
86.	IBI	6,183	107.	ZURU	5,308
87.	DANHASSAN	6,176	108.	ZONKWA	5,304
88.	JIBIYA MAJE	6,092	109.	BAKURA	5,273
89.	YARKO	6,065	110.	BABEJI	5,231
90.	BICI	6,012	111.	JIGAWA	5,200
91.	TAKUM	5,914	112.	KIYAWA	5,094
92.	IKWHI	5,863	113.	KANYA BABA	5,085
93.	KWANKWASO	5,749	114.	GAMMO	5,066
94.	WUDIL	5,713	115.	KIYAYA	5,028
95.	DANALHAJI	5,672			

B. Eastern Nigeria

1.	ONITSHA	76,921	23.	ETEH	11,367
2.	PORT HARCOURT	71,634	24.	AWKA	11,343
3.	ENUGU	62,764	25.	AMASSAMA	11,185
4.	ABA	57,787	26.	ABONNEMA	11,092
5.	CALABAR	46,705	27.	OMOKU	10,645
6.	ENUGU-UMOZI	35,846	28.	IGBO-UKU	10,255
7.	EHA AMUFU	29,434	29.	ENUGU-EZIKE EZODO	10,191
8.	NNEWI	28,777	30.	INYI	9,795
9.	IHIALA	24,290	31.	ABAKALIKI	9,687
10.	AKU	20,809	32.	IBAGWA-AKA	9,512
11.	EHA ALUMONA	19,580	33.	OWERRI	9,331
12.	UGEP	17,567	34.	IFIAYONG	9,303
13.	OKRIKA	16,671	35.	BODO (BORI)	9,061
14.	OGUTA	14,761	36.	ENUGU-UKWU	8,875
15.	NSUKKA	14,674	37.	NANKA	8,783
16.	BUGUMA	14,609	38.	MGBOWO	8,625
17.	ORON	13,641	39.	MBU	8,371
18.	OPI	13,417	40.	OVOKO	8,114
19.	OBA (East)	13,370	41.	IFETE	7,904
20.	UKEHE	12,167	42.	MAKU	7,879
21.	ENUGU-ITODO	11,645	43.	TOMBIA	7,843
22.	NIMO	11,419	44.	OBOLO EKE	7,824

45. EKURI	7,810	63. EDE	6,391
46. OBOLO-AFOR	7,787	64. OTU-OCHA	6,303
47. OBOLO-OYE	7,463	65. UYO	6,256
48. IMILIKE	7,208	66. EKET	6,096
49. IKEM	7,206	67. ITCHI	6,020
50. OMOR	7,196	68. UGBENE	5,672
51. EKWULOBIA	7,177	69. ULELE	5,666
52. SEIBIRI	7,105	70. IGBO	5,661
53. IKOM	7,058	71. EGBEDA	5,635
54. NNOBI	6,978	72. ETINAN	5,540
55. ABBOH	6,966	73. IHEAKPU	5,503
56. ABAGANA	6,814	74. MKPANI	5,409
57. LEKE	6,791	75. OGOJA	5,399
58. IBAGWA-ANI	6,625	76. AGBOGUGU	5,199
59. IHAKA	6,547	77. UMULOKPA	5,142
60. AKWEGBE	6,515	78. ENWEN	5,131
61. BAKANA	6,513	79. EGWANGA	5,106
62. OBUKPA	6,506		

C. Western Nigeria

1. IBADAN	459,196	26. IKARE	25,239
2. LAGOS	267,407	27. ADO-EKITI	24,646
3. OGBOMOSHO	139,535	28. IJEBU-IGBO	24,166
4. OSHOGBO	122,728	29. FIDITI	23,636
5. IFE	110,790	30. SHAKI	22,983
6. IWO	100,006	31. UROMI	22,339
7. ABEOKUTA	84,451	32. GBOGAN	20,480
8. OYO	72,133	33. IKIRE	20,118
9. ILESHA	72,029	34. WARRI	19,526
10. BENIN	53,753	35. IGBO-ORA	19,294
11. ISEYIN	49,680	36. ASABA	17,387
12. EDE	44,808	37. ADO	16,381
13. AKURE	38,853	38. OGWASHI-UKU	15,900
14. ILOBU	38,322	39. EJIGBO	15,851
15. ONDO	36,233	40. OKEIHO	15,807
16. IKERRE	35,584	41. IRAGBIJI	14,629
17. SAPELE	33,638	42. IDANRE	14,615
18. MUSHIN	32,079	43. AIYETORO	14,090
19. OWO	30,662	44. IFON (OSHUN)	13,708
20. SHAGAMU	30,099	45. IBUSA	12,857
21. OKA	28,524	46. AGEGE	12,844
22. IJEBU-ODE	27,558	47. ISHARA	12,568
23. ILORA	26,122	48. ILARO	12,373
24. IKIRUN	26,005	49. EFFON	12,367
25. ILLA	25,745	50. ODEOMU	11,701

51.	ILE-IGBO	11,597	94.	UBIAJA	6,716
52.	ILERO	11,168	95.	IGBESSA	6,615
53.	ILAWE	11,084	96.	OYAN	6,610
54.	IGBETTI	10,955	97.	IFON (OWO)	6,573
55.	OKITIPUPA	10,697	98.	OTAN	6,552
56.	IGBARA-OKE	10,615	99.	IRESSI	6,489
57.	OMUO	10,573	100.	OTU	6,440
58.	IRELE	10,413	101.	EDUNABON	6,377
59.	APOMU	10,400	102.	AGO-IWOYE	6,369
60.	IPETU-MODU	9,898	103.	AYE	6,362
61.	INISHA	9,803	104.	AJILETE	6,317
62.	IPERU	9,642	105.	ALADE (AKURE)	6,257
63.	IKOLE	9,469	106.	AJEGUNLE	6,241
64.	IGANNA	9,138	107.	ODE REMO	6,201
65.	BOJI-BOJI	9,109	108.	ABBI	6,136
66.	IKORODU	9,018	109.	UYIN	6,088
67.	ILE-OLUJI	8,972	110.	ESA-OKE	6,068
68.	OTTA	8,914	111.	OKE MESI	6,063
69.	IFO	8,765	112.	LAGUN	6,013
70.	IPETU-IJESHA	8,510	113.	IKENNE	5,995
71.	IGBOHO	8,476	114.	OGBAGI	5,974
72.	EPE	8,422	115.	BADAGRI	5,971
73.	ILUTITUN	8,325	116.	AWE	5,928
74.	IRE	8,295	117.	ISHUA	5,916
75.	ERUWA	8,154	118.	ODE	5,876
76.	IPOTI	8,153	119.	IFAKI	5,805
77.	IGBARA-ODO	8,142	120.	ILARA	5,783
78.	OLUPONNA	7,855	121.	ARANOKO	5,757
79.	KISHI	7,827	122.	AKUNGBA	5,721
80.	ISE	7,756	123.	ENWE	5,579
81.	UMUNEDE	7,708	124.	EMEDE	5,517
82.	IJEBU-IJESHA	7,693	125.	IKORO	5,514
83.	OBIARUKU	7,658	126.	KUTA	5,450
84.	IJERO	7,586	127.	AIYETORO	5,434
85.	AKINMORIN	7,461	128.	OKAINGBA	5,417
86.	OMIFINFUN	7,417	129.	OKE-AGBE	5,383
87.	IGBAJO	7,162	130.	IDDO	5,323
88.	UBULU-UKU	7,126	131.	IDOANI	5,262
89.	ODOGBOLU	6,867	132.	OTUN	5,258
90.	ARIGIDI	6,863	133.	OZORO	5,251
91.	ERIN	6,847	134.	IREUKPEN	5,200
92.	BURUTU	6,784	135.	FUGAR	5,174
93.	OKE-IGBO	6,774			

Appendix 2 (See Fig. 14)

ZONE I consists of an area of low-lying land fringing the coastal swamps and creek areas across the whole of southern Nigeria, beginning as a narrow strip in the west and widening out in Warri Province and the Eastern Region. It embraces the eastern part of Ijebu Province, the southern part of Ondo and Benin Provinces, the non-creek areas of Warri and Rivers Provinces, the southern part of Onitsha Province and the whole of Owerri and Calabar Provinces. The oil palm dominates the economy of the zone and the bulk of the population is engaged in activities connected with the collection and marketing of palm produce, both oil and kernels; the production of foodcrops is designed solely to meet the needs of the local population. The principal food crops grown are cassava, yams and maize and, in addition, there is a variety of minor crops such as *telfairia*, okra, peppers and melon.

ZONE 2 is confined to the Western Region and covers Ikeja Division of the Colony, part of Abeokuta Province, western Ijebu Province, the southern part of Ibadan Province, Ife and Ilesha Divisions of Oyo Province and the central part of Ondo Province. Cocoa exerts an influence on farming similar to that of palm produce in Zone 1, and kola is also of considerable importance in the south-western part of the zone. The principal farm crops are similar to those grown in Zone 1.

ZONE 3 is a transitional zone on the fringe of the high forest area and consists of a number of isolated areas on the northern edge of Zones 1 and 2. Generally speaking the production of cash crops for export is not important in this zone, although cocoa is found in isolated parts and the oil palm abounds throughout the area. There is, however, a greater tendency to concentrate on the production of food crops, and yam takes the place of cassava as the principal crop. Maize is grown throughout the area and tobacco and cotton are important in certain areas in the west.

ZONE 3A, a small, isolated zone in the Eastern Region, corresponds roughly to the Udi Plateau and, for the purpose of the census, has been taken as occupying the whole of Onitsha Province, with the exception of Onitsha Division itself and the lowland areas of Nsukka Division. The soil on the plateau is poor and farming is purely on a subsistence basis. Cash crops are not grown and the principal food crop is yam.

ZONE 4 is the main yam-producing area of Nigeria extending across the whole of the country immediately south of the Niger and Benue Rivers, although in places, for example, Minna and Abuja Divisions of Niger

Province and the southern parts of Lafia and Nasarawa Divisions of Benue Province, it extends north of the Rivers. In addition to yams, grains are also grown in large quantities, with maize predominating in the more southerly areas and millet and guinea-corn in the north. Much food is exported from the zone to other parts of Nigeria, particularly the large towns of the Eastern and Western Regions. Most of the minor crops grown farther south flourish, and groundnuts and other northern crops are grown in small quantities. Rice is important in the flood plain of the Niger, and the production of benniseed is concentrated in Tiv Division of Benue Province. The production of cash crops for export is not important in this zone.

ZONE 5 is primarily a grain-producing area, extending across most of Nigeria immediately north of Zone 4, and in places as far south as the Niger and beyond. Farming is mainly on a subsistence basis and there is little movement of food from this area to other parts of Nigeria. Millet and guinea-corn predominate, but groundnuts are grown in small quantities and there is some cotton in the north of Niger Province. The swamp area of Bida Division of Niger Province is an important rice-growing area.

ZONE 6 is the main cotton-producing area of Nigeria, covering the southern part of Sokoto, Katsina and Kano Provinces, the northern part of Niger, Zaria and Bauchi Provinces, and also Gombe Division of Bauchi Province. In addition to cotton, groundnuts are a cash crop of considerable importance, while guinea-corn, millet and cowpeas are the principal food crops. In parts of the zone dry season farming is carried on along the banks of the rivers, a wide variety of useful vegetables being grown.

ZONE 7 extends across the whole of the extreme north of Nigeria and is the main groundnut-producing region of the country, although by far the greatest production of this crop is concentrated in northern Kano Province. Guinea-corn, millet and cowpeas are again the principal food crops.

ZONE 8 covers the high plateau area of Jos and Pankshin Divisions of Plateau Province. The soil here is inferior, having suffered much from erosion, and will support only the poorer type of crop. The principal crop is *acha* (an inferior kind of millet), while millet (*dauro*), *tamba* (another variety of millet) and some yams are grown. The production of European-type vegetables is important in this part.

ZONE 9 is the area enclosed within a radius of 30-40 miles around Kano City in which the pressure of population is such that cultivation of a more or less permanent nature is undertaken with the aid of manuring; for that reason it has been treated as a separate zone. Similar principal crops to those of Zone 7 are grown, with groundnuts as the export crop and millet, guinea-corn and cowpeas as the principal food crops. Market gardening, based on irrigation, is also very important in the immediate vicinity of Kano City.

ZONE 10 covers those areas of the Cameroons administered as part of the Northern Region of Nigeria, with the exception of two small areas, one in the extreme north and one in the south. Although conditions do vary to some extent throughout this zone, farming practice is, on the whole, similar to that in Zone 5, subsistence farming being the general rule, with guinea-corn and millet as the principal crops. Groundnuts are fairly important in the northern part of the zone.

ZONE 11 covers the mountain grassland area of Bamenda Province and the Mambila Plateau of Adamawa Province. The abundance of grassland encourages the immigration of the Fulani herdsmen during the dry season and many Fulani have now settled permanently in the area. A wide variety of crops is grown by the local inhabitants, including yam, cocoyam, cassava, maize, bambarra groundnuts and many kinds of African and European vegetables.

ZONE 12 is a small, specialized zone covering the north-east corner of Bornu Province on the fringe of Lake Chad, and cutting across Bornu Division (Nigeria) and Dikwa Division (Cameroons). The area is characterized by the black cotton soil known as *firki*, which favours the cultivation of *masakwa* or dry season guinea-corn. This crop is planted towards the end of the rains when most of the land is flooded and it ripens as the floods recede during the dry season.

Appendix 3

NIGERIAN TOWNS (1952 CENSUS)

MATRIX OF INTERCORRELATIONS AMONG NIGERIAN TOWNS
(For key to variables, see Table 19, p. 153)

Variable No. and Name	1	2	3	4	5	6	7	8	9	10	11	12
1. TOTPOP	1·000											
2. TOTM	0·149	1·000										
3. TOTF	-0·149	-0·998	1·000									
4. HA/FU	-0·072	0·009	0·010	1·000								
5. IBO	-0·038	0·047	-0·050	-0·395	1·000							
6. YORUBA	0·172	0·080	0·080	-0·510	-0·431	1·000						
7. ONORTH	-0·026	0·127	-0·113	0·341	-0·218	-0·350	1·000					
8. OSOUTH	-0·033	0·213	0·216	-0·249	-0·033	-0·151	-0·089	1·000				
9. NONNIG	0·244	0·548	-0·544	0·149	0·011	-0·180	0·277	0·170	1·000			
10. STDII	0·268	0·376	-0·382	0·521	0·228	-0·259	0·213	0·372	0·330	1·000		
11. RANDW	0·174	0·124	-0·129	0·424	-0·203	-0·175	0·277	-0·049	0·297	0·176	1·000	
12. MLESS2	0·077	-0·317	0·313	-0·159	-0·217	0·402	-0·306	-0·129	-0·431	-0·224	-0·256	1·000
13. M2-6	-0·053	-0·534	0·529	-0·139	-0·076	0·139	-0·114	-0·008	-0·421	-0·155	-0·182	0·590
14. M7-14	0·007	-0·301	0·297	-0·315	0·193	-0·123	-0·384	0·089	-0·330	0·162	-0·138	0·305
15. M15-49	0·019	0·506	-0·503	0·101	0·263	-0·340	0·230	0·108	0·511	0·218	0·192	-0·808
16. M50+	-0·001	-0·232	0·237	0·349	-0·563	0·227	0·164	-0·265	-0·189	-0·361	0·095	0·194

	13	14	15	16	17	18	19	20	21	22	23	24
17. MAG/FH	−0·363	−0·489	0·488	0·077	−0·073	0·059	−0·174	−0·304	−0·595	−0·662	−0·350	0·365
18. MTD/CT	0·352	0·382	−0·383	0·202	−0·216	0·008	0·232	0·080	0·415	0·390	0·397	−0·332
19. ADMIN	0·320	0·441	−0·439	0·143	−0·034	−0·097	0·251	0·180	0·618	0·515	0·441	−0·461
20. OOCCUP	0·229	0·539	−0·534	0·096	−0·018	−0·118	0·280	0·223	0·619	0·485	0·370	−0·523
21. OMALES	0·023	−0·402	0·403	−0·341	0·191	0·096	−0·167	0·096	−0·289	0·086	−0·214	0·377
22. FLESS2	0·115	−0·016	0·012	−0·245	−0·183	0·443	−0·318	−0·030	−0·282	−0·041	−0·240	0·902
23. F2-6	0·044	0·018	−0·028	−0·353	0·125	0·143	−0·145	0·182	−0·104	0·306	−0·104	0·385
24. F7-14	0·174	0·061	−0·064	−0·540	0·230	0·305	−0·390	0·149	0·116	0·430	−0·165	0·319
25. F15-49	−0·145	0·145	−0·141	0·259	0·242	−0·473	0·270	0·021	0·335	−0·061	0·135	−0·785
26. F50+	−0·005	−0·366	0·370	0·406	−0·560	0·163	0·179	−0·286	−0·228	−0·447	0·104	0·166
27. FAG/FH	−0·112	−0·266	0·265	−0·572	0·328	0·271	−0·447	0·011	−0·407	−0·024	−0·474	0·291
28. FTD/CT	0·158	0·178	−0·181	0·115	0·281	−0·206	−0·032	−0·025	0·175	0·169	0·096	−0·026
29. OFEMLS	0·034	0·130	−0·126	0·478	−0·203	−0·332	0·484	0·003	0·278	−0·072	0·408	−0·263
30. MOSLEM	0·069	−0·016	0·020	0·844	−0·618	−0·164	0·391	−0·338	0·097	−0·538	0·310	−0·033
31. XTIANS	0·057	0·119	−0·124	−0·682	0·127	0·486	−0·343	0·316	−0·038	0·718	−0·067	0·098
32. ANIMIS	−0·109	−0·223	0·222	0·659	0·659	−0·045	−0·267	0·153	−0·273	0·066	−0·442	0·071

Variable
No. and name

1. TOTPOP
2. TOTM
3. TOTF
4. HA/FU
5. IBO
6. YORUBA

Correlation matrix (lower triangular):

	7	8	9	10	11	12	13	14	15	16	17
7. ONORTH	1·000										
8. OSOUTH	0·424	1·000									
9. NONNIG	-0·773	-0·550	1·000								
10. STDII	-0·023	-0·234	-0·416	1·000							
11. RANDW	0·275	0·158	-0·362	0·203	1·000						
12. MLESS2	-0·310	-0·265	0·286	0·115	-0·698	1·000					
13. M2-6	-0·391	-0·238	0·437	-0·078	-0·741	0·603	1·000				
14. M7-14	-0·493	-0·410	0·541	-0·060	-0·769	0·618	0·742	1·000			
15. M15-49	0·556	0·500	-0·465	-0·173	-0·030	-0·337	-0·241	-0·405	1·000		
16. M50+	0·422	0·236	-0·640	0·077	0·222	-0·212	-0·323	-0·348	0·241	1·000	
17. MAG/FH	0·667	0·383	-0·432	-0·301	-0·107	-0·104	-0·092	-0·130	0·406	0·452	1·000
18. MTD/CT	0·187	0·657	-0·347	-0·246	-0·051	-0·131	-0·093	-0·159	0·303	0·381	0·407
19. ADMIN	-0·558	-0·430	0·836	-0·325	-0·144	0·141	0·277	0·326	-0·345	-0·788	-0·562
20. OOCCUP	0·082	-0·172	-0·395	-0·170	0·245	0·059	-0·135	-0·150	-0·065	-0·010	-0·357
21. OMALES	0·241	0·277	-0·235	0·110	0·465	-0·483	-0·501	-0·456	0·198	0·267	0·172
22. FLESS2	-0·076	-0·081	0·031	0·154	-0·261	0·504	0·227	0·261	-0·279	0·049	0·038
23. F2-6	-0·172	-0·250	0·189	0·154	-0·294	0·170	0·378	0·310	0·038	-0·285	-0·192
24. F7-14	-0·106	-0·336	-0·022	0·512	0·080	0·263	0·114	0·075	-0·322	-0·129	-0·394
25. F15-49	0·101	0·297	-0·094	-0·255	-0·288	0·128	0·123	0·113	0·215	0·235	-0·508
26. F50+	0·172	0·278	-0·031	-0·387	0·248	-0·500	-0·352	-0·331	0·336	0·055	0·512

Additional variables: 18. MTD/CT, 19. ADMIN, 20. OOCCUP, 21. OMALES, 22. FLESS2, 23. F2-6, 24. F7-14, 25. F15-49, 26. F50+, 27. FAG/FH, 28. FTD/CT, 29. OFEMLS, 30. MOSLEM, 31. XTIANS, 32. ANIMIS

Variable No. and name	25	26	27	28	29	30	31	32
5. FI5-49	1·000							
6. F50+	−0·262	1·000						
7. FAG/FH	−0·211	−0·206	1·000					
8. FTD/CT	−0·044	0·054	−0·388	1·000				
9. OFEMLS	0·208	0·216	−0·701	−0·342	1·000			
0. MOSLEM	0·122	0·564	−0·512	0·188	0·404	1·000		
1. XTIANS	−0·311	−0·346	0·249	0·116	−0·292	−0·672	1·000	
2. ANIMIS	−0·002	−0·360	0·577	−0·324	−0·394	−0·772	0·156	1·000

Appendix 4

NIGERIAN TOWNS (1952 CENSUS). FACTOR ANALYSIS OF THIRTY-TWO
VARIABLES: TABLE OF COMMON VARIANCES.

No.	Eigenvalue	*Percentage of Communality Over*			
		All (32)	Factors	7 Rotated Factors	
1.	8·510	29·6	29·6	35·1	35·1
2.	5·901	20·5	50·1	24·3	59·5
3.	3·878	13·5	63·6	16·0	75·4
4.	2·124	7·4	71·0	8·8	84·2
5.	1·612	5·6	76·6	6·6	90·9
6.	1·209	4·2	80·8	5·0	95·8
7.	1·006	3·5	84·3	4·2	100·0
8	0·893	3·1	87·4		
9.	0·728	2·5	89·9		
10.	0·623	2·2	92·1		
11.	0·533	1·9	94·0		
12.	0·489	1·7	95·7		
13.	0·391	1·4	97·0		
14.	0·283	1·0	98·0		
15.	0·196	0·7	98·7		
16.	0·171	0·6	99·3		
17.	0·154	0·5	99·8		
18.	0·100	0·3	100·2		
19.	0·076	0·3			
20.	0·061	0·2			
21.	0·032	0·1			
22.	0·027	0·1			
23.	0·003	0·0			

Trace of Original Matrix   *28·752*
Communality Over   *32 Factors* = *28·752*
                              7 Factors = *24·240*

Appendix 5

NIGERIAN TOWNS (1952 CENSUS)
FACTOR ANALYSIS OF THIRTY-TWO VARIABLES
UNROTATED FACTOR MATRIX

Variable No. and name	Communality 10 factors	1	2	3	4	5	6	7	8	9	10
Sum squares over variables		8·510	5·901	3·878	2·124	1·612	1·209	1·006	0·893	0·728	0·623
1. TOTPOP	0·312	-0·126	-0·163	-0·353	-0·030	0·061	0·023	-0·227	-0·204	-0·060	-0·208
2. TOTM	0·953	-0·550	-0·476	-0·195	0·237	-0·531	-0·154	-0·043	0·055	0·070	0·119
3. TOTF	0·952	0·546	0·481	0·198	-0·236	0·533	0·146	0·043	-0·060	-0·067	-0·114
4. HA/FU	0·941	-0·521	0·688	-0·017	-0·184	-0·245	0·247	-0·105	0·164	-0·008	-0·065
5. IBO	0·929	0·147	-0·542	0·587	-0·158	-0·049	0·121	-0·269	-0·282	0·271	-0·040
6. YORUBA	0·948	0·378	-0·092	-0·537	0·476	0·298	-0·210	0·004	-0·105	-0·370	0·038
7. ONORTH	0·709	-0·495	0·279	0·035	-0·300	-0·080	-0·153	0·218	-0·250	0·065	0·389
8. OSOUTH	0·917	-0·047	-0·446	-0·046	-0·188	-0·003	-0·162	0·488	0·564	0·207	-0·229
9. NONNIG	0·544	-0·641	-0·304	-0·118	-0·061	-0·107	-0·021	-0·015	-0·076	0·007	-0·069
10. STDII	0·850	-0·132	-0·802	-0·328	-0·062	0·262	-0·052	-0·046	0·026	-0·048	0·021
11. RANDW	0·404	-0·481	0·080	-0·226	-0·252	0·100	0·063	-0·154	0·033	-0·102	0·051
12. MLESS2	0·937	0·722	0·230	-0·428	0·015	-0·297	-0·045	-0·007	-0·134	-0·026	0·265
13. M2-6	0·889	0·682	0·176	-0·217	-0·445	-0·027	0·192	0·291	-0·140	-0·027	0·080
14. M7-14	0·878	0·608	-0·213	-0·100	-0·318	0·093	0·245	0·366	0·360	0·011	0·140
15. MI5-49	0·966	-0·748	0·345	0·463	0·203	0·005	-0·012	0·037	-0·032	-0·167	-0·032
16. M50+	0·927	-0·034	0·691	-0·377	0·210	0·245	-0·270	-0·028	0·006	0·341	0·111

17. MAG/FH	0·916	0·566	0·532	0·390	0·280	−0·163	0·016	−0·002	0·145	−0·098	0·160
18. MTD/CT	0·731	−0·616	−0·159	−0·474	0·029	0·201	0·196	0·002	−0·084	0·123	−0·028
19. ADMIN	0·725	−0·679	−0·328	−0·291	−0·174	0·158	−0·021	−0·083	−0·062	0·012	−0·076
20. OOCCUP	0·777	−0·743	−0·359	−0·233	−0·015	0·110	−0·069	0·057	−0·091	0·109	−0·034
21. OMALES	0·687	0·558	−0·111	−0·031	−0·542	0·137	−0·103	−0·014	−0·081	−0·076	−0·161
22. FLESS2	0·913	0·602	0·005	−0·509	0·134	−0·444	−0·092	0·017	−0·124	−0·033	−0·226
23. F2-6	0·858	0·464	−0·373	−0·343	−0·376	−0·264	0·157	0·271	−0·154	−0·036	0·228
24. F7-14	0·846	0·503	−0·520	−0·275	−0·029	−0·057	0·015	0·407	0·205	0·085	0·165
25. F15-49	0·966	−0·645	−0·054	0·666	0·048	0·163	0·140	0·090	0·010	−0·200	−0·083
26. F50+	0·920	−0·019	0·781	−0·275	0·093	0·318	−0·228	−0·024	0·014	0·267	0·027
27. FAG/FH	0·761	0·685	−0·215	0·332	0·352	0·035	−0·112	0·000	−0·034	0·042	0·012
28. FTD/CT	0·862	−0·234	−0·045	0·475	0·321	0·106	0·645	0·191	−0·029	0·112	0·009
29. OFEMLS	0·918	−0·523	0·264	−0·052	0·581	−0·059	−0·433	−0·121	0·031	−0·165	−0·020
30. MOSLEM	0·912	−0·455	0·771	−0·221	−0·010	−0·148	0·139	−0·096	0·052	−0·087	−0·049
31. XTIANS	0·792	0·279	−0·667	−0·337	0·077	0·274	−0·101	0·108	0·086	−0·153	0·147
32. ANIMIS	0·843	0·530	0·401	0·536	−0·001	0·071	−0·101	0·065	−0·172	0·251	−0·048

Appendix 6

SCORES OF NIGERIAN TOWNS ON FACTOR ONE

Scores from −2·0 to −1·0

	North	East	West
Group A.	—	—	2. LAGOS −1·177
Group B.	— —	9. ONITSHA −1·001 13. ENUGU −1·027	— —
Group C.	27. JOS −1·009	—	41. IJEBU-ODE −1·004

Scores from −1·0 to −0·5

	North	East	West
Group A.	4. KANO −0·882	— —	1. IBADAN −0·676 8. ABEOKUTA −0·998
Group B.	15. YERWA −0·556 16. ZARIA −0·789 19. SOKOTO −0·634	14. ABA −0·616	11. ILESHA −0·622 17. BENIN −0·633

Group C.

— —

Group D.

59. BIDA — -0·598
74. TALATA MAFARA — -0·583
93. MINNA — -0·726

Group E.

130. FUNTUA — -0·617
165. BUKURU — -0·867
214. KAFANCHAN — -0·954
247. KEFFI — -0·500
287. KONTAGORA — -0·645

— —

135. ABAKALIKI — -0·600
144. OWERRI — -0·540
146. IFIAYONG — -0·730
254. UYO — -0·713
325. EGWANGA — -0·855

Scores from -0·5 to 0

32. SAPELE — -0·887
34. MUSHIN — -0·854

58. WARRI — -0·948
92. AGEGE — -0·694
—

166. EPE — -0·605
224. BURUTU — -0·691
255. AJEGUNLE — -0·617
— —

Group A.

— — —

— —

3. OGBOMOSHO — -0·111
5. OSHOGBO — -0·191
6. IFE — -0·435
| |

Group B.

18. KATSINA — -0·343
24. ILORIN — -0·289
25. GUSAU — -0·258

	North	East	West
Group C.			
50. NGURU	−0·150		
54. OFFA	−0·212		
39. NNEWI		−0·118	
26. AKURE			−0·067
29. ONDO			−0·488
31. IKERRE			−0·273
35. OWO			−0·209
36. SHAGAMU			−0·186
42. ILORA			−0·265
46. ADO-EKITI			−0·152
48. IJEBU-IGBO			−0·284
49. FIDITI			−0·208
Group D.			
61. KAURA NAMODA	−0·217		
62. GOMBE	−0·428		
69. WURNO	−0·331		
75. POTISKUM	−0·306		
90. SHINKAFI	−0·056		
99. BIRNIN KEBBI	−0·411		
115. JEGA	−0·283		
116. ISA	−0·078		
123. HADEIJA	−0·311		
127. AZARE	−0·256		
64. ASABA		−0·249	
68. OGWASHI-UKU		−0·048	
73. OGUTA		−0·325	
106. NIMO		−0·287	
108. AWKA		−0·264	
98. EFFON			−0·111
117. OKITIPUPA			−0·124
124. IRELE			−0·138
Group E.			
134. YARTSAKUWA	−0·112		
138. LAFIA	−0·366		
141. ARGUNGU	−0·176		
156. ENUGU-UKWU		−0·034	
213. IKOM		−0·067	
215. NNOBI		−0·482	
131. IPETU-MODU			−0·243
132. INISHA			−0·028
150. BOJI-BOJI			−0·087

Group A.

		Scores from 0 to +0·5
145. MALLUMFASHI	−0·213	—
147. RINGIN	−0·188	—
171. BAMA	−0·025	—
186. RIMI	−0·188	—
189. ABUJA	−0·235	—
196. GWANDU	−0·140	—
202. IDAH	−0·478	—
203. KABBA	−0·164	—
204. ALIERO	−0·107	—
208. DAURA	−0·171	—
218. BAKORI	−0·137	—
226. FADANKWOI	−0·155	—
229. DUTSIN-MA	−0·265	—
235. RIJAU	−0·056	—
249. RUWAN DORUWA	−0·198	—
252. GUIMA	−0·066	—
269. BICI	−0·110	—
313. ZONKWA	−0·137	—
251. OTU-OCHA	−0·079	—
304. OGOJA	−0·266	—
152. IKORODU	−0·470	
159. IFO	−0·137	
173. IPOTI	−0·360	
174. IGBARA-ODO	−0·186	
188. IJEBU-JESHA	−0·090	
192. KOKO	−0·144	
195. IJERO	−0·194	
210. IGBAJO	−0·006	
227. UBIAJA	−0·345	
232. OYAN	−0·239	
241. IRESSI	−0·154	
257. ODE REMO	−0·100	
266. OKE MESSI	−0·219	
270. IKENNE	−0·219	
272. BADAGRI	−0·436	
274. ISHUA	−0·022	
278. IFAKI	−0·139	
280. ARAMOKO	−0·301	
282. AKUNGBA	−0·006	
296. IKORO	−0·101	
305. OKE-AGBE	−0·058	
309. IDDO	−0·001	
7. IWO		0·042

Group B.

North	East	West
—	—	10. OYO — 0·179
—	—	20. ISEYIN — 0·335
—		22. EDE — 0·157

Group C.

North	East	West
38. KUMO — 0·091	37. EHA AMUFU — 0·410	28. ILOBU — 0·156
—	47. IHIALA — 0·147	40. OKA — 0·225
—	53. AKU — 0·314	43. IKIRUN — 0·192
—	—	44. ILLA — 0·027
—	—	51. SHAKI — 0·022
—	—	55. GBOGAN — 0·008
		56. IKIRE — 0·335

Group D.

North	East	West
72. GALADI — 0·150	57. EHA ALUMONA — 0·492	60. IGBO-ORA — 0·443
80. GUMMI — 0·067	63. UGEP — 0·239	67. ADO — 0·267
81. GANDI — 0·100	76. NSUKKA — 0·407	70. EJIGBO — 0·040
83. JANGERU — 0·210	88. ORBA (East) — 0·382	71. OKE-IHO — 0·446
89. GAYA — 0·207	104. ENUGU-ITODO — 0·482	78. IDANRE — 0·363
94. NAFUCE — 0·080	—	82. AIYETORO — 0·138
101. GWADA BANA — 0·341	—	84. IFON (OSHUN) — 0·340
113. GEIDAM — 0·381	—	96. ISHARA — 0·081
121. GASHUA — 0·130	—	103. ODE-OMU — 0·177
122. MORIKI — 0·168	—	105. ILE-IGBO — 0·394
125. GUMEL — 0·389	—	110. ILERO — 0·351
—		112. ILAWE — 0·202

Group E.

142.	DANBATTA	0·274
143.	KURYA	0·269
148.	MAIKULKI	0·252
153.	BIU	0·292
162.	WUKARI	0·174
170.	GORA	0·324
182.	KIRU	0·456
191.	KATAMI	0·138
194.	DARKI	0·443
197.	YADAKWARI	0·430
200.	GORA	0·081
217.	RIMI	0·471
228.	GIYAWA	0·245
233.	GARKO	0·273
242.	KOFA	0·358
256.	BIRNIN KUDU	0·202
258.	IBI	0·003
262.	JIBIYA MAJE	0·377
265.	YARKO	0·317
275.	TAKUM	0·235
281.	KWANKWASO	0·256
283.	WUDIL	0·250

139.	IBAGWA-AKA	0·224
157.	NANKA	0·161
160.	MGBOWO	0·106
167.	MBU	0·414
177.	MAKU	0·250
181.	OBOLO-EKE	0·417
183.	EKURI	0·329
184.	OBOLO-AFOR	0·365
205.	IMILIKE	0·409
206.	IKEM	0·341
209.	EKWULOBIA	0·297
216.	ABBOH	0·440
222.	ABAGANA	0·127
237.	IHAKA	0·338
266.	ITCHI	0·295
297.	IHEAKPU	0·410
303.	MKPANI	0·288
323.	UMULOKPA	0·481

119.	IGBARA-OKE	0·149
120.	OMUO	0·095
126.	APOMU	0·470
136.	IPERU	0·084
140.	IKOLE	0·100
155.	OTTA	0·169
163.	IPETU-JESHA	0·032
164.	IGBOHO	0·357
168.	ILUTITUN	0·162
169.	IRE	0·098
178.	OLUPONNA	0·453
180.	KISHI	0·244
185.	ISE	0·028
187.	UMUNEDE	0·149
190.	OBIARUKU	0·276
198.	OBOLO-OYE	0·290
219.	ODOGBOLU	0·001
220.	ARIGIDI	0·103
221.	ERIN	0·215
231.	IGBESSA	0·102
234.	IFON (OWO)	0·097
236.	OTAN	0·035
243.	OTU	0·449
245.	EDUNABON	0·287
248.	AYE	0·105

North		East	West	
291. WURNO	0·198	—	250. AJILETE	0·166
293. AMBURSA	0·081	—	253. ALADE (AKURE)	0·276
298. INDABO	0·318	—	259. DANHASSAN	0·256
299. RIKADAWA	0·261	—	260. ABBI	0·364
307. GARUNATI	0·251	—	263. UYIN	0·123
308. BARBURA	0·194	—	264. ESA OKE	0·472
311. KWARRE	0·016	—	268. LAGUN	0·476
312. ZURU	0·316	—	271. OGBAGI	0·176
314. BAKURA	0·185	—	273. AWE	0·052
318. BEBEJI	0·034	—	276. ODE	0·340
326. KIYAWA	0·410	—	279. ILARA	0·126
327. KANYA BABBA	0·302	—	295. EMEDE	0·379
328. GAMMO	0·407	—	301. AIYETORO	0·113
329. KIYAYA	0·346	—	315. IDOANI	0·195
		—	316. OTUN	0·019
		—	317. OZORO	0·241
— — —		—	319. IRUEKPEN	0·361
			322. FUGAR	0·242

Scores from +0·5 to +1·0

Group C.	—	30. ENUGU-UMOZI 0·650

Group D.

No.	Town	Value	No.	Town	Value		Town	Value
87.	OPI	0·654	77.	IRAGBIJI	0·518		—	
100.	UKEHE	0·627	97.	ILARO	0·543		—	
107.	ETEH	0·685	114.	IGBETTI	0·557		—	
129.	ENUGU-EZIKE	0·604		—			—	

Group E.

No.	Town	Value	No.	Town	Value	No.	Town	Value
133.	INYI	0·515	149.	IGANNA	0·562	158.	GWARZO	0·704
176.	IFITE	0·735	172.	ERUWA	0·652	310.	SAYA-SAYA	0·503
175.	OVOKO	0·545	199.	AKINMORIN	0·516	320.	JIGAWA	0·686
207.	OMOR	0·719	201.	OMIFUNFUN	0·533		—	
223.	LEKE	0·669	300.	KUTA	0·602		—	
230.	IBABWA-ANI	0·723	302.	OKAINGBA	0·599		—	
238.	AKWEGBE	0·873		—			—	
240.	OBUKPA	0·696		—			—	
244.	EDE	0·726		—			—	
284.	UGBENE	0·770		—				
288.	IGBO	0·542						
321.	AGBOGUGU	0·653						
324.	ENWEN	0·594						

Group A—Towns with population over 80,000.
Group B—Towns with population between 40,000 and 80,000.
Group C—Towns   „   „   „   20,000 and 40,000.
Group D—Towns   „   „   „   10,000 and 20,000.
Group E—Towns   „   „   „   5,000 and 10,000.

Index

The figures in italic refer to illustrations